CO-DEPENDENTS ANONYMOUS
Second Edition
Second Printing

Co-Dependents Anonymous, Inc.
P.O. Box 33577
Phoenix, AZ 85067-3577
602-277-7991
www.coda.org

Second Edition
Second Printing 2009

For additional copies of this book, or to order other
CoDA Conference endorsed literature, contact:
CoRe Publications
P.O. Box 670861
Dallas, TX 75367-0861
Phone: 214-340-1777
Fax: 214-340-6066
E-mail: coreorders@coda.org

Order online at: www.coda.org/estore

Library of Congress Catalog Card number: 95-69158
ISBN: 0-9647105-0-1

To a loving Higher Power

*To each member of the Fellowship
of Co-Dependents Anonymous*

To the codependent who still suffers

Acknowledgments

We, the members of the Fellowship of Co-Dependents Anonymous, would like to express our heartfelt appreciation and gratitude to all who have committed time, energy, gifts, and talents to CoDA. To you who worked so diligently to develop and establish CoDA as a program of recovery from codependence, and to you who continue to arduously support and maintain CoDA's growth, we say "Thank you."

The heritage of the Twelve Steps and Twelve Traditions of CoDA are found in the program of Alcoholics Anonymous. We wish to express our sincere gratitude to Bill W. and Dr. Bob, the founders of A.A., and to the successors of Alcoholics Anonymous for the work you have accomplished, the struggles you have endured, and the successes you have experienced as you walked this path before us.

The Twelve Steps and Twelve Traditions are reprinted and adapted with permission of Alcoholics Anonymous World Services, Inc. Permission to reprint and adapt this material does not mean that A.A. has reviewed or approved the content of this publication, nor that A.A. agrees with the views expressed herein. A.A. is a program of recovery from alcoholism *only*— use of the Twelve Steps and Twelve Traditions in connection with programs and activities which are patterned after A.A., but which address other problems, does not imply otherwise.

CONTENTS

Foreword i
Preamble ii
Welcome iii
Twelve Steps of Co-Dependents Anonymous iv
Twelve Traditions of Co-Dependents Anonymous v
Twelve Steps of Alcoholics Anonymous vi
Twelve Traditions of Alcoholics Anonymous vi
Twelve Promises of Co-Dependents Anonymous vii

Chapter 1
Beginning Our Journey 1
Chapter 2
Our Spiritual Dilemma 13
Chapter 3
A Suggested Program of Recovery 23
Chapter 4
Service to Others 83
Chapter 5
Commonly Asked Questions 95

PERSONAL STORIES
1. My Story 127
2. My Thanksgiving Story 137
3. David & The Lions 147
4. God, Please Help Me 155
5. Freedom from Denial 165
6. Cecile's Story 171
7. Tap Dancer No More 187
8. A Door of Hope 193
9. To Tell the Truth 205
10. The Die Maker/Accountant 219
11. The Joy is in the Journey 233
12. Chameleon 247
13. CoDA Comes to Maryland 257

14. Gay, Catholic, and Codependent 269
15. Painful Journeys 285
16. No More Secrets 297
17. Men Don't Cry 309
18. Trial by Fire 315
19. Off the Roller Coaster 321
20. Bobby's Hope 327
21. Finding My Child Within 337
22. Listen to the Wind 343
23. Finally Stopped the Abuse 351
24. Ken's Story 365
25. Bill's Story 385
26. Codependence Manifested as
    Multiple Addictions 399
27. I Couldn't Stay and I Couldn't Leave! 409
28. Mary R's Story 419
29. The Gift 439
30. John's Story 445
31. Two Lives, One Relationship 463
32. Bob's Story 485
33. Beth's Story 489
34. I Am a Miracle 497
35. Tim's Safe Place 509
36. A Story of the Original Sin 513
37. Life is Positive 523
38. Once Upon a Time 531
39. The Only Child 543
40. The Celebration of a Spiritual Journey 551

APPENDICES
1. CoDA'S First Six Years 572
2. How to Get in Touch With CoDA 583
3. CoDA Materials Available from CoRe 584

Foreword

Co-Dependents Anonymous is a worldwide Fellowship of men and women who come together to solve their common and individual problems of codependence. The need for such a program as CoDA was so great that in the first six years of CoDA's existence the program grew to more than 4,000 meetings worldwide, with a membership of approximately 100,000.

In the infancy of Co-Dependents Anonymous, the Board of Trustees turned to the founders to draft the first version of a book to reflect the experience, strength, and hope of the Fellowship. This version began the process leading to the book you're reading today. This book, *Co-Dependents Anonymous*, is the culmination of many years of work involving members of several Boards of Trustees and others in the Fellowship. This work is not a product of any one time or place. It is an ongoing evolutionary process, produced by countless meetings of group conscience.

We offer this book, not only as a practical guide, but as a symbol of our own collective journey. It represents a cross section of our experiences, both joyous and painful, and it stands as a beacon to the codependent who still suffers. There is hope for changed relationships with a Higher Power, ourselves, and others. We can move out of our current, perhaps lifelong pain and into a new way of living.

We now invite all who suffer from codependence to read our book in the hope that each of you may find what many of us have found—the hope and freedom of recovery.

Preamble

Co-Dependents Anonymous is a Fellowship of men and women whose common purpose is to develop healthy relationships. The only requirement for membership is a desire for healthy and loving relationships. We gather together to support and share with each other in a journey of self-discovery—learning to love the self. Living the program allows each of us to become increasingly honest with ourselves about our personal histories and our own codependent behaviors.

We rely upon the Twelve Steps and Twelve Traditions for knowledge and wisdom. These are the principles of our program and guides to developing honest and fulfilling relationships with ourselves and others. In CoDA, we each learn to build a bridge to a Higher Power of our own understanding, and we allow others the same privilege.

This renewal process is a gift of healing for us. By actively working the program of Co-Dependents Anonymous, we can each realize a new joy, acceptance, and serenity in our lives.

Welcome

We welcome you to Co-Dependents Anonymous, a program of recovery from codependence, where each of us may share our experience, strength, and hope in our efforts to find freedom where there has been bondage, and peace where there has been turmoil, in our relationships with others and ourselves.

Most of us have been searching for ways to overcome the dilemmas of the conflicts in our relationships and our childhoods. Many of us were raised in families where addictions existed—some of us were not. In either case, we have found in each of our lives that codependence is a most deeply-rooted, compulsive behavior, and that it is born out of our sometimes moderately, sometimes extremely dysfunctional family systems.

We have each experienced in our own ways the painful trauma of the emptiness of our childhood and relationships throughout our lives. We attempted to use others—our mates, our friends, and even our children, as our sole source of identity, value, and well-being, and as a way of trying to restore within us the emotional losses from our childhoods. Our histories may include other powerful addictions, which at times we have used to cope with our codependence.

We have all learned to survive life, but in CoDA we are learning to live life. Through applying the Twelve Steps and principles found in CoDA to our daily lives and relationships—both present and past—we can experience a new freedom from our self-defeating lifestyles. It is an individual growth process. Each of us is growing at our own pace and will continue to do so as we remain open to God's will for us on a daily basis. Our sharing is our way of identification and helps us to free the emotional bonds of our past and the compulsive control of our present.

No matter how traumatic your past or despairing your present may seem, there is hope for a new day in the program of Co-Dependents Anonymous. No longer do you need to rely on others as a power greater than yourself. May you instead find here a new strength within to be that which God intended—precious and free.

The Twelve Steps of Co-Dependents Anonymous*

1. We admitted we were powerless over others—that our lives had become unmanageable.
2. Came to believe that a power greater than ourselves could restore us to sanity.
3. Made a decision to turn our will and our lives over to the care of God as we understood God.
4. Made a searching and fearless moral inventory of ourselves.
5. Admitted to God, to ourselves, and to another human being the exact nature of our wrongs.
6. Were entirely ready to have God remove all these defects of character.
7. Humbly asked God to remove our shortcomings.
8. Made a list of all persons we had harmed, and became willing to make amends to them all.
9. Made direct amends to such people wherever possible, except when to do so would injure them or others.
10. Continued to take personal inventory and when we were wrong promptly admitted it.
11. Sought through prayer and meditation to improve our conscious contact with God as we understood God, praying only for knowledge of God's will for us and the power to carry that out.
12. Having had a spiritual awakening as the result of these steps, we tried to carry this message to other codependents, and to practice these principles in all our affairs.

The Twelve Traditions of Co-Dependents Anonymous*

1. Our common welfare should come first; personal recovery depends upon CoDA unity.
2. For our group purpose there is but one ultimate authority—a loving Higher Power as expressed to our group conscience. Our leaders are but trusted servants; they do not govern.
3. The only requirement for membership in CoDA is a desire for healthy and loving relationships.
4. Each group should remain autonomous except in matters affecting other groups or CoDA as a whole.
5. Each group has but one primary purpose—to carry its message to other codependents who still suffer.
6. A CoDA group ought never endorse, finance or lend the CoDA name to any related facility or outside enterprise, lest problems of money, property and prestige divert us from our primary spiritual aim.
7. Every CoDA group ought to be fully self-supporting, declining outside contributions.
8. Co-Dependents Anonymous should remain forever non-professional, but our service centers may employ special workers.
9. CoDA, as such, ought never be organized; but we may create service boards or committees directly responsible to those they serve.
10. CoDA has no opinion on outside issues; hence the CoDA name ought never be drawn into public controversy.
11. Our public relations policy is based on attraction rather than promotion; we need always maintain personal anonymity at the level of press, radio and films.
12. Anonymity is the spiritual foundation of all our Traditions, ever reminding us to place principles before personalities.

---

*The Twelve Steps and Twelve Traditions are reprinted and adapted with permission of Alcoholics Anonymous World Services, Inc. Permission to reprint and adapt this material does not mean that A.A. has reviewed or approved the content of this publication, nor that A.A. agrees with the views expressed herein. A.A. is a program of recovery from alcoholism only—use of the Twelve Steps and Twelve Traditions in connection with programs and activities which are patterned after A.A., but which address other problems, does not imply otherwise.

The Twelve Steps of Alcoholics Anonymous

1. We admitted we were powerless over alcohol, that our lives had become unmanageable. 2. Came to believe that a Power greater than ourselves could restore us to sanity. 3. Made a decision to turn our will and our lives over to the care of God *as we understood Him*. 4. Made a searching and fearless moral inventory of ourselves. 5. Admitted to God, to ourselves, and to another human being the exact nature of our wrongs. 6. Were entirely ready to have God remove all these defects of character. 7. Humbly asked Him to remove our shortcomings. 8. Made a list of all persons we had harmed, and became willing to make amends to them all. 9. Made direct amends to such people wherever possible, except when to do so would injure them or others. 10. Continued to take personal inventory and when we were wrong promptly admitted it. 11. Sought through prayer and meditation to improve our conscious contact with God *as we understood Him*, praying only for knowledge of His will for us and the power to carry that out. 12. Having had a spiritual awakening as the result of these steps, we tried to carry this message to alcoholics, and to practice these principles in all our affairs.

The Twelve Traditions of Alcoholics Anonymous

1. Our common welfare should come first; personal recovery depends upon A.A. unity. 2. For our group purpose there is but one ultimate authority—a loving God as He may express Himself in our group conscience. Our leaders are but trusted servants; they do not govern. 3. The only requirement for A.A. membership is a desire to stop drinking. 4. Each group should be autonomous except in matters affecting other groups or A.A. as a whole. 5. Each group has but one primary purpose—to carry its message to the alcoholic who still suffers. 6. An A.A. group ought never endorse, finance or lend the A.A. name to any related facility or outside enterprise, lest problems of money, property and prestige divert us from our primary purpose. 7. Every A.A. group ought to be fully self-supporting, declining outside contributions. 8. Alcoholics Anonymous should remain forever nonprofessional, but our service centers may employ special workers. 9. A.A. as such, ought never be organized; but we may create service boards or committees directly responsible to those they serve. 10. Alcoholics Anonymous has no opinion on outside issues; hence the A.A. name ought never be drawn into public controversy. 11. Our public relations policy is based on attraction rather than promotion; we need always maintain personal anonymity at the level of press, radio and films. 12. Anonymity is the spiritual foundation of all our Traditions, ever reminding us to place principles before personalities.

The Twelve Promises of Co-Dependents Anonymous

I can expect a miraculous change in my life by working the program of Co-Dependents Anonymous. As I make an honest effort to work the Twelve Steps and follow the Twelve Traditions...

1. I know a new sense of belonging. The feelings of emptiness and loneliness will disappear.
2. I am no longer controlled by my fears. I overcome my fears and act with courage, integrity and dignity.
3. I know a new freedom.
4. I release myself from worry, guilt and regret about my past and present. I am aware enough not to repeat it.
5. I know a new love and acceptance of myself and others. I feel genuinely lovable, loving and loved.
6. I learn to see myself as equal to others. My new and renewed relationships are all with equal partners.
7. I am capable of developing and maintaining healthy and loving relationships. The need to control and manipulate others will disappear as I learn to trust those who are trustworthy.
8. I learn that it is possible for me to mend—to become more loving, intimate and supportive. I have the choice of communicating with my family in a way which is safe for me and respectful of them.
9. I acknowledge that I am a unique and precious creation.
10. I no longer need to rely solely on others to provide my sense of worth.
11. I trust the guidance I receive from my Higher Power and come to believe in my own capabilities.
12. I gradually experience serenity, strength, and spiritual growth in my daily life.

CHAPTER ONE

Beginning Our Journey

Perhaps some of these thoughts are yours...

"If he/she changed, everything would be all right."

"I can't control this pain, these people and what's happening."

"It's all my fault."

"I keep getting into the same bad relationships."

"I feel so empty and lost."

"Who am I?"

"What's wrong with me?"

Our sadness and loss bring us here. We want change, and we want it now. We want to escape our misery. We want to feel good about ourselves and live abundant, fulfilling lives. We want happy, healthy relationships.

If any of the preceding thoughts are yours, then you're not alone. Many of us in the Fellowship of Co-Dependents Anonymous have felt deep sadness, anxiety, despair, and depression and have turned here—to each other and a Higher Power—for our sanity to be restored.

What brings us here may be a crisis such as divorce, separation, imprisonment, health problems or attempt at suicide. Some of us are feeling weary, desperate or devastated.

If you're new to recovery, this moment may not seem like something to remember, but someday you might consider it a celebration. Many of us find our pain to be a gift, for without these feelings of emptiness and despair, we can't experience a real desire to change our lives. Without this desire, many of us know we won't make the decision to change. We want balance, happiness and peace, but to change we must acknowledge these feelings and decide to climb out of this pit of pain.

Once we make this decision, many of us ask, "How do I go about this change? Where can I get help?" At first, many of us think we can solve our problems by just trying harder or by studying techniques to change people. Often our pride or upbringing cause us to think that we can do this ourselves. These two approaches, however, block our road to a better way of life.

What is codependence?

Somewhere along this road we learn about codependence. We hear about it from a friend or therapist. We see it mentioned in the news. Many of us wonder if codependence describes who we are.

Codependence is a disease that deteriorates our souls. It affects our personal lives: our families, children, friends, and relatives; our businesses and careers; our health; and our spiritual growth. It is debilitating and, if left untreated, causes us to become more destructive to ourselves and others. Many of us come to a point when we must look beyond ourselves for help.

When we attend our first meeting of Co-Dependents Anonymous, many of us find a source for help. Each of us arrives here from different directions. Some of us are urged by family members or friends. Some of us come to CoDA when our physicians, psychiatrists, or therapists see the need. Many of us reach CoDA's doorstep after treatment for codependence or other addictions.

Whether it's crisis or curiosity that brings us to CoDA, many of us learn about the characteristics of codependence at our first meeting. These characteristics help us determine what unhealthy patterns weave in and out of our lives. Do we live in extremes instead of balance? How do we, our mates, children and friends suffer because of our behaviors? Do our codependent behaviors cause our relationships to stagnate, deteriorate or destruct? If the answers to these soul-searching questions cause us to admit, "I am codependent and I need help," then we're beginning to locate recovery's path.

It all begins with an honest look at ourselves.

The following characteristics of codependence outlined in the CoDA pamphlet, "What is CoDA?" can help us to identify to what degree this illness affects us:

> Many of us struggle with the questions: What is codependence? Am I codependent? We want precise definitions and diagnostic criteria before we will decide. As stated in the Eighth Tradition,

Co-Dependents Anonymous is a nonprofessional Fellowship. We offer no definition or diagnostic criteria for codependence. What we do offer from our experience are characteristic attitudes and behaviors that describe what our codependent histories have been like. We believe that recovery begins with an honest self-diagnosis. We come to accept our inability to maintain healthy and nurturing relationships with ourselves and others. We begin to recognize that the cause lies in long-standing destructive patterns of living.

These patterns and characteristics are offered as a tool to aid in self-evaluation. They may be particularly helpful to newcomers.

Denial Patterns: Codependents...

- have difficulty identifying feelings.

- minimize, alter, or deny their feelings.

- perceive themselves as being completely unselfish, dedicated to the well-being of others.

Low Self-Esteem Patterns: Codependents...

- have difficulty making decisions.

- judge their thoughts, words, and actions harshly, as never being good enough.

- are embarrassed to receive recognition, praise, or gifts.

- are unable to ask others to meet their needs or wants.

- value other people's approval of their thoughts, feelings, and behaviors over self-approval.

- do not perceive themselves as lovable or worthwhile.

Compliance Patterns: Codependents...

- compromise their values and integrity to avoid rejection and other people's anger.

- are very sensitive to others' feelings and assume the same feelings.

- are extremely loyal, remaining in harmful situations too long.

- place a higher value on others' opinions and feelings, and are afraid to express differing viewpoints or feelings.

- put aside personal interests and hobbies to do what others want.

- accept sex as a substitute for love.

Control Patterns: Codependents...

- believe most others are incapable of taking care of themselves.

- attempt to convince others what they should think or feel.

- become resentful when others refuse their offers of help.

- freely offer advice and guidance without being asked.

- lavish gifts and favors on those they care about.

- use sex to gain approval and acceptance.

- have to be needed in order to have a relationship with others.

Many of us are shocked when we read this list because many of the characteristics describe us. Some of us are relieved to see these feelings and behaviors on paper because there's hope we might have discovered a way out of our pain. Some of us are embarrassed, as though someone is reading our personal mail or journals. We wonder, "How did they find out?" and, "If these are the characteristics of codependence, then the whole world is codependent."

At our first meeting, we listen to people talk about their struggles and how their lives have changed from working a program of recovery. We hear of relationships healing—those with ourselves, our Higher Power, and others. We learn how we can experience freedom and an inner peace.

We listen with wonder as they seem to be telling our stories, describing our problems, and talking about our most secret feelings. This may be one of the few times we don't feel strange or alone. Armed with the knowledge that we're like other people, we realize that if they can work the program and improve their lives, we can too. As we attend more meetings, we hear a message of hope loud and clear; we hear it through CoDA literature and the stories of those around us. This message of hope tells us that we can also have the gifts of recovery, if we're willing.

We also learn that all of us suffer from this illness to some degree, so recognizing codependence can be difficult. Understanding codependent behaviors and attitudes can be especially tough because many of them are not destructive; as children we may have used these behaviors to survive abuse or neglect. For example, we might have developed internal detectors to read our parents' moods and then developed behaviors based on their moods to keep them happy.

For many of us, codependence became worse as we grew up. Behaviors that may have served us well in childhood are now causing our lives to deteriorate. As our codependence gets worse, we lose our ability to acknowledge this pain and its harm.

Once we acknowledge our feelings of pain, we can begin to make the decision to change. We must also try to be patient, loving and forgiving of ourselves while we begin this road to recovery. Each of us will recover in unique ways and at a different pace. Our paths are as individual as our personalities and circumstances, but while we start from different points, we share a common recovery goal.

The Fellowship of CoDA

The road to recovery is filled with fellowship; the people of Co-Dependents Anonymous become our dear companions on our journey. Where we may have felt isolated and helpless, we can now feel friendship and strength.

One of the program's greatest blessings is this journey we take together. We try to understand and support one another. We're able to renew our trust and faith in humanity; we see growth in people who work the program and look to the Fellowship of CoDA for support.

New faces are always welcome at CoDA. They give us hope because we know more people will journey with us to live more fulfilling lives. In CoDA, there is understanding and acceptance, not judgment and advice.

With the love, support, and safety the CoDA Fellowship provides, we can begin to describe our own codependent characteristics and discover their sources. We learn to accept the support and guidance from others and begin to trust in a Higher Power or God of our own definition. We acknowledge our troubled past and accept where it might have begun. For many of us, this can be found in the abuse and neglect we experienced in our significant childhood relationships. We may be reluctant to call some of these experiences "abuse" and "neglect," but we might need to recognize them as part of our personal history.

These issues might apply not only to our childhood—emotionally and physically—but sexually, intellectually and spiritually as well. They affect us as adults in our ability to love ourselves and others, and to be loved. We often get caught in negative situations that impact our mental and physical health and the well-being of others. Some of us may be unable to recognize our feelings and comprehend the disastrous path we're on. We call this denial.

Denial

Denial of ourselves—our past and present—is often a great stumbling block to our early recovery. It's a term often used when we don't accept our codependent behaviors as we learn about their patterns and characteristics or as we hear them described in another person's story. Often in our frustration, we clearly see what everyone else is doing wrong, but we can't recognize our own wrongdoing. Some of us come to a place of despair and think of nothing else but giving up. We isolate from our friends and families, many times rejecting their love. Some of us go to elaborate degrees to create the "all together" act in our homes, marriages, families, jobs, friendships and social lives. Try as we might to do otherwise, we often experience devastating marriages, parenting and family relationships, friendships and careers. Sometimes, even then, our denial continues.

We may become so entangled in denial and control that we're forced to accept the hand of recovery through formal intervention and treatment. Eventually, we may get involved in separation or divorce, legal action, imprisonment, attempted suicide, hospitalization for physically related illnesses, mental problems, job loss or a sidelined career. We walk an extremely lonely and empty path in denial, whether we suffer severe devastation or try to appear "all together."

We usually reach a point where denial no longer works. We finally determine "enough is enough." We seek the hand of others in CoDA and, if necessary, professional help.

Acceptance

As we break through our denial, we're better able to determine the degree of our problem. We recognize our denial as a symptom of codependence and see it as a process that continually emerges, subsides and evolves throughout our lives.

As we continue our recovery in CoDA, we replace denial with acceptance. We progressively embrace our past and current life with honesty, openness and a willingness to change. We move beyond denial and identify the harm our codependent decisions and behaviors have caused us personally, as well as our families, careers, physical health, and spirituality. We see how codependence has allowed us to become trapped in unhealthy situations and relationships. It affects every aspect of our lives. As we see our direction more clearly, we recognize that our journey is not advanced by force, will, intellect or even strength of character. At some point, most of us acknowledge a Higher Power as the guide on our journey, the source of our progress. We may become more aware that we're on a spiritual journey.

We know we're not alone when we accept our codependence. Together, we're learning how to love and be loved, and how to live life rather than merely survive it. Recovery in CoDA is an ongoing process. It's a life that constantly challenges us. Recovery isn't earned like a merit badge; it's a way of living that evolves with us every day.

The *Serenity Prayer* expresses our awareness that recovery is about living life as it unfolds. These simple phrases affirm that our recovery is lived one moment, one decision, one day at a time:

God, grant me the Serenity to
accept the things I cannot change;
Courage to change the things I can;
and Wisdom to know the difference.

Some of us become nervous at the mention of spirituality and a Higher Power. Even if you've given up on a Higher Power or wonder if such a being exists, you are welcome to the program of Co-Dependents Anonymous. This is not a religious program, but a spiritual one; it's a program for finding peace within. Over time, most everyone who makes a conscious choice to work this spiritual program decides what their Higher Power should be.

With the help of a loving Higher Power, the program of Co-Dependents Anonymous, and those who join us on this journey, each of us can experience the hope of recovery. We find the willingness to change, grow, and evolve toward the positive, loving potential that lies within us. Through the guidance of our Higher Power, the program of Co-Dependents Anonymous, and the CoDA family, each of us can experience the hope of recovery and a life filled with peace and joy.

CHAPTER 2

Our Spiritual Dilemma

Codependence causes a dilemma to boil inside us. For many of us, our pain and despair are signs of a deep inner need. This need, hunger or desire gnaws at the core of our being. It could be a cry for unconditional love, respect, nurturing, acceptance or joy. Many of us turn to other people, drugs, alcohol or other addictions to fill this need to gain some sense of safety, self-worth and well-being.

Our answers to the following questions can help us determine how we've looked to other people or addictions for our emotional well-being.

• Do I control others to relieve my fears?

• Do I let others control me for fear of their abuse or neglect?

• Do I adapt or change my behavior for others?

• Do I validate my value and worth as a person through them?

• Do I avoid others in order to feel safe?

In CoDA, we learn that our self-worth and well-being come from our Higher Power. When we attempt to codependently control or manipulate others, we turn ourselves into a Higher Power to maintain our sense of safety and well-being. When we codependently avoid others, as well as adapt or change our behavior for others, we give them, instead of our Higher Power, this control and strength.

13

As we turn ourselves into a Higher Power or give this power to others, we leave little room for our Higher Power to work in our lives. This is our spiritual dilemma.

The following paragraphs describe how our spiritual dilemma may involve control and avoidance, especially when circumstances become stressful.

Controlling people and circumstances

Many of us take pride in controlling circumstances and those around us. If we think we might be abandoned, abused or neglected by others, we label them as the problem and manipulate them. Specifically, we may overcontrol our mates, children, family members, friends or associates by dominating them. Another way we control them is by being "nice," passive or quiet for long periods of time. Then, when fear or other feelings overwhelm us, we rage, isolate or allow others to act out our feelings for us.

We become a Higher Power when we control others, to any degree, either quietly or aggressively. We may even reinforce our control with an attitude of arrogance, authority or prejudice. We value others' beliefs and behaviors as foolish, selfish or worthless. We establish ourselves in a "better-than" position. Our way is the only way, we think.

In giving the power of our Higher Power to other people, we may seek others' approval, often to the point of abandoning our own needs and desires. We live in fear of those we put in power. We dread their anger or disapproving looks. We fear their disappointment, avoidance or control. In essence, we lose our sense of self (or never gain it) because we become obsessed with their attitudes and behaviors toward us.

Avoiding people and circumstances

Some of us may fear others so much that we avoid any degree of closeness or intimacy. We work hard to prevent placing ourselves in a vulnerable position. We become skilled at hiding our fears, especially when things seem out of control. We may remain silent even when we experience injustice or abuse.

We may fall into martyr roles or act helpless to avoid confrontation or accountability. We may place ourselves in a subservient position and judge ourselves harshly. We may believe we're not acceptable enough to live a life with relationships, purpose or happiness.

Our codependence worsens; our fear and shame overwhelm us. We control and avoid others even more. But these behaviors are temporary fixes; our fears always return and our shame is ever present.

Many of us seek false gods. We numb our feelings with alcohol, drugs, food, sex or work; these often turn into chronic addictions and compound our problems. None of them provide us freedom or peace.

Regardless of whether we position ourselves as "better than" or "less than," as a controller or avoider, we behave in self-centered ways. Equality is lost.

What drives our need to control and avoid others?

Many of us ask, "Aren't some of these behaviors healthy?" The answer can be found in the motivation for our behaviors. Our behaviors toward ourselves, others and our Higher Power may be appropriate if they are by choice with healthy boundaries. For example, we may leave the premises of a person who is verbally or physically threatening us. We behave codependently, however, if we allow fear or shame to dictate our lives, causing us to rely on past survival instincts such as control and avoidance.

Fear

For many of us, fear is our guardian; it helps protect us from harm. As codependents, we habitually use fear to protect ourselves from any opportunity of being shamed by others. Our fear may be cloaked in anger or resentment, rage, pain or loneliness. Oftentimes our passivity, silence, manipulation, isolation, rage, violence, denial or even deceit are our expressions of fear. Other feelings that show up as fear are: concern, anxiety, nervousness, and feeling uptight or scared.

Shame

Shame causes us to believe we are "less than," stupid, foolish, worthless, inadequate or unwanted. It diminishes our true sense of identity and destroys our belief that we are loving human beings. It erodes our self-esteem and sense of equality in the world.

Experiencing fear and shame as children

As children, our identity as well as our relationships with our Higher Power, ourselves and others were damaged each time we were abused or neglected. We felt shame and naturally feared its reoccurrence, yet we allowed our sense of self and well-being to be shaped by those who abused and neglected us. As children, we had no choice.

As we continued to experience abuse or neglect, our fear and shame intensified; we gave more of ourselves away. Over time (most often without our knowing), our abusers became our Higher Power. We learned to fear their authority. As the abuse and neglect continued, the possibility of developing an emotionally fulfilling relationship with ourselves, others, and our Higher Power diminished.

We learned survival skills in order to cope. We controlled or avoided potentially volatile circumstances. We cast away our childhood, tried to become little adults or rebelled. Many of us didn't understand our actions because they were often instinctive.

Over time, we learned how to alleviate our fear and shame by controlling and/or avoiding ourselves and others. When we felt overwhelmed or stressed out, we relied on what we knew best to survive. In this devastating codependent cycle, we took greater control of life, allowing less room for a power greater than ourselves to work through us.

Continuing this behavior as adults

Without some form of help, we carry these emotional conflicts and survival patterns into our adult lives. We hope to find peace and happiness and leave the past behind; but instead, we recreate similar or opposite circumstances in our adult relationships. Neither extreme is healthy. We unknowingly transfer the characteristics and power of our childhood abusers to significant people in our lives today. Sometimes we transfer abusive characteristics to our Higher Power, too.

In our adult relationships, we fearfully guard against any sign of shame, abuse or neglect. We become manipulative or avoid other people and circumstances. This fear can grow stronger than the shame itself. It forms a shaky foundation for relationships. We continue to draw others near us (hoping for intimacy) but when they get too close, we push them away because of our fear of shame.

Building our own concept of a Higher Power

Many of us participate in organized religions or learn various doctrines and concepts of God or a Higher Power. Some of us may hope to cleanse our sense of shame by living righteous lives. Even controlled behavioral change combined with our religious beliefs are not enough. Our motives may be virtuous, but we're still emotionally bound to the abusive, neglectful people in our lives—most deeply to those from our childhood.

Some of us are atheists or agnostics. Organized religion may remind us of an abusive, authoritarian God. Some of us may be angry at our Higher Power for the negative experiences we faced, or we may discover we've been angry at this Higher Power for years but didn't know it. Some of us believe we're undeserving of God's love or grace.

We must ask ourselves, "Is my life filled with honesty and serenity?" "Am I working toward a safe, healthy and loving relationship with my Higher Power, myself and others?" Most often, we say, "No." Our fear and shame drive us to behave in devastating ways.

Wherever our codependent course takes us, we find we're left with no other recourse than to seek a safe power greater than ourselves—one that can restore us to sanity. To continue recovery, we must become willing to consider this endeavor.

If we haven't experienced a Higher Power before, our concept of a safe being can begin to take shape. If we already have a relationship with God, we can help strengthen it. Whatever our past beliefs, we can begin building a spiritual foundation for our program of recovery.

Beginning the journey of recovery from codependence

In our codependence, we excessively place our faith and hope in ourselves, our mates, children, relatives and friends—even our careers and lifestyles. We do this for our safety, value, worth and well-being.

In recovery, we learn to build faith and hope, and progressively surrender our lives to the care of a loving Higher Power. We learn to let go of our controlling and avoidance behaviors, to resolve our feelings about what we do, and to emotionally detach from those on whom we compulsively rely.

Some of us gladly reach for our Higher Power's hand. Some of us reach in desperation. Some of us realize that our ability to trust anyone or anything has been so greatly diminished that it may take time. We may need to feel some sense of safety. We may have to act as if we have faith until it becomes a reality.

Many of us pray or meditate when our fear is so overwhelming that we're unable to surrender even a small part of our will or lives to our Higher Power. Often, time will allow only a simple prayer such as, "God, please help me find the willingness to let go."

As we continue our recovery, many of us can surrender more easily to our Higher Power and experience this power's heartfelt presence within us. Surrendering and letting go doesn't mean that life's circumstances will happen the way we want. It means we're better able to accept life as it is and handle problems with a newfound strength from our Higher Power. This enables us to experience a growing personal empowerment and a humble, yet truer, self-esteem.

We learn that our Higher Power doesn't create bad people. Goodness dwells within us all, even those responsible for the broken promises and betrayals, abuses, hurts and fears of our past. It's possible to love these persons, yet not condone their negative behaviors. We can even love and forgive ourselves. In our own way, we're all learning how to love and be loved.

Even with our Higher Power's help, none of us loves or lives life perfectly. Our humanity continues to evolve. We begin to realize that perfectionism is merely an illusion. Over the long haul, we make many mistakes and, at times, "slip" into our former codependent behaviors.

When we're unable to maintain our emotional balance, strength or self-esteem, we reflect on the work we must do and that recovery is a lifelong process. We remember that comparing our progress with others is self-defeating; each of us is learning at our own balance and pace.

To keep our relationship with our Higher Power in perspective, we find it helpful to prioritize our relationships. Our relationship with our Higher Power must come first. Once we establish and begin to develop this relationship, we're better able to develop one with ourselves. As the relationships with our Higher Power and ourselves gain in strength and balance, we begin to heal and develop loving relationships with others. When we accept a healthier priority for our close relationships, we allow our Higher Power to work in our lives. We draw on strengths that far exceed our own.

As we continue to strengthen our relationship with our Higher Power throughout our recovery, our overwhelming tiredness, depression, anxiety, despair and hopelessness are replaced with an increasing strength and resiliency. Step by step, our fear of shame diminishes. Our childhood wounds and feelings progressively heal. We experience richer encounters of prayer and meditation. It becomes easier to let go of our control and avoidance behaviors, and to allow our Higher Power to guide our life's journey.

The miracles of recovery unfold. Loving

relationships with our Higher Power, ourselves and others improve and evolve. We begin to feel more assured that our deepest needs will be cared for. We don't turn as often to other people or to an unhealthy lifestyle to satisfy our spiritual hunger. Like the light of dawn, our Higher Power's will radiates through us with reassurance and trust.

CHAPTER THREE

A Suggested Program of Recovery

Codependence is an illusive and devastating problem that requires simple yet specific solutions. Many of us believe these solutions can be found within the program of Co-Dependents Anonymous. The CoDA program consists of the following: the Fellowship, CoDA meetings, sponsorship, literature, conferences, conventions, service work, the CoDA Twelve Steps and Twelve Traditions.

The CoDA Twelve Steps have been adapted from the Twelve Steps of Alcoholics Anonymous for our use, as well as for many of other Twelve Step programs. Millions of people worldwide have applied these concepts to their lives.

These Steps hold the strength and spirit of personal recovery. We become willing to work them to the best of our ability. We're as honest as possible with ourselves, our Higher Power and another person. Halfhearted attempts to work the Steps often leave us feeling self-defeated; the changes we seek may not last long.

If we attempt to complete the Steps alone, we may perpetuate isolation: a common codependent behavior. In time, many of us seek the loving help of those who have traveled this path before us— sponsors in CoDA who can offer us insight, encouragement, and support. They help us see that these Steps cannot be completed quickly or absolutely; they are not quick fixes.

The Twelve Steps steer us from a path of self-defeating behaviors toward healthy and loving relationships with God, ourselves, and others. They offer us growth, a priority for our relationships and a guide for living healthy and loving lives. Through their simplistic nature, we can discover who we are and how to become involved in healthy, loving relationships. The Steps help us to see how our past experiences of abuse and neglect have formed and reinforced our codependent behaviors and lifestyles. We learn how to turn over our self-claimed power, addictions and problems to a loving Higher Power. We give our lives, will and healing into the care of that Higher Power.

We become accountable for our codependent behaviors which reinforce patterns of devastation in our lives. We grow in humility as we learn of our own shortcomings and defects of character and recognize our skills, talents and successes. From this humble state, we do all within our power to right our wrongs. We also try to complete the work which helps heal our wounds and perhaps those whom we have hurt.

In our Step work, we strive on a daily basis to maintain accountability for our own behavior. We learn to strengthen and deepen our relationship with our Higher Power. We rely more freely upon our Higher Power for our true value, worth and well-being. Finally, we realize if we want to keep what we've gained through our Step work, we must strive to pass on the experience, strength and hope of our recovery to those who still suffer from codependence.

Our journey through the Steps may be the most difficult work we ever attempt, yet the rewards and the healing we receive cannot be measured. In time, the Steps become an integral part of our daily lives as we practice these principles in all our affairs.

Listed below are the Twelve Steps which are the suggested program of Co-Dependents Anonymous for personal recovery from codependence:

1. We admitted we were powerless over others— that our lives had become unmanageable.

2. Came to believe that a power greater than ourselves could restore us to sanity.

3. Made a decision to turn our will and our lives over to the care of God as we understood God.

4. Made a searching and fearless moral inventory of ourselves.

5. Admitted to God, to ourselves, and to another human being the exact nature of our wrongs.

6. Were entirely ready to have God remove all these defects of character.

7. Humbly asked God to remove our shortcomings.

8. Made a list of all persons we had harmed, and became willing to make amends to them all.

9. Made direct amends to such people wherever possible, except when to do so would injure them or others.

10. Continued to take personal inventory and, when we were wrong, promptly admitted it.

11. Sought through prayer and meditation to improve our conscious contact with God as we understood God, praying only for knowledge of God's will for us and the power to carry that out.

12. Having had a spiritual awakening as the result of these Steps, we tried to carry this message to other codependents, and to practice these principles in all our affairs.

At first glance, some of us see these Steps as overwhelming tasks that can never be accomplished. Some of us see them as quick, easy instructions that can be achieved in an afternoon or a few days. Some of us avoid them entirely until we become overburdened with crises and our codependent behaviors. Ultimately, we must be willing to move forward and embrace these Steps as part of our personal recovery if we want our lives to get better.

Step One

We admitted we were powerless over others—that our lives had become unmanageable.

> **On powerlessness**—Until now we had applied self-control, obsessiveness, and our own clouded thinking to our problems of living. When our relationships broke down, many of us just tried harder, applying our arsenal of misinformation with a vengeance. Our self-will took many forms. We were overbearing. We were people-pleasers. We conformed. We rebelled. We blamed. We hurt ourselves and we hurt others. Some of us had to

go to the edge of insanity or death before we were willing to admit our powerlessness. And all the while we were convinced we were doing the right thing. Where was success?

On unmanageability—Chances are that by the time we reached CoDA our lives were out of control. The coping skills we had relied on for a lifetime were no longer working. We were the victims of a compulsive way of behaving so subtly powerful and damaging that no ordinary means could break it. Our lives were truly unmanageable. It was at this point that our old ideas began to crumble and we became open to the possibility that there might be another way.

excerpt from Step One in the
CoDA *Twelve Steps Handbook*

All journeys begin with a first step. Our journey of personal recovery in CoDA begins with the CoDA First Step.

To understand the growing devastation of our powerlessness and unmanageability, we must explore our past and how we arrived at this point. Maybe we're devastated by a divorce, separation, or a loved one's death. Maybe we tried killing ourselves or slowly "bottomed out" from drugs or alcohol. Many of us are overwhelmed and weary. Once we make the decision to change, we start our recovery journey with Step One, the Step of admission and acceptance.

This Step helps us to identify our lifetime of experiences, feelings and behaviors, to pinpoint how we avoid, control and manipulate ourselves, other people and circumstances. We learn how we've become our own Higher Power or placed others in that role. We begin to see that God has not given us ght to control another person's behavior, but we have been given the responsibility to set limits and boundaries for ourselves with others. To explore how we control and avoid ourselves and others, we search our personal histories. We ask ourselves the following questions to see if they apply to our lives:

- What neglect and abuse did I experience growing up?

- Where did I learn to turn my head when I and/ or other people were being neglected or abused, and why?

- Who in my childhood displayed these behaviors or instructed me not to tell or share my feelings about it?

- Where did I learn that avoiding others was safer than being involved?

- Where did I learn to control others for my sense of well-being?

- How did I learn that I wasn't good enough or was better than others?

- When, where and how did I learn to deny my own thoughts, feelings and needs for the sake of others or, conversely, to demand that the world revolve around me?

- How did I know never to tell the family secrets and why?

- Where did I learn to behave in neglectful and/ or abusive ways that are intellectually, emotionally, physically, sexually and/or spiritually harmful?

- Where did I learn to express these behaviors

which are often communicated in the extremes from silence to violence?

- How did I learn to allow them to be expressed toward me?

- Where and how did I learn that having a relationship would make me whole?

- Did I learn these things through others' words or actions? If so, whose?

- How had I come to survive life through codependent behaviors rather than living life through a sense of freedom?

- What are my true feelings about all of these questions?

By answering these questions, we gain an understanding of how our powerlessness developed in our childhood, but knowing this is not enough. We must see the unmanageability of the codependent behaviors we carry into our adult lives.

To explore our unmanageable adult codependent behaviors, we find it helpful to review the first chapter and its outline of the denial, low self-esteem, control and compliance patterns. We specifically list those patterns which represent our adult codependent behaviors. It's important to be honest with ourselves to change our unmanageability.

By exploring the powerlessness of our childhood and the unmanageability of our adult lives, we come to understand more about our personal heritage. Our denial of codependence fades, our acceptance increases and we're better able to see our destructive adult behaviors.

It is extremely important to remember that our First Step is not to be used to assign blame to others or to ourselves. We're not on a witch-hunt. By holding on to blame, we react codependently and remain powerless.

Rather than blame, we attempt to review our childhood and adult experiences that are the roots of unhealthy behaviors. We acknowledge how powerlessness and unmanageability developed in childhood and gradually manifested themselves in our adult behavior and relationships. We accept that our lives get crazier the more we try to control and avoid ourselves and others. Rather than blame others or ourselves, we become accountable for our feelings about our childhood and adult experiences, as well as our progressive adult codependent behavior.

We find it helpful to list the losses we've experienced in our childhood and adult life. We allow ourselves to grieve these losses—the pain and anger we've held so long. As we release these feelings, we begin to release the energies that drive our codependent behaviors. We see that our codependent behaviors of manipulation, control and avoidance have only left us in despair.

Many of us share our First Step with our sponsors and friends in recovery. We share our past experiences, losses and grief. In doing so, we begin to release the emotional depths of our powerlessness and unmanageability. Once we do, we can begin to accept our past, think more positively and act in healthier ways with ourselves and others.

By understanding and accepting our codependent powerlessness and the unmanageability of our lives, we open the door to possible solutions. We admit that our best efforts in these areas have failed and that we need greater help than our own limited abilities can provide.

From this position of admission and acceptance, we are ready to reach for the help of a power greater than ourselves to restore us to sanity.

Step Two
Came to believe that a power greater than ourselves could restore us to sanity.

Came to believe—In the beginning, we came to believe by attending meetings and listening. We heard others as they described a relationship with a Higher Power. We noticed that those who maintained a regular connection with this Power experienced what we sought—RECOVERY. Because we were members of a Twelve-Step program, the form of this Power was left to each of us to discover. We became willing to entertain the possibility there was something that could do for us what we could not do for ourselves.

Restore us to sanity—With the help of others in the program, we began to look more clearly at our own behavior. We discovered a great truth in Step Two: that continuing to act in a self-destructive manner, no matter how well-meaning we believed we were, was insane. And once this behavior became compulsive, any belief we held that we could control it on our own was equally insane.

Becoming honest with ourselves was at times painful. The reward was magnificent. As we came to believe and embrace the simple and profound truth offered in this Step, the seed of humility produced by our admission of powerlessness in Step One was nurtured. We experienced a sense of freedom and hope by our willingness to have a true Higher Power. At this point our faith emerged.

excerpt from Step Two in the
CoDA *Twelve Steps Handbook*

In Step One, we recognize our failure in our own attempts to play God. We also allow others to be our God. We recognize that we must seek help beyond ourselves and those to whom we've given authority. In doing so, we become ready to develop a belief in a power greater than ourselves—a power that can restore us to sanity and health.

In Step Two, we begin establishing or strengthening this belief. For those of us who do not know a Higher Power, we embark on a new and wondrous relationship. For those of us who have a relationship with a Higher Power, this Step can help us strengthen its weaker areas.

Through our work in the First Step, we learn that as children, we may have prayed often for God's help, but the neglect and/or abuse continued. The authority figures in our lives were often unavailable and absorbed in their own addictions and codependence. As adults, we try to leave those circumstances behind, only to find ourselves in adult relationships where similar or extreme opposite behaviors occur.

We keep praying to God, but nothing changes until we turn away from our addictions and from the people with whom we're obsessed. We may continue to look to others for solutions, peace, hope, and our sense of identity and worth. We begin to feel more worthless because our humanness won't allow us to be our own Higher Power or we give that power to others. We are left with few choices. Only one offers us the freedom, strength and serenity we so desperately need.

Some of us come to CoDA already believing in a loving God. We may feel God's loving presence through hardship, or believe that God abandons us in times of need. Many times, shame causes us to believe we're not good enough to warrant God's love, goodness or grace.

Some of us have little or no concept of a Higher Power, or we may have forgotten or abandoned our learned concept of God.

A review of Chapters One and Two can help us clarify our concept of a Higher Power. In our childhood, our Higher Power may have had personality traits similar to authority figures. At times, God may still resemble a punishing or shaming person like a tyrannical spiritual leader, family member or friend. We find it helpful to list the personality characteristics and traits of a Higher Power with whom we do have or would like to have a relationship. This can help us determine if we have transferred personality traits and characteristics from our former or present abusers to our Higher Power. To better understand these concepts, we talk with others in CoDA and learn from their experiences. Some people choose nature, the universe or their home groups of Co-Dependents Anonymous as their Higher Power. Others choose, renew or strengthen a belief in a Higher Power of religious convictions. We learn how they struggle, just like us, and how they experience many miracles in their lives and relationships with God and others, often in spite of their doubts and fears. We learn of their spiritual discoveries and how God works in their lives, even when they ignore God's presence. We learn how their lives are restored through faith and even divine intervention, sometimes in the face of life threatening circumstances. For some people, placing faith and belief in a Higher Power may be difficult because it means letting go of illusionary safeguards. It means believing or being willing to believe that a power greater than ourselves can do for us what we're unable to do for ourselves.

We remember we're being asked in Step Two only to believe or be willing to believe that a power greater than ourselves can restore us to sanity. We're not required to believe in another person's personal God, religion or spiritual concept. Our Higher Power must feel right and safe to us. Our Higher Power must be one of our own choosing and concept. As we begin placing our faith in this renewed or newly established relationship, we begin to feel relief and a new sense of hope. We no longer need to control or avoid ourselves or others. We begin placing this relationship first to gain the strength and peace necessary to maintain recovery and live life rather than survive life.

In Step Two, we experience a newfound faith and responsibility. Our Higher Power does not accomplish our recovery work for us; we must do our share. Every day, we must attempt to renew and strengthen our relationship with our Higher Power and share our newly fortified experience, strength and hope with other codependents.

With the help of a loving Higher Power, we are now ready to begin Step Three.

Step Three
Made a decision to turn our will and our lives over to the care of God as we understood God.

Made a decision—We had admitted our powerlessness over the compulsive behaviors we had practiced for so long. We were beginning to believe a Higher Power could relieve them. The next Step was obvious. If we believed we were powerless and that a Higher Power could transform us, why not accept it? Why not give God a chance where we had failed? Besides, what did we have to lose but our misery?

Our will and our fives—Our old ideas called out to us to return to self-will. Once again, we attempted to play God in our lives and the lives of others. Old doubts sometimes challenged our new thinking. We began to believe that even though this program worked for others—we were different. Losing hope, we questioned our ability to change.

It was this experience that led us to acknowledge that this program of recovery was not a "flash in the pan," something nice to do on a pleasant afternoon. It represented our opportunity to live as whole human beings. And if we wanted it, we would need the willingness to go to any lengths—even if it meant asking God for help more than once.

excerpt from Step Three in the
CoDA *Twelve Steps Handbook*

In this Step we continue to develop and strengthen our relationship with God.

We pause to read this Step and what it suggests we do. We reflect upon its wisdom and our feelings about surrender.

We are asked to make a decision to let go of ourselves and others. We decide whether we can trust in God to care for all we consider precious and important. Trust does not come easily for many of us. For years, we put our faith and hope in ourselves and others. We relied on everything but our Higher Power to provide us peace, happiness and well-being.

Control and avoidance have demanded a great deal of our time, attention and energy. We know we've abandoned ourselves and given others the power of our well-being. Some of us pray and hope that God will help. But until we let go on a heartfelt level, our codependence continues.

Through our work with Steps One and Two, we realize that our control and avoidances no longer work and that others are no longer responsible for our happiness and well-being. We realize how our playing God or giving the power of God to others is short-lived, painful, and, ultimately, self-destructive. We gain a better or new understanding of a power greater than ourselves. Until we turn our emotional attention to God, we are still bound by our codependent thoughts, feelings and behaviors.

We may be frightened by the thought of allowing God to take care of us and the other people in our lives. What if God doesn't do what we think best? What if things don't go the way we would like? What if "they" don't change? What will happen if others don't like us as we change in recovery?

As codependents, our fears are understandable. They lay beneath our intense need to control and avoid ourselves and others. In letting go of our control and avoidances, these fears often surface and we are emotionally faced with our spiritual dilemma. Once we face these fears, we are at a crossroads: Do we return to playing God in ours and others' lives or do we turn our will and life over to the care of God as we understand God?

We remember that we are asked only to make a decision. We are not asked to instantly experience total faith and trust in God. Our ability to trust in healthy ways has, more than likely, been negatively affected by the codependence in our lives. We cannot expect to make this decision without some reservation and fear.

To cope with our fears, we ask God for courage and strength. We seek the support and understanding of our sponsors and recovery friends. Some of us may create a special time and place to complete this Step. In any case, when we are ready, we may find this prayer to be helpful:

> *God, I give to You all that I am and all that I will be for Your healing and direction. Make new this day as I release all my worries and fears, knowing that You are by my side. Please help me to open myself to Your love, to allow Your love to heal my wounds, and to allow Your love to flow through me and from me to those around me. May Your will be done this day and always. Amen*

When we make this decision, our fears, concerns and reservations subside, and our relationship with

God grows. Our trust grows stronger by continuing our recovery work and experiencing how God helps us to change our codependent behavior. We feel a healthier sense of well-being. Our tendency to control and avoid others and ourselves decreases.

As we progressively release our control-and-avoidance behaviors and refocus our attention and energies on our own personal recovery, we're not as overwhelmed by life's circumstances. We experience a growing sense of serenity. We more effectively release the lives of others to the care of God, as well.

We may not realize how dramatic the changes have been in our lives and circumstances because they're so often subtle. They happen day-by-day, and we may not see them. A review of just how far we've progressed over the past month, six months, and year(s), can reassure us of God's continuing presence and care.

We may experience circumstances when we think God cannot or will not help. We may revert to our former codependent survival patterns. If we look closely, we find that fear, shame, or fear of shame are at work once again. We can walk a path toward serenity again by praying for God's help and guidance, talking with our sponsors and recovering friends, and reviewing these first three Steps.

Day by day we strengthen our relationship with God. We become more responsible for our recovery by placing this relationship first. Every day, we find it helpful to renew our decision to turn our will and our lives over to the care of God.

As we continue to do this, our trust in God grows. With our Higher Power's help, the program of CoDA and the care and support of our sponsors and recovery friends, we can strive for a life of balance, strength, and serenity.

Having brought an end to our spiritual dilemma, and having developed a growing trust in the loving care of God as we understand God, we are ready to begin the healing of our relationship with ourselves. Step Four begins this healing process.

Step Four
Made a searching and fearless moral inventory of ourselves.

Searching and fearless—Searching meant to look over carefully in order to find something lost or concealed; to come to know, to learn, to seek; to conduct a thorough investigation. And fearless meant courageous, bold, and unconquerable. If "searching" meant to look for something lost or concealed, we were really on the brink of a great adventure, the discovery of our true selves. But this word "fearless" was another story. Many of us still believed it was impossible to approach this process without fear. We were comforted by others who had felt as we had. We realized that we were not alone, that we were embarking upon this journey with God who would guide us gently along our way.

Moral inventory of ourselves—The first part of this Step defined the attitude we adopted as we worked it—one that was searching and fearless. The second part of Step Four gave us our focus and direction. This inventory would be only of ourselves, and it would pertain to our personal behavior in as many life experiences as we could recall. The word "moral" had many synonyms; among them were words like honest, straightforward, fair, and open. The message in Step Four was clear. This inventory of ourselves was to be honest and straightforward, not critical or abusive.

If this was to be a thorough inventory, we would need to list our assets and our liabilities. That meant we would have a truly balanced picture of ourselves. For some, it was more difficult to discover good points than to face shortcomings. For others, acknowledging positive qualities made the task less painful. Whatever our feelings were about this, we were encouraged to do both, as each was an important aspect of a thorough inventory.

excerpt from Step Four in the
CoDA *Twelve Steps Handbook*

Until now, we've focused on establishing or renewing our relationship with God as we understand God. In Step Four, we begin a spiritual journey of healing our relationship with ourselves.

Many beliefs, religions and philosophies speak of cleansing the soul to spiritually evolve. Just as we boil river water to remove impurities for drink, so must we go through this process to drink more fully from life. As we do, we're better able to separate and appreciate our goodness from our unhealthy thoughts and behaviors.

Our cleansing begins with an honest and thorough self-assessment through the work of Step Four. We look to this Step to continue our process of freedom and to help us become all that God intends us to be.

Step Four may appear overwhelming because it often causes memories to surface, particularly memories with feelings of pain, shame and guilt that we tried to avoid. We review our first three Steps. We remember our powerlessness and unmanageability. We think about the strength and hope we experience in our relationship with our Higher Power. We look to our sponsors and others in CoDA for their support and guidance. We know we're not alone. Many before us have completed this Step. We rely on God to lead us on this difficult inward journey.

We remember that our courage to complete this Step doesn't come from the absence of fear but our willingness to walk through it. We work toward understanding our strengths and weaknesses, our internal assets and liabilities, who we are and what we've become as a result of our codependence. We look for understanding, not fuel to fire self-condemnation.

This Step is part of our healing—a form of emotional surgery that requires gentleness and care. We find it helpful to refer to Step Four in the CoDA *Twelve Steps Handbook* for insight, and to seek the support, guidance and experience of our sponsors and recovery friends.

A variety of methods are available to complete Step Four. One method is diagrammed on pages 44 & 45. In reviewing our lives, both the past and present, we list those people who have been affected by our codependent behaviors. We include God, ourselves, our mates, children, friends, family members, co-workers and people who participate in our various activities. In a second column, we list our codependent behaviors with each person throughout each relationship. Specific behaviors may be difficult to remember. This is defined in five areas: emotional, physical, sexual, spiritual and intellectual. Our behaviors could have included these:

Lying	Distancing
Manipulating	Punishing
Avoiding	Discounting
Denying	Offending
Passiveness	Bitterness
Aggressiveness	Abusing
Resenting	Enmeshing
Raging	Hypervigilence
Silence	Overcontrolling
Victimizing	Overpleasing
Abandoning	Teasing
Judging	Helplessness
Neglecting	Shaming
	Hating

The list above is not inclusive; we offer it as a beginning for exploration. To be honest and thorough we must ask ourselves if we've treated God, ourselves and others in these ways. Have we abused, abandoned, become enmeshed with, or neglected God, ourselves or others emotionally, physically, sexually, spiritually or intellectually? Because we may have reacted or responded to mistreatment by others, it's easy to rationalize or justify some of our codependent behaviors. Doing this only serves to maintain and continue these behaviors, and doesn't cause us to become accountable and responsible for changing them. We then create a third column to gain insight into what feelings drove our codependent behaviors. A fourth column can help us determine the consequences of our codependent behaviors; to that person, ourselves and the relationship. And a final or fifth column can help us determine our feelings about our codependent behaviors, the feelings that drive them and their consequences. The following two pages are an example of such an outline.

Person	My codependent behaviors & reactions	My feelings that drove those behaviors	Consequences to the person, myself & the relationship	My feelings about my behaviors & consequences
Mother	I made up lies to get her to give me money when I was broke 3 different times.	Shame about being irresponsible for my own finances. Fear of her judgments of me. Fear and anger about having to be financially responsible and having to get help.	Abandonment and neglect of my own financial responsibilities kept me financially and emotionally dependent on her. Manipulated her to be financially responsible for me. Kept me in the child role in our relationship and not equal.	Sad, ashamed, guilty.
Father	Stayed resentful, angry and bitter about his sexual, verbal and physical abuses of me without seeking help or resolving these. (He would pretend that everything was fine when I was with him.) Etc.	Fear, anger and shame about facing these issues. Fear of being abused or abandoned by him if I told him I was in CoDA or therapy. Fear of being labeled crazy and of being the "bad guy" in the family.	Continued loss of love and intimacy with him. Risk of my kids acting out my emotional secrets about him. Abandoned and neglected my own feelings about this. Needed to use anger, resentment and bitterness to cover my hurt, fear, and shame about being abused. Didn't learn to stand up for myself either with him directly or in some healthy way to gain a sense of empowerment with abusive men.	Lonely, sad, ashamed, scared, angry.
Joan (wife)	She raged at me at the park and I stayed silent for a couple of days.	Fear and terror of her raging or abandoning me if I stood up to her. Fear she might look for someone else. Fear and anger that she would make me out to be the wrong one.	Abandoned and neglected my own feelings about this. Neglected myself and the relationship by not standing up for myself. Enabled her to continue raging. Controlled her through silence. Maintained lack of intimacy by punishing her with silence.	Lonely, sad, scared, ashamed, guilty.

Person	My codependent behaviors & reactions	My feelings that drove those behaviors	Consequences to the person, myself & the relationship	My feelings about my behaviors & consequences
Bonnie (Daughter)	A couple of days after Joan raged at me in the park, I raged and dumped all over Bonnie for not emptying the trash. Everything was fine between Joan and me after that!	Months of anger, resentment, pain and shame about Joan's ragings that I never shared with Joan or addressed at all.	I abandoned and neglected my feelings about Joan's behavior and raging. I reinforced the role for Bonnie as my emotional scapegoat. I drove Bonnie and I further apart. I reinforced fear and lack of trust in Bonnie toward me. I reinforced the message to Bonnie that raging is part of a relationship and is OK.	Sad, ashamed, guilty, scared.
Allen (Boss, Friend)	He told my co-workers about something confidential that I shared with him, and I became angry and called in sick the next day, so that I wouldn't have to face them.	Fear that I might be fired if I told him how angry I was. Fear of losing the friendship if I told him how angry I was. Fear of him reacting to me in front of my co-workers. Fear of being judged by him and any co-workers as being too sensitive. Pain that my friend broke my confidence.	I abandoned and neglected my own feelings. Loss of trust and integrity in myself to stand up for myself and in him. Loss of intimacy with my friend. Loss of integrity within my friendship by not being honest. I reinforced the value that it's OK for people to violate my confidences.	Sad, lonely, angry, guilty, ashamed, scared.

45

As we progress in this work, we see our codependent patterns emerge. Many times we react to people in similar or extreme ways—just as we reacted to a parent or authority figure from our childhood. We often put another person's face on this individual, not allowing us to see their true selves. We unknowingly recreate similar or unhealthy and abusive patterns within our adult relationships. We must become responsible and accountable for these behaviors today even though we learned them from our childhood.

To thoroughly explore and understand the relationship we have with ourselves and to bring balance to the work of our Fourth Step, we must also explore our strengths, assets and positive behaviors. For this purpose, it's helpful to return to the previous outline. We do so with the intent of making a new list of these people and identifying our positive, healthy, appropriate and loving behaviors in our relationships with each one.

In this new list, we add individuals who did not experience our codependent behaviors—people who have experienced our strengths, assets and positive behaviors. It is helpful also to include a column for our feelings about our strengths, assets and positive behaviors in each relationship. We might also want to include a column to identify when we behaved in a healthier manner than we did previously, to show progress on our recovery journey.

Some of us find it difficult to identify these behaviors. It can be insightful to ask our sponsors, recovery friends, mates and family members about our strengths and positive behaviors. With an open heart and mind, we must strive to listen to what they share. At times, it's easy to become downtrodden with shame and fear from our past. Just as a tablecloth covers the beauty of a fine oak table, shame and fear cover our ability to witness our own God-given beauty, talent and goodness.

When we look at our relationship with ourselves from a more balanced perspective, we begin to realize we're not bad people at all. The shame messages we learned about ourselves as children are untrue. This is the way many of us learned codependent behaviors.

We must remember not to use our strengths and positive behaviors to minimize our feelings about our codependency. We must maintain accountability and responsibility for these behaviors and our feelings about them in order to change them. Today, we're not victims. We can't blame people, places or things for our problems or codependent behaviors anymore.

We become more humble as we explore our relationship with ourselves through the work of Step Four. It helps us open the door to see, accept and begin loving ourselves as we are. From this place of humility, we've become ready to complete Step Five.

Step Five
Admitted to God, to ourselves, and to another human being the exact nature of our wrongs.

Admitted to God, to ourselves, and to another human being—At the suggestion of CoDA friends who had already worked these Steps, we decided to risk this exposure we feared in the safest possible way, with our Higher Power. By admitting first to God, we were reminding ourselves that the primary element in our recovery was spiritual.

> Encouraged by other CoDA members, we stuck with this section of Step Five and, eventually, the pressing weight of what we had locked inside began to lift. This self-admission had become a vehicle for self-acceptance.
>
> **excerpt from Step Five in the CoDA *Twelve Steps Handbook***

In Step Four, we began our cleansing process by becoming aware of ourselves and our codependent behavior and addictions. We struck and held a match to shed light on those aspects about ourselves we've been unable or unwilling to see.

In Step Five we continue our cleansing process. Becoming accountable to our Higher Power, to ourselves and another person for our feelings, behaviors and addictions is imperative to our recovery. Without accountability, our spiritual program is incomplete, and we continue to play God or give others that role.

Many of us experience strong feelings as we consider working this Step. Some of us fear sharing our inventory with another person, believing no one else could have been as bad. Some of us fear being criticized, judged or shamed for what we've done. Some of us want to defend and minimize our inventory, blaming others for our behaviors. Some of us fear how we might feel about ourselves as we share our inventory.

These fears are natural in completing our Fifth Step for the first time. Though we may have strong feelings in approaching this Step, many of us find that in sharing our strengths and weaknesses with

God and another person, we experience newfound acceptance, humility and compassion for ourselves.

We find it helpful to give time and thought to finding the right person with whom we may complete Step Five. Is there someone with whom we feel safe sharing our secrets? Is there a person we can trust to maintain our confidences? Many of us complete our Fifth Step with our sponsors. Some of us share this Step with clergy, a spiritual advisor or a therapist. In any case, it's important to complete our Fifth Step with someone outside our families who can be objective, loving, caring and compassionate. We look for someone who has an understanding of codependence, its devastation and the recovery process.

In completing Step Five with the person we have chosen, we must remember we're allowing our Higher Power to cast a healing spiritual light on our darkness. We must be thorough and honest. Withholding aspects of our past continues to enslave us. By sharing our past with God, ourselves and another human being, we may understand God always knows what we keep concealed or are unable to see. We learn how God never abandons us, but we do abandon ourselves.

Upon completing Step Five, we often gain an even deeper awareness and a healthy respect for our powerlessness and unmanageability. Many of us experience a great sense of relief and a new spiritual and emotional freedom from the bondage of our past. For some, this is immediate; for others, it is a gradual awakening as we continue our recovery journey.

We may feel a deeper gratitude for God's help and the recovery process. In quiet reflection, we become aware of our losses but we realize that only through God's grace have we come this far.

We're not ignorant anymore of who we are and what we've done. Enlightenment always brings responsibility. We must continue to strive to change our codependent thoughts and behaviors with our Higher Power's help.

We remember that this Step is not an instant cure for our past and present problems. We must continue our recovery journey and our cleansing process by strengthening our willingness through the work of Step Six.

Step Six
Were entirely ready to have God remove all these defects of character.

Entirely ready—We were reminded that "entirely ready" meant completely prepared. Having completed our Fifth Step was a large part of that preparation. We examined this phrase more closely and found we could test it in our daily lives.

The answer came to us, that all of our character defects were, in some way, products of our own self-will. They were survival tools from our past and, while they seemed to provide for our apparent well-being, they were no longer enough. We wanted to live, not merely survive, and for that we would need a clean slate.

To have God remove all these defects of character—It was suggested that we view these shortcomings as a protective shell that we had outgrown. Hanging onto them would be as self-defeating as a bird keeping some of its shell or a butterfly clinging to a bit of its cocoon. At this point in our recovery, our character defects didn't protect us at all. They were excess baggage that dragged us down, often blinding us to our potential.

excerpt from Step Six in the
CoDA *Twelve Steps Handbook*

Step Six asks us to begin taking positive action toward changing those defects of character we outlined in our Fourth Step. It is a part of our cleansing process. Now we must apply the faith and trust we developed while working our Second and Third Steps and put them into greater action. In doing so, we take the decision of turning our will and our lives over to the care of God and advance one Step further by becoming willing and ready for God to remove all our defects of character.

Our defects of character may have served us well, even though they're destructive. By reviewing our Fourth Step outline, we can see the horrible consequences of holding onto them. We're left with little choice but to let these character defects go.

To complete Step Six, we question our readiness and willingness. Will we continue relying on our codependent behaviors to relate to God, ourselves and others? Or, do we accept the challenge of change in our lives?

Many of us question, "Do I have to become a saint?" "Do I have to work a perfect recovery program?" "How will I protect myself?" "What will I do?" In time, we learn that perfectionism is unachievable in this life and is a characteristic driven by a codependent past. Instead, we must devote ourselves to progress, with its ups and downs, in whatever stage of life we may be. We find it important to avoid using "progress" or "trying" as excuses or disguises for fear and an unwillingness to move forward.

For some of us, considering our readiness and willingness causes us to become fearful because we don't know how to behave in healthy ways. Some of us become resistant to change or fearful of losing our power.

In one way or another, our character defects emerge to provide us a sense of power—false as it is. To make the transition from self-powered/powerless individuals to healthier human beings requires the help of our Higher Power. Only our Higher Power can remove our defects of character that have provided us unhealthy defenses, protection and false power.

In exploring our readiness and willingness to complete Step Six, we find it helpful to once again share our thoughts and feelings in CoDA meetings, with our sponsors and our recovery friends. Above all, we seek the help and guidance of our Higher Power through prayer and meditation. We remember again that courage doesn't come from the absence of fear but the willingness to walk through it. It is only through God's power that we make true and significant progress. At times, we may be barely willing to let go. Yet even the smallest amount of willingness opens the door to the power of God's healing.

Readiness and willingness are key attitudes in our process of experiencing change from our character defects. Our experience has shown that many defects may be removed by God without effort. Some may require our conscious attention and work with the guidance and support of God and our Fellowship. Some of our defects may be complicated and require the additional guidance of the professional community.

If we are entirely ready, or thoroughly prepared and willing to have God remove all our defects of character, then it's time to continue our positive actions and move to Step Seven.

Step Seven
Humbly asked God to remove our shortcomings.

> **Humbly asked God**—After much consideration, we defined humility as freedom from false pride and arrogance. True humility allowed us to see things as they were. We would not instruct our Higher Power to remove our shortcomings. Neither would we beg. Instead, we would gently, peacefully ask.
>
> **To remove our shortcomings**—Having asked God to remove our shortcomings, many of us experienced their loss with sadness. We had never expected to grieve for what we had come to believe was detrimental to our happiness. We began to see that these "old friends" had served us well. Like a childhood life preserver that no longer fit, we put them aside. With the help of God, we were learning to swim.
>
> excerpt from Step Seven in the
> CoDA *Twelve Steps Handbook*

Step Seven helps us to complete our spiritual cleansing process in our relationship with ourselves.

It opens our hearts even more deeply to a relationship with God.

Heartfelt humility is a vital part of this Step. Without it, there is little room for a Higher Power to work within us and through us. Step Seven helps us to acknowledge our imperfections. Each of us is different, but humility allows us to experience true spiritual equality with others.

In one way or another we each reach our unique "bottom" in our codependence. We feel a deep level of powerlessness. We learn that God can help us if we are willing to do our part in helping ourselves. We surrender to God's will for our lives. We open our eyes to the devastating effects of our codependent behaviors in all of our relationships. We share the exact depths of our codependence with God, ourselves and others. We recognize we have failed in our best attempts to participate in truly loving and intimate relationships with God, ourselves and others.

Each aspect of our Step work has brought us an ever deepening understanding and experience of our humanness. Our heartfelt humility fuels our desire, readiness and willingness to have God remove our character defects. It is from this heartfelt and humble posture that we are ready to complete Step Seven.

In doing so, many of us search our hearts for the prayer and communication with God that express what we truly feel. Some of us find helpful the following prayer from Step Seven in the CoDA *Twelve Steps Handbook*:

> *In this moment, I ask my Higher Power to remove all of my shortcomings, relieving me of the burden of my past. In this moment, I place my hand*

in God's, trusting that the void I experience is being filled with my Higher Power's unconditional love for me and those in my life.

In completing Step Seven, we allow our Higher Power to guide our lives and the healing of our codependent behaviors. We begin to understand that our recovery can continue only through our Higher Power's love and care. We no longer play God or place others in that role. We become partners with our Higher Power. We ask for God's help as we apply healthy new behaviors in our relationships with God, ourselves and others.

Though we may behave in some of the same codependent ways, we become convinced, regardless of the timing and ways, that God will continue to remove these shortcomings. We ask God to remove them as they happen and seek additional help when necessary. We must try to be consistent in our readiness and our willingness. In doing so, our maturing, healthier selves will continue to emerge.

By completing these first seven Steps, we establish strong foundations in our relationships with God and with ourselves. We begin to experience choices in our lives. We become aware of our self-defeating thoughts and behaviors and begin replacing them with positive thoughts and healthy behaviors. We move farther from shame and fear to an even greater acceptance of ourselves and others. As this transformation continues, we notice a growing inner strength. People and situations that frightened, angered, overwhelmed or overpowered us become less powerful. We develop self-acceptance and personal integrity.

With these greater strengths, it is time to begin the work of healing our relationships with others through Step Eight.

Step Eight
Made a list of all persons we had harmed, and became willing to make amends to them all.

Made a list—In the first half of Step Eight we were asked to list everyone who had been harmed by our personal unmanageability. Our name came first and the reason was obvious. We had been the least able to escape from our own codependence and, therefore, in most cases, we received the greatest injuries. A change in behavior toward ourselves would have to come first.

Nothing we could have possibly done as children ever warranted the abuse we'd received. What was important here was to discover if we had harmed ourselves or others as a way of venting our rage, grief, or hurt at these past injustices.

Became willing to make amends to them all— The purpose of Step Eight was to focus our attention on becoming ready to face those we had harmed. And it was in becoming willing that we got stuck. We wondered what action we could take to prepare ourselves for this new task.

This self-forgiveness would be instrumental in moving us out of our codependence and into healthy, whole relationships with God, ourselves, and our fellow human beings.

excerpt from Step Eight in the
CoDA *Twelve Steps Handbook*

To this point, we have made great strides in establishing or renewing and healing our relationships with God and ourselves. It's time to turn our attention and energy to healing our relationships with ourselves and others, both past and present. Step Eight helps us to prepare to be accountable to others in a direct and positive manner for our codependent behaviors.

Step Eight consists of two parts. First, we concentrate on making our list. Then, we focus on becoming willing to make amends.

As we make our list, we find it helpful to refer to our Fourth Step inventory. We review our inventory and highlight the names of all those whom we have harmed—including God and ourselves. We may think we can avoid highlighting some aspects of our Inventory. After all, some people may not know we had harmed them. However, we find it important at this stage of our recovery work to include even the smallest inappropriate behavior. As in all our previous work, we need to be thoroughly honest with ourselves about those people we've hurt.

Because we were raised in families where abuse, abandonment, neglect, enmeshment, alcoholism, sex addiction, eating disorders or any other addiction may have existed, we need to be clear about how these influences have affected our adult lives. Have we ignored our relationship with God or taken it for granted? Have we blamed God, ourselves or others for our life experiences? Have we, as a result of emotional abuse, become critical and judgmental of ourselves or others? Have we, as a result of neglect, ignored our personal needs or those of our mates and children? Have we secretly held onto resentment, bitterness or hatred toward those who had neglected, abused or abandoned us in our childhood and adult life? Can we let go of fear and resentment as false power and establish healthy boundaries?

We must ask ourselves these types of questions as we prepare our list and discuss it with our sponsor. As we do, we may add more names. Once we feel we have thoroughly completed our list, we move on to the second half of Step Eight.

This part of the Step asks us to become willing to make amends. Once again, we have an opportunity to let go of our will or control and allow our Higher Power to guide us. We remember why we entered the program of Co-Dependents Anonymous. Most of us made a commitment to be willing to go to any lengths for our recovery. Making amends for our past wrongs is important and vital to this process.

In many cases we find willingness to be the most difficult part of this Step. It's natural to feel some fear as we consider our willingness to make amends; we're literally facing our codependent past head-on.

Some of us fear facing the members of our families of origin or people we have skillfully avoided for many years. Some of us fear how others will react to our amends. There are those of us who fear the consequences of our past codependent behaviors.

No matter how severe the consequences, we must be willing to address them all. We must be willing to become accountable in all areas of our lives: our spirituality, our families and friendships, as well as our sexual, social, business, financial and legal lives. We must face the reasonable consequences of our codependent behaviors. We're not helpless victims or offenders anymore. Rationalizing, judging, procrastinating, explaining, avoiding, minimizing and manipulating are now useless tools of our codependent past. They've been replaced with willingness and honesty.

Our emotional wounds and boundaries may require more work and healing before we are ready to complete this Step with some people on our list. Our willingness will come in time. We must commit, however, to healing these wounds and boundaries and to completing Steps Eight and Nine when we have the strength.

Our job is to list the exact nature of our wrongs, to accept and forgive ourselves for our wrongdoings, to be willing to make amends to those we have wronged, and to be willing to face the reasonable consequences for our actions. We leave the outcome of these efforts to God. We have come to trust in God's time and way that the outcome of our willingness and honesty always works for the benefit of all involved.

We remember that making amends is meaningless without the willingness and effort to change our codependent behaviors. Otherwise, we're simply putting a temporary bandage on the problem. Sooner or later the problem always returns.

In our efforts to complete this Step, we find invaluable the strength and support of our sponsor and recovery friends. Our sponsor is helpful in determining what, and in how much detail, to share with each person on our list. We may practice our amends with our sponsor, whose experiences offer us hope and add to our willingness. Most importantly, we rely upon our Higher Power for the courage to maintain our willingness to make amends.

Through our self-forgiveness, and with our integrity and dignity humbly and spiritually fortified, we can address those whom we have harmed and attempt to make right our wrongs. We are ready to complete Step Nine.

Step Nine
Made direct amends to such people wherever possible, except when to do so would injure them or others.

> **Made direct amends... wherever possible—** And so we arrived at a method of making amends—to acknowledge our harmful behavior and the other person's feelings in the matter, and to follow that with a change in our own behavior.
>
> **Except when to do so would injure them or others—**We looked at this statement in several ways, and included ourselves in the word, "others."
>
> We could not afford to enter into this amends-giving with expectations of those to whom we owed amends. By doing so, we could be injuring ourselves with disappointment and possibly resentment.
>
> excerpt from Step Nine in the
CoDA *Twelve Steps Handbook*

To complete our part in the healing of all our relationships, we must complete Step Nine. It is the work we had prepared ourselves for in Step Eight. We will have fallen short in our preparations if we approach Step Nine with any motivation other than to ask for God's highest good. We make amends only for the healing of our codependence, not to manipulate others in any way.

In addition, we risk failure if we approach this Step with expectations of how our amends will turn out. Some of us expect personal accountability first from those who have harmed us. We believe our pain will be relieved if other people make amends too. If our motives for our amends and changes are based on expectations that others will now like, forgive, accept or become available to us, we're likely to be deeply disappointed. Nor can we expect everything to go our way.

These expectations can vary from person to person and are usually rooted in fear—fear that the outcome will not be of our choosing. Just as we addressed our fears about possible consequences in Step Eight, we must clear our minds of our expectations, offer our fears to God, seek the support of the Fellowship, and ask for God's help in letting go.

When we approach each of our amends, we remember God is working through us, and we ask for our Higher Power's presence and guidance. We seek the help of our sponsors and recovery friends to determine the best possible attitude to serve God, others, and ourselves through our amends. We allow our Higher Power to be in control of our lives.

In making our direct amends, we recommend simple, direct and specific communications. We approach God, ourselves and others with compassion and understanding, maintaining our humility, spirituality and boundaries to the best of our ability.

Our Higher Power has been there for us always. If our behaviors have been inappropriate toward God in our past, it is God to whom we owe our first amends. Some of us complete this Step with God through guidelines set forth by our religious and spiritual organizations. Some of us complete these amends by writing them in a letter and reading it to God in God's presence. When we do, it's important to make time for ourselves to meditate with God to experience God's love, care and forgiveness.

Although there are many creative methods to approach our amends with God, the best way is to live progressively healthy and loving lives.

If we have been codependent with others, we probably have been codependent with ourselves. Our next step is to make direct amends to ourselves for our self-abandonment, self-neglect and self-abuse.

We may find it helpful to write a letter to ourselves outlining our inappropriate behaviors toward ourselves. We may imagine ourselves and/or our child selves in the room with us while we read our letter of amends. We may ask our sponsor to be there during this time. Or, we may create time to face ourselves in the mirror and, while making eye contact, share our wrongs and make our amends. However we decide to complete this Step with ourselves, it is important to begin treating ourselves with love, respect and care.

Next, we approach all others on our list. We find it helpful to first tell them how we have reached this point in our lives and recovery. We then share our wrongs and make our amends. It is not a time to argue, debate, criticize or judge others. We leave judgments to God. As we outline our inappropriate behaviors and amends, other people may react angrily. They may be hurt or understanding. Our job is to listen and acknowledge their feelings.

A simple formula and guideline for completing each amend is found in Step Nine in the CoDA *Twelve Steps Handbook*:

> "...to acknowledge our harmful behavior and the other person's feelings in the matter and to follow that with a change in our own behavior."

We recommend that we share what we are specifically doing to change our behavior. Over time, as our behaviors match our words, the people we have harmed will come to trust us more fully.

Some people may see our codependent behaviors as normal and want to discount them and our amends. Accepting this lack of insight, and reaffirming our wrongs and amends, helps us to keep our boundaries and recovery perspective in order. We remember we are cleaning up our part in each relationship, no matter how others may see the situation.

Some people to whom we owe amends may not be living or can't be found. Writing letters and reading them to God and our sponsor helps us to complete this Step. We remain prepared, however, for the opportunity to complete this Step with those we can't find, should the opportunity present itself in the future.

Some of our wrongdoings may involve financial restitution, legal or business issues, emotional or sexual problems, or other sensitive areas. These amends may require investigation first. Talking with our sponsor and recovery friends, and seeking the guidance of spiritual, legal, therapeutic and other professional communities can be extremely helpful in determining the best possible approach to each amend.

We also need to recognize there are some doors that are better left closed. Though we may be willing, some people and their families would be further injured in our amends-making process. Asking our Higher Power for discernment and discussing each situation with our sponsor and recovery friends will usually lead us to appropriate decisions.

When there is no possibility of making direct amends, being of service to others is our amends. In giving, we receive. Through God's grace, and in gratefully offering our service to others, we gain peace in a spirit once filled with remorse and pain.

With the help of God and the CoDA Fellowship, we complete our Ninth Step and free ourselves of the laborious burden of our codependence. Our relationships with God and ourselves stand on new firm ground, even more spiritually empowered and free. In time, many of our relationships with others heal. True acceptance and forgiveness become sound precepts in our approach to life.

Our greater challenge now is to work consistently toward changing and improving ourselves as human beings. By applying our willingness to this challenge, we are ready to incorporate Steps Ten, Eleven and Twelve into our daily recovery program.

Step Ten
Continued to take personal inventory and when we were wrong, promptly admitted it.

Continued to take personal inventory—There were times it seemed we were being nagged by feelings of fear, rage, hurt, or shame with no clear explanation. During these situations we put the first three Steps into action. We acknowledged our powerlessness over this condition and affirmed our belief in God's power to bring us to balance. Then, we asked our Higher Power to reveal what we needed to know about the situation. Usually the answer came and we could take whatever action we thought was appropriate. If it seemed slow in coming, we asked for patience and faith.

And when we were wrong, promptly admitted it—Step Ten seemed to suggest that we had made some progress, that we had become capable of handling our lives with even greater maturity than we believed possible. "When we were wrong," reminded us that not every unpleasant situation was our doing. It suggested we could cultivate the willingness to admit our wrongs when the fault was ours and the courage to set boundaries when the fault lay elsewhere.

excerpt from Step Ten in the
CoDA *Twelve Steps Handbook*

As part of our daily maintenance program, practicing Step Ten helps us to maintain daily accountability, health and continued growth in all areas.

Steps One through Nine helped us to heal our relationships with God, ourselves and others. We shifted the focus from ourselves and others to God. Spiritual empowerment is now our mainstay. We no longer live one-up, one-down lives. We strive to change our unhealthy, inappropriate behaviors, and Step Ten helps us to remain focused on that goal.

This Step offers us not only consistency, but also continued progress in our present relationships. Continuing to take our personal inventory keeps us ready to change our codependent behaviors. Some of our habits are ingrained. Our goal, however, is to make consistent progress. We look for familiar codependent behaviors and areas where our boundaries with others need strengthening.

For many of us, a daily journal is a practical tool for this work. A journal becomes a record of our progress, growth and areas of our personality that still need attention.

At the end of the day and with our journal in hand, we take time for reflection. Some of us say a short prayer, asking God to reveal everything we should know about ourselves from this day. With gratitude, we review events from the past 24 hours. Though this Step is intended to focus on our wrongs, we find it helpful to give some attention to our assets and accomplishments in growth and recovery, as well.

We ask ourselves if we've remembered to check in with our Higher Power periodically. Are we able to maintain gratitude to God for all that has been given us this day?

Have we been short with our co-workers or families after a long day at work? Have we been feeling sorry for ourselves or isolated from others? Did we rage, overreact, or passively abuse someone? Did we take on others' feelings or responsibilities? Have we been controlled or manipulated by people, not said anything, and then resented them?

These and similar questions help us to take an honest daily look at our codependent behaviors and feelings toward God, ourselves and others. We look to see if we have been building fear, shame or resentments toward others. Have we abandoned, abused or neglected ourselves in any way?

Once we're sure we have been honest and thorough in completing our inventory, we remember not to shame ourselves, but to be gentle. To shame ourselves would be indulging, once again, in our own self-abuse.

We determine what amends we need to make and the most appropriate ways to accomplish this. We remember to include any amends to God and ourselves. If we're unsure of the healthiest way to approach a situation, we share the circumstances with our sponsor and recovery friends.

Promptness is very important in completing this Step. If we procrastinate, we run the risk of not following through at all. Knowing what we need to do for ourselves and neglecting it becomes a form of self-abuse. To progress, we must continue working.

Because promptness is so important, we make any amends we owe God and ourselves each evening as we take our inventory. We ask, as well, for God's help and grace to accept and forgive ourselves, and for God's strength and courage to correct our wrongs and change our behaviors.

Over time, we find it helpful to review our journal. As we do, some of us may see consistent areas where we avoid responsibility and accountability in our relationships with God, ourselves and others. Often these are areas where we hold greater fear, shame and resentments. A review of the values and willingness we established in Steps Eight and Nine will help provide healthier solutions with these concerns.

At times, our resistance may be greater than the strengths we gained from working Steps Eight and Nine. We may be bucking against strongly rooted protective defenses from our childhood. Talking with our sponsor and recovery friends can help determine if the person or situation may be triggering deeper, unresolved feelings and patterns about people or situations from our past.

In these circumstances, and with other strongly held codependent patterns, repeating Steps One through Nine is our next alternative. In some areas where we seem to find no resolve at all, the professional community can offer support and guidance. Many of us find it helpful to balance professional support with our strengthening spiritual life.

As we continue to practice Step Ten in our daily lives, we gradually apply it to our experiences throughout the day. In our growing awareness, we learn to see our wrongful behaviors as they happen. Asking for God's assistance, we make our amends immediately and make note of healthier behaviors for similar situations in the future.

We develop an instinctive sense of when to set boundaries with others. With boundaries in place, we are less likely to passively or aggressively react to others, take on others' feelings, attitudes, or realities, or give away our own sense of self.

As a result, the remnants of our self-centered codependence start to disappear. We begin to accept and forgive ourselves and others more naturally. We become better equipped to experience progressively loving intimate relationships with ourselves and those around us.

Having added the daily practice of accountability through Step Ten to our recovery program, it's time to expand our relationship with our Higher Power through Step Eleven.

Step Eleven
Sought through prayer and meditation to improve our conscious contact with God as we understood God, praying only for knowledge of God's will for us and the power to carry that out.

Sought through prayer and meditation to improve our conscious contact with God as we understood God—In the beginning, some of us needed direction. We weren't clear where prayer left off and meditation began. It was explained to us that prayer was talking to God. Meditation was listening for God's guidance.

How we chose to meditate and pray would be an individual decision. Because our conscious contact with God would be continually improving, our methods might change as we grew spiritually.

Praying only for knowledge of God's will for us and the power to carry that out—Just as each of us had to take our own inventory, request that our own character defects be removed, and make our own amends, so we learned that the purpose of the Eleventh Step suggested we improve our own bond with God.

excerpt from Step Eleven in the
CoDA *Twelve Steps Handbook*

Step Eleven guides us as we grow and evolve in our spiritual program. Remembering that codependence is a spiritual dilemma is crucial to our recovery. Through our codependent behaviors, we made people, places and things our gods, giving them importance and power. To avoid the possibility of returning to our former codependent ways, we must pursue a greater relationship with our Higher Power on a daily basis.

By the time we reach Step Eleven, many of us have learned or reaffirmed that we are not alone. We may never have experienced a relationship with God or we may have avoided our Higher Power through our codependence, but God has always been there for us.

Throughout our Step work, we have been renewing or establishing a relationship with God. As in any fulfilling relationship, if we want a strong and healthy relationship with God, we must devote time and attention to it. We find this is best accomplished through daily prayer and meditation.

For some of us, praying on a daily basis is a new experience. Some of us have many years of practice. Before recovery, many of us who prayed often wondered why things weren't changing or were getting worse. The answer is obvious. Either we weren't listening for answers, or we were unwilling to carry out the answers we were given.

Most of us understand prayer simply to be our way of communicating with God. Some of us follow the guidelines and specific prayers of our religious and spiritual organizations. Those of us who have no religious affiliations may find help from the experiences shared by our sponsor and recovery friends.

If we are still unsure how to pray effectively, asking God directly to teach us will surely bring us what we need. As with all learned things, if we speak from the heart and practice daily, we will develop our own personal, unique and effective communication with God.

If we previously expressed our codependence in our communications with others, it is reasonable to think we would continue these behaviors in communicating with God now and then. As subtle as codependence can be, we must be on guard for this even in our prayers.

Praying only for God's will for us may be difficult. It means we must be willing to let go of others and trust the outcome for their lives and ours to God.

Some of us, often without noticing, try to control the outcome of situations in our lives and others' through our prayers, because of our fears or other feelings. We have learned in recovery that we aren't in charge of others' lives nor will we benefit from trying to control God's will. To continue on our spiritual path, we must release our control to God.

Each of us is different; we come from varying backgrounds and have distinct life circumstances. God's will for one may not be the same as God's will for another. When we seem led to pray for others, asking for God's love, will and the highest good is usually sufficient. Our lives become much simpler when we emotionally and spiritually let go, pray only for God's will for us, the power to carry that out, ask God to guide us and direct us throughout our day, and trust the outcome of ours and others' circumstances to our Higher Power's care.

In our relationship with God, meditation is our way of listening for God's will and experiencing God's presence. Some say we pray through our words; we listen with our hearts. To hear with our hearts, we must step out of our fast-paced, daily activities, quiet ourselves and focus our attention on God as we understand God. To aid the quieting of our internal dialogues, some of us use music. Some of us rely upon physical and mental disciplines. And some of us simply sit quietly, close our eyes and allow our thoughts to rest.

There are many forms of meditation. Finding one that fulfills our needs may take a little time. Whatever the form, it's important to allow ourselves to feel a heartfelt and spiritual connectedness with our Higher Power.

By meditating and/or praying daily to improve our conscious contact with God, we become more aware of God's presence in all aspects of our lives. We begin to see and hear answers to our prayers through surprising sources. It may happen directly in our meditation or prayer. At times, we may find answers we never prayed for, nor ever imagined.

Though we may have set aside specific times in the morning or evening to practice this Step, we also find that checking in with our Higher Power throughout the day helps us to improve our conscious contact with God. We might utter a prayer of gratitude for something that just happened or ask

God's assistance when we're unsure of which path to take. We may even take time during a break or lunch to quietly meditate and renew our connection with God's presence.

In seeking God's will for us for specific situations, we may be led to let go emotionally and do nothing— neither taking nor making changes in our circumstances. When we are unsure of the right path, we review the possibilities with our sponsor and recovery friends. Often a different perspective sheds light on God's will for us.

Once we are assured of God's will, we ask for God's grace, strength and courage to carry it out. This is especially important when circumstances are emotionally overwhelming. We must remember that God's power is always present for us. With daily application of this Step, we come to believe that the power of God always carries us through wherever God's will leads us.

As we grow through our daily practice of Step Eleven, we are truly allowing God to control our daily lives and recovery. Our fears decrease and we come to trust that all we need to meet each day is provided for by our Higher Power. Our strength and spiritual empowerment grow more present in all our relationships. Our faith in God is continually renewed as we watch God's miracles unfold in our lives. Our spirit progressively comes to know peace and well-being.

With our daily practice of trusting and strengthening our relationship with God in place, it is time to begin passing on to others all that we have been given in our recovery. Step Twelve shows us the way.

Step Twelve

Having had a spiritual awakening as the result of these steps, we tried to carry this message to other codependents, and to practice these principles in all our affairs.

Having had a spiritual awakening as the result of these steps—The first words of this Step were often glossed over in our eagerness to "carry the message." Upon reflection, however, we could see that these words described the very foundation of our recovery. We came to understand that as a result of putting the Twelve Steps to work in our lives, we were transformed and that no matter what we believed about ourselves, as long as we put these Steps into action, the result would be our spiritual awakening.

We tried to carry this message to other codependents—By living this program, one day at a time, we became the message we had hoped to carry. We shared our experience, strength and hope with other codependents at CoDA meetings or when asked.

It was our process, what we did, rather than our personality, that was the message. The way we "carried it" was by being where we could share it—with other people.

And practice these principles in all our affairs—The final phrase in this Step reminded us that we could not separate our spirituality from the rest of our lives. The principles embodied in the Twelve Steps and Twelve Traditions were not the private domain of CoDA meeting rooms. They were meant to be practiced in ALL our affairs.

excerpt from Step Twelve in the
CoDA *Twelve Steps Handbook*

Many of us come to our first meeting of Co-Dependents Anonymous with the hope that we can find help. We hear other CoDA members talk about their experience, strength and hope in working the Steps. We see the transformation that has happened in their lives and hear how they handle situations now that previously paralyzed them. We hear of their trust in their Higher Power, how they walk through their fears, hurts and anger, believing that God will see them through.

We hear of the spiritual principles found in CoDA and how CoDA is a spiritual program. Some of us wonder what they mean by spiritual principles and spiritual program. Not realizing it, we are about to embark on a journey of spiritual transformation. Now eleven Steps and a million miles later, we're embracing Step Twelve of the program of Co-Dependents Anonymous. In completing these Twelve Steps, we come to understand the meaning of spirituality in our lives.

Some say spirituality is how we allow our Higher Power to be expressed through us. Some say it is an expression of our own spiritual nature. Through our recovery, many of us believe it is both. However we define it, we now know it is a vital power which has helped us to sustain life, to heal, grow and become healthy human beings.

Each of us experiences spiritual awakenings by completing the first eleven Steps. Some of us call it "change in progress." Each step of the way, the spiritual doors of our being open more, and we experience a conscious awakening and greater awareness of God, our own spirit and spiritual nature.

It is the process of enlightenment, illuminating the greater truths of life, God and God's way.

As a result, we become more consciously aware of ourselves and the physical life in which we live. We see God and our spiritual way of life with all its dimensions through new and different eyes. We understand living, codependence and recovery with greater spiritual depth and wisdom.

If we had been searching for a spiritual awakening, we probably wouldn't have found it; it is a by-product of our work. As we concentrate on our immediate task of living our life day to day, we trust that God will continue healing and changing our spirit.

Spiritual awakening brings greater responsibility. Through our Step work, we gain a greater ability to respond to life, with its joys and difficulties, in more spiritually sound, mature and healthy ways. Part of our greater responsibility includes carrying the message of hope of recovery to other codependents.

Throughout our recovery, God has continued to touch our lives through others. We have received a great gift. If we want to keep what we have been given, we must be willing to let go and give it away. We are a vessel for God's love and healing energy. We must try to pour out our gift of recovery and pass it on to others. We become the message, the experience, strength and hope of recovery. Through our own enlightenment, we become God's light—a beacon for those who still suffer.

Service work is what we call giving what's been given to us. Someone else in CoDA may have reached out to us long before we became a member. Someone else paid the rent, opened the door, made coffee, and prepared the meeting room. Many people share their experience, strength and hope through sponsorship, individual sharing and in meetings. They have touched our hearts in many ways. Many have been of service in CoDA organizational work so that CoDA continues to be available to us. Each experience is a way of carrying the message.

In applying this Step to our recovery program, we see it is time to decide how we will carry the message of recovery to others. We determine in what ways we'll pass on what we have been given.

It's important to explore our feelings about being of service. Do we avoid this part of the program? Do we tend to jump in when others won't? Do we attempt to use this part of our program to exercise a desire to be in control or find ourselves trying to "fix" others? If our motives in this area are codependent-bound, practicing these principles in all our affairs is our guide to a greater purpose in carrying our message.

We carry our message to other codependents in many ways. First and foremost, we do so through the attraction that we provide by practicing these principles in all our affairs. We offer ourselves to whatever level of service work we seem led—from the individual CoDA meeting to CoDA's international organization. Whenever possible, we offer no hesitation when asked to chair a meeting, to share our experience, strength and hope, or to help organize a meeting or other CoDA event. Organizational service work is so important that the next chapter of this book is devoted to this message.

In other areas, we make ourselves available. When appropriate, we reach out to both the newcomer and experienced member with understanding, compassion and care. We share our joys and triumphs, struggles and hurts, experiences and hopes of recovery.

When it is right for us, we make ourselves available in sponsorship to others. Our own sponsor and recovery friends can help us with this decision. There is no greater satisfaction than seeing God working through us to support the recovery of other codependents and watching them become all that God intended.

Both inside and outside of CoDA, we find no need for promotion, banners or streamers. Like a bee naturally drawn to honey, the quiet humility of our experience, strength and hope usually draws the newcomer, experienced member and non-member who may need what we have been given. Our job is to share our story with them, invite them to a meeting and be available to them in healthy ways.

As we continue to give to others what God has given to us, we continue to receive greater gifts. Our recovery becomes an exciting and rewarding journey of spiritual fulfillment. We gain a balance of all life's experiences, from joy and delight to sorrow and loss. We no longer live life in the extremes. We allow ourselves to become more open to God's continuing miracles and spiritual transformation.

We are about to complete the Twelve Steps of Co-Dependents Anonymous. With gratitude, we recognize God's love, healing and guidance throughout our journey. We should pat ourselves on the back for our recovery efforts. But we are not finished; we are just beginning. We must continue to practice these principles in all our affairs. It is a lifelong process.

We must continue to apply the Steps and the spiritual principles found in Co-Dependents

Anonymous throughout our daily lives and in all our relationships.

When our well-being is directly and negatively affected by a person or situation, we must admit, at that moment, we are powerless once again. Momentarily, our lives have become unmanageable. Whether formally applying the Steps or applying the principles found in the Steps to the moment, the Steps always show us the way.

We may never be free of our codependence. Remember, we are human and progress, not perfection, is our goal. We are not alone. God is always with us. We are joined in this journey by thousands of others. Individually and together, we express the spirit of recovery from codependence.

CoDA offers us a guide for living healthy and happy lives. By completing these Twelve Steps, again and again, and practicing these principles in all our affairs, we experience a new freedom from our self-defeating lifestyles and find a new strength to be what God intended—precious and free.

The Journey Continues

Our program of recovery is meant to be taken seriously, but we find balancing our recovery work with play, laughter and fun is also important in our daily lives. These are some of God's most healing medicines. Rest, productivity, recreation and exercise require our attention, as well. The benefits of these, we think, are obvious.

Responding to all our needs in healthy ways is an important part of our program for living. For some of us, responding to various needs may require time and practice. Eventually we become skilled in these areas.

As we progress in meeting our needs and sincerely continue our recovery program, our lives take on a well-rounded balance. This is the balance many of us have sought most of our lives.

Through God's abundant love, the spiritual principles of our program and our willingness to be rigorously honest in continuing our recovery to the best of our ability, we will come to know a new sense of belonging. We will begin to trust and believe in ourselves and that the healing of our past is possible. We'll no longer be controlled by fear and shame. We will find we are able to respond to life's challenges with courage, integrity and dignity. Others will no longer be our gods. We will experience a new love and acceptance of ourselves and others. We will become capable of developing and maintaining healthy and loving relationships, and we will learn to see ourselves as equal to others. We will learn that it's possible for our families to mend and become more loving and intimate. We will come to know that we are each a unique creation of a loving Higher Power, born with beauty, value and worth. And, we will progressively experience spiritual strength and serenity in our daily lives.

Some of us question if all this is just too much to hope for. Many of us on this journey do experience the fulfillment of these promises in our lives if we work each of the Steps to the best of our ability, particularly Steps Eight and Nine when we make amends to ourselves and other people we have harmed. We find further hope for our recovery in the promises stated on pages 83 and 84 of the book of *Alcoholics Anonymous* (reprinted with permission). These promises are being fulfilled daily by many recovering alcoholics and codependents. They are:

> *We are going to know a new freedom and a new happiness. We will not regret the past nor wish to shut the door on it. We will comprehend the word serenity and we will know peace. No matter how far down the scale we have gone, we will see how our experience can benefit others. That feeling of uselessness and self-pity will disappear. We will lose interest in selfish things and gain interest in our fellows. Self-seeking will slip away. Our whole attitude and outlook upon life will change. Fear of people and of economic insecurity will leave us. We will intuitively know how to handle situations which used to baffle us. We will suddenly realize that God is doing for us what we could not do for ourselves. Are these extravagant promises? We think not. They are being fulfilled among us—sometimes quickly, sometimes slowly. They will always materialize if we work for them.*

In CoDA, spiritual transformation is our way of life. Being human, we make mistakes. We may have codependent slips from time to time. Remembering this, we approach recovery with love, acceptance, compassion and care for ourselves and others. We remember that love and codependence cannot coexist. Progress is our goal. We give ourselves to God and ask to be guided throughout every moment of our day. We work our program to the best of our ability and help others to recover.

In this way, we are the experience, strength and hope of recovery in Co-Dependents Anonymous.

CHAPTER FOUR

Service To Others

THE TWELVE TRADITIONS OF CO-DEPENDENTS ANONYMOUS

1. Our common welfare should come first; personal recovery depends upon CoDA unity.

2. For our group purpose there is but one ultimate authority—a loving Higher Power as expressed to our group conscience. Our leaders are but trusted servants; they do not govern.

3. The only requirement for membership in CoDA is a desire for healthy and loving relationships.

4. Each group should remain autonomous except in matters affecting other groups or CoDA as a whole.

5. Each group has but one primary purpose—to carry its message to other codependents who still suffer.

6. A CoDA group ought never endorse, finance or lend the CoDA name to any related facility or outside enterprise, lest problems of money, property and prestige divert us from our primary spiritual aim.

7. Every CoDA group ought to be fully self-supporting, declining outside contributions.

8. Co-Dependents Anonymous should remain forever nonprofessional, but our service centers may employ special workers.

9. CoDA, as such, ought never be organized; but we may create service boards or committees directly responsible to those they serve.

10. CoDA has no opinion on outside issues; hence the CoDA name ought never be drawn into public controversy.

11. Our public relations policy is based on attraction rather than promotion; we need always maintain personal anonymity at the level of press, radio and films.

12. Anonymity is the spiritual foundation of all our Traditions, ever reminding us to place principles before personalities.

Many members of the CoDA Fellowship have enhanced their understanding of the Twelve Traditions by working through *The Twelve Steps & Twelve Traditions Workbook of Co-Dependents Anonymous*. This can be done individually, with a sponsor, or in a study group meeting with other recovering codependents.

What is service work?

Our Twelve Steps and their spiritual principles help us to establish our recovery in our relationships with God, ourselves and others. They offer us spiritual guidelines to help us work with others. Service work in CoDA enables us to put these spiritual guidelines into practice. It embraces a healthy spirit of giving and enables CoDA to exist. Through service work, we acknowledge and esteem every person and their recovery, talents and abilities. Service work enables us to deepen the recovery we experience and allows God's gift of recovery to touch the hearts and minds of other codependents.

Each of us in CoDA has a variety of talents and skills to offer. CoDA offers a variety of service opportunities, from sponsorship and interactions with CoDA friends to group participation at local, regional, national, and international levels.

Determining our participation in service work is an individual decision. Once we choose the activity or role, we become open to another dimension of our recovery. As we review service opportunities and talk with our sponsor and recovery friends about various areas of service, we experience ourselves becoming a part of CoDA's spirit of giving. It's this spirit that assists CoDA members to work together for the good of CoDA in all of its areas of needs. Some of us may know exactly what service work we wish to pursue. Some of us may be unsure if we should do service work at all. We may feel overloaded with activities from our daily lives, not wanting to add on one more responsibility. Some of us may find it difficult working with others if we're not in charge, or we may feel we have nothing to offer. Whatever the case, each of us has a talent to share or an opportunity to give of ourselves. When we do, we grow in our recovery even more. No gift of service is better or less than others. They all have equal value—from setting up chairs for a CoDA meeting to participating in the CoDA Service Conference. Without all of us participating and giving of ourselves in some way through service work, CoDA cannot survive.

Our Traditions tell us that CoDA is self-supporting through our own contributions. We may think this Tradition refers to financial resources only; however, it includes our talents, ideas, abilities, time and care. The more we attend CoDA meetings, the more aware we become of the services provided by our membership. Pamphlets and newsletters for our local groups are paid by members' donations. These materials are written by members of CoDA who donate their time. Secretaries and treasurers of local CoDA groups prepare reports and handle expenses such as rent, anniversary chips and literature. Community offices and committees are operated and supported by CoDA members to help coordinate CoDA efforts in local areas. One of the ways we celebrate our recovery with other CoDA members is by attending local, regional, national and international conventions, all of which have been created, facilitated and supported by volunteer members and their contributions. With each passing day, CoDA benefits from the service work of others. The following are examples of areas in CoDA in which we may consider providing service:

- Sponsorship.
- Providing information on meeting times and locations.
- Listening to others.
- Starting a new meeting.
- Preparing chairs, literature, and refreshments for a meeting.
- Chairing a meeting.
- Greeting a newcomer.
- Cleaning up after a meeting.
- Volunteering as secretary or treasurer of a home group.
- Leading a meeting.
- Helping with CoDA workshops or social events.
- Updating meeting lists.
- Spreading the message of recovery to those who still suffer.
- Participating in a hospital or institutions meeting.
- Offering financial support through the Seventh Tradition.
- Establishing a Community Service Office.
- Starting or assisting with a local or regional newsletter.
- Working with local, regional, national, or international service offices.

- Writing articles and providing services for the Co-NNections newsmagazine.

- Volunteering for local, regional, national, or international conference and convention preparations.

- Improving the communication channels between local, regional, national, and international levels.

- Participating in committee work for local, regional, national, and international committees, such as Outreach, Hospitals and Institutions, Issues Mediation, Service Structure, Finance, Literature, Co-NNections, CoDA event committees, and others.

- Volunteering as a group representative, community representative, Voting Entity delegate, or CoDA, Inc. Trustee.

- Practicing and upholding the Traditions.

- Appropriately addressing Traditions violations.

Some may view this list as overwhelming, but when each of us contributes just a little to service work, we can accomplish so much together.

As we embark on the path of service work, we soon discover its benefits to CoDA, its members, and our personal recovery. We enhance our recovery to practice loving and healthy behaviors with those we join in service. We see the benefits of healthy reliance upon one another. We learn to accept our differences and similarities. We come to recognize that each of us has a purpose and path, all deserving of love and respect.

Codependence and service work

In our codependence, some of us use service work and other CoDA activities as a way to gain our value, worth and identity. We satisfy our hunger for an identity, or to feel needed, by becoming overinvolved in our families, relatives, friends, careers and other activities—many times to the detriment of our own needs. We literally give until it hurts our well-being.

Some of us isolate or avoid being available to others, fearful of our abilities or the judgments of others. Some of us are working to replace our controlling behaviors with healthy ones. Balance and workaholism are other issues with which many of us struggle. "How do we devote our time and talent in service work in healthy ways?" we ask.

Our answer is simple. Our Twelfth Step suggests we practice these principles in all our affairs. It doesn't matter if our codependence focuses on fixing, controlling, avoiding or isolating. We can experience more personal recovery through service work by applying our recovery tools. Service work is a safe place to practice our recovery. It can become a mirror that reflects which areas of our personality may need refinement or change.

Each of us involved in service work in the CoDA Fellowship addresses our own recovery concerns at some point. It's a wonderful opportunity for growth. Service work allows us opportunities to practice setting boundaries, working with and accepting others, refraining from behaving in self-defeating ways, and developing healthy and loving relationships with other recovering codependents. It also helps us to become more sensitive to differences between caregiving and caretaking, responding and reacting, becoming a human being versus a human-doing.

At times, we place high expectations on the service work we provide, only to feel disappointed or disillusioned. At this extreme, we may vow never to do service work again. This is a terrible loss. By addressing our unrealistic expectations, we can expand our growth and recovery. Our groups can experience this as well. An uninformed group conscience may build unrealistic expectations about meetings or CoDA groups. Members may control, manipulate, or intimidate other members or violate the Traditions. In these cases, unrealistic expectations and resulting behaviors become self-serving and sabotaging. The good of the whole of CoDA becomes jeopardized. These unhealthy motives or unrealistic expectations can perpetuate codependence within our program. Exploring our motives with our sponsor and CoDA friends prior to engaging in service work is important. Regardless of whether or not we desire or avoid service work, our sponsor can also help us identify the weaker areas of our personal recovery that might be affected.

Before we participate, it helps for us to understand our expectations, weaknesses and strengths. CoDA offers few specific guidelines for the amount of time a member should remain involved in any service position. We each need to remain aware of our length of service and when it is best to step aside. Others need to rise through the service organization to experience the benefits and growth. Sometimes we hurt ourselves when we remain active in a role or take on more tasks when no one offers to help. When this happens, we run the risk of relapsing into our codependency.

To find out how long we should take on a certain task or role, it's helpful for us to recall our spiritual and personal reasons for engaging in service work. We may journal our thoughts and feelings, pray for insight, and talk with our sponsors and CoDA friends. We need to be sensitive to the appropriate time for us to end our service work in a given area and allow others the opportunity to experience the growth and the spirit of giving that service work offers. For recovering codependents, our service work is a valuable tool. It's not a fix, penance or an arena for control. It's our way of passing on to others what has been given to us.

The Traditions in service work

Our Twelve Traditions are the spiritual principles for the membership of CoDA as a whole and the spiritual guidelines for the provision of service work. They help CoDA to remain spiritually centered and to operate from a state of integrity. They provide us a clear and specific path so that CoDA will continue to be available for us all.

Applying the Traditions and their spiritual principles in service work means learning to speak for ourselves, practicing spiritual equality with others and maintaining boundaries. We learn to accept others' differences, to lovingly confront passive and aggressive abuses and to work together with others for CoDA's highest good. We learn to be a part of a team working toward, and developing unity within, the CoDA program.

We risk hurting CoDA if we do service work without the guidance of the spiritual principles found in our Traditions. We can prevent this by applying the knowledge and wisdom of the Traditions as well as sharing the experiences of our membership. Understanding and implementing the Traditions is the responsibility of every CoDA member. We find it helpful to study and discuss them with our sponsor and CoDA friends. We also enhance our study by exploring how the Traditions apply to various aspects of service work. Some of the ways individual members or groups can support the healthy functioning of CoDA are through these actions:

- Promoting the use of CoDA Conference endorsed literature at meetings.

- Donating amounts over a group's prudent reserve in the Seventh Tradition.

- Using the group conscience to resolve issues.

- Involving ourselves in service that positively impacts other groups or CoDA as a whole.

- Honoring the anonymity of CoDA members.

Each of us is harmed every time a member or group breaks or modifies any of our Traditions; and each time we ignore, disregard, or overlook Traditions violations, we perpetuate that hurt. The ripple effect can hurt other CoDA groups in the local, regional, national, and/or international communities. It is important to speak up when Traditions violations occur. We find it helpful to do so in non-shaming and loving ways. No one is on trial; perhaps the individual or group is not even aware of the

Tradition violation. We ask our group to hold a business meeting. We share our knowledge and experience with the Traditions and the issue. We listen as others share their thoughts and opinions. We discuss the issues and look for solutions that best serve CoDA. After all discussions have taken place, we then take a group conscience vote and trust in our Higher Power's will to be expressed through that vote.

Service work is both a gift and a responsibility. As we continuously rely upon the wisdom and guidance of our Twelve Traditions, conditions that can negatively affect CoDA's safety rarely appear. In practicing these principles throughout our service work, we become responsible for safeguarding the spiritual integrity and the future of CoDA. If each of us offers a small contribution of our time and talent to service in CoDA, the needs of CoDA will surely be met and CoDA will continue to grow. Throughout our service work let us remember: We have but one ultimate authority, a loving Higher Power as expressed to our group conscience, and but one primary purpose—carrying the message to the codependent who still suffers.

CHAPTER FIVE

Commonly Asked Questions

Beginning recovery in CoDA can seem confusing at times. We ask questions and sometimes the answers bring up more questions. CoDA's Fellowship is comprised of a wide variety of people who have gained valuable experience through their lives. This chapter is a collection of our questions and answers over the years. We've found it helpful to refer to these questions and answers throughout our recovery, not only in the early stages, but as a useful reminder as we walk our recovery road.

We're not suggesting that the following paragraphs contain all of the questions about recovery raised by the CoDA Fellowship or that these answers are definitive; however, it's helpful to discuss these topics in meetings or with our sponsor and friends. By doing this, we can hear a wider variety of experience, strength and hope from our Fellowship, and generate more discussion. As we evolve and grow, our questions and answers will change, too. This chapter, therefore, represents part of the experience, strength and hope of the Fellowship of CoDA. It is important to remember that the Fellowship of CoDA is not attempting to provide professional or therapeutic help. We're simply offering our understanding of how we've applied these ideas and concepts to our recovery programs.

Why do I need meetings?

The CoDA pamphlet, "Attending Meetings," describes the "building blocks" of recovery: meetings, working the Steps, sponsorship and service. It also lists how we gain the most benefit from attending CoDA meetings: speaking, sharing and listening.

Meetings are where we hear the experience, strength and hope of other recovering codependents. We learn to join the camaraderie of people supporting each other in healing. We learn to listen and experience being heard. We find out how others have worked the Twelve Steps and how the Twelve Traditions have influenced their lives.

We learn about ourselves and our relationships with others by hearing other people share about growth and change. We can be present, loving and supportive of ourselves and each other in healthy and fulfilling ways. As we attend meetings and apply what we learn to our daily lives, we become more loving, caring, accountable and responsible. Most importantly, meetings remind us from where we've come and how far we've grown. They provide us with a continuous support network throughout our recovery process.

How long do I need to go to CoDA meetings?

Many of us believe we may need to attend CoDA meetings the rest of our lives; others disagree. It's a personal choice and one that requires contemplation. Our decision may vary from year to year as our recovery progresses. No matter how long we're in recovery, we may experience episodes of codependence, although they're not usually as strong or long-lasting as in our early recovery. Whether or not we choose to attend meetings for the rest of our lives, we believe CoDA always will be there for us.

What is a CoDA birthday?

A CoDA birthday is the annual acknowledgment and personal celebration by each of us of the day we started our codependence recovery within the CoDA program. This birthday can represent our first CoDA meeting or the day we first called ourselves "a codependent." Members at our CoDA meetings often recognize people celebrating birthdays and present them with a medallion for the number of years they've been a part of CoDA. When they do, we recognize that it's a special time for all of us. We can congratulate each other and acknowledge our continued commitment and effort to gain personal recovery and happiness.

What are sponsors?

Sponsors are people within the CoDA program who help guide us through the Twelve Step recovery process. These people are recovering codependents whose personal recovery is their first priority. They continue to learn how to live happy and fulfilling lives and are willing to share their experience, strength and hope with us. They've usually walked the road of recovery longer than we have. They're who we call for help when we're confused or overwhelmed. They can also be friends who work the program with us.

Sponsors are able to remain objective and detached from feeling responsible for our happiness and recovery. They also refrain from behaving in abusive, critical or controlling ways that can result in fixing, rescuing, acting as therapist, sexual manipulation or personal gain. Sponsors are role models for recovery, sources of loving support, and respectful of our anonymity and individual pace in working the program.

More information about sponsors can be found in available CoDA literature.

How do I find a sponsor?

The CoDA pamphlet, "Sponsorship In CoDA," lists some suggestions for finding a sponsor when there are few old-timers within our Fellowship:

> New CoDA groups usually have members with long histories in other Twelve Step programs, both as members and as sponsors. While they may not have experience with CoDA's application of the Steps, they do understand what it means to work the Steps in daily life. Such a person may be a candidate to sponsor you. There is a form of sponsorship arising out of this kind of situation called "co-sponsorship." If you choose this method, you and another CoDA member will sponsor each other. You can meet regularly to share what you are learning about the Steps from others and from reading CoDA literature. As you discuss various aspects of the program, you may become aware that each of you has some answers within. Some CoDA members have started sponsorship groups which meet weekly or bi-weekly. This group consists of people who make a commitment to work on the

Twelve Steps together. Discussion is focused on applying the Steps to specific issues that are related to recovery from codependence.

Do I have to believe in God to recover?

Codependence involves a spiritual dilemma, meaning that we've made people our Higher Power, just as alcoholics make alcohol their Higher Power for their sense of well-being. Anything to which we give our power and well-being can become our god. We find this to be true whether we've experienced a belief in a Higher Power or not.

Many of us find that recovering from codependence means believing in a power greater than: Ourselves, another person, behavior, addiction, place or thing. Some of us try to recover without this belief but fall short. Through our faith, trust and belief in a Higher Power, we're able to experience a rich and rewarding recovery from codependence.

As we attend meetings and listen to CoDA members describe their recovery, we hear them talk about a relationship with a Higher Power and notice that those who maintain a regular connection with this power experience the recovery we seek. The form of this Higher Power is ours to discover—whether it be unconditional love, divine intelligence, God, nature, music, an image of an ocean, river or tree, or our own CoDA "home group." Above all, it's important that we become willing to entertain the possibility there is something that can do for us what we cannot do for ourselves.

What is the purpose of prayer and meditation?

Since so much of codependence is tied into our spiritual dilemma, we find that consistently praying and meditating (in whatever form that works for us) improves our conscious contact with our Higher Power and helps keep us on our recovery journey. We can allow fear, projection, blame and shame to overpower our relationship with our Higher Power if we don't include some type of prayer, meditation or contact in our daily routine.

Through prayer and meditation we can experience a sense of peace and serenity in our lives, and strengthen and nurture our relationship with our Higher Power. It's a time we can be ourselves with our Higher Power and affirm that this God of our choosing is there for us. We can focus on our daily purpose, asking that our Higher Power's will be done in our lives and for the power to carry that out.

Why doesn't CoDA refer to God or our Higher Power as He or She?

Many CoDA members have spiritual beliefs that do not interpret God as masculine and/or feminine. Many people in our Fellowship have been discriminated against or suffered physical, sexual or verbal abuse from the males and females in their lives who were authority figures. Many people have experienced religious abuse in situations where God was referred to in a masculine sense.

As a result, many CoDA members have difficulty separating the messages, shame, fear and pain from their concept of God. To them, God has the personality of these abusive and/or neglectful individuals because they held the authority status, so it may be difficult to hear God referred to as "He" or "She."

Given the wide variety of people, cultures and countries, CoDA chooses to extend respect to all people and their varied spiritual beliefs. In short, CoDA simply refers to God as our Higher Power.

Do I work the Steps only one time?

Throughout the recovery process, we work the Steps many times. They're not meant to be a one time fix. Our Twelfth Step tells us to practice these principles in all of our affairs, which is our guidance to work the Steps every time we discover an area of our lives over which we're powerless. Each time we give someone the power to affect our well-being, the Steps help us to regain our empowerment and learn from the situation.

The Steps are our guides to living and maintaining healthy lives. By following this guidance we are given tools to use for a lifetime.

What is "Thirteenth-Stepping?"

This term originated in several other Twelve Step programs to describe unhealthy and inappropriate sexual behaviors that take place within the Fellowship. One person could be taking advantage of another when they're in a vulnerable or painful spot, or someone may be using a nurturing hug for sexual gratification. It could apply to sexual innuendoes or sexual joking in order to control, embarrass or subtly negotiate sexually with another.

Thirteenth-Stepping also occurs in meetings when members flirt, dress inappropriately or attend just to find dates.

In an attempt to approach the subject without shame and blame (because many people are unaware of these behaviors) some members of the Fellowship make announcements or engage in discussions concerning Thirteenth-Stepping and the potential damage it can cause. Whether we're engaging in inappropriate behaviors, receiving or witnessing them, we must all work together to create and maintain CoDA meetings where the members can feel safe to be vulnerable, share their thoughts and feelings, and receive support for their recovery without manipulation or control.

What does childhood have to do with our lives today?

The habits and beliefs of a lifetime, from how often we brush our teeth to ideas about God, country and our place in the world, are established in childhood. As we continue our recovery work in CoDA, we find many of the thoughts, feelings, and behaviors of childhood are present in our adult lives. Until we consciously examine each, we may unconsciously continue these habits and adhere to the beliefs we learned as children. The CoDA *Welcome* states, *"...that codependence is a most deeply-rooted, compulsive behavior, and that it is born out of our sometimes moderately, sometimes extremely dysfunctional family systems."* The roots referred to in the phrase, *"...deeply-rooted, compulsive behaviors"* can often be uncovered and traced to the experiences of childhood. More importantly, the way we interpreted these experiences and the coping devices we created to overcome our distress allowed us to survive or even thrive. We continued to use and perfect these methods of coping until they became unconscious parts of ourselves.

In our current relationships with others, we tend to repeat our dysfunctional patterns of the past. As adults, especially when our lives become difficult, we often revert to the old familiar behaviors to deal with current feelings and situations rather than question our long held beliefs. For example, if, as children, we experienced a raging parent, as adults, we may experience fear of anger—our own or others. Rather than express ourselves directly or honestly, we may go to great lengths to avoid confrontation. Conversely, if we identify with the aggressor, we may become argumentative and controlling. Codependence is about extremes.

If, as children, we were emotionally or physically neglected, we may find ourselves attracted to people who are consistently preoccupied, absent, or emotionally unavailable. Or, we may perpetuate the abuse cycle through our own actions or inactions. If, as children, we were physically abused, as adults we may become attracted to insecure, aggressive partners because their behaviors are familiar— reminding us of one or more of our caregivers. Or, we may justify and imitate their behavior, using physical force in our attempts to control others.

If, as children, we were emotionally abused, we may verbally abuse our partners or we may choose partners who emotionally abuse us. If, as children, we were sexually abused, we may have learned to use our sexuality in a manipulative way to get what we wanted or we may be indiscriminate in our sexual relations because we confuse sex with love. We may not feel able to refuse sex or we may avoid sexual situations entirely. If, as children, we were expected to be perfect, we may continue this illusion and rarely, if ever, feel satisfied with our own or others' performances, looks, and/or accomplishments.

We answer the Step One questions in Chapter Three to begin understanding how our powerlessness developed in childhood. Working the First Step helps us to gain an awareness of the effect our behaviors have had on our lives. ("We admitted we were powerless over others—that our lives had become unmanageable.") As adults continually focusing on our recovery, we work the Fourth Step, which helps us to further identify and admit to these behaviors. As we take a long, hard look at ourselves, deeply buried feelings begin to surface, bringing about the awareness that, at times, we have acted as a victim or victimizer due to our childhood experiences.

Searching for clarity and becoming more aware of the adverse effects of our childhood behavioral patterns, we seek help. We use the tools of the program; i.e., we call our sponsor, attend and share at meetings, keep a journal, and seek out supportive CoDA members or friends. Most importantly, we rely on our Higher Power for guidance. Our recovery work helps us move forward in our healing process and release the powerful hold of the past.

What is the child-within?

The child-within is the sum of all of our childhood experiences, memories, perceptions, beliefs, and emotions. It is the part of us that 1) experienced both the positive and the negative aspects of childhood; 2) retains the unexpressed feelings generated by our childhood experiences; and 3) reacts strongly, either passively or rebelliously, to the difficult situations we encounter in our adult lives.

The child-within, or our inner-child, is that part of us that carries the innocence of life, curiosity of nature, and the spirit of who we are. Our inner-child can be delightful, spontaneous, creative, playful, joyful, mischievous, tender, and loving. It may also appear as the hurt, embittered, shamed, scared, or angry part of us.

When unsettling feelings connected with the past are triggered, the child-within often reacts impulsively, immaturely, or aggressively. Our unresolved issues erupt as overwhelming thoughts and/or feelings that drive our behaviors, often leaving us wondering, "Why did I act like that?" or "Where did *that* come from?"

For example, if criticized by someone, we may overreact in anger or we may be passive. We might go into a shame spiral without realizing that we are actually reacting to a similar event from childhood, when we were shamed or criticized. A minor loss may bring on bouts of uncontrollable crying and subsequent depression, which actually relates back to unexpressed grief from childhood. For instance, if as a child, we experienced the death of a loved one, but were told not to cry.

The solution lies, not with trying to eradicate the child-within, but by embracing this often unpredictable, sometimes unwelcome part of ourselves. With help from our Higher Power, as we experience and accept our inner-child, we are able to heal our pain from the past and discover our authentic selves. Learning to accept and love ourselves is a gift we give ourselves, allowing us to live healthier, happier lives. We are able to experience what it means to love and to be loved. Recovery work is vital if we want to free ourselves from our all-consuming fears and resentments of the past. Attending meetings, following others' examples, learning to have fun, journal writing, and seeking professional assistance, if necessary, are some of the ways we use to connect with the precious little child within.

What is meant by parenting ourselves?

Parenting or reparenting ourselves means recognizing we are capable human beings who are choosing to become fully-functioning, emotionally healthy adults. Growing up in dysfunctional families left us with many unmet needs and we may not have felt valued or loved by our parents. As adults in recovery we become aware of our childhood wounds and we have the opportunity to fill those childhood voids. We learn to take care of ourselves by honoring and setting limits with our inner child. We use our recovery tools to nurture ourselves, develop healthy boundaries, and become accountable for our actions. As we come to love ourselves, we are capable of loving others and accepting love in return. We place our faith in a Higher Power and ask for help in addressing the fears, hurts, shame, and anger of the child-within.

Parenting ourselves means reflecting on and responding to situations, rather than reacting. It means practicing acceptance and asking for what we want and need in relationships. We strive to let go of self-shame and blame and take responsibility for ourselves, our happiness, and our sorrow. As we become more able to take care of ourselves, we discover how to stop expecting others to fulfill our basic needs.

Healthy parenting self-talk is filled with honesty, strength, understanding, compassion, and wisdom. If we make a mistake, our parent-self or inner parent refrains from making self-shaming statements. Instead, we address the mistake with a compassionate inner dialogue such as, "I know I made a mistake; I feel sad and guilty about it, but I'm human— sometimes I make mistakes." We nurture ourselves with loving behaviors and thoughts.

Learning to parent ourselves is a continuous process requiring a variety of teachers. Observing and listening to healthy mothers and fathers talk to their children provides models of good parenting skills. For those of us who were shamed by our parents, we discover we can reparent our inner child with a nurturing inner parent we choose to create for ourselves. We let go of negative shame-based beliefs and reparent ourselves with affirmations and permissions that help us recover from childhood wounds. Recovery allows us to be our authentic selves.

We can read books that cover parenting, assertiveness training, affirmations, and building self-esteem. Sponsors and CoDA friends may share with us their own self-parenting journey. Such examples can help us learn about loving behaviors and dialogue between our inner parent and inner child. Along with the wisdom, love, and accountability found in our Twelve Steps and Twelve Traditions, a loving Higher Power is our greatest teacher.

What are boundaries?

A boundary is a limit or border. In CoDA, boundaries relate to imaginary borders that surround each individual's body, spirit, energy, behaviors, thoughts, and emotions. We set boundaries to help insure our personal safety, comfort, and self-respect. If our boundaries are violated by ourselves or others, we experience various feelings of discomfort. Thus, we use our boundaries to care for ourselves and to be respectful of others.

We distinguish between external and internal boundaries. External boundaries focus on physical and sexual aspects. Internal boundaries concentrate on protecting our emotional, mental, and spiritual well-being. If our boundaries are intact and functional, then we can say: "I know where I stop and where you begin," "I know what is my business and what is none of my business," "I know the difference between my emotions and others' emotions," "I recognize what is and is not my responsibility," and "I am aware of what is and is not comfortable or safe for me."

An example of a physical (external) boundary is

a personal comfort zone: the distance of space that feels comfortable between two people. If we do not know a person, we might not feel safe if the person gets too close, tries to hug us, or physically touches us. When we close or lock a door for privacy, or tell someone we do not want a hug, we are setting a physical boundary so we can feel safe. Our physical boundary (comfort zone) can also be flexible. It can vary for different relationships and it can change within a relationship because of circumstances. We are all unique and only we can determine what physical boundaries feel safe and appropriate for us.

We are also responsible for and have the right to determine our sexual boundaries. As stated in the *Newcomers Handbook*, "Healthy and safe sexual boundaries are recommended from the very beginning in CoDA. It is not wise to begin new sexual or love relationships when first attending CoDA. Anesthetizing the pain of failed codependent relationships by immediately beginning a new relationship is a part of the disease. Staying out of new sexual relationships is a good stop-gap to end the dysfunctional behavior long enough to figure out what is going on inside."

Some of us may have experienced sexual abuse at some time during our lives and may not recognize healthy sexual boundaries. In recovery, we take our time getting to know our true selves and determining what is safe and comfortable for ourselves. We also take time to know a potential partner before deciding if it is appropriate to be sexual with that person. Even if we have previously been sexual with someone, we have the prerogative to say "no" to additional sexual encounters. No one has the right to be sexual with us without our permission. We do not have to engage in any type of sexual activity that feels unsafe, inappropriate, or uncomfortable. We always have the right to say "no" or tell someone to stop at any time before or during sexual activity.

Our internal boundaries define and contain the unique personal characteristics of our thoughts, feelings, opinions, behaviors, beliefs, and spirituality. Boundaries help us recognize, honor, and respect our individual wants, needs, and desires. They help us define our separateness and give us safety in our intimate communications with others. If someone verbally attacks us, we maintain our internal boundary and practice self-containment by moderately expressing our thoughts and feelings about their behavior using "I" statements. Or, we may choose not to respond and silently remind ourselves that how another person acts is about that person, not about us. If someone confronts us about our behavior, we use our internal boundary to listen to what they say. We do not internalize what is said before deciding if any of it rings true for us. If we have wronged the other person, we make amends. In either situation our self-worth is not diminished because we have maintained our internal boundaries.

We use internal boundaries in various ways. An example is deciding how much personal information, such as personal history or financial information, to share with others. Conversely, we refrain from delving into others' personal business. We might really want to ask a question or say something to someone, yet we do not because we know that person's private life is none of our business.

When we have healthy internal boundary systems, we recognize that each individual is responsible for his or her emotional, mental, and spiritual boundaries. We allow ourselves and others to have their own thoughts, feelings, opinions, behaviors, beliefs, and spirituality. With functional boundaries we are able to meet our needs without infringing on others' abilities to meet their needs. Our internal boundaries can be flexible and we decide what is safe and comfortable for ourselves.

We are the only ones who can engage our own boundaries. We cannot expect others to recognize and respect them if they do not know about them. It is our responsibility to communicate our boundaries to others in a gentle and firm way, remembering that if someone hasn't dealt with their own lack of boundaries, they probably will not recognize boundaries in others. If we encounter a perpetrator or major offender who does not respect our boundaries, then it might be necessary to create a "wall" between us and that person for our personal safety. Conversely, some of us may avoid forming healthy and loving relationships by shutting ourselves off from authentic interactions with others. We may believe we have created boundaries when we have actually created walls that impede our ability to have healthy relationships.

Creating healthy boundaries is essential for our recovery. We learn this by attending meetings, socializing after meetings, talking with our sponsor, working the Steps, and participating in service work. With the guidance we receive from our Higher Power, we create healthy boundaries for ourselves and learn to respect others' boundaries. We are then able to form and sustain healthy and loving relationships with ourselves and others.

What is enmeshment?

Enmeshment occurs in relationships between people who have not developed their own clear identities and/or boundaries. Each person's sense of wholeness and self-worth is intertwined with those of the other person. It is as if there were only one identity, and it is difficult for either to function fully without the other. When we look to another person to define our values, and we accept their needs, feelings, or opinions as our own, we are enmeshed. Statements of enmeshment such as, "I'd die without you," "You're my everything," "Without you, I'm nothing," "I need you," or "You make me whole," are found in everyday conversations.

Enmeshment is common among family members, lovers, friends, and in caretaking situations. An enmeshed relationship doesn't allow for individuality, autonomy, wholeness, or personal empowerment. Healthy relationships with ourselves, others, and with our Higher Power are hindered by enmeshment because our focus is most often outward, towards someone else.

The antidote for enmeshment is developing healthy boundaries, keeping the focus on ourselves, and working to define our unique identities, wants, needs, and opinions. Maintaining a relationship with our Higher Power, participating in CoDA meetings, and using the Twelve Steps and Twelve Traditions in our relationships with others all help us let go of our enmeshment behaviors and become our authentic selves.

What is detachment?

Detachment is the act of disengaging or disconnecting from another person, group of people, or situation. Detaching allows us to emotionally and/or physically separate ourselves from people, events, and places in order to gain a healthy, objective point of view. If we don't like the behavior of others, we can detach, recognizing that we are separate from them with our own distinct identity and set of boundaries. We endeavor to detach with love and respect for ourselves and others, especially when detaching from family or friends. We ask our Higher Power to help us focus on maintaining our boundaries. Even though we care, we remember that we are not responsible for other people's behaviors, nor are they responsible for our well-being.

What is the difference between detachment and avoidance?

Another way of stating this could be, "What is the difference between letting go and running away?"

In CoDA, detachment is a conscious act of self-care. We choose to disengage emotionally from people and/or leave situations that could harm us. Avoidance is often an unconscious, dysfunctional coping mechanism that allows us to avoid self-accountability, ignore people or situations, hide from the truth, or run away from our responsibilities. Avoidance is often driven by our fear of experiencing rejection, anger, disappointment, abandonment, or shame. Simply put, detachment is an action based on love and strength while avoidance is based on fear.

Am I ever recovered from codependence?

We can become very disappointed if we believe we can stop all of our codependent behaviors. Our program reminds us to show up, work our recovery process and turn the results over to God. When we do this and release perfectionism, we can experience the hope and miracles of recovery: a life progressively filled with serenity, acceptance and love.

What is a codependent slip?

Dictionaries tell us that the word slip means to stumble, fall, make an error or mistake. When we apply that to our codependence, we find the same meaning; we momentarily return to using codependent behaviors to deal with interactions or life's circumstances. (A codependent slip is also called backsliding.)

We remember there's not complete abstinence in our recovery; we're human and make mistakes. How we deal with those mistakes is what's more important. Our Tenth Step helps us to address this: "Continued to take personal inventory and when we were wrong, promptly admitted it." We also try to remember that our mistakes help us to determine what aspects of our recovery we should work on, and ask our Higher Power for help.

If we continue to slip, we may consider reworking the Steps on that issue. This will enable us to reach a deeper level of healing and understanding about the problem and work toward healthier behaviors. We've also found it helpful to avoid shaming or punishing ourselves for our slips. Remembering that shame is a large part of codependence, we find we only fuel the fire when we add self-shaming and punishment to our mistakes. Forgiveness, love and perseverance from our self-parent are the keys to working with our codependent slips.

What is meant by bottom-line behaviors?

A "bottom-line behavior" is a situation or a specific behavior that is likely to trigger our codependence. In order to maintain emotional sobriety and advance recovery we avoid these situations and behaviors. For example, an alcoholic avoids taking that first drink; a gambler avoids casinos, lottery tickets, etc.; and a compulsive eater avoids foods or behavior that can cause an eating binge.

For codependents, our bottom-line behaviors can manifest in different, complex forms depending on how we act out in our disease. We look at behaviors that have been offensive or hurtful to ourselves and others. These may include remaining in relationships with toxic people, accepting sex as a substitute for love, trying to rescue others, pleasing others at our own expense, obsessive thinking, fantasizing, attempting to control people or circumstances, and condemning ourselves.

We ask our Higher Power for guidance, talk with our sponsor, read inspirational literature and review our Fourth Step for renewed awareness of these behaviors. Each one of us determines what our individual bottom-line behaviors are. We seek out and create guidelines for ourselves—recovery tools to help us abstain from acting-out these behaviors. If we have a codependent slip and engage in one of our bottom-line behaviors, we practice self-love by forgiving ourselves. Our fear and shame subside as we become more accountable for our behaviors and actively work on changing them.

What is a shame spiral?

When we experience overwhelming feelings of worthlessness, apathy, or panic, we may believe there is no solution or end to our pain. Our feelings/beliefs seem to take on a life of their own and we feel isolated, rejected, foolish, or stupid. We may berate or push ourselves harder to meet someone else's expectations, engage in unhealthy sexual behavior, compulsively eat or starve ourselves, or try to escape from a situation by avoiding people. All of these behaviors cause our negative feelings to intensify and we feel more pain and confusion. We call this a shame spiral. Without intervention, our shame will spiral even more and may result in a crisis situation.

To counteract the shame spiral, it is important to reach out for guidance and support—to our Higher Power, to our sponsor, and to our non-judgmental recovery friends. Writing about our thoughts and feelings, talking with people we trust, attending meetings, and nurturing our inner child with affirmations can help decrease the intensity of our shame. With recovery, we choose to focus on our strengths and possible solutions in order to regain a sense of empowerment and self-esteem.

What is fear of shame?

Fear of shame is our fear of being shamed again by our boss, mate, family members, friends or parents. It has much greater control of our lives than shame itself.

We may be afraid to hear about our mistakes or shortcomings and, in turn, become defensive or critical, possibly avoiding or lying about a situation. We become terrified of being discounted or abandoned. We control others out of fear of their disappointment or anger with us. The shame we fear most is the same type of shame we experienced in our childhood.

Many of us find it helpful to share these fears with our sponsor or friends. When we confront these feelings and the resulting progressive fears, we're able to soothe and possibly eliminate their intensity.

What is projection?

Projection is a type of denial we use to cope with our unrecognized characteristics and/or unresolved issues, both present and past. It is as if we are a movie projector and a present life situation and/or another person functions as the screen. We may project a painful memory or a disowned characteristic onto this "screen" and convince ourselves that what we are "seeing or experiencing" is reality.

One form of projection is when we react from our history by re-creating an unhealthy childhood relationship or situation. We take an unresolved feeling/issue from our past and believe it is happening now in our current relationship. In essence, we are unknowingly projecting our past onto the present moment.

Another form of projection occurs when we displace an unresolved past or unwanted present feeling, such as anger, onto others. In projecting one of our disowned behaviors or feelings onto others, we might either accuse them of being angry or we might convince ourselves that they are angry with us. For example, we may lie to a friend. In order to avoid experiencing the feelings (regret, anxiety, guilt, shame) that might accompany our admission of lying, we instead accuse the friend of lying to us. We remain in denial by accusing others of behavior that is our own to correct.

What are physical and aggressive forms of abuse and control?

Some people say that identifying physical and aggressive forms of abuse and control is a simple task. We've found there are many forms of abuse and control that are difficult to recognize. Outlined below are three areas of obvious and subtle forms of physical and aggressive abuse and control.

> **Physical pain:** Any physical behavior that results in creating physical pain in ourselves or another, including pinching, scratching, biting, slapping, hitting, kicking, or repeated injuries due to physical activities such as overexertion, forcing the body to attempt to reach unrealistic expectations,

unnecessary surgeries and/or medical treatment that would result in physical pain.

Physical restraints: These include: Obsessive tickling, ganging up on another, holding someone down against his/her will, hair pulling and restraining any physical movement or physical freedom against someone's will.

Sexual touch: Fondling, being forced or coerced into sexually touching or kissing another person, sexual hugging, unwanted kissing or touch, molestation, rape and sexual violence or any sexual behavior used to control another.

What are non-physical and passive forms of abuse and control?

We've found eight areas which help identify some of the nonphysical forms of abuse and control.

Criticism: Shaming, put-downs, mocking, blaming, name-calling, imitating or taunting others, insinuations, and using meaningless words or gestures.

Verbal abuse: Shouting, being vulgar, continuously raging, using profanity, angry expressions or gestures to control.

Misrepresenting: Falsifying, exaggerating, distorting, lying, withholding and/or misstating information and being unfaithful.

Dominating: Domineering, controlling, claiming to know the truth, commanding, or analyzing others' behavior through logic or shame.

Suppressing others emotionally: Refusing to offer support, attention, respect or validation of others' feelings; not offering affirmations or compliments.

Denying self-care: Needlessness, or not asking for

help and support; addictions to alcohol, drugs, food, sex or other substances; people-pleasing, caretaking or isolation.

Financial constraints: Controlling the spending of others; non-support of a partner's desire to work; withholding money; using money or resources as punishment; making financial promises with no intention of keeping them.

Power tactics: Hurrying others to make decisions; shaming, accusing, pouting, threatening, or manipulating others; abusing feelings; gathering forces to control others; using money, sex, children or religion to control.

What's the difference between being codependent and being thoughtful?

Very simply, our motivation tells us the difference. If our motivation for being thoughtful is fear-based and of any need to fix, caretake, control, manipulate or avoid abandonment, we're behaving codependently. If our motivation is a sincere desire to give to another person with no fear of shame, abandonment or neglect of our needs and boundaries, then we're being thoughtful.

When we find ourselves pleasing other people and behaving in ways that can be harmful to our needs, we should ask ourselves, "Have I taken care of myself?" This question can help us discern our motivation to care for others.

What's the difference between blame and accountability?

We blame others when we're using victim-like behaviors, when we refuse to take responsibility for our lives, safety, well-being and happiness. We may believe the unhappiness in our lives is caused by our mates, parents, jobs or even God, but our unhappiness is actually caused by our own feelings and thoughts. As long as we blame other people, we're powerless to do anything constructive toward recovery. We're like a mouse caught in a maze of our own creation. Accountability is taking responsibility for our feelings, thoughts, behaviors and solutions. We stop longing for others to make us happy and look to ourselves and our God.

How do I learn to trust?

Many of us are never taught when or how to trust. The words we heard from our childhood may have been, "I love you," but the behaviors we saw weren't loving. So as children, we learned early not to trust. Today, we may isolate from interactions, or become overly trusting, setting ourselves up for hurt and disappointment. Learning to trust others appropriately doesn't happen until we're able to trust ourselves and our Higher Power. These relationships need to be in order first, so that we're better able to understand the trustworthy behaviors of others. This enables us to develop trust within our relationships.

Do I have to forgive those who hurt me?

There's a saying within CoDA: "Blame keeps wounds open, and forgiveness lets wounds heal." If we want to heal, we must learn to forgive. Not forgiving at all keeps us bound to blaming. It serves only to perpetuate our resentments and hurts. Quickly seeking and/or forgiving early in our recovery often becomes a quick fix. We must first do

Steps One through Seven before approaching Step Eight. If not, personal and emotional growth do not take place. Forgiveness or not, our same codependent patterns eventually repeat themselves.

How do I apply my recovery to my relationships?

All healthy relationships require our consistent time, patience, attention and nurturing. Many of our relationships have been devastated by our codependence. How do we begin the process of healing? How do we move from being fearful human beings to becoming loving, healthy and empowered individuals who allow others to be the same? The Steps give us the guidance and direction we need.

We may find it helpful to look at our relationships in their order of importance to us, focusing first on our relationship with ourselves, our Higher Power, our mate; then children, family, friends and finally those at work. We work the Twelve Steps with our sponsor about each relationship—past and present. We may discover that their order of importance changes as we become healthier human beings. We look at our powerlessness within and about each relationship, and focus on what we've experienced with them. We look to see where we've projected our childhood experiences into our adult relationships and how we've recreated these patterns again. We ask our Higher Power for help and insight.

Many of us take time to imagine what our behaviors might be like if our relationships were loving, healthy and equal. We note what positive changes we've done, so that we can focus on new positive changes each day.

Our Step work may include issues of powerlessness and unmanageability about the relationship. We explore our definitions of what we've been taught about relationships. We look at our roles within them, as well as our expectations of the other person's roles.

We talk with our sponsor about learning new ways to communicate with others. We take responsibility for our feelings, needs and wants and share them within our relationship. We search for meetings where topics focusing on relationships can help us learn how to improve our behaviors in these areas. Some of us feel additional need to seek professional help for overwhelming issues beyond the guidance and support that CoDA can offer.

When both individuals (or a family) are willing to recover—both individually and together—then healthy, loving, caring and truly intimate relationships can emerge. Developing and maintaining healthy and loving relationships is a lifelong process. It helps us as individuals to develop mutual support and respect for the relationship and one another's growth. We understand how we all grow and evolve, and that we deserve each other's patience and care. Recovery and the Steps offer us the tools to maintain this process.

Can I use CoDA for all my addictions?

Though codependence is considered the root of all addictions, CoDA doesn't address specific information or aid in the recovery from other addictions and compulsive behaviors. Members of our Fellowship who identify other compulsive and/

or addictive behaviors should also attend the appropriate Twelve Step program that can help them address their issues. Results can be disastrous when CoDA members attempt to circumvent their need for other Twelve Step programs by using CoDA as their sole recovery program.

As we begin our recovery from codependence, some of our discoveries and experiences can become emotionally overwhelming. When this happens, those of us who have other addictive and compulsive behaviors, and who are not doing Twelve Step recovery work for these behaviors, can find that our addictions intensify. This may lead us to get involved (or re-involved) in Twelve Step programs that are applicable for our unique recovery.

Some of us relapse with other addictions before we're willing to get involved with another program. Regrettably, some members of the CoDA Fellowship have died as a result.

It is strongly suggested that we not use CoDA as the sole recovery program for all our addictions and compulsive behaviors.

What is the difference between CoDA, Al - Anon, Adult Children of Alcoholics (ACA/ ACoA) and Al-Anon Adult Children (AAAC)?

Al-Anon, Adult Children of Alcoholics and Al-Anon Adult Children are Fellowships for those who are spouses, family members or friends of alcoholics. CoDA is a Fellowship for those who have difficulty in maintaining healthy, functional relationships with others, regardless of whether those others have alcohol, drug or other problems. Members of CoDA may also be members of these other Twelve Step Fellowships.

Do I need professional help because I'm codependent?

Many members of CoDA's Fellowship seek the help of the professional community. It's an individual choice, not a requirement. CoDA is a nonprofessional organization and cannot assess a member's need for professional guidance, counseling or therapy. Many of us seek professional help for issues related to our codependence that are beyond the scope of the experience, strength and hope that the CoDA program and our Fellowship offer.

When considering this choice, we find it helpful to ask our Higher Power for guidance and to talk with our sponsor and recovery friends for their experience and support.

Can you recommend any books about codependence? ...or a therapist, hospital or treatment center?

We recommend that members of the Fellowship read CoDA Conference endorsed publications and listen to the stories of CoDA members in recovery. These publications and audio recordings are available from CoRe Publications. Other books, of course, are read and used by CoDA members, but CoDA, as a Fellowship, cannot recommend or endorse specific books outside approved CoDA literature. We honor Tradition Six by not endorsing any other literature, program, individual, or institution.

MY STORY

The question comes to me why more of us do not share the truth of our existence. Fear was my answer—fear of others knowing me. Through CoDA, I have learned the paradox that only through sharing my more vulnerable parts, can truth and healing occur. CoDA has provided me with many opportunities to face my fear and shame, to discover much truth. I am grateful to have this opportunity to share my experience, strength and hope. Sharing is how I identify myself, and through my sharing I hope you may also find some benefit. Please take what you want and leave the rest.

I was born in a small town in north central Missouri. I left at age 1-1/2 and, to this day, have no idea what my birthplace looks like. I suspect that seeing it would kindle memories preferably forgotten. Those memories were similar to many others in my life that I would rather not remember. A sad beginning, perhaps, but the truth is necessary to free me from the past. I have come to believe that pain and the associated difficulties and crises are required to attain lasting happiness in one's life. The pain becomes a door to healing. As I continue on my journey, the truth of this concept becomes more clear. My beliefs about my past do affect how I view my present. I now choose to see my past with less pain. The day when I have accepted my past in total, no longer holding any resentment, will be a graceful day in my life.

There are the stories told about Jack in a hushed voice to me by my Grandmother. Our family called mom "Jack," short for Jacqueline. My mother did not want to be called "Mom." Jack used to let me, as a newborn, cry in my crib until I would finally cry myself to sleep. When I was a little older, we went to bed no later than 7 p.m., because Jack was "fed up" with me and my brother. I have no memories of any expression of affection, much less love, in our family. There were no hugs or pats on the back. I remember Jack as unhappy; "things" were never right. I believe I was unwanted from birth. Being unwanted, from my experience and from what I have read, leaves me with lifelong self-esteem issues. These issues are like chronic heart problems; with good practice they are minimized, but they never go away.

Our family moved to a large city early in my life, where my memories began. I remember the house. My earliest memories are of being beaten. I remember making the decision when I was four never to cry again, no matter how hard or how many times my Dad beat me with his "fraternity" paddle. Jack was as cruel as Dad. She set me up for all my beatings with Dad. During the week while Dad traveled, she would keep a "list of my infractions" (talking back, not doing what she wanted exactly when she wanted). When Dad returned on Friday night, she would read the list, and out came the frat-paddle. Dad was a salesman for a big corporation. I was glad he was not home during the week.

My history would be of little relevance, except that the behavior I learned manifested itself in some insidious ways. My two marriages and my deteriorated relationship with two daughters are the best examples. Through these, I discovered what "dysfunctional family" means.

I found out what an addictive personality is all about. I found out what happens when a little boy named Andy does not get the love and nurturing he needs and deserves. As a child, in order to defend myself in the kind of environment I grew up in, I developed psychological defenses. Primary among these defenses is denial—denial that the abuse occurred or that the abuse had any significant impact. Beyond the denial was the acting out to try and work out these psychological traumas. A good example of these defenses is my denial (not consciously) until after I was 40, that Jack was an alcoholic. Dad is an enabler, someone who made it possible for Jack to practice her addiction. Telling the whole truth about Jack and Dad was and is important to understanding the true impact of my past.

Dysfunctional families do lots of unusual things. Children get to play adult roles because the adults do not know how to act like adults. My early role was "dad." I got this part because someone had to fill the void created by Jack not receiving love and attention from Dad. I understand this to be called emotional incest. Jack and Dad never slept together. They always had separate beds and later separate rooms. As a child, I tried hard to please Jack, and then she set me up for beatings. The impact of inconsistent behavior and incest on trust are difficult to overcome. I have vague memories of being physically incested by Jack, but I cannot remember. Much recovery remains for me in this area. Trusting is hard for me.

We moved to another city while I was in third grade and then back to the previous city after fifth grade. I grew angry with my early role. Who would not? A new role began to emerge; I became the one who acted out all the family problems, the rebel. I was good at it. I started smoking at 11 and drinking at 14. I smoked a pack a day by 14 and still participated in sports. At night I used to sneak out often. One summer, after my parents finally gave up on beatings, I was grounded for the "rest of my life" because I just kept sneaking out. During this time period, Jack and Dad yelled at each other often. No wonder I had a temper (later I learned it was rage). I got involved with women early. I took the advice of grown-ups and did not get a girl pregnant. I was 14 when I first started borrowing Jack's car. She went to bed early, and Dad was "out of town." My rebel role continued when my family moved to the west coast in 1965. I was 16 and living life in the "fast lane." In retrospect, I think about how different my life would have been if I had put my limitless energy into educating myself or helping society.

Next was college, then quitting college, followed by Vietnam, then back to school. The "achiever" role was starting to develop—I would prove to the world and me that I was OK. Achievement was a compulsive coverup for low self-esteem. I would get a B.S., an M.B.A. and a C.P.A. Success in business was important. As my responsibilities grew in business, work replaced partying as the preferred method of escape. I became a workaholic, just as effective as any other addiction at encouraging denial and preventing intimate relationships. During this time, two marriages failed. The estrangement of my children which occurred due to my second divorce (my ex-wife is from a dysfunctional family, too) subtly began the process of "recovery" for me. Through trying to understand the pain my children were encountering due to divorce, and what I could do for them, I came to understand the pain of my childhood. The moment at which that occurred was simultaneously one of the most painful and graceful moments of my life. It became clear that I had learned few skills for interpersonal relationships. My family of origin, where I learned my skills, only understood the use of control and manipulation. Love, growth, kindness and encouragement were not present. No difficulty or argument was ever resolved in our family; rather, an edict was issued by one of the parents. I learned to "tell people what to do," not to work with them or accept their differences. That is how I learned to relate to people; my history is no surprise, accident or stroke of fate.

Shortly after that graceful moment when I began to truly understand my childhood, a failed relationship became the final straw. My life was unmanageable. I needed help and a safe place to share. The pain finally drove me out of isolation and into a CoDA meeting which was the second moment of grace. The first six months were painful. One day at a time was the only way I survived; I spoke the *Serenity Prayer* over and over. My weekly meeting became the one thing I looked forward to. This was early in the CoDA movement. Sponsors were not recommended yet, so we all worked together as collective "buddies."

Then came the next moment of grace. I felt the need to become involved in a Twelve Step Study Group, but none was available. God acted through me and a group formed. Within a short time, 24 of us divided into four sub-groups or "families," and we were on a six-month path to work the Steps in detail. We met weekly and used a workbook to structure our efforts. As I write, my heart feels the love and struggle we shared. The power of the Steps is indescribable to me. Working the Steps encouraged growth and compassion; my passage to genuine self-love had commenced. One member of my "family" and I have adopted each other as brother and sister. Truly this is and was my family by choice. The family that CoDA offered has so encouraged the love within me to be found. During the time of this study group, I was to face some of the most difficult times of my life. Without CoDA and my family, I am unsure what I would have done. I sometimes think my Higher Power provided me the challenges to help me learn to ask others for help, a task which continues to challenge me.

The Steps were the beginning of finding a spiritual path. That path has let me know myself enough to leave behind a career that was motivated only by the desire to make money. I have traveled extensively, an act of cleansing. My travels allowed me time to consider my spirit and those things which brought me joy. I returned and began the process in earnest to decide on a new career. Many thought my efforts were commendable. I was often in pain from trying to control when and how my Higher Power would direct my path. Patience, and taking the time to listen, is so difficult for me. Yet it is another opportunity to learn that my Higher Power does not operate on the time schedule I desire. As I write, my shame for not developing a more intimate relationship with my Higher Power surfaces. I can now feel this and not run away from the feeling. Patience that my recovery happens at its own pace and is not comparable to others' is a truth difficult for me to accept. Many of the truths of recovery are difficult to accept. Letting go of old beliefs and loving myself are still challenging tasks for me. I have truly had to accept my powerlessness over my false beliefs and inability to love myself. Only with my Higher Power's assistance does a chance for change and growth come.

Spirituality is the core of all the Twelve Step programs. My knowledge of this core continues to grow. Developing a relationship, the relationship discussed in the Eleventh Step, is and has been an ongoing process. I have some interesting revelations regarding my Higher Power. First among these was accepting that anger with my Higher Power was OK. Being angry at God (someone like my parents) just did not seem possible. Then a friend said, "What kind of relationship would it be if anger was not allowed?" Allowing my anger has deepened my relationship. Feeling the anger has also allowed me to have what I call a pre-memory experience. On two occasions, while being angry, I came to feel that I had severed my relationship with God at a very early age. I felt that, as a child, I reached the conclusion (really a choice) that I could not be worthwhile if all these terrible things were happening to me. I felt that God would not allow this to happen to a little boy unless he deserved it. And so I need a spiritual recovery.

As I approach my fourth year in recovery, I see how far I have come. My recovery is an ongoing process. Many days I do enjoy the process, and some I do not. The time to work my way through the Steps is again upon me. My Higher Power helped me to know it was time again. Another long-term relationship has failed, at least temporarily. For a change, I am feeling the sadness and doing my best to grieve the loss. Since crying is such a challenge, I was proud when I could shed genuine tears and tell my inner child I loved him, that somehow we would find a way to prosper. I was able to hug my former lover and feel little if any anger. She, too, is a child of God, and our challenges make her no less than that. I know that our relationship had become unhealthy; and I trust, with the help of my friends in CoDA and other Twelve Step groups, that I am all right and can feel the pain. I still fight feeling "less than," but I no longer believe that my value comes from another. When the spirit is within me—when the light burns inside—I know that I am worthwhile just as I am. I know that one day at a time, I can trust that my life will work. Not only work, but prosper.

My new adventure into the Steps will center on my powerlessness over myself, my powerlessness to change beliefs and love myself unconditionally as I deserve. I see more than ever how my addictions and control have kept me from letting go. Codependence and my addictions have indeed been cunning, baffling and powerful. I have used work, play, alcohol, food and compulsive thinking to keep myself from feeling. Fear strikes me as the feeling I most avoid. As I look deeper, fear is everywhere: fear of intimacy, fear of success, fear of failure and fear that I cannot even succeed at recovery. Perhaps the fear of being with myself intimately and in peace is greatest. I long for the few days I remember as a child where I could lay in the grass and watch the clouds go by for hours. Being at peace with me, accepting where I am at this moment and enjoying it, are goals I would like to achieve. I believe I will achieve that by turning over my care to a Higher Power.

I have recently read the "Big Book" from AA. I recommend it for all. The book has been the inspiration for me. There is much wisdom between its covers. I find that where it mentions alcohol, I can substitute my codependence or any of my compulsive behaviors. I have discovered my other compulsive behaviors to be so cunning, baffling and powerful, and yet, I have seemingly overcome them. As a late adolescent and in my 20s, I behaved as an alcoholic, yet today I drink little. I have quite a number of various ways of "acting out." As the layers of the onion peel back, I can see that I am attached in an unhealthy way to my way of suffering and my false beliefs. This vision is how my Higher Power has helped me to see it is time to work the Steps again.

Next to the Steps, I would consider sponsorship the second most important aspect of recovery.

Because I was an early CoDA member, and for reasons I'm probably not yet willing to inventory, I did not have a sponsor until recently. Part of this was due to my difficulty finding a sponsor within CoDA. My recommendation, regardless of the program, is to find a sponsor. Take your time—follow the time-tested recommendations of all the Twelve Step programs. Make mistakes and then move on. The benefits of sponsorship are real. I look forward to the day when I feel the confidence to act as a sponsor. Some would certainly have acted sooner than I; I know my ability to be of service will come when the timing is right.

I leave you now with the hope that you will be fearless and thorough. Face your truth with rigorous honesty. Finally accept your powerlessness over other people and your compulsiveness. Let go that your Higher Power may bring grace into your life. Laugh, too; allow yourself to enjoy life. These are my hopes for you and for me. I also hope that our Higher Power's love will fill us with self-love so that we may live each day in peace and love and, thus, be free to be of service to our fellows.

by Andy D.

MY THANKSGIVING STORY

The date is November 22, 1990, Thanksgiving Day. All of our children and friends have gone home and the dishes are done. Suddenly this seems like the perfect time to express my thankfulness by sharing my story of abuse, codependence, and recovery with my CoDA friends.

I was born in 1944, an only child in an alcoholic family. My father was in the Army and my mother and I lived with my maternal grandparents. I came from multi-generations of alcoholism and abuse; it seems many of the men and women in my extended family were addicts and codependents.

I want to say up front that I do not blame my caretakers for the pain I suffered as a child. I realize that they, too, were victims and didn't have the advantage of recovery. They could only pass on to me what they knew. I take full responsibility for my life and all the pain, believing that I chose this lifetime to grow in specific ways. This belief does not diminish the terrible effects of my abuse and the creation of a codependent and addicted adult.

The first time I saw my father I was about four months old and had become his incest victim. I had always known that I was a survivor, but it wasn't until I went into hypnotherapy in 1979 that I discovered how early the abuse had started and how brutal the attacks were. Incest with Daddy went on until the summer I was 13. It included fondling, rape, oral sex, shared sex with other men and children, threats with burning and knives, and forcing me to watch while he raped and butchered animals. I felt really "crazy" while all this was going on, and I dissociated a great deal. Sometimes Daddy was gentle and quiet; sometimes he was brutal and added beatings with his fists to the rapes. Always I felt like I wasn't there, like I was nothing, a nobody.

There were other sexual abusers: my maternal grandfather and uncle, five family friends, two priests, and my mother. The abuse I received from these people was sometimes less traumatic and lasted a shorter time than with my father, but served to tear down my trust and any feelings of self-worth. Every time someone touched me, I froze. I wanted so badly to scream, "NO!!!" But I was too afraid. I just went deep inside myself with rage and self-hatred.

My mother was very abusive, both physically and verbally. She also came from an alcoholic family and was a victim of incest, although she still denies it. Her methods of punishment included slapping, kicking, and knocking me down with her fists; screaming at me; shaming and humiliating me; locking me in my room or my closet, not allowing me to come out to go to the bathroom; and forcing me to get up in the middle of the night to tell my drunken father to go away.

I felt totally worthless and hopeless with my mother. I have no memory of ever being held and nurtured by her. When I got sick, she made me stay in bed and brought food to me with her face covered by toilet paper so that she wouldn't catch my illness. She would lay the food down and leave.

She denied that she knew that I was being sexually abused until I told her, when I was 12. Last year, when my memory of a specific event returned spontaneously, I learned that her denial was not true. She had caught me with my father when I was three years old and almost killed me by beating and kicking me as he fled the scene. I felt totally abandoned by her.

I believe that mother also sexually abused me. Daddy often worked at night. When I would get up to go to the bathroom, Mother would call me to come and get in bed with her. It always felt "creepy" and made me get real warm all over. I can recall a few of the details, but then I must have dissociated because I still don't fully remember. I don't "know" for sure what happened. I only know that those were frightening and unpleasant experiences. I feel terrible shame in sharing that secret.

My mother's family was southern Baptist and so was I, until Mother got interested in the Catholic church when I was nine years old. She put me in a parochial school and forced me to be baptized. I screamed and yelled, but was held over the baptismal font by the priest and my godparents, all of whom kept telling me that I really did want this. They were wrong. I was torn between my mother's desires and my grandmother's hatred of my mother's new religion. I was terribly afraid I would lose my grandmother.

The fight between her and Mother finally got so bad that I was not allowed to see my grandmother for two years. Between the two denominations, I was taught to fear a God who was judgmental and who condemned people to hell for all eternity. I tried hard to fulfill expectations, but I knew I was never good enough. My spirit was crushed. I often sat on the floor of my prison/closet and wondered what I had ever done to be hated by God. That was a horrible ordeal for a bewildered child to endure.

My grandmother, who I call Mamaw, was the saving grace of my childhood. Even though she had her faults, she gave me a sense of self-worth and self-esteem that I found in few other places. I lived with her until I was almost three years old and spent as much time with her after that as I possibly could. I have no idea whether or not she knew about any of my abuse. I wanted to tell her, but I didn't until I was an adult. I went back to live with her and my alcoholic grandfather when I was 17. I stayed with them until I married at 19. There are few things in this life that I'm as grateful for as I am for her presence. She sustained, supported and expressed love for me as no one else did. "Thank you, Mamaw."

I went all the way through parochial school and graduated when I was 18. I was too emotionally insecure and had been sheltered too much to be able to go to work or to college, so I got pregnant instead. I married my childhood sweetheart who was several months younger than me. He also was from an alcoholic home.

We didn't have much chance. Our first baby was a stillborn son and that was a crushing blow. My young husband struggled to get an education and work while I worked at several jobs at home. In three years I got pregnant again. This time I was doubly blessed with twin boys, but my marriage was in deep trouble, and I began taking out my rage on my children. I became the verbally and physically abusive parent my mother had been.

By the time my children were three years old, I divorced my husband and went to work outside the home. I put my boys into an excellent day care center run by the city in which we lived. We all received wonderful care from the staff and a social worker. Eventually, I was able to stop abusing my boys. For that I am deeply grateful.

I remarried three years later. This time my codependence took another twist; I married a man who was nineteen years older than me, with five children. We both brought tremendous baggage to the marriage. We have persevered by the grace of God and have been married for eighteen years. We've worked out a successful and rewarding relationship. Our families, however, have never blended, and we have experienced a lot of heartache.

It is very important for me to acknowledge that my husband has been my strongest supporter. He came into CoDA just three months after I did and is very active. He has taken care of me through many serious illnesses, and I will always be grateful. We share a common spiritual philosophy which is of the utmost importance to both of us. We have grown tremendously in CoDA. We no longer expect each other to meet all of our individual needs. We attend CoDA meetings together and separately. We enjoy each other and our CoDA friends.

As a codependent adult, I have experienced lots of problems that I will share with you: drug addiction, love and sex addiction, compulsive spending, people-pleasing, caretaking, child-abusing, isolating, arrogance, dishonesty and an eating disorder, to name a few. One of my biggest problems has been prescription drug addiction. I certainly was genetically predisposed to alcoholism, but my drugs of choice turned out to be codeine and halcion. I became addicted after numerous surgeries. I remained on drugs for about five years after which I went through rehabilitation and still struggle with this.

I was in CoDA for a year before I finally got off drugs. It was one of the scariest things I have ever done. I had an incredible amount of intractable pain in my legs and back and had no idea how to survive without drugs. I really didn't know how much emotional pain was being dulled by the drugs. It was my CoDA program and friends who sustained me through that battle.

One of the ways codependence manifested itself in my life was through illness. My mother is a hypochondriac and taught me early that I was weak and prone to illness. I developed diabetes when I was ten years old. I learned that getting sick got me out of having to deal with a lot of life.

I rarely faked illness. It was already deep within the fabric of my life. I had hepatitis when I was 11. I had migraine headaches at 13, vaginal and bladder infections at 15, and a dislocated sacroiliac at 17. I had flu and colds frequently. I have undergone 17 surgeries for eyes, breasts, wrists, and ankles as well as a C-section and hysterectomy. I developed ulcers and a severely contracting colon. I have diabetic neuropathy which causes the nerves in my legs to die. By the time I was 36, I was trying to cope with the stress of my codependence combined with long-term diabetes that resulted in total blindness in both eyes. That was also the point at which the pain in my back and legs became unbearable. I had fought long and hard. I had undergone a great deal of therapy and had read every self-help book I could find. I had availed myself of alternative healing methods of many kinds. Nothing had helped.

When I was 37, I tried to kill myself with an overdose of drugs and alcohol. When I was 41, I tried again. I was serious about it. I had given up and had no will to live. My Higher Power obviously had different plans for me and brought me through, miraculously, both times.

During all those years of chaos, I worked to put myself through college. I was stopped many times with illness and three episodes of blindness, but each time I came back and kept going. In 1986, I finally graduated with a 3.79 grade point average and a Bachelor of Science degree in Counseling and Guidance. I thought the day would never come. It had taken me ten years.

About four years ago, I was in group therapy for incest recovery. Our therapist was very good about informing us about things she thought we might be interested in and might find helpful. I remember the night she brought a copy of a popular book on codependence to the group. I had been in Al-Anon and ACA for several years, but I had never heard the term "codependence." That same evening she also told us about Co-Dependents Anonymous. Thank you, Diane. I attended my first CoDA meeting in August of 1987.

When I first started attending meetings, I was still on drugs. I had not admitted that I was an addict. My first year in CoDA was pretty dull, but I did learn a lot. I sort of stored the information until I could get sober enough to use it. I worked through a Step study and made my first amends. I had no way of being very honest, but at least it was a start. After I came out of drug rehabilitation, I worked the Steps again with a sponsor and started to make my amends again. This time the program really began to work.

I had already been blessed by a close relationship with my Higher Power before I came to CoDA. Even after my unpleasant childhood experiences with religion, I continued to search, trying a number of western-style religions as well as atheism. I went through a 10-year "dark night of the soul" and then my Higher Power brought me to an eastern philosophy—one that answered all my needs.

This philosophy was gentle and kind, overflowing with love and acceptance. It opened my heart and taught me compassion, understanding, forgiveness, tolerance, and truthfulness. There was no threat of judgment or punishment and no condemnation of other spiritual expressions. This prepared me perfectly for the Twelve Steps. It opened me to the phenomenon of paradox and taught me that we are all a part of the One. Finally, I had come to my spiritual home, and for that I am deeply grateful.

I began to take risks by doing Twelve Step work in CoDA. That was when I really began to grow up. I felt terribly inadequate and unworthy, and that I had nothing to offer, but I offered anyway. I remember how absolutely frozen I felt the first time I spoke, the first time I facilitated a meeting, the first time I answered calls on our meeting line. Somehow I was given the courage, and once I got a taste of service, I knew I would never stop. I spend about 25 to 30 hours a week doing CoDA service work at the community level and have recently volunteered at the state level. I am truly thankful to be able to give back in some small measure with what I have been blessed.

I know that I will be working on my recovery for the rest of my life. The deep scars from the abuse I received do not heal quickly. For the first time in my life, however, it doesn't matter how long it takes. I'm on the road to recovery, and I have hope. I have CoDA and the Twelve Steps. I have my Higher Power. I have the Fellowship of Co-Dependents Anonymous. I am learning to release the past and old negative thought patterns that have continued to harm me through the years. I am finally learning that I'm worthy of affirmation, love and respect. I will be OK, and, in the meantime, I am in great company.

I continue to work on areas of denial, especially in regard to being diabetic. I still have a great deal of trouble eating in a healthy way, testing blood sugar levels and keeping accurate records for my doctor. Even though I've suffered a great deal of damage due to diabetes, I still don't value myself enough to take the care I deserve. I also still tend to get enmeshed in relationships with people who take advantage and abuse me, although this doesn't occur as easily as it did. I find it very difficult to say, "no" and find it very hard to call and ask for help. Consequently, I still live with a lot of emotional and physical pain. My attitude has changed about these kinds of things, however.

I no longer need to be perfect. I know that I'm growing and developing at the rate that's right for me. I know that my Higher Power is the essence of all that comes into my life in all ways. I have come to believe that I'm not only a precious child, but a divine child. I no longer fear that I was created to be tortured and punished. Since coming into CoDA, I have discovered that I was created out of the beauty and splendor of the universe. I am a beautiful and sparkling soul. I am deeply grateful to my Higher Power.

I want to say how thankful I am to the founders of Alcoholics Anonymous for giving us the Twelve Steps. I'm especially grateful for the program of Co-Dependents Anonymous. Last, but by no means least, I thank the CoDA community in Dallas, Texas, for all the love, support and opportunities to grow and share. I am grateful to be "that which God intended—precious and free."

by Jenny C.

DAVID & THE LIONS

In my 49th year (1985), four traumatic events occurred. In March of that year, I was negotiating over the phone for a very well-paid senior consulting position with a prestigious Washington, D.C., research firm. At the time I was living in the mountains 40 miles west of Denver, Colorado, and it was snowing. As I negotiated the terms of my employment, I saw through the sun bubble over my kitchen that my chimney was on fire.

Not knowing a burning bush when I saw one, I excused myself to my future employer, hung up, filled a bucket with water, ran up a ladder onto the roof and poured water down the chimney, successfully dowsing the fire. Some years before, I had asked God for right livelihood, and I knew that this job, however well-paid and prestigious, was not right livelihood. At that point in my life, however, livelihood mattered most and $45,000 plus benefits was not to be ignored.

At the time I did not know that being a workaholic for 8, 10, or 12 hours a day and drinking, smoking dope, and engaging in or fantasizing about sex the rest of the time was out of line. After four months, I gave up the fancy job in D.C. to return to a similar, but less well-paid job in Colorado. The mountains were worth the difference in salary. I had risen nearly to the top of my third career, and I gave it up without a pause. I told myself I was too old for "Potomac Fever."

In October, it turned out that my wife of ten years (my third) was pregnant. At first that was not joyous news. We had raised the two children from my first marriage under very difficult circumstances with indifferent results. We had been forced to throw out of the house our 18-year-old because he was using every drug he could find, and "Tough Love" was the only faintly appropriate policy we knew. It was much later that I came to understand that he was chemically dependent, and that condition is probably inherited. He is still not in recovery, although I pray for that regularly.

When my wife was undergoing amniocentesis, I saw the new baby's foot running up and down the barrel of the hypodermic needle that was withdrawing the amniotic fluid, and at that point, my heart went out to him. I felt a joy that overcame my previous reservations about having another child. I considered that having a new child at 50 might well be a blessing.

I continued along, working, doping and drinking, until February of '86 when I completed a workaholic's dream/nightmare assignment for a major computer company and returned home to have a heart attack. I spent eight days in cardiac care and eight more days in the cardiac ward before I was allowed out of the hospital. I remember how wonderful the Colorado mountains looked as my wife drove me home, and I knew that I had received a major warning from God, but I didn't know what to do with it or how to relate it to my life.

The baby was born a month before my 50th birthday in July. By that time, I had been fired from the job I had held while I had the heart attack. I drank far less than before, had stopped smoking tobacco, but still periodically had a puff of a joint. I stopped that about the time the baby was born when I learned it contributed in a major way to the chest pains I had been experiencing. I was left with liquor, depression, a fearful attitude about sex (normal for a cardiac patient, I'm told), infrequent work and a lot of worry.

On my 50th birthday, my alcoholic, abusive, prescription drug-addicted mother wandered away from her home and had to be returned by the state police. Later in the summer, some friends in another city hired me to install a new computer system for them; and while I was doing that work, my mother attempted suicide. Her act brought me home to a far away state to look after my father who was 79, suffering from diabetes and other health problems. We became close then, and I was grateful for that opportunity to heal some old wounds.

The following August (1987), my wife, new baby and I left the Colorado mountains, my all-time favorite place to live, and moved to the upper Midwest where my wife had secured a very good job with a branch of a major university. We knew it was temporary, but my heart sank to leave the mountains.

I was lost on the banks of the upper Mississippi a year and a half after a heart attack, with three abandoned careers behind me, the prospect of writing a book of some sort, and tending an 18-month-old baby. I started to drink more and to think of suicide. I literally could not go into the basement to run laundry without looking at the rafters and thinking of hanging myself. I did not know that I was bottoming out.

My self-esteem was gone. In the past I had valued myself because of my work record. I had finished a difficult Ph.D. in three and a half years when the national average was eight years. I had been published in highly regarded professional journals. I had taught myself to make films in less than six months. I had become a senior technical writer and editor very quickly. None of this work mattered. I was still a scared and (seemingly) helpless three year old caught in a trap set by his parents. I still saw myself as a victim, still felt isolated.

Somewhere in October of that year, one of my wife's students who was very active in the program and in her own recovery suggested very subtly to me that I might want to attend the Saturday meeting. This suggestion happened as an aside while I was giving her a ride home from baby-sitting one day. She didn't say whether it was AA, N.A., ACoA or what, but she knew a soul in trouble when she saw one.

That Saturday meeting turned out to be an ACoA meeting, and I knew I had found friends—or at least people I could hear and who could hear me at the first meeting. I attended faithfully every Saturday after that and came to depend on the spirit of that meeting. I came to understand that having an alcoholic and abusive mother, a workaholic and (largely) absentee father, and an abusive Catholic childhood was commonplace for many people.

Even though I felt less isolated as I learned more about the program and more about other adult children and codependents, my relationships at home worsened. I was in my third marriage, and I had a new baby. I was desperate to give that baby a better shot than I had had, even though I had no real idea of how to do it. My marriage was no longer an emotional support system, if it ever had been one. Nonetheless, I was addicted to it. It took a long time and a lot of Third Step work to understand that one.

While I learned about the program, I still didn't progress far enough to give up alcohol. It took until the spring of 1990 to do that. That winter I had tried returning to my first career of university teaching only to find that I had been honest with myself in leaving it in 1977. After fourteen years I had discovered I no longer had the heart for it. Two sections of freshman composition reinforced the accuracy of my decision.

I finished the semester and had a balloon angioplasty to increase the circulation in the arteries surrounding my heart. Two weeks after that operation my father died, and I had to return home to bury him, and to settle my crazy mother in some kind of extended care facility. She was 77 and more dysfunctional than ever, although dry since her suicide attempt.

After nearly a month of dealing with my father's affairs, I returned to the midwestern hospital where they thought my arteries were closing up again. It turned out that they weren't, but the high stress and drinking had not been good for me. Nine months of program helped me to give up alcohol. That step eliminated the rest of my obvious addictive crutches and forced me to look at myself. My "less than" feelings ruled my life at that time.

Later in the summer I went back to Colorado where I met with a very dear friend who started to talk to me about CoDA. He had tried ACoA and AA, but felt that he had finally found the right program when he started CoDA. He also started to talk about the magic of doing a week-long program at a treatment center in the Southwest. The idea was that if I was getting some recovery from ACoA, I should try CoDA. There were no CoDA meetings around me in the upper Midwest short of the cities, and they were 120 miles away. So I burned up a lot of long-distance time with my friend and co-sponsor in Colorado until we went to the week-long program in January.

That week introduced me to the idea of my own childhood abuse more thoroughly than I had ever seen it before. I also came to reflect on the many addictions that had filled my life, how I had bottomed out two falls ago because my addictive support system had been largely removed by my physical condition and by my Higher Power. That heart attack was like a two-by-four across the back of the head. I had needed an unequivocal warning to wake up, and my Higher Power gave me one.

I returned to the Midwest at the end of January after the week-long intensive program and started a CoDA group with a friend who had experienced treatment at another facility. He also had about twenty-five years in AA recovery behind him. In the summer, my family and I moved to a midsized Southwestern city where there is plenty of recovery. I went to two CoDA meetings a week, one of them a men's group. I went back to the treatment center in January of 1990 for another week of treatment. Today, I continue to work my program daily.

I am aware of my Higher Power in my life on a daily basis, and it is with God's help that I am putting together a book about men and recovery. I know I am alive, thanks to the program and the spiritual center it has given me. One of my current practices is to keep a log of when my Higher Power intervenes to help my life along. On the flipside of that page, I keep a list of lessons that occur. That type of accounting keeps me aware that my Higher Power is ever present in my life.

Years ago, I had asked God for right livelihood, and He led me to recovery. Little did I know of the uphill path that would take me there, but the moderation of recovery is worth every step of that long path. Borrowing an image from a CoDA friend, "to think of going back would be like stepping down from the mountain onto a plane where a pride of lions is quietly digesting a kill. They are quiet and well-fed now, but God help us if we stir their appetites."

by David

GOD, PLEASE HELP ME

When I first came to CoDA, I had just gone through an experience I will never forget as long as I'm on this planet. I was asked to go on a business assignment to another state. This meant I would be leaving behind my husband and son to take care of themselves. My thoughts were, "How are they going to manage without me there?" I had already spent a good portion of my life taking care of others and fixing everyone else's problems. My nursing job had allowed me to escape all my own problems and place the focus everywhere else.

As I completed my day's work and returned to my hotel room, I began to feel physically ill. I wasn't happy with the job because it required me to leave behind my family. In addition to that, the job did not allow for complete honesty to the customers. The combination of these two things created a lot of discomfort in me. As the discomfort increased, I got sicker. My head hurt to the point where I thought it was going to explode. My sinus congestion hindered my breathing. I had chest pain, back pain, stomach cramps, bloating, leg cramps, nausea and a lot of confusion. I remember saying "God help me." I contemplated calling my boss and telling her I needed to fly home. The thought of staying in this hotel room for 60 days made the symptoms more exaggerated. I really thought I was going to die.

I laid down on the bed and listened to a soothing tape of spiritual music. I felt so miserable, I couldn't lay still. I sat up and started to write. I wrote for three hours. Then I sat there and kept staring at what I wrote.

What I wrote out were all the symptoms I had and what I was feeling. I made a list of every illness I had ever had. The longer I stared at it, the more I realized my symptoms came out of my fear of being alone and that every time I had ever been sick, it was in conjunction with lonely feelings. My life had been spent thinking, believing, and living that I was nothing without a man in my life, and that my caretaking allowed me to bury those issues. What I was facing in that hotel room was my biggest fear—being totally alone. I sat for hours looking at my history of emotional issues and physical symptoms, putting the connections together. I realized that night that my codependency was the root of all my problems.

I tried to find meetings near the hotel I was staying at, but nothing was available. I decided to give my recovery everything I had in me until I could return home where there were CoDA meetings. I listened to cassette tapes about getting my history straight about where my problems originated. I realized my family of origin was more dysfunctional than I thought. I had taken many looks at my family in the past but never really saw things as clearly as I did this time. Now, I know why people in the neighborhood talked about us as that "crazy" family. I kept hearing how important it was to acknowledge but not blame. So I dug deep inside and listened to those tapes over and over again.

My job was flying me home on the weekends, so I was able to spend time with my husband and son. We were all unable to communicate effectively due to active alcoholism on my husband's part, adult child issues on my son's part, and blooming codependency on my part. I am also a recovering alcoholic.

Soon the business assignment was over, and I was home to stay. I began to go to CoDA meetings and worked on my history. I realized there was every kind of abuse possible in my family. I had already been to a treatment facility a year prior to my first CoDA meeting and had really started the digging there, but put it out of my mind for whatever reason. The inventories had revealed four known generations of alcoholics, food addicts, illness addicts, as well as the latest two generations who added drug and sex addiction to the alcohol, food and illness. Somebody had to be the one to stop this craziness. There was no such thing as being close in our family.

I realized then that every man I attracted into my life fulfilled two or more of the addictions that I had been raised with. I knew I had to tackle many areas in order to make a change in my life, as I could see how a lot of the family illness, addictions, alcoholism, and just plain suffering had been incorporated into my life.

I started with a chart on the wall of things I needed to do daily to make the change. As I would do each thing, I would check it off so I could start to see my accomplishments. As I went to meetings and talked about my present habits that came from my history, I got in touch with my personal characteristics and patterns of codependency. I had a lot of anger that had to be released, so I walked, swam, exercised, and wrote out feelings. I kept having to admit my powerlessness over my anger and resentments, just to mention a few. I kept doing this every day, every minute sometimes. Eventually I would get rid of the anger enough to see the codependent issue that was at the root of it all.

It became clear to me that the Steps in the program could help me get out of being controlled and out of controlling others. I started every morning with Steps One, Two and Three, and continued calling on the first three Steps in every crisis. I had to admit my powerlessness over the specific character defect I was experiencing or else I would never be able to let go of any negativity.

I identified the negative characteristics, and slowly they would begin to change as I did whatever needed to be done to practice the opposite. I learned how to release people-pleasing issues by becoming aware of my behavior. My list of patterns and characteristics was constantly around me at work and at home, so I could look at it in a crisis and find which one applied to me at the time. As I did this, I realized I had chosen each one of my three husbands so I could be the peacemaking fixer of their problems, so I could get the approval I never had at home. The trouble was that it didn't turn out that way. There were still crisis episodes in our house as recovery began, as it took time to learn how to work the Steps.

After I would identify my patterns and characteristics using Step Four, I still had to go deeper to find the feelings. Some feelings were there, some were not. The more inventories I did, the more feelings began to surface. I made it a practice to identify at least one feeling at each meeting. There was a lot pent up inside, tightly linked to abandonment and physical abuse, as well as emotional and sexual abuse.

I dove into inventories like some people would dive into a swimming pool, but it wasn't always that way. I came into the concept of recovery kicking and screaming like there was nothing wrong with me— it was all the other person. If he would change, I wouldn't have to act the way I do.

My Step Five was difficult at times. I had a lot of lack of trust issues, so sharing with a sponsor was not easy. She was tough with me at times to keep me focused on myself rather than others. I remember going to her one day complaining about my husband. She told me it didn't become me and that she didn't have time for that. I got her message real fast. I was off track. There were a lot of awarenesses I had about myself as I shared with my sponsor. We had a pretty good relationship until one day I could sense and feel control issues coming up between us. I realized I was OK in her eyes as long as I did everything her way. I needed that in the beginning, to have someone lead me by the hand. But as I grew I began to have a mind of my own and needed to exercise it and make my own mistakes and have my own successes. I truly began to believe there was only one authority in my life, and it wasn't going to be another person again. I learned a person can only learn from a sponsor as far as that sponsor has learned about themselves. It was time to move on.

As I informed her I was going to release her from being my sponsor, she became very manipulative. I knew I had made the right decision. Moving on was all about not allowing myself to be someone else's victim again. The CoDA program was getting me in touch with situations I contributed to that kept me someone's victim.

There were times I wasn't really ready to give up being others' victim as there was so much ground to cover and I couldn't do it all in a day. One day at a time, with a lot of pain at times, got me closer to being entirely ready to give up the victim role. I had been the victim of all my husbands, my family members, different employers and friends. My whole life had been lived for everyone else. This was the scary part. I had never learned it was OK to be me. My childhood was lived according to my parents' desires. How could I be me and still be "a part of?" This is where I learned I cannot be a part of a dysfunctional family and expect to be me.

I was missing boundaries. I had to step away from my dysfunctional family to get strong. It has been three years in CoDA, and my biological family still denies there are problems, so I have little communication and contact. In CoDA, I learned it's OK to start a family of choice. I couldn't possibly expect myself to be entirely ready to have my defects of character removed if I was still surrounding myself with people without recovery.

The program also taught me what humility is. I couldn't go any further unless I made myself teachable to new ways of living. That was the hard part. I learned that what I said, did, thought, and felt was not in alignment. So it was like being a baby in an adult body learning how to walk again. There were thousands of old tapes in my head running my life. The trick was to identify the tapes and to put boundaries in place. That's pretty hard to do when there's no trust for others.

I also had spent most of my life learning on my own—intellectually, an "all-A-student," emotionally, a mess. Becoming teachable meant I had to shut up and listen. That's why I like being at a meeting where there's no feedback and crosstalk. It allows me freedom to share and the space to listen without a "parent" giving advice. I need to hear messages brought to me through others' experiences.

As time went by in the program, I learned I also played a role in negative impact on others. Amends were necessary. As I began to make amends to those I had harmed, in some cases I felt a sense of freedom. Sometimes people are accepting and sometimes not. One family member actually started to add to my list of wrongdoings. I learned making amends is not for what the other person thinks or how they act. It's about acknowledging my stuff and clearing myself. Some people may not be ready to acknowledge my changes, and that has to be OK. If it isn't, then I'm their victim again. Some friends and family members were not ready to see me outside of the old pictures they had of me in their minds. So I was back again to that "family of choice" stuff. It kept coming up in various places in the program.

There are still people on my amends list, and when the time is appropriate the amends will happen. The program has taught me not to rush into things, as was so much a part of my codependency. Apologies are not the same as amends. I have apologized in the past to win the good graces of the person again. Making amends, for me, is about acknowledging my behaviors without having to do penance, but with having to demonstrate how I have changed in my walk of life. I can't just talk about it; I have to live it. Living it gets easier, even though in the beginning it was real tough.

That's why I have to constantly do Tenth Steps. Without my inventory to tell me what needs to be changed, it's too easy for me to listen to another codependent give me sick advice. The more awareness I began to have by using the Tenth Step the more I was able to release my negative behaviors. After doing Tenth Steps in writing many times, I was able to take that process and quickly apply the Tenth Step to a situation at the time it was happening, sort of like in my head. Quickly identifying my anger and releasing it allowed me to not have to carry it around all day. Considering how full of anger my body was, I did not need to hang on to it all day until I got to a meeting. I would have exploded. Sometimes my Tenth Steps did not come on a timely basis, and I would carry stuff around. I had to learn that the program was one of progress, not perfection. There were times that I wanted to say, "_____ the program!" That was usually when I waited too long to look at my part in a situation. This is the Step that kept me from internalizing my pain and getting sick again.

The more I got in touch with my feelings, the more comfortable I felt with me. I began to pray a lot and meditate. It was very difficult to pray and meditate with thousands of old movies running in my head telling me what to think—everyone else's movies. Soft music with an oriental blend seemed to catch my focus, so I used it a lot and still do. It was the only thing that I could focus on without scenes from my childhood creeping in or the happenings of the day getting in the way of my relaxation. It got better as time went by. For me this Step energizes my body. Without that, I can spend a lot of time feeling tired.

As more time went by, I began to hear this little voice talk to me about codependency and how I hide behind other people with my feelings, so I don't have to take risks. It seemed that every time a codependent situation occurred, and I meditated about it, I would get the answer from within. Sometimes I would resent that voice within and want to solve the problem my way. I soon learned the little voice was "right on" with the healthiest solutions. That's why I like this Step; if I use healthy solutions, then I feel good inside.

Step Eleven has taught me to use my feelings as a guideline, feelings I never knew I had before I came to CoDA.

As I have gone along in the program, I have done Twelfth Step work from the beginning. Making coffee, setting up tables, cleaning up, telling my experiences were all part of my growing process. The more I gave away, the better I felt about me. My emptiness started to get filled with this magical feeling of liking who I was when I looked in the mirror.

In the course of time I became the state delegate for CoDA. This level of work brought me many interesting experiences. I saw the work necessary to keep CoDA alive across the world and learned the global picture of how worldwide growth happens in a healthy way. My involvement in helping CoDA grow in our state helped me to walk through more old tapes of "not being as good as others" and "it's not OK to tell the truth" just to mention a few.

Three years of working with others and sharing ideas, experiences, strengths, and hopes has turned on many light bulbs inside my head. There is no turning back now. As time goes by, I still uncover more issues, but now I have a program to follow that allows me to live in a healthy way. I can be myself, regardless of what anyone thinks.

This program has brought me the gift of freedom of self-expression, no matter the number of people who think differently than me. I learned taking risks is important in my growth process. And best of all, I am never alone. I have a partner wherever I go, my Higher Self.

by Sue J.

FREEDOM FROM DENIAL

It is an honor and a privilege to be asked to share my story with you. Not too many years ago, I didn't know I even had a story. My denial actually served a purpose. It allowed me to survive through the pain I was really in, until I could reach a place on my journey to see the truth.

Today, I believe that my codependency is about my human condition. To define it is like trying to define God. And to feel the depths of its boundaries allows me to encompass all of my feelings and extremes.

Once I arrived at the time in my CoDA journey in which I could finally see "the nature's of my wrongs," it was time to deal with what has always motivated me—*fear*—the fear that stems from the lost identity I felt.

Now I didn't wake up one day and have all this knowledge pour through me. It has taken many years, and lots of inventories, to understand the dynamics that really keep me from freeing myself from the lie. It has taken time to see where I play out my roles, over and over again, and to understand how I create the many situations in my life.

One of the most important things I learned in my recovery process was from my beloved sponsor. She stated that in order to really be able to make healthy choices for myself, at any given time, I would have to own my motives. Sounded simple. Well it wasn't. Many times I have found myself in situations again, because I wouldn't own my motives. And what usually lies under all of that "disowning" is my *fear* of someone either leaving or hurting me. My fear of abandonment has been the worst thing for me to deal with.

Part of my history includes a very sick mother who had to undergo shock treatments because she had a fear that she wanted to kill me. That was my first impression of what my caregivers had to offer me. From then on, not only my family, but also my ethnic community, educational system, religious community and social groups gave me messages of nonapproval. My father even chose to leave and join a war he didn't need to go to at that time.

Today, through many times of working through my history as it emerges, I have been able to put the pieces of my story together. I am grateful that both of my parents have been able to be accountable for their part in this drama. What that has allowed me to do, over the years, is to finally empathize with the pain they truly live in. And how that was done for me was to see how I lived out all the "truths" of my family system. I thought I was different from them because I went to opposite extremes in many ideas and things. The fact was I was still coming from the same place.

Today, I know that I can only come from what is stored in my vast file system within. From that knowledge, only certain conclusions can form when situations arise. For me, when time came to make decisions, I usually made poor ones, because of the negative information I had stored in my system.

Recovery has not been easy for me. It held a lot of fear. The fear to move forward is difficult. I was so totally spiritually abused that just the thought of turning my life over to God was terrifying. I was brought up in a world where I was afraid to stay, afraid to leave, just afraid. Even today I still feel like people are watching me, even when I am totally alone. My mother has become accountable for doing what she did to me in order to control me, but I still have to live the repercussions.

I don't know about you, but for me, I had this belief that if I just went to enough meetings, did enough inventories, workshops, read all the self-help books I could, everything would go away because I would finally have all the answers. Well, one day a rude awakening happened; it wasn't going to be that way for me.

Again, my sponsor was there to tell me that my characteristics were mine, and that my history made me who I was. I didn't want to own all of that. There were pain and loneliness, and many other things to deal with, including rage. But within that conversation, I remember her telling me that in order for me to really know what it was like to love, I would first have to go through the rage. I want to tell you, from then on, I tried everything I knew not to deal with that stuff, but it wasn't going to go away. I had choices. I could go back to using my chemicals and other addictions, or I could go on. There was something inside of me that I could now feel, very slightly. It supported me to go on.

Many times I wanted to scream, "That's enough! No more!" and I would rest for awhile. Now there is this yearning to return to what I know is the real truth, the acknowledgment of Annie, God's manifestation. And the only way I can get there is to keep walking through the many situations that get put in my life to teach me what the lie feels like.

The only time today that I get into addictive type behaviors is when I am caught in fear, failure or potential. I have had to learn to be responsible for my behavior. That was tough. First of all, I had always thought I was responsible for the world, and that wasn't true. Others gave me that job. I bought it. Then, I realized that the reasons I did most things for others in my life was to protect myself so they wouldn't leave, reject me, hurt me, or kill me.

The truth was I did have to walk through that rage, and it was not easy. Up came the depths of all my history and secrets. And along with it came the understanding of how this all tied into my everyday decisions in the now. Today I can love myself enough to understand that after all the raging I did, at and to others, the real rage lay within me. The rage from that inner being, "me," was screaming about the fact that I had sold myself out, over and over again. I knew I had been taught that I had no identity. The freedom from all of that was when I claimed my responsibility in this whole trip.

Today I believe that I chose to come to this earth and participate in this lifetime. Not too long ago, I had the privilege of thanking my father and mother for walking this journey with me, and for what happened between us. It was the most wonderful feeling to release what I had been carrying. You see, even after all the history went together and everyone had become accountable, there was still this anger toward my mother. One day she said, "What do you want from me? I have given you all that you asked for. I don't know what else to do." I realized that what I was doing was holding onto the old and familiar because I didn't want to take responsibility for myself. I still wanted to blame her. Once I got that honest with myself, it just went. Becoming responsible for me was where the freedom came.

I am glad I don't have to live it over again. Once was enough. Yet because these things are imbedded in my very being, emotionally as well as physically, I find that each day I have to use the tools I have gathered, because I still get into situations. It is so much better. And I can't stay in situations too long before I feel the old feelings and reactions, but I can finally take care of myself to change what is going on for me.

Today I can leave. Or I can stay and confront gently. I know that if it is time for someone or a situation to leave, it will go. I don't look at that negatively. It means that my lessons are finished, and I can thank the other person for their participation and let go. Moving on is about growing. It is part of the process.

I return this gracious gift by walking through life interacting with many people, sharing who I am with them. I believe, for me, this is what I am to do with my gift. Whenever I reach out and share with another, I always get much more in return.

I wouldn't trade my life with anyone else. I absolutely love how I am and what I am about. And coming from where I have come from, that is the truth for me. Everything in this universe just waits for me to use it. And in that belief, I can let others "use me" on the journey. It's called interdependency.

by Annie D.

CECILE'S STORY

The setup

I grew up in a mid-size town in the South where people settled from all parts of the world. Like many people in Twelve Step programs, my parents were Irish-Catholic. I am their second child and only girl.

My parents divorced in the first year of my life. I found out later (typical of the "don't talk rule") that my parents were excommunicated from the church because of their divorce. I'm told that my father also became a conscientious objector avoiding the draft. It wasn't popular in those days to object to war, and it added to our ongoing family shame. I was never to know my natural father, except through letters and an occasional phone call. He married again but never had any more children.

I believe the God of my understanding put a mentor in the midst of all the early "stuff" to show me love, strength and care, and to sustain and keep me going. That person was my maternal grandmother. Without her, I have no doubt my life would have been a greater struggle than it was. From my earliest memories of her, she was always available to me. She seemed to possess a lot of common sense, good character and a strong faith in the God of her understanding. She did not force her religious beliefs on me in any way.

She had a twin sister who died in the childbirth of her second child. Grandma had four children, but only my mother survived. I feel certain that by experiencing the loss of loved ones, and with only one surviving child, there was a great deal of pressure on my grandmother to overdo her care with her daughter.

Because of financial, emotional and dysfunctional needs, Mom took me and my brother to live with our grandmother sometime in the first year of my life. My grandmother made most of the decisions concerning my welfare. I always craved knowledge about my father, but they would put me to bed early to avoid talking about him when I could listen. I would lay awake in the next room, trying to decipher their words.

Today, I'm as far removed from my mother as I can be. I'm able to focus on myself better and to work out my own issues with trusted people, counselors and with my Higher Power.

When I reached the magical age of 18, Grandma finally told me why there were no early baby pictures of me even though there were plenty of my brother. The reason concerned my physical appearance; I was drastically underweight. Grandmother told me that

I weighed less than a pound more at six months than I did at birth.

My grandmother had become very concerned about my weight but was instructed by Mom to "stay away." Evidently nothing was being done by my parents to discover what was wrong. Grandma knew she had to take matters into her hands or risk watching me die. She and one of her nieces went to my parents' house and rescued me from their negligent care. They took me to a pediatrician, who discovered the problem; I needed corrective surgery to open my esophagus for food. I wasn't getting any nourishment.

To compensate for my parents' neglect, my grandmother excused the actions of her only child by saying that "she tried" to find out what my weight problem was, but "couldn't." Apparently my mother had become extremely depressed and withdrawn and could not handle a newborn. This is where I began to comprehend why I felt such a huge distance from my mother. Now I see it as a cover-up for severe child neglect.

I'm just now beginning to understand more clearly why I used to get so angry with my grandmother about some of her behavior, too. She seemed to do anything and everything for my mother. She made decisions for her, and I watched and wondered why. Was my mom acting like a doormat?

Grandma was very supportive of me, continually urging me to take care of myself and make something of myself, no matter what others said. This was a 180-degree turnaround from her behavior with her own daughter. I am told this is very typical for dysfunctional families.

Money was not plentiful in my family at that time. Of the two of us, I excelled in school, but my brother usually got the new toys (bikes, roller skates, etc.), and I would get used things and hand-me-downs. I was told that was all they could afford. I had a second-place feeling and accepted it as part of my role in life.

My brother and I only took one vacation with our mother. This occurred when I was four years old and my brother was six. Mom took us to New Jersey to be with her fiancee, a New Jersey doctor, because she wanted to see how we'd all get along. She and her friend had taken many trips together, and upon returning, she would promise to arrange to take us one day. This trip turned into a disaster for me. It also ended their engagement; they broke up two weeks later.

As a result of that trip, I was locked up in a room for a week. I was told I was being punished for walking into the bathroom where her fiancee was standing at the sink. I couldn't understand the punishment because the door was open when I went in. I had no way of knowing that others were not allowed in. I was only four years old at the time and had never spent time in the presence of an adult male. I remember crying and sobbing the whole week, begging Mom to let me out. She refused and wouldn't tell me why. This was another traumatic event of feeling abandoned and rejected by her.

Ironically, she met her second husband (the man she married five years later) on the train back from New Jersey. I remember the trip, even at an early age, and knew from the start that I didn't like the man. Things were drastically dysfunctional in my life, but I was powerless to do anything about it.

The Drama Begins

When I was about 9-1/2 years old, Mom announced to all of us that she was going to get married again. I remember feeling so much anger and fear over her decision and begged her not to do it. I cried and ran outside of my grandmother's little house and began to beat on the siding, sobbing and pounding the wall, asking God for help. I couldn't understand my mother's desire for a crazy man.

For more than four years, I underwent the most horrible times I've ever experienced. Because of my mother's decision, I felt like I was being forced to live in prison, yet I was told to call it "home." Almost anything was better than living with my mother and her alcoholic/rage-aholic husband. Everything that has happened in my life since this time has been tremendously better by comparison.

Today, I know that I'm slowly gaining a greater feeling of freedom, and I owe this to my contact with God and my Twelve Step program. Could it be that freedom does come once I learn that a power greater than me is in control of my life? I don't play as many of the old tapes; that's recovery in action.

For years, I wasn't able to feel good about buying things for myself or receiving gifts from others, because there was always some kind of guilt or shame attached to it.

Part of my mother's reasoning to marry again was for economic security and promises of fatherhood for my brother and I. Like all other growing children, we needed new shoes and clothing every year. Prior to her marriage, it seemed that Mom and Grandma saw to it that we had clothes and shoes to wear. Though we didn't get a lot of clothing, we knew we were cared for with the essentials.

It wasn't long before my mother and her new husband announced to us that they wouldn't be buying us any new clothes that year; we had to make do with what we had or find a way to earn it ourselves. I had just turned 10 years old and my brother was 11-1/2. I couldn't fathom how we could possibly earn enough money to buy our own clothes. This problem surfaced just six weeks after school started, and I felt awful about it.

I was on my way home from school one day and looked for my neighborhood friend to play with, but she wasn't home. My mom and stepfather were gone, too. With the house locked and my friend not there, I found someone else to play with for awhile and then went back to my friend's house. She was there with bags and boxes scattered all over her bedroom.

As she was showing me everything, I got so excited for her. I wanted to tell my mother in the hope she would do the same for me. I told my friend that she was very lucky to have a mom who cared for her so much that she would leave her job to come home and take her shopping. Then she told me what had happened: it had been my mother and her husband who had purchased the clothes and shoes for her.

Wow! Talk about feeling unloved! It was like someone had run a dagger through my heart. Crying, I ran out of the house to find both my parents at home. I asked them if they took my friend shopping. They said "yes." I asked if they were going to take me and my brother shopping too. They told me "no." "Why?" They said they did it to teach me a lesson: don't ask for anything. They said it was time that I learned to take care of myself, and that there were no free rides in life. I said I didn't expect a free ride, but how could they expect me to provide for myself when I had just turned 10?

At that point, I gave up on my relationship with them. My walls went up, high and thick. I realized that my mother would never be available to me. She wasn't available to herself. The pain of this event struck me hard. I made a vow that if anyone was going to help me, it would be someone like my grandmother. I knew from that point on that the little trust I placed in my mother had disappeared.

Soon after this event, my stepfather began drinking heavily. Everything we did made him angry. Since his job took him out of town quite a bit, we knew we could count on him ranting, raving and drinking heavily whenever he returned. We paid for his anger though by his emotional and physical outbursts. Within a short time, he began to ritually beat my brother with a water hose, garden hoe, belt, or anything he could lay his hands on. During these episodes my mother never stepped in, only looked on. I'd beg him to stop, but he'd just tell me to shut up if I knew what was good for me or I'd be next. Since no one else lived in the house besides us, there was no one to help me defend my brother.

This man's abusive behavior continued in waves. Just as soon as he started badgering us, we gave our power to him. Our mother told us she could do nothing for us, that we needed to make the best of it. He soon began to hit her when my brother wasn't around. All this time I had to witness his abusive behavior toward us, and I felt myself beginning to die inside. I kept praying diligently to God for help, to get me out of this mess. I didn't know that my prayers were to be answered, but three years later.

At the age of 13, after living within this extremely dysfunctional family environment, I told my mother that I'd no longer be witness to any kind of abuse and that I was leaving her house. This was the one and only time that I can remember that my mother actually came alive and listened to me. She said she wouldn't leave, but understood why I could not stay. In my opinion, she was "hooked" on an addictive person. She said she would do everything she could to assist me to find a place to live because she did not want me on the streets. I told her that if that were my only option, I was willing to be on the streets. I had no idea what it would be like, but I was not going to live in the environment she had us living in and would do anything to get out of it.

She discussed the situation with my grandmother and they agreed that I would complete the school year and then move into her home. I felt like my God had listened to my prayers and had worked out the details between those two women. I could return to my grandma's home where I felt like I had a real mother. She told me that no granddaughter of hers would ever live on the streets as long as she were alive and able to provide a place to live.

I spent the next several years with her. My mother and stepfather objected constantly to me about taking advantage of her. My grandmother assisted me in every way she could. I got the chance to go on to college in my senior year, but my parents objected. They said that I should be out working somewhere, supporting myself totally and not allowing "that poor woman to do it all." I worked at several part-time jobs to help support my personal and college expenses.

The irony here is that Grandma was willing to take the responsibility of caring for me, and helping me gain a better chance in life, while my own mother balked at providing me with much more than a tormenting environment. I'm amazed every time I speak of what happened to me and how far I have climbed out of the mire.

After finishing high school, I began to believe in me, believing that I was a valuable person and had something to offer to life. A cousin was instrumental in helping me secure a scholarship from a woman's club that paid my class tuition for the first two years. The scholarship was based on academic standing and personal need. Mom and my stepfather were not happy about Grandma's insistence that I continue my education; they didn't want me to change.

My grandmother was ecstatic when I completed two years of college. I blossomed under her tutelage and guidance. She gave me free reign to make decisions about my life and where I wanted to go. What she was unable to do with her daughter she accomplished in her guidance with me. I give her full credit as being my first and very dear mentor. I know God had her close by me to keep her watchful eyes on me and to assist me when the time was right. She was always available to me, and I have warm feelings about her today. A therapist helped me understand, several years ago, that I can recall her personal essence any time I want and gain strength from our relationship, even though she has gone on to another place.

Real Life Begins

During that latter part of my sophomore year, I met a man who was to become my husband in the next seven months. As he and I entered into a relationship, we both had high hopes that it would be a good mix. Neither one of us had any idea about the dysfunctional families we came from, nor did we know about any recovery programs. And, little did we know, until after the years went by, that our choices were pre-determined by the nature of our families of origin. Both of us were children of alcoholics raised in severely dysfunctional family systems.

I found that this young man provided the exact thing I needed and had dreamt about for years: a way to escape from my dysfunctional family. Being codependent, I had no source of recovery at that time. I provided the same to him. I had made a private promise to myself that I would *not* get into the craziness that my mother did in her marriages. I was to escape from some of the dysfunction, but not all of it.

What I found was that none of us escape dysfunction until we're prepared to step out of it. It takes a lot of courage and effort to make better choices and move on. Most of us think we know more and can improve on the dysfunctions in our lives from our families of origin. I'm not saying that each new generation can do things better, but we can if we're willing to change. Just look at the history of Twelve Step programs and how they've evolved from generation to generation.

Keeping my identity was the thing that I valued most in my struggles to move away from dysfunction. I became overly supportive of my husband, which is a main characteristic of being codependent. For example, I put my education on the back burner to assist my husband with his. In my crazy thinking I rationalized that I was "investing in my future." Now I see that the only future I have is right now and not in some different time.

After being married two years, we found out we were going to be parents. I was totally excited about the prospect of having a child and was not prepared for the response that I got from him. He wasn't happy about being a parent at all, but succumbed to the inevitable fact. As we continued our marriage, I found myself compromising my values and staying in a relationship that should have ended long before. It's obvious now that we stayed together until we had learned as much as we could from each other.

Fortunately for any other children we might have had, we did not produce any more. I love my only child, a daughter, and know I did the best job I could in raising her. She and I are more friends than mother and daughter. By working on my recovery, I may have avoided imprinting my dysfunction onto her. However, she continually reveals to me what family issues still lurk in the background.

After being divorced eight years, I "put my money where my mouth is" and began completing my education. I did this at a time in my life that was best for me. Because I was working hard on my recovery, I was able to complete my education without the help of another man, giving me a great feeling of accomplishment. One of my main objectives in self-improvement is to help others, and for me, completing my education is part of this journey.

I've found that because I'm willing to be vulnerable and be shown a better way, I'm also willing to see things I need to correct in myself. I do this by observing what my daughter gets involved in and by listening to others tell their stories in CoDA meetings. I also receive good feedback from friends and a very trusted sponsor. What a great source of personal awareness I have so close to me.

I know I'm not perfect and still have much to uncover, but I believe that because I've worked a Twelve Step recovery program for fifteen years, I'm able to see things more clearly than before. By following the Twelve Steps along with other areas of spiritual enlightenment, I continue to emerge as a new person everyday. People, places and things don't have as much a hold on me as before. I'm certainly much less materialistic than just a few years ago. I find joy and happiness in the little things of life. I have a more personal relationship with God than I ever thought I could.

Unfortunately, one member of my family, my older brother, didn't make the choice to start a recovery program. He committed suicide after marrying and divorcing the same woman many times, leaving a large family behind.

If you want recovery from your dysfunctional family, stop at nothing to achieve the peace that passes all understanding. Find the program that will assist and support you and get to work. To do my program, I had to go to a lot of meetings, starting out in one Twelve Step recovery program and walking through the door of four programs in all before I found CoDA. It takes what it takes. It may take 90 meetings in 90 days to really have a light turn on, or it may not. I encourage at least two to three meetings a week to start. This helped me to stretch, push my parameters and take the risks I needed to take.

For me, discovering people with whom I find common bonds can be one of the most healing things to happen. I'm not alone anymore. After I walked through the doors of my first CoDA meeting, almost 15-1/2 years ago, I've discovered that the God of my understanding talks to me through other people and their stories. In the past, God didn't let me down; it had been me.

I've found that having a sponsor and becoming a sponsor are extremely important too. It took me quite a while to get to a point where I could ask someone to be my sponsor. Even though I had a few very trusted friends in the program, having a sponsor really got me into working the Twelve Steps. I needed to process more of the real issues with a true friend, and through the years, that meant changing sponsors. Each sponsor provided something I needed to hear, and I had something to give back. Sponsorship is a two-way street. I doubt that my recovery would have been as good without those trusted servants.

My first sponsor started me at Step One and helped me progress through Step Twelve. The big hurdle to get through was my First, Fourth and Fifth Steps. Wow! What a cleansing feeling once it was over, but the pain to get through it was horrendous. I cannot recommend it enough. All the counseling in the world cannot do what my program has done for me, though I still seek counseling when I know I need it, and it's right for me. The rewards that come in recovery far outweigh staying where I am.

By all events that took place in my early life, I shouldn't be here today. My recovery has been a long, uphill climb, much like climbing Mt. Everest. Many times I've felt that for every inch of recovery, I lose a foot. I'm sure it's that way for many of us, since no two humans are alike and our recovery isn't the same either. I'm told that God doesn't make junk and that our recovery is built on faith and trust. Faith and trust in a Higher Power are all I really have.

Since I'm on my own path, using the Twelve Steps as my guide helps me to continue adjusting my path's alignment. This recovery process isn't easy because there's usually no gain without first passing through pain. But this process helps me pass to the other side and into a better way of living. It's beyond our imagination. However, with the recovery process comes risk and with the risks I can take a giant leap of faith, move out of my old ideas and into the new.

Recovery is a lifetime process and worth every Step. There is no graduation as far as I know, but

I'm worth recovering from my dysfunction and so are you. Today I'm letting my God do for me what I cannot do for myself, one day at a time.

by Cecile

TAP DANCER NO MORE

I was born into a white, middle class family in the Midwest in the mid-fifties. My hometown is situated on the border of the South, and the border of the East. I was the middle child of four and was raised to live in the middle ground of life where civility, manners, and right and wrong matter more than authenticity or self, calling, and path.

At an early age, I can remember knowing inside my heart of hearts that I liked girls more than I liked boys, (you know, in "that way"...). I began my exploration of the mysteries of gender at an early age. I returned the dolls the elders gave to me as gifts. I refused to wear dresses unless it was absolutely required by the powers that be. And I played with the boys in the neighborhood as hard and as long as they played. I was a tomboy, as good as any boy at the boy stuff and damned proud of it.

But growing up gay was against the rules and I knew it. There is an insidious way that homophobia (the fear of and oppression of gay people in this culture) seeps into the consciousness of young people. Somehow, I just knew I was "the worst," I was the scum of the earth, and that being a lesbian was probably both my father's and mother's worst fear. So I incorporated an incredible arsenal of coping skills around this particular part of who I was becoming. My codependent "false self" got lots and lots of practice from about age eight on.

Slowly, I became one of my family's secrets. The "no talk" rule was steadfastly in place: "If we don't talk about it, we won't have to feel too uncomfortable." Over time, I automatically began to carry the shame of my family, feeling their embarrassment for them, and doing all kinds of tap dancing, so they would not have to feel too ashamed of me, their budding "queer" daughter and sister.

I excelled in high school with straight A's and took leadership almost compulsively. This was a way to make them proud of me, to get attention, to hide out in the sanctuary of books and intellectualism, mentally shutting off the feelings of loss, shame and low self-esteem that were just underneath the surface. If I was "not good enough" in all the "normal" ways of courting male attention, dating, eventually marrying and settling down into a "normal" lifestyle everyone could understand, then at least I furnished my family members with the fixings of pride in raising an honor student who surpassed all family standards.

I was the "smart" one of the four children. Having smarts was one of my covers and a form of tap dancing. It was safe behind a book, and I did not have to feel the abandonment that was looming in and around the unspoken regions of my unacceptable persuasion.

Also during the high school years, I discovered the safety and power in focusing on others, their problems, and their feelings. This deflected all attention off me, and I got a lot of juice from being able to "be there" for others. A different "me" surfaced, the one who was fed at the core by a motivation to belong, to fit in with other people. I needed to be needed; this was a growing hunger and emptiness that had to be filled up on a daily basis. Focusing on others became the source of my worthiness, to cover up the ways I felt deep down underneath it all: filthy, wrong, sick, disgusting, and "less than" all others of the heterosexual world. The wounding that came from "being different" and not feeling that I belonged was deep and at the core of how I lived those long years before recovery.

I was literally "disowned" several times by my family because of my sexual preference. I was taken out of the will and asked to go into therapy to get "cured." Being in therapy constantly and working on myself became one of the ways I codependently tried to control and manage my family's impression of me. If they thought I was "getting help," and seriously rooting out all the blemishes that made me the way I was, then maybe I would be tolerated, and someday loved. Maybe I could grow and change in some specific or resounding way so that they would finally love me.

In my 20's, I went from relationship to relationship looking for validation. I became addicted to relationships, using my highly developed people-pleasing "skills" to keep lovers and friends alike from leaving me. I've heard folks in meetings describe holding their lovers hostage with the neediness and fear of abandonment that resides in the belly of every codependent. That was the kind of gnawing energy that would rise and rule every time a relationship got to the breaking point. I went into high gear, where I was willing to do and be anything for the "other," just so that they wouldn't reject or abandon me as my family of origin had.

My relationship history had become a full-blown array of hooking up with alcoholics, drug addicts, sex addicts and workaholics. People "needed me" but, for whatever reason, they were all unable or unwilling to be fully present in the relationship—the classic "unavailable" lovers. My addiction to them, as the "co-queen," grew and became finally uncontrollable. My life became unmanageable and I was in a cesspool of spiritual bankruptcy.

Several therapists and many years later—plus thousands of dollars spent on therapy—I discovered the Twelve Step programs. The tortures were not working any longer—I came in on my knees and have been on them ever since. Thank God!

It was in CoDA that I first unveiled my pain and eventually myself in front of entire rooms full of people who would not judge, or criticize me for being who I was. I was invited to participate in the healing as much as I was willing to—and it actually took me a long time to let this invitation sink into my untrusting, flinching soul. I did not have to tap dance, accommodate, hide out or take care of others to be accepted as I am nor was I intended to carry and shoulder all of the sexual shame of the times and culture. I was supported and encouraged by others to shed this conditioning one step at a time, with a vital and vibrant sense of community and belonging enfolding me every inch of the way. The solutions and the process were human; the path was also human and, of course, very spiritual.

Turning my will and my life over to the care of God allowed me to enter into a way of life where my worth was no longer tied to external sources. Depending on God to guide and sustain me represented an amazing change in my approach to daily living and, thus, allowed me to slowly rewrite my own story. With help from my sponsor, Higher Power and all my friends in the Fellowship, I am learning that my wounding as a young person is not my destiny. The trick is not to try and reshape or reconstruct myself into someone else (as I had been conditioned to believe), but rather it is to reknow who I am, as a whole and worthy child of God.

CoDA has given me the tools and fellowship, internal ego structure, and spiritual context to draw strength from, strength which helps me no longer run from life's past and present pain, but instead to simply feel it. When I stop trying to fix and control others and my own life, everything lightens up. I grow in faith and trust in universal order and good in God's will for me on a daily basis.

So I tap dance a lot less now, and life is calm. I am no longer the drama queen doing anything and everything trying to secure others' love and attention.

Serenity is good on my nervous system, and truly it all just gets better and better as I move along. There is room in God's garden for all of us, regardless of one's lifestyle.

by Laura J.

A DOOR OF HOPE

I did not make a conscious decision to find out about codependence. My own awareness of this dysfunctional way of life was thrust upon me by painful circumstances. Our family was in therapy together to address the problems of a troubled son. As the months went by, in spite of my resistance, an inner painful reality began to surface, slowly, dimly, but surely. I had joined the family counseling with the purpose of returning a son to a healthy life. Now I could not honestly reject the new light that was dawning in me, pointing to my own need for restoration. This awakening process took me through family therapy, codependency treatment and finally to the Twelve Step program of Co-Dependents Anonymous. I had never known how to ask for help or that I was in need of it. The fact that I was able to reach out and take the hands of so many is nothing less than a miracle to me.

This story is about how I am discovering what is happening to me in my nice, comfortable, respectable "family-of-origin," how subtle the messages were and how well I learned and adapted to what was expected of me. The forces that drove my life were in place at an early age. I began to see that still functioning within me, decades later, were "emotional programs" I had adopted as a child, as an adolescent and as a young woman in an effort to make a secure place for myself in the world. This included decisions to be nice at all costs, to keep the surroundings peaceful, and basically to make my world a happy place to live in. Without knowing it, I had set myself up to live dishonestly. With the emotional agenda I had, my attempt to live out these goals succeeded only at great cost to me spiritually, emotionally and physically, and deeply affected the lives of my children. I learned to bury my painful feelings to keep the "nice" image, to suppress the spontaneous life within me and to say "yes" when I meant "no" in requests from family and community. In this way, I set up dishonesty in my relationship with myself and in my relationships with others.

Even more damaging was the failure to know what was going on within me. I kept myself enmeshed with people and with nonstop activities which totally distracted me from my own "reality." I focused carefully on the behavior of others and learned how to act and respond. I believe that I was always watching, and chameleon-like, and adapting. I tried to make myself as invisible as possible in asserting my own thoughts, opinions and feelings. These patterns kept me from being fully alive and had, in part, reaped their harvest in the depressed son facing us in that counseling room.

My "birthing" into codependence began early in

life. My father was a beloved physician who took care of the needs of others 12 to 18 hours a day, including weekends. Though dedicated, he was fulfilling his own codependent and work-addicted needs. As a child with such a parent, I felt a large measure of pride, but I am learning that, essentially, I was abandoned in this primary relationship.

I was eager to take care of my father when he returned in the evening, and my sister and I hovered over him. Added to this was an older brother who expected his little sisters to wait on him hand and foot. We vied for his attention and I discovered that the only time he noticed me was when I was doing something for him. Between these first two male relationships, my lifelong patterns of taking care of men were set up.

I think my mother needed me to be good. The behavior of my siblings was much more demanding and lively than mine. I decided at a young age to get her approval by being quiet and invisible. I believe my mother compensated for her own unmet emotional needs with community affairs and many social activities. As I grew older, I noticed that whenever there was a crisis in my family, my mother would give a party. Of course, nothing was ever acknowledged as a crisis or a difficulty. The denial patterns in my family were immense. Anything that did not fit the acceptable family image or was painful was either ignored, discounted or rationalized away. There was no process for dealing with or grieving. My mother gave a great deal of form to my life in outward appearances and observances. It was as if she were saying, "This is the way we live. This is the way we act, dress and speak," essentially communicating, "This is who we are." These messages were all conveyed with the utmost of "Southern" charm and graciousness. There was an abundance of activity and physical presence of Mother in our home, but little inner emotional substance available to any of us. I learned how to "act" loving, how to "act" close by caretaking and how to "act" happy without the corresponding inner feelings. I mistook the performance for the real thing.

I became who my parents wanted me to be. As I grew up, I became increasingly more separated from the self that I believe God had created. I was taught manners, morals and good behavior by my family and the society around me, including my church. The development of my own inner reality, my true self, suffered. I became "other" oriented and grew up with a need to look good, to be strong and to take care of others.

Because of this orientation, I did not allow myself feelings, spontaneous responses or opinions which disagreed with the authority figures in my life. A kind of death set in—an inability to engage in life at any meaningful level. I became more and more obedient, adaptive and conforming. I learned to carefully watch the behavior of others, preparing myself to respond in a way that would be pleasing and acceptable. I was so "nice" and accommodating to others; not only did I not know who I was, neither did anyone else.

Because of this "good behavior," I believed I was loved, accepted and valued by my family, society and God. At a deep inner level, the split between who I was and who I thought I was included the way in which I needed others to perceive me. This "false self" became the identity I took into my adult life. All the pieces were in place for full-blown codependence.

Not surprisingly, I married a man much like my father—a hardworking medical student who was an answer to all my hopes for a husband and family. I adapted well to his life and needs. If I stopped short of making him my God, at least I made him the sun around which my world revolved. The enmeshment that developed felt like a wonderful intimacy, and my codependence found a comfortable home in which to flourish.

The years that followed were a whirlwind of activity. His centered on receiving extensive training and establishing a surgical practice; mine was divided between the care of four children and creating a design business. My own need to look and feel worthwhile was fed by both. I kept a beautiful home. My husband was highly respected in his profession. We embodied all the external trappings of "success." I experienced my life as being rewarding and stimulating. Those about me affirmed me in this perception.

I arranged the world of my children much as my mother had ordered mine, with the "right" schools, camps, friends and activities. I drove in countless carpools as part of my commitment to be "supermom," but the restlessness driven by my clamoring inner needs controlled my life more and more and began to take its toll. My creative endeavors began to dominate my decisions. I became increasingly unable to spend quality time with my children. I seemed to be powerless to stop and join their world and cherish them in their development.

Instead, I designed one house after another. I sewed and painted, produced beautiful needlepoint and quilts and became a consultant for the creations of others. I found a very seductive drug in all of this activity. I discovered the immense gratification of taking an idea from my mind and bringing it into reality through the works of my hands. I grieve that this was not enough for me. My disease demanded that ideas and busy hands also serve to feed an insatiable activity addiction. The long unattended feelings within me were kept at bay, and the denial processes remained intact.

If I would have been able to see, I would have noticed cracks appearing in my "perfect" little world. My husband was showing signs of depression, our second son was beginning to "act-out" in negative and destructive ways and our daughter and eldest son were overachieving in many areas. I was turning more and more to our youngest son for companionship as my husband became less and less available in his depression. I minimized everything that was not acceptable to the way I wished to perceive my family. It finally became very difficult to ignore the drug abuse of our son. I resisted the truth. I tried harder and harder to cover the painful reality with shreds of activity and beauty. I painted rooms the color of sunlight to dispel the increasing gloom and I decked myself in self-made finery to create an outer appearance that would belie the insecure, frightened person inside me. Every means I had developed to feel alive and safe was external and transitory.

When I became less and less able to make my old familiar line of defense protect me, I turned to one I had learned well in my childhood, namely to be strong and invulnerable. In my need, I embraced the God of my understanding with renewed commitment. I became a "strong" Christian. I shared my developing fear and pain with no one. In this relationship with God I became the "good little girl" I had been with my parents, and worked hard at being "saintly." This took me farther away from myself and contributed to my denial processes. I then switched my activity addiction from my home to the church. I was available for all requests for service, said "yes" when I should have responded "no," and expended great energy trying to change others. My full-blown codependency became runaway codependency.

I believe my body began to take the brunt of the unaddressed codependence with its lifelong symptoms of denial, repression and isolation. I had developed chronic low back pain which inhibited many of my activities. By the time I was 46 years old, I had a malignancy. The surgery was successful, but did not, of course, touch the underlying emotional and spiritual dysfunction. During the inactivity of my recuperation, I had a recurring thought which seemed to be telling me that if I did not find a new way to deal with life, this would probably happen to me again. It was a very sobering time for me.

I had joined my husband in addressing the gathering problems of the family by focusing on our troubled son. He served as a "scapegoat" although, of course, we did not see that then. In my illness I began to wonder what I needed to do to change myself. I had no idea how to respond to life differently.

God was faithful. I can only surmise that He had been waiting for me to be willing to be open to a new way and to risk peeking out of my tightly controlled world. This was not easy for me, but I was finally ready to explore new terrain. God used my husband to pave the way. Through his own distress, he became willing to address his work addiction and debilitating depression. In seeking help for our son, he responded to suggestions that he enter treatment and, afterward, a Twelve Step program. In a relatively short time, I saw the depression of a decade lift and a new energy and creativeness come into his life. I observed this strong, reserved, independent person begin to share his feelings and to lean on a supportive group of men. As he modeled this remarkable change, I received the courage to step into these strange waters myself. I wish I could say that I embraced the recovery process as quickly as he had, but I dawdled along the way, putting a toe in now and then. Again, a crisis pushed me into another decision.

The tragic life of our son ended suddenly, and the years of drug abuse took their victim. The grieving process was both racking and healing. In this death, it was as if waters of birth broke and brought forth new life into the devastation of generations. I believe now that this terrible dysfunction that had been passed down to us and had finally taken such a toll was indeed codependence. The entrenched patterns of denial, betrayal of our true selves and the estrangement from healthy bonding and intimacy had produced a family that could only act externally and die internally. The drug abuse, the work and activity addictions, the dependency problems were only symptoms of the underlying codependence. I did not see this all at once. The process of this understanding has been painful and yet the most rewarding pilgrimage of my life.

Many gifts began to come out of my son's death. The first were in the shape of two prayers that came to my mind almost immediately. One was that I would be able to feel the pain; the other, as radical, was that I would not try to do it alone. With these requests, I began to break the isolating patterns of the past and to question the way in which I had been taught to be strong. As I journeyed down into the pain, I began to experience renewed energy and a new sense of myself. The deadness that I had felt for so long began to lift. In its place came a new connection with life. I could hardly believe that the very thing I had built such impenetrable defenses against, namely the acknowledgment of any sadness or hurt, was now the carrier of deep healing. Losses of a lifetime, so carefully buried, began to emerge one at a time. The loss of my son had opened the dam through which the stored up pain of decades began to pour. In this grieving process, I was being given back my life.

Another gift was given on the heels of this initial healing. It came wrapped in the package labeled, "Co-Dependents Anonymous." I will be forever grateful to my Higher Power for providing this program when I was feeling like a toddler trying to learn how to walk. The CoDA Fellowship has provided me with a structure and a process upon which to build a new life. It has given me a family in which to grow, one that supports me in risking new behavior, brushes me off when I fall and cheers me on. In these safe surroundings, I can risk being spontaneous, speaking my own opinions and experiencing my own feelings. When I get "too visible" in all this new behavior and the old shame surfaces, I can share this, too, instead of withdrawing into my old busyness to quiet my discomfort.

More and more, I am accepting my powerlessness over the need to look good and to perform well. This awareness is helping me to resist that old "false self" and the deadness that it brings. The more I find that "child" within who had to go into hiding so long ago, the less I have to live my life from a place outside myself. Increasingly, I can give up my false gods; my husband, my addictive need to project a certain image of myself with all the control that entails, my compulsive busyness that borders on debilitating work addiction and my dependency needs on others, which takes the form of being a "savior." Instead, I can let God be God and learn what being truly human is all about. This ongoing learning process is yet another gift that CoDA offers to me. I find I can take the fruits of being a part of the Fellowship and enhance every facet of my life.

I no longer have to project a "strong" image to the world or in my church. Instead, I have discovered the most paradoxical truth: Part of my own brokenness has been the lifelong need to believe that I am "all together." My move toward wholeness is the realization that I am a broken person. Only as I live out of this place can I draw on the grace of God and experience the strength that comes from Him. To learn about my own powerlessness and false strength has been an invaluable gift of the CoDA Fellowship. I can truly receive the love of God in a new and different way.

I no longer believe that I am loved because I am an obedient, adaptive "good little girl." Through CoDA, God is helping me to address the very heart of the codependence that almost took my life. I had always believed that the choice was about goodness or badness. Now, I know it is about life or death. I am grateful that in recovery I am increasingly able to choose life.

by Jenny B.

TO TELL THE TRUTH...

Last night I received my four-year CoDA medallion at my home group. My birthday in CoDA was a couple of weeks ago, and each day I put my three-year medallion in my pocket, I felt disappointed that I did not have my fourth medallion yet. Each year in recovery is important to me because I still sometimes hear that little voice inside that tells me it is no big deal. Part of my recovery is to honor my progress, so celebrating each year is one way to remind myself this is a big deal!

I grew up in a family that looked great on the outside, and most people thought we were a "happy, loving family." We created that image so well that even I believed it for a long time. I knew we had some problems, but no more than most people—in fact probably fewer. The only real obvious problem to me (and the rest of the family) was that my brother was rebellious and drank, used drugs, and ran away a lot. And that didn't happen until I was an adolescent.

I cannot tell you much about my childhood before my adolescence because I don't remember a lot of it. I remember bits and pieces—some pleasant, some painful, others neutral. But until this past year, I never saw that as having large gaps in my memory. One of the painful memories I do have is of being called "Little Sarah Bernhardt" by my parents. I had no idea who she was until I finally asked and was told she was an actress. I was usually called "Little Sarah Bernhardt" when I was expressing some feeling, and I suppose, at some level, my parents' message became that much clearer after I found out who she was. The message was that I was dramatic, and that I was making a big deal out of nothing. That was how they conveyed that otherwise unspoken "don't have any feelings" rule. So I dutifully tried to hide my feelings. Since I never became very adept at doing so, I learned to spend a lot of time alone in order to conceal my emotions.

Some of the pieces of memory I have discovered over the last several years are about being incested and molested. I remembered the incest, which occurred when I was an adolescent. Since that time, I have worked through those memories and have gained a lot of healing. For the most part though, the memories are only in small bits and pieces. I do not know who my molesters/perpetrators were, and the bits of memory still haunt me.

After surviving my adolescence, which in retrospect felt dark and lonely, I decided to move to the West Coast with the intent of attending college. My boyfriend at that time wanted to join me, and so, at 19, I moved 3,000 miles away from my family. At some level it seemed to be the only way I could begin to live independently. It was several months after the move to California that I began to notice myself changing. I was becoming more and more fearful, and was acting more and more irrationally. I was becoming more obsessed with my boyfriend's drinking and increasingly scared of his behavior when he was drunk. He became violent when he was drunk and would shake, push and grab me, but I didn't know he was abusing me, because he was not hitting me. I loved him, so leaving him never entered my mind. I became more and more housebound and isolated out of my terror. My primary connection was still to my family 3,000 miles away. Less than a year after I moved away, my brother became suicidal and ended up shortly thereafter in treatment for chemical dependency. That provided enough of an opening in my shame for me to begin talking a little about what was going on in my life. With my family's encouragement, I called my first Twelve Step program the night following another violent episode and began attending meetings. The changes I experienced came slowly, but within nine months, I faced a decision as to whether or not I should leave this man. Part of what prompted the question about leaving was that I began to be concerned about my own well-being. I had discovered that my boyfriend was ripping off the drugstore he worked for and was dealing the drugs. My concern was whether I would be charged if he were arrested.

For the first time, I truly practiced the Third Step and turned my will and my life over to my Higher Power. The following day, I knew in my heart that the answer was for me to leave.

That was only the beginning of a number of

changes I made as I continued practicing recovery through the Twelve Steps. My life changed over time, but I noticed one area of my life was not changing much—the relationship part. I seemed to continue to attract and be attracted to men who were addicted to something and seemed to have no emotional lives other than anger. No matter what I did, this did not seem to change. I began to believe there was something wrong with me, and that somehow it was my fault. I believed in the illusion that my family was healthy and did not have problems like mine. They began to make comments like, "You have been in recovery this long and you are still doing that?" But for me, that translated to, "What is wrong with you?"

Every once in awhile, something would happen and I would catch a glimpse of truth, that things in the family had not really changed much. Like the day my brother commented that he wanted to drink, even though he had been sober at least five or six years, and each person in the room instantly found something to do, a nonverbal change of subject. I thought that was an odd response, especially since my mother worked in a chemical dependence treatment center developing family treatment programs. I commented that I thought what he had said was important, and we ought to listen. Their response to this and similar incidents only added to my confusion, and I felt crazy.

I went to graduate school and noticed how smoothly my life went when I did not have time for dating or any relationships with men. I was in a stressful job within several months after graduate school, back into dating and into a brief relationship.

I was also back into unmanageability and terror. I felt very quiet and dead inside, yet I was seething with rage. I knew I needed to be hospitalized, which had been one of my biggest fears. When I was an adolescent, I was afraid to talk about what went on inside, because I believed if I did, my parents would lock me up in a psychiatric hospital and I would never get out. So here again I was afraid it would happen. Instead, I took a couple of days off from work, continued going to my Twelve Step meetings and found a therapist. I lost my job right after that, which allowed me to focus on my healing. About all I would do was get up, sit on the couch and maybe by late afternoon finally get dressed. My sponsor calls it the "sitting-on-the-couch-in-your-bathrobe-stage."

I started thinking about suicide because it was the only way I could think of to get the pain to stop, and the pain seemed endless and overwhelming. I knew my boyfriend had a gun and figured that was how I would do it. I had tried to kill myself when I was about 16 by drinking and taking a handful of pills, but I only slept extra soundly that night. I just knew there was something horribly wrong with me if I had been working on recovery for seven years, and I was feeling like this.

At the same time, something was beginning to change for me—my therapist and my support system in recovery were chipping away at my denial about my family. Maybe they were not so healthy and loving; maybe they were actually abusive. As the illusion about my family started to crumble, I felt more and more pain, and I began to get in touch with my rage.

I tentatively began talking about my new awareness with my sister and brothers and met with mixed results. Sometimes they seemed to understand, and other times, they discounted me. Because my family's pattern seemed to be that we did not get help until one of us was suicidal, things did not change until my sister, and later my brother, got in touch with their pain and went to treatment. The whole family was asked to participate, and I made a commitment to myself that I would use the opportunity to further my recovery.

My father is a minister and my mother is a family therapist who specialized in chemical dependence treatment, and before going to my sister's "family week" of treatment, my mother told me I was going to the family week to work on my sister. I responded I was not going to work on my sister, I was going to work on me, and she argued with me. I felt crazy until I realized how crazy-making the argument was. My mother told her client family members that they were powerless over the addicts in their lives and, therefore, needed to focus on themselves; yet here she was telling me just the opposite.

What I discovered during that family week was a number of family secrets that I had no idea existed. Like the fact that we all had been molested by someone inside or outside our own family (except my mother, who does not remember ever being molested). And that my father was a sex addict. That was something I would never have thought of in my wildest imagination—ever. This was my father who objected to premarital sex, was a minister, and ran marriage encounter weekends for couples with my mother, and was very much opposed to pornography.

This was my father who, along with my mother, told me (when I was in my first year of college), that if the congregation found out I was staying with my boyfriend on weekends, he could lose his church. I believed him and felt mountains of shame even though part of me knew that would never happen. So how could he be a sex addict? No one in the family knew—except my mother. So the bit about the congregation getting rid of him because I was "living in sin" was really about the fact that if they found out what he was doing, he would not just lose the church, but would stand to lose everything. He voluntarily shared, "I'm a sex addict." No one had suggested that to him.

Denial runs so thick in my "family-that-looked-so-good," however, that nine months later when I was home visiting, we had a discussion of why Dad can't eat "just one chocolate." My mother seemed to have difficulty grasping this. She finally decided that was not such a big issue; there were worse possibilities as she indicated by her next statement to my father, "Well, honey, at least you're not a sex addict. At least you're not an alcoholic." I could not believe what I was hearing, and the old "I'm crazy" feeling resurfaced.

Fortunately, God works in ways that allowed for more changes and healing in the family. Through a series of events, my brother, mother and father went to treatment. And shortly after that, I discovered CoDA. By then I was attending a few different Twelve Step programs and each of them helped, but when I read through the starter packet for CoDA I was amazed. This program fit me exactly. It was not one of the programs where I identified with parts; I knew this was what I had needed for a long time. I identified with the patterns and characteristics of a codependent. In fact, I could do an immediate inventory based on those patterns and characteristics.

I knew I wanted to be able to attend a CoDA meeting in my city, and since there were none here, I began talking to my friends who were in recovery and showing them the packet to see if they were interested in helping me start a meeting. So we started the first meeting here. For a long time, only about eight people showed up, and I worried about that and wondered why more did not come. It seemed that when I reminded myself I was powerless over that and let go, the meeting began to grow. Today, there are 14 meetings in or around this area and I truly appreciate being able to have a choice of meetings to attend.

I already had the basic tools of recovery, so it was relatively easy to apply them to my CoDA program. My understanding of what I am powerless over has expanded considerably over the years. I know now I did not create my inability to have healthy relationships; I learned that from my family. In CoDA, I was relearning how to have relationships. One of the things I liked about CoDA was that I could focus on my relationship with myself. That became a focus of my recovery: who was I, how did I or could I best take care of myself, what were my wants, needs, desires, and dreams.

Part of my learning meant I needed to stay out of relationships with men for a period of time because at that point, I was not able to focus on myself in a relationship. I had to work so hard just to survive or maintain in a relationship that there was no energy left for me. While I stayed out of relationships with men, I was able to develop relationships with women. I had never had very many friendships with women because of my need for male attention. Women and girls were not valued in my family, so why would I want to be friends with them? And then one day I had the overwhelming realization that in the core of my being I carried the belief that, "If I had been a boy I would have been loved." I believe those realizations are part of how God restores me to sanity. I need to know the messages that I operate from if I am ever going to have a chance of changing them.

I had struggled with working the Steps in the years I had been in recovery. Working the Steps in CoDA was eased some when I had an opportunity to read the first Step literature that was available. Tears came to my eyes as I read the first three Steps. It was the first time I had read Step literature and identified so clearly with it. My experience and beliefs were reflected in those Steps; they even contained things I had said about the Steps in the past. When CoDA changed the language of the Steps to make them nongender-specific, I was overjoyed! Having grown up in a religious family, God was virtually shoved down my throat, and that God was defined in very specific ways. Those ways did not work for me and made it difficult for me to connect with a Higher Power at times. A male God no longer worked for me; that was not a safe or nurturing concept of a Higher Power for me.

As I worked the Steps in CoDA, I became more aware of how little I trusted in a Higher Power. I was out of a job for quite a while and had tried to work the Third Step on that particular issue. I finally realized I was afraid that if I turned my will and my life over to God, God would give me a job at Burger King. Now it is not that there is anything wrong with Burger King; I had had a job working fast food several years earlier. It was that I had this graduate degree, and out of my shame and feelings of worthlessness, I thought that was all I deserved. It was not about what God wanted for me; it was what I thought I deserved. And then it dawned on me that God probably wouldn't have guided me through graduate school in order to give me a job at Burger King.

I had attempted to do my Fourth Step countless times but had given up because I was overwhelmed. I was overwhelmed because I was sure I was doing it wrong. I wanted to know the right way to do it, and I thought I had to write it all down—at once. My sponsor finally said to me, "What do you think you've been doing when you've been writing about what happened to you, and how you feel about what's happened, and what your part in it was?" For me the Fourth Step started and stopped and came out in bits and pieces and fills many notebooks. I have talked to my sponsor about each piece as I've done it. Again, my shame told me I was doing it wrong because I wasn't doing it the way everyone else said to do it, or the way the original Twelve Step program suggested. In CoDA, I was able to begin to validate that how I do it is OK and is the best for me. It might not work for anyone else, but it doesn't need to. It only needs to work for me.

CoDA was the first place I learned about affirmations and the importance of affirming myself.

I see this as another tool that is a means for God to remove my shortcomings. I've realized God doesn't magically pluck them from my being, and I'm suddenly free. My Fourth Step allows me to see and identify my shortcomings. My Fifth Step allows me to admit them and not keep them a secret (not that they really are a secret to others). And, the Sixth and Seventh Steps help me to be willing and ready to let go of them. Usually that means I become painfully aware of them as I practice them over and over, and feel some mild level of horror that here I am, doing this again, until finally, one day, God provides me with the energy to see the impending defect, and I discontinue practicing it. And then I learn more tools to deal with the defects.

Yesterday at work, I was in a meeting where we were asked to introduce ourselves to a prospective employee. I was the first to go. I included my name, title and the comment that, "I'm fairly new to the department." As everyone else introduced themselves (some of whom were newer to the agency than I am) no one else made any comment like that. I felt embarrassed and started thinking, Why did I say that? I'm discounting myself by saying that (which is a shortcoming of mine). That bothered me for a little while. Several hours later, I had the thought, I wasn't discounting myself. I was validating what is true for me. I am new to the department, and I need to remember that so that I can maintain realistic expectations of myself. By doing so, I can validate that I am still in a transition period. Whew! So that is how God removes my shortcomings.

Anyway, since I've been in CoDA, I have developed a good support system. I have several women friends willing to take risks with me, and I with them, on practicing being real. My relationship with my family has improved greatly. It makes it much easier that they are all in recovery now, too. But that still doesn't mean it's easy. I have some difficulty being around my parents for long periods of time. When old stuff surfaces, or I start hearing crazy-making messages, I tend to protect myself in old ways, and I can say mean things. I have learned that one of the ways I can make amends to my parents is to not put myself around them for extended periods of time. I do fine with phone conversations.

As for relationships with men, I have had a couple of relationships since I've been in CoDA. I was able to stay more focused on myself and not become quite as desperate and clingy as I used to be, which is a great improvement. And I was able to take many risks with a male friend in recovery. I was able to say who I was, talk about my feelings and be vulnerable. I developed a deeper level of intimacy with him than I had ever experienced in a relationship with a man. It was scary, but it was worth every risk involved. Although that particular relationship has since ended, or at least is on sabbatical, I would not have had the joy of knowing I am capable of that kind of relationship without risking it.

My life on this particular day is calm and I feel content. I am not in an intimate relationship with a man, nor does my life depend on that. One of my desires is that I will be able to have that at some point in my life, but I don't have to wait for it. Today I know I will be OK if it never happens. There was a time when I first started in CoDA when I frequently wondered if the pain I felt would ever end. There was a time in recovery when I thought that feeling that much pain meant I was not doing recovery right. My sponsor frequently reminded me that feeling the pain within me was possible only through recovery. (That was one of those "gifts" of recovery I found questionable at the time.) Well, the pain did lessen and most of the time I feel content now. My life is not perfect, though. There are many issues I still need to address. But my life is OK, and that I can attribute to the tools of this program.

by Kathy T.

THE DIE MAKER/ACCOUNTANT

The progression of a career that goes from tool and die maker journeyman, to engineer, to certified public accountant may seem strange to most people. That is only because it is strange to anyone who engages in accepted norms of logic. It is not so strange, however, if one understands the dynamics of codependence.

My first codependent relationship was with my father. As far back as I can remember, I always wanted or needed to have my father love me, be proud of me, pay attention to me, teach me things and not yell at me, watch me participate in sports and spend quality time with me. When, on the very rare occasions (perhaps a half-dozen in my life while in his house) he paid me a compliment—I felt good. Then I felt life was worth living; I was exhilarated. Most of the time, however, I felt otherwise. I lived all my life until the time I entered high school, trying to get my worth from how my parents (primarily my father) treated me.

When I got to high school, I switched from trying to get my parents' approval to trying to get my sense of worth from the approval of my peer group. I became the ultimate overachiever—the resident hero. In my senior year, I was the student body president, president of the InterConference Student Council of all the high schools in our conference, all-state in football, a starter on the basketball and baseball teams, wrote for the local newspaper on teen events and voted the best dancer in school.

The prime example of my father's lifelong attitude toward me was illustrated by an incident I recall that happened toward the end of my senior year. We were driving out of the driveway in his new Cadillac (which I was convinced he cared more about at the time than he did me) when I slipped back into that "needing-his-approval" mode. I verbally listed off all the aforementioned high school accomplishments and asked, "Gee, that's pretty good, isn't it Dad?" His only response was, "Aw, you're spending too goddamn much time at that school!"

It felt to me, that in his mind, I simply never measured up. If I started to feel good about myself, started to do something creative or wanted to explore and try something new, he would discourage me by saying, "Aw, what do you want to do that for? Stop thinking about having fun all the time, and do your homework or cut the grass," etc.

I learned it wasn't OK to be who I was. I had to be what he thought I should be. Of course, my mother was really no better. She fostered me up to be her surrogate spouse and drove wedges between my dad and me which simply made things worse. They were often at cross purposes. My mother would rebel against my father through me by telling me that I didn't have to do as he had said.

The position of being in between them all the time became very confusing. It was as though there were no rules in the house, but God help me if I broke one of them.

I did, however, get the message that I was to be what they wanted me to be, do what they wanted me to do in the manner they wanted me to do it. My ideas simply were not good enough. When there was a confrontation between them and/or among the three of us, I always assumed it was my fault and kept on trying to get it right.

In the mode of trying to get it right, I served an 8000-hour tool and die maker apprenticeship. Why? Because my grandfather was a tool and die maker and my father was one of the most respected die engineers in the automobile industry at the time— naturally! All of my young life, I was told the "only" way to do something really worthwhile in my life was to be a professional in the automobile industry. My dad used to say, "To be an engineer where you're involved in the kind of manufacturing where 400 automobile doors per hour are produced is the finest kind of engineering there is."

It didn't occur to him that I might be much better suited to do something else with my very own life. There really were other ways to make a living and people really were happy doing them and making genuine contributions to the human race.

I remember when I did finish at the top of my class, the four-year apprenticeship that was so almighty important to my dad, I didn't receive so much as a graduation card or even a "Good job, I'm really proud of you." At the time I needed to hear those words, but they never came.

Prior to serving my four-year apprenticeship, I went to a Big Ten university to study engineering because my dad wanted me to. I recall the horrible feeling of abandonment I felt when I was dropped off at the dorm. I felt totally unprepared emotionally and academically.

I was "big-man-on-campus" in my small high school, but a little fish in a big pond at the university. It was a terrible experience for me. I wanted to hide all of the time because I felt so inadequate. Then I found alcohol, or perhaps it found me.

Alcohol did all kinds of wonderful things for me for the next eighteen years. I used and abused alcohol to get me out of a feeling that I didn't want to feel, or to feel feelings I suppressed because of shame. I could sing and dance without concern over what "people might say." It gave me relief from the fear I experienced on a daily basis.

I was the periodic type of drinker. Most every weekend, I would drink to excess. Yet when I was working in the factory on the afternoon shift, I drank almost every night after work. It is hard for me to recall how I did it when often I was working seven days a week, going to college four mornings (or nights depending on which shift I was working), and drinking. Amazingly, I graduated at the top of my class with a straight-A average and didn't get hurt while working in the shop around very dangerous machinery. I believe that God was watching over me.

I might mention here I have experienced other addictions, like work. I am on record as having worked in the plant for 147 days without a day off. Of course in my family, that was the mark of a true man—you were what you did. And the more you did it and the harder you worked, the better man you were.

It didn't occur to me until much later in life that I could actually "go against" the family system. That system was so sick and dysfunctional. Living in that capsule apart from the real world seemed normal. That was reality. It was certainly my reality. That was my view of how the world operated. It was my view of how relationships worked.

The sick views that my parents held were, of course, what they were taught, and they passed them on to me with such conviction and fervor there simply was no other way for me to live except to be loyal to that system at all cost. It was sick, dysfunctional, abusive, etc., but it was familiar because of my family, and my inner child; be magical and non-logical; keep "trying to get it right."

My parents did the very best that they could. They were not internally ugly, nasty, sadistic, noncaring, morbid people. They loved me to the extent that they could. Of that, I am very sure.

This narrative on what happened to me is not about blame. It is about my disease: how it occurred, what it did to me and my family, and about my recovery from that disease. I know that if I continue to blame anyone on this planet (including myself), I give myself permission to stay in my addiction, whatever that addiction may be. For an alcoholic, like myself, I could always "reason" that they treated me so badly, that the ill treatment gave me such justifiable anger and resentment that I could go get "drunk at them." What I was doing, of course, was giving them a great deal of power, so much power that I could never get in touch with my own feelings.

So what did I do when I couldn't feel my own feelings? I learned to play a role which is what I did all of my life until I finally got into recovery. I knew how to play the "good" son role. I could figure out rather quickly what it was my parents wanted to hear, and I would tell them that to get the desired result.

Role-playing was a real setup for the way I lived my life. It was the method by which I habitually gave away all my own personal power. I was always in the position of reacting to what other people said or did, rather than acting in a positive way from a posture of self-awareness and/or being self-motivated.

There I was with three basic ingredients: (1) tremendous God-given potential, (2) no self-concept and (3) a people-pleaser. Those three ingredients in me created a con man. I would "know" what the person in a given situation wanted to hear; I would tell them that, then they liked me. The result of their liking me in my mind, was that "I was OK." I got my esteem, therefore, from others. It was so insidious that it all happened in a heartbeat, and I was the one in control. The person I conned the most was me.

That way of living my life created a high level of fear in me. I felt so inadequate so much of the time. That "one-down, less-than" feeling caused me to create an immediate required persona for the given situation. I wore so many masks.

I had no idea I was so ill. What I really believed I needed was to be married. I wanted to be married. To have that one person I could devote my life to. So, three days before my 28th birthday, God answered my most earnest prayer.

"It's a perfect match," I thought. We thought the same way, had the same value systems in many ways, and she was an alcoholic, just like me. We had the same goals in life in many areas. I had not finished college at the time we married. So we set out together on the project of my finishing college. I did so and went on to graduate school and completed a master's degree in science.

We both worked very hard during those years and did without a lot of the material things in life. She completed a master's degree during that time. She helped me by typing papers for me, and she worked a full-time job the entire time.

Eight years into the marriage, our first child was born; a wonderful son. Four years later, we were blessed with our beautiful daughter. Everything seemed just perfect. By all outward appearances, I'm sure that our situation looked just perfect.

I had bought what I call the "great American myth for men." That is, if you get letters after your name, have a pretty wife (which she was), have beautiful healthy children in private schools, live in the right part of town, have two new cars in the driveway and an impressive job with a good company—you will be happy. We had done all of that and I was absolutely miserable and so was she. I literally did not know how to change any of my negative feelings.

Shortly before our son was born, we quit drinking. Then through a set of circumstances which I now know to be divine circumstance, I, then she, found Alcoholics Anonymous. We had separated for a short time at that point. To say our relationship was strained and lacked intimacy was an understatement.

I had an extremely difficult time identifying myself as an alcoholic. It had been essentially five and a half years since I'd had a drink of alcohol. When it was suggested that I try AA, the only thing I could do at that moment was cry. I thought, "How could I be an alcoholic with so much time being dry?" I tried to prove that I was not an alcoholic. After my first AA meeting, I bought two six-packs of tall cans of beer, thinking that if I could drink three cans and look at the other nine, I could control my drinking and therefore, I was not an alcoholic.

So why did I buy two six-packs? At some level I knew that I would drink both of those six-packs, which I did and got very drunk. They told me in the meeting that the disease was progressive even if I wasn't drinking. I proved them to be right. I picked up right where I had left off, five and a half years before. As I write this story, that was ten years ago.

Entering the program of Alcoholics Anonymous, I was sure it was going to be my crucifixion, but it became my resurrection. I had been looking for some answers to questions that had lain deep within me for years. I had tried church, talking to priests, and learning about religion, thinking that I wasn't religious enough. I tried Bible study; I did that compulsively for three years, which included three different studies a week. I learned a lot, but there was still a hole inside me. I had tried psychiatrists. I was blessed with an uncle who had been one of the best. Yet nothing seemed to work to give me the peace and serenity that I sought. Someone once said, "Within each of us is a God-shaped vacuum." I tried to fill that vacuum with everything else but God.

AA did give me tremendous relief in showing me that I was sick and not evil or insane. I lived all of my life up to that point thinking I was unique in thinking the thoughts that I did, when it was really a "simple" matter that I was a compulsive, addictive person who was raised by parents who were alcoholic.

A little over three years in AA, I went to a treatment center for my codependency at the strong suggestion of my AA sponsor at the time who happened to be a Catholic priest. That was in November 1985. The very week that he made that suggestion, I lost a six-figure income job, my wife cleaned out our bank accounts in a prelude to our divorce and my sponsor moved out of town. I thought that I was going to come apart.

What I heard in the treatment center was amazing. I had no idea that people knew so much about the dynamics of families where there was addiction. I learned the meaning of a whole new set of terms like: family of origin, dysfunctional family systems and enmeshment. I learned about what abuse really was and all the issues that come from being a shame-based codependent person.

The problem was that I heard everything for my wife. I thought this was her problem, this codependence. I recall dragging her up to the center to see a videotape about shame. I thought it was an honest effort on my part to save our marriage. Obviously, my denial system was very strong about my own codependence. I just could not see it as it related to me.

Two months after my visit to that treatment center, in January 1986, I moved out of our house into a dump of a place that was at least close to my children. I thought that I was going to come unglued. In that one act of moving, I had lost all the roles I had been playing for nineteen years. I was no longer in the husband role, the father role, the provider role and the good-son-for-staying-married role.

I had literally lost every reason for living that I had up to that point. My total identity was wrapped up in those roles and what I did in those roles. My identity was also wrapped up in the things that I owned like the beautiful home, the motor home and classic Jaguar. All of those things went as well. Eventually, I wound up filing personal bankruptcy after nearly 30 years of hard work.

During the next two years I worked very little. All that I could do was attend AA meetings, talk to my sponsor and begin to sponsor people. I did that compulsively as well. It was amazing what I learned from the people that God put in my life to sponsor. At some level, I knew that I had to hang on to the program. I believe today that it was the gift of faith from God. Somehow I knew that it would get better, and it did.

In late October 1986, I attended my first meeting of Co-Dependents Anonymous. It was CoDA's second meeting. What a blessing to have been directed to move to Phoenix, Ariz., some 20 years before. I truly began to understand what was meant by spiritual recovery. AA could keep me sober, but the CoDA program began to get me in touch with the true me, the person that I believe God intended me to be. I was finally getting in touch with my feelings.

There were many times I would come home from a meeting, however, drop to my knees at the end of my bed and cry like a baby. I had loaded, cocked and placed a gun to my head at least a half-dozen times. The only reason I didn't commit suicide was because of my children. I had heard a man tell his story at a meeting about how devastated he had been all of his life because his father had committed suicide when he was a boy of five.

Because of the CoDA program, I was able to break through my denial and feel the grief of my many loses, feel the terrible sadness, get in touch with the pain that I used to medicate with alcohol and work. I embraced those feelings and began to work through them. I have learned that it is only through our wounds that we are healed; there is no other way. For me, my recovery could have happened in no other way. Carl Jung said, "The basis of all neurosis is the avoidance of legitimate suffering;" and "The evil isn't the shadow, it's the shadow denied." I had to own my new awareness. If I didn't own it, I could not give it to God in Steps Six and Seven. How could I give away what I didn't own?

I began to relate to some of the scriptures that I remembered from years before in Bible study. I must paraphrase here: "Seek ye first the kingdom of God and all things will be added unto you;" and, "The kingdom of God is within." To me, those are the Third and Fourth Steps of the program.

I learned that God's justice is allowing me to live by the consequences of my own decisions. He has given me a free will and an intellect and He will never take them away from me. I have had to make a conscious decision to recover. I had to do the First Step at a gut level and realize that I was powerless over many things. When I was finally able to do that, I dropped the walls that I had put up against God's love. I had then invited all of the power of the universe into my life.

I had a strong belief in God for many years and I knew that He worked miracles in my life. Yet, there was a part of me that had a very negative concept of God. That part knew that God knew that I was not measuring up. The God of my understanding today is a loving God and only wants my highest good. He is not the God I was taught to fear and to beg things from. The God that was in a church where the church told me to do these seven things and those nine things and the church would then give me God back. I now believe there is nothing I can do to earn God's love. It's a gift from God and from no other. I must do my part to live my spiritual life. Once I have been shown the way, I can do nothing else. I know when I fall short of the mark, God lovingly brings me back to center.

It is also written, "We all are created in God's image and likeness" and "God is Love." I reasoned that out for myself; either it is true or it isn't. There could be no in-between. I chose to believe those things to be true, and realized I was coming from a position of love. I wasn't being who I was designed to be.

In order to go through the process of recovery, I had to have the "faith of a child" to enter the kingdom, and the faith, like His love, is a gift from Him. I had to have that faith of my inner child, to acknowledge the child within—that child which is of God's divine design.

Thank God the program is one of progress and not perfection. I thank God He is so patient with me. If He weren't, He would have given up on me long ago. But He hasn't, and for that I am very grateful. Today, I believe life is about learning many things, but most especially, learning to become who we really are. Therein lies the joy. I have great joy in my life today. I would never want to repeat what I had to go through, but I would never trade it for anything at all.

I learned something that sums it up for me: They went to Michelangelo when he finished the statue of David and asked, "How did you do that?" Michelangelo replied, "Well, I took a block of granite, these chisels and a hammer and chipped away everything that didn't look like David, and that's what I got."

Today I believe, with myself as a willing block of granite—the Twelve Step programs, the people in the programs as the tools and God as the Master Sculptor—that He's chipping away everything that doesn't look like Chuck. So far, this is what He's got.

Chuck M.

231

THE JOY IS IN THE JOURNEY

As Groucho Marx once said, "I'd never be a member of any club that would have me as a member." I believed that for most of my life, until the past three years. My original club was my family, and much of my childhood was spent daydreaming that my family would be mysteriously overcome by some magical cloud that instantly changed everyone. Since that never happened, I tried my best to make things different by being funny, hypervigilant, in control, making Mom and Dad happy and keeping them from fighting with each other. I not only thought I could make my home life safe, secure and happy, I also came to believe it was my responsibility—my life's work! This belief was to haunt me through most of my life, which often resembled a Woody Allen movie.

My parents were both products of dysfunctional homes. They attached to one another like magnets. Both were needy and tried their best to let no one in on their neediness. In addition, each one played the role of a victim very well, powerless over the entire world around them. My role models taught me to trust no one or nothing and to be fearful of others. I learned that the world was not a safe place and that I should trust only my parents. Of course, they both lied to me. My mother beat me. Each resented me in their own unique way, and both abused me in overt and covert ways. This is not to indict them or pass judgment, rather to state what really was as I lived it.

I grew up in an era when TV sitcoms showed Americans the ideal family life. My family was nothing like those people on TV, but I watched and imagined how I could make my home life great like the TV families. I fantasized extremely well as a child, and my ability to "space out" became a major issue in my adult life. I made believe that life was really OK; I relieved the pain that way.

My mother was an extremely anxious woman. She was a child of an alcoholic father and didn't have much of a childhood. My father was quite fearful and tense as well, but covered it up by drinking daily. Mom didn't like herself very much, and she took her tension and self-dislike out on me. Today I understand, but as a child, what she said about me stuck. I was told that:

- I was responsible for my father's drinking.
- I brought shame to my family by acting so badly.
- I was too slow, too sloppy, too much to handle.
- I was trouble, a burden, and evil.
- She wished I had never been born.

- I was the reason my mother's life was such a burden.
- God was going to punish me.
- How dare I have fun while my mother was suffering so much.
- Nobody likes me.
- I was selfish and ungrateful.

After much therapy and more than a decade of program, I know that she would have told that to anyone in my place. She was acting out her illness, but to that child, it all went in very deeply.

Being raised in this type of environment made it virtually impossible for me to be anything else except codependent. You might say I'm a thoroughbred codependent—I just don't have any pedigree papers. I was taught to feel responsible for other people's feelings, behaviors, dysfunctional habits, and illnesses. In a negative way, I was led to believe that I was the center of the universe. I became the dark Sun.

This sense of enormous responsibility for others accompanied me wherever I went. I could feel guilt or shame as easily as navy blue picks up lint. I was able to feel uncomfortable, confused, ashamed, etc., for other people, as well. My antennae were always out, so I could know what was happening around me. I needed to know so I could fix it, to make me and others safe. If I was unable to fix a person or situation, I became extremely scared; I ran. Sometimes I stayed put physically, but numbed out and emotionally disappeared.

I felt responsible for the safety of both my parents. I would save my mother from my father beating her, and I would be beaten by her when he left. I was always trying to persuade my father not to drink and was afraid that he was going to die and leave me alone with my crazy mother. The roles shifted many times, so that I became the parent, and they were my children. My relationship with my parents was topsy-turvy. There was little sense of safety, security, nurturing, acceptance, caring, warmth, or love present in my family of origin. Nonetheless, I created a fantasy that told me all was going to be fine tomorrow.

Life outside my home was less stressful than being at home. In school I was an entertainer, usually labeled the class clown. I was friendly with the children in my class but seldom felt connected to others. I told lies about my family so my classmates would think I lived in a normal home.

Wherever I went, I usually felt shame. I didn't like myself very much and hid my low self-esteem through humor. Other children liked me, for the most part, but my parents tried to "shelter" me from them and the "trouble" they could get me into.

We moved around a lot while I was growing up. That compounded my socializing problems. Just when I would get a few friendships established, it was time to leave.

High school found me socially backward. I was interested in girls and very scared of them, too. Sports was a way to be with other guys and not have to get very close. Even my closest "friendships" were antagonistic. When I reached high school, my self-esteem was extremely low. I constantly worried about what others thought of me. I tried to make schoolmates like me by being funny and telling them what they wanted to hear.

Upon entering college, I had my first opportunity to live away from home. I went home on the weekends, for holidays and the summer. The attachment to my parents and the craziness of my home was clear to any objective observer. That aside, I got a taste of what living in a more peaceful environment was like. I was granted a view of freedom that helped me partially detach from my parents. In college, I started to feel better about myself. Unfortunately, as I started to feel more confident, I began to drink and experiment with drugs. These substances, I soon learned, had the magical power to make me feel better and to take me far away from my emotional pain. My attachment to and frequent use of these drugs grew, which soon compounded all my problems.

While in my second year of college, I met my wife to be. I had "fallen in love" with a few women, but this time I became very attached and "in love" almost overnight. For two years we spent most of our time together. That seemed normal to me. Besides, I was so insecure that I was sure I would lose her to another man if I didn't "keep an eye on her." I mistook possessiveness, manipulation, and desire to control as an indication of the depth of my love. We were enmeshed and without boundaries—remarkably codependent. Of course, we both thought this was what true love was supposed to be. In our fighting daily with words meant to hurt and belittle, each of us was actually loving the way we learned to love in our parents' homes.

This relationship so fulfilled my dysfunctional needs that we got married. Our reason for marrying when we did was so we could travel across the USA together. Her father wouldn't let us go otherwise. It doesn't make much sense to me today! Our communication methods grew worse as the years passed. We enjoyed traveling, and the only good times we had together were on our trips. By our tenth year of marriage, I was about as low emotionally as I could get. Our marriage was a mess; neither of us took responsibility on the outside. Deep down inside, I felt it was all my fault. My wife, who was very much like my mother, was more than happy to tell me how all the problems in our marriage were my fault.

Finally, I left my marriage to be with another woman. At last, I would be loved, accepted, nurtured, and appreciated—if life were only that simple! Within eight months, my insecurities and instabilities put an end to that relationship. I ran back to my wife, and she welcomed me with open arms. Just before I returned, I was picked up for a DUI. This arrest was to change my entire life, because it forced me to become involved in AA and look honestly at my way of relating to life.

I was forced to go to AA by the state if I wanted to keep my driving privileges. While at first I felt I'd just play their game, soon I came to believe that I needed to change. There were no thunderbolts, but I did experience a few spiritual awakenings and stopped feeling suicidal. God became a loving force that wanted me to enjoy living, rather than the punishing God my mother taught me about. The obsession to drink and drug was lifted from me very quickly, for this, I was and still am enormously grateful to my Creator. Fortunately, I also came to realize that controlling the world around me doesn't work. Of course, I still kept doing it quite often, but my awareness of my thoughts and actions was the beginning of my codependence recovery. "Let go and let God; I can't change anyone but myself," became a mantra for me which helped diminish my need to manipulate. It was clear, as my time in AA increased, that my life had become truly unmanageable, and that if I applied the Twelve Steps to my life, I could get better day by day. Self-talk is another issue I became aware of in my AA recovery, and I began to replace the negative tapes in my head with kind, understanding ones.

After about 18 months, I intuitively knew AA was not enough. An AA friend told me about Adult Children of Alcoholics meetings. Even though most AA members told me I'd get drunk if I went to ACoA, I followed the wisdom of the guidance inside me. Like Columbus, I had discovered a new world. While I felt accepted in AA and am eternally grateful for my life being saved there, ACoA felt so much like the home I always wanted; I knew I belonged. ACoA was a wonderful way to learn about the illness of codependence and experiment with how to relate to others. In those days there was no CoDA, and no one used the term codependence, but I was gaining information about codependence regardless of the terminology.

Through the support of friends in both programs, the Steps and God, I was granted the strength to leave my 14-year-old marriage. I felt guilty leaving, but also knew my recovery could go no further if I stayed. I was much less enmeshed than I had been, thanks to the counsel of friends, therapy, the answers to my requests for guidance from God, and my constant focus on my powerlessness over another person. I was repeating the CoDA First Step before it had been written.

One and one-half years after my separation from my wife, something I was totally unprepared for happened. I got a call that my mother had suffered a stroke. I was in disbelief. I thought they meant my father because he had been ill and often close to death for five years. To my horror, when I arrived at the hospital, it was my mother. She died ten days later, and my father died eight days following her death. Thank God for the recovery I had. It gave me the strength I needed to take care of all the complicated matters that follow death. More importantly, I was able to take care of myself. I allowed myself to grieve without trying to figure out why or judge the process. A year after my father's death, I filed for divorce. This was the beginning of a difficult legal battle.

While I knew, thanks to recovery, that I was not totally responsible for the problems in our marriage, my disease told me differently. My wife was more than happy to bolster in defense of my disease. The year that the divorce dragged on was painful and brought invaluable lessons to me about my codependence. Regardless of how nice I was, how understanding, how fair, how willing to sacrifice, nothing changed how my wife viewed me. She was into blame, full of rage about my freedom from her control, and nothing I could say or do would stop the waves. I was told as a child, "Don't make waves, Butch." Well, this time I had to choose between going back to her (which would have killed me) or continuing forward to gain full freedom, which meant making many waves. I struggled through my fear. Praying for God's help and guidance was a practice that kept me going.

Just before I filed for divorce, I "fell in love." This would turn out to be a most painful relationship. After the death of both parents and with my pending divorce, I was extremely needy and vulnerable. I picked a woman who walked all over my boundaries— and I let her, even encouraged it. It was this relationship, the death of my parents, and the experiences with my wife during my divorce that taught me many emotional lessons about letting go of those, both living and dead.

My new love would totally invade my boundaries, then retreat and need a lot of space. This pattern went on for 15 months. Then, finally, I got it; I couldn't fix or change her. By that time, I was divorced and my parents had been dead for two and a half years. Now I was completely alone. Well, not really; I had me, God, and my friends.

Now came a time to face my fears of being without a family, a marriage, and a romantic relationship. This was a great period of growth for me, during which all my worst fears surfaced. I learned to be alone in a new way. I started to feel better than ever. Soon I was dating without attaching and taking a hostage. During this time, I started feeling my feelings even if they felt overwhelming. I began to feel and live the motto: "I am responsible for my life and only I can change me." This period of being alone continued for about two and a half years. Then I met the beautiful woman who motivated me to work on my codependence issues.

When I met Laurie, after seven and a half years of recovery, I thought I was ready to have a healthy relationship. Boy, was I mistaken! There were red flags early on, but I totally ignored them. She was separated from her husband only a brief time when I met her. I emotionally supported her through her divorce. Laurie was extremely enmeshed with her mother and I constantly gave her advice about that. This beautiful woman also had tons of other problems, like work, former boyfriends, difficulty with her sister, and constant abuse from her ex-husband. Oh, a codependent's dream come true! I spent most of my time trying to solve her problems— I was getting my identify from "saving" her. My self-esteem was really other-esteem. Of course, she loved the "help" and kept needing more daily. I abandoned my friends, gave up my interests, and felt like I lost the self I had taken eight years to find. I felt like a hamster in one of those wheels that just keeps spinning.

About six months into this relationship, intuitively I knew our exclusive involvement was not exclusive. So I got scared, denied my feelings and disbelieved my intuition. As the months passed, my ability to deny how I felt and my willingness to shut off my inner voice diminished. Finally, I confronted her about a co-worker with whom she spent a lot of time.

She, of course, told me nothing was going on. I wanted to believe her because the thought of "losing" her was terrifying, so I denied my own reality in favor of her words. Well, I was right all along, she finally told me when all that was left to her was the truth.

This relationship showed me how I denied both my feelings and that voice inside, and gladly gave up my interests for another person. I came to CoDA just before the end of this relationship. I had attended a codependence workshop and read a book on the disease, which made me realize I was a codependent, so CoDA became my new program. I thank my Creator for this program! It has brought new meaning and depth to my life. I'm not surviving; I'm truly living life.

CoDA allowed me to just be a member without needing to help another person in the group. That was such a relief! I also was able to say whatever I wanted to without anyone telling me what to think, feel, or believe. It felt very safe to speak without crosstalk or even covert crosstalk called "help." Through CoDA recovery, I learned to acknowledge that my feelings were often based in shame. Also, I came to see that when I was "helping others," it was usually to get something I needed or to manipulate them. I began to realize how dependent on others' approval I had become and that I often was quite needy. Oh, yes—I discovered that I felt like a victim and gave my power to others as well.

What I needed to do in order to change was to stop judging myself and expecting perfect behavior from myself and others. I learned to nurture the inner child and love him in spite of his fear, sadness or anger. Reparenting that little soul of God's was a full-time job which I hated at first. Another difficult change was to let other people take care of themselves. Letting others suffer the consequences of their actions, words, etc., was not easy, but has paid off royally. Letting go of dysfunctional habits that have protected me in the past has been difficult, but well worth the struggle.

My CoDA recovery has brought me to a new way of viewing the world. I don't have to be in control of others if I trust in my Higher Power. Serenity no longer means that I am always calm. It is that feeling of safety and security that comes when I "TCB" (Take Care of Business). In life, things come up and I am responsible for taking care of all matters in my life. With the help of God, I have learned to push past my fears and do what I need to do to TCB—even confront friends whom I fear will abandon me. My recovery has taught me to stick up for myself, to speak my truth without judgment of me or others. I've been able to take risks that I never would have dreamed of before CoDA. This change came about because I've become willing to listen to the voice inside. I'm more ready to trust in my Creator, because I know I'm worth it!

Spontaneity is a reward of recovery for me. I am more flexible and no longer afraid of what will happen. I can let go of control. I plan ahead and ask for what I want and need, but I'm much less attached to outcomes. Today, I believe that when one door closes, another one opens. In other words, there are many choices for me. Now I can see a variety of options, with no one perfect or right choice. This change has brought an incredible sense of freedom to me.

A reality for me in CoDA recovery is that being good to myself isn't *selfish*, as I was taught as a child. Rather, it is only when I love, honor, accept, respect, and treat myself well that I can do that for anyone else. Forgiveness has been an important part of my new life. When I am able to forgive myself and others, my life is much less complicated, happier, and more joyous.

When I first began recovery, I said, "progress, not perfection," but I didn't feel good enough if I didn't appear perfect. Today, I accept who I am, as I truly am this day. By liking me as I am, I can feel the same about the world around me. I seldom feel a sense of shame anymore. My sense of profound sadness that was with me for the first two years of CoDA recovery, has been lifted. I still cry, but basically about the present.

Gradually, I'm getting to know what I want and need. My haunting sense of ambivalence is giving way to clear-cut decisions. I second-guess myself much less often, which allows me to be in the present more often. My life works well most of the time, and I accept the times it doesn't work the way I'd like. Crises are opportunities to learn and grow!

Presently, I don't have a romantic relationship. That's OK for now. When the time is right, I will receive what I need. For now, I'm enjoying my friends, nature, traveling, and just plain being alive.

Today I try to show up, be present, tell my truth without blame or judgment, and not be attached to outcomes. I have come to believe that:

- I am responsible for my thoughts, actions, and words.

- God will help and guide me if I ask.

- I must express my needs and wants to others.

- I respect the dignity of others when I let them make their own mistakes.

- I need to respect, honor, and love myself just as I am today.

- I feel good when I talk nicely to myself.

- God's love is mine.

- I am empowered, not a victim.

I hope that my experience, strength, and hope have been helpful. Happy trails to you!

by Arnold B.

CHAMELEON

I'm a codependent, an adult child of a dysfunctional family, and a recovering alcoholic. I believe my codependency and alcoholism developed as a means of coping with my childhood fears, as a way of attempting to control my environment and my feelings to avoid the pain of shame and the terror of abandonment.

My acute fears of abandonment developed in infancy and were reinforced throughout my childhood. My father was sent away when I was six weeks old. He had resented my existence, and one day, he released my stroller with a push at the top of a steep hill. My mother believed this was an attempt to kill me. Shortly after my father left, Mother went away for six weeks, the time required to establish residency for a Nevada divorce in those days.

My earliest memories are about life with Mother and my grandparents in the waning months of World War II. They were good people in many ways, and we were an affluent family with many advantages. My grandparents had a small estate near an Eastern city, a farm about two hours' drive away, and a cottage at an exclusive mountain resort.

My childhood was filled with places to go, things to do, and happy times, and while these things were very nice, they contributed to my confusion when, later in life, I tried to understand what had happened to cause so much pain. I now know we were a "looking good" family, characterized by rigid rules, repression of feelings, excessive concern about keeping up appearances, and an air of smug superiority. The first thing I remember learning was to be afraid of what other people would think of me. I now understand that this is what it means to be ruled by shame.

In many ways, my family didn't possess tolerance for the normal behavior of children. From early childhood, I was expected to conduct myself as an adult. I was to do as I was told to do, without protest. I was to feel what I was told. I was to know what was expected, sometimes without being told. The consequences for thinking or feeling differently from what was expected were the same as those for overt misbehavior; they included shaming criticism, physical punishment, and threats of abandonment.

Some of the things actually said to me were, "children should be seen and not heard. Spare the rod and spoil the child. Speak when you're spoken to. Don't act like that; people will think you're ill-bred. We'll have to send you back where you came from."

I had no siblings and no playmates in the first five years of my life. I learned to entertain myself and live in the company of adults. I didn't know how to relate to peers, and I was painfully self-conscious and shy. I felt middle-aged.

I was about five when my mother married again. Her husband was a compulsive perfectionist who demanded socially correct behavior at all times. He was cold, rigid, and humorless; I liken him to an evil character from a Charles Dickens novel. His way of relating to me (and to my three half-sisters, who appeared in orderly five-year intervals) was by constant, unrelenting, shaming criticism of our manners, behavior, judgment and attitudes.

Mother was mentally ill most of her life, but as a child, I had no way of understanding that fact. I believe she lived in a state of fear and denial, and carried intense shame, especially about her sexuality. When she found me involved in sexual exploration normal for a seven year old, she became hysterical. Completely out of control, she beat my legs severely with branches from a willow tree, then she sent me outside in short pants everyday until the wounds healed, to show everyone how bad I was. I carried shame about my sexuality for the next 40 years.

Other normal feelings and my expressions of childhood needs were shamed as well. Sometimes my mother or stepfather would beat me if I sulked, or if they thought I had a "bad attitude." This amounted to being punished for being unhappy. I was rarely punished for what I did because I was usually obedient, rather, I was abused for how I felt and for who I was.

I learned not to feel, talk, trust or be spontaneous. I learned to hate myself because I believed I was worthless. I learned to mistrust my feelings and perceptions because I was always wrong. I learned to feel what others expected me to feel and to deny what I really felt. I learned to fear everyone, sure they would disapprove of me. I learned to survive by isolating as much as possible and by being compliant with others.

I reached adulthood not as a person, but as a chameleon, skilled at changing myself to fit my environment. I also became a perfectionist; I had to be perfect to avoid disapproval, criticism, and shame. Other people could make mistakes (I was "perfectly" tolerant of others' humanity), but I had to look right, be right, and have the right answers. I would beat myself without mercy for mistakes, especially social errors such as being late, making an inappropriate remark, or wearing the "wrong" attire. I had to have the "right" accessories, too. I believed others' opinions of me would be influenced by my house, my car, my choice of friends.

Paradoxically, as much as I believed I needed to manage others' impressions of me, I deliberately rejected opportunities to learn the requisite skills. To this day, I don't know what the "right" clothes are, and I rejected the upper-class lifestyle I was expected to pursue. I can appear to fit in anywhere for a while, but I've always preferred a backyard barbecue to the country club scene.

My codependency is subtle and pervasive. I'm not overtly caretaking or manipulative, nor visibly dysfunctional. I know how to make a living and how to look good. I'm reasonably competent and successful. But on the inside, driven by fears of other people's disapproval, I try to control others' thoughts by manipulating myself, and by (very subtly) steering others to think what I want them to think.

As might be expected, my personal relationships have been a series of disasters.

From the moment I noticed the opposite sex, I developed a pattern of forming attachments that were obsessive, compulsive and exclusive. I would try to get all my needs met within these relationships. Lacking any real identity, not sure of my own values, needs, likes and dislikes, I allowed my partners to define me. I was jealous and possessive, but not outwardly, so my fears of acting on my own feelings inhibited overt attempts to control. I'd do almost anything to avoid disapproval and prevent being abandoned—yet, often I abandoned others when things didn't go my way. Unaware of my own feelings, I was often insensitive to those of my partners.

One of my shortcomings was an inability to identify people who would be safe and appropriate for me. My first wife, for example, perceived life much differently than I, and seemed to find many of life's normal activities difficult. She was also gay, but she didn't admit that to herself or others until many years after we separated. She practiced a religion which was foreign to me, and I disagreed with most of its major tenets, but to please her, I practiced it too. I even became soloist at Sunday services.

Our marriage lasted five years; we had one child. I recreated the roles of my original family, and abused my daughter emotionally in the same ways I had been abused. Not knowing about my wife's latent homosexuality, I felt hurt and confused about the lack of intimacy in our relationship. I alternated between blaming myself and blaming her. Driven by shame, frustration, and low self-esteem, I gradually withdrew physically and emotionally. In the end, I impulsively abandoned my wife and child for a woman I met only a week before.

I didn't see my daughter again for nine years. That was obviously the right thing to do, wasn't it? My father had not interfered in our lives after he left, so that must be the way to handle such situations. (Fortunately, my daughter is dealing with her abandonment issues in recovery today, and we are close friends.)

True to my pattern, I attached myself to this new woman in what I thought was the great love affair of all time. I not only had a willing sex partner, I had a drinking buddy as well. I moved in with her immediately, and my alcoholism and codependency flourished. Our relationship was characterized by intensity, extremes, excesses, and conflict. Even though I abhorred conflict, I could not detach. Ignoring the fact that our relationship reminded me of "Who's Afraid of Virginia Wolff," I married her and made her my Higher Power.

My wife and I denied our unresolved childhood issues and our alcoholism, and blamed our problems on my problems. We played a game called, "Let's Fix Peter and Then Everything Will Be Fine." We "agreed" that my values had been warped by my family and set out to correct them. Actually, with a few drunken or codependent exceptions, my values and conduct have been well within societal norms, but she wanted me to believe that shoplifting and cheating were OK.

I complied in every way imaginable to make myself acceptable to her. I once helped her steal a dress from an expensive boutique; on another occasion, I put in a false claim on my insurance. I reluctantly supported her insatiable demands for money, alcohol, pills, and merchandise. Replaying my family of origin issues, I tried desperately to find out who I was supposed to be to prevent being criticized and abandoned, feeling shamed and worthless every time I failed in this impossible mission.

After three years playing scapegoat, I attempted suicide because I couldn't think of any other way to stop being abused. I survived to invest another seven years in our hopeless dance, which sometimes included physical violence. Only after two years in recovery from my alcoholism was I able to gather enough self-esteem and courage to walk away.

Before leaving, I experienced the despair of trying to control someone else's addictions and help someone who doesn't want help. I somehow progressed in early recovery while living with the rage, manipulation, and psychosis of an addict in denial. During this time, my wife developed the interesting habit of following me around the house with knives.

I remained confused about what happened in that relationship until I began recovering from codependency some 10 years later. In the interim, I was married and divorced a third time. My parenting skills were inadequate to cope with two stepsons. Not having accepted myself as a child, I had trouble accepting them, and as they entered adolescence I tried vainly to control their sometimes serious misbehavior. The family became increasingly dysfunctional, and eventually collapsed over unresolved childhood issues brought into the marriage by both my wife and myself.

I did not want the divorce, and the ensuing feelings of abandonment and shame forced me into a deeper level of recovery. I sought out Co-Dependents Anonymous and began to understand myself, my relationships, and my compulsive need to control. Shortly after my wife left me, my mother died; I was overwhelmed with the grief of accumulated losses. I recognized sadness as an old, familiar feeling which I had never understood nor resolved. Unable to meet my normal responsibilities, I placed myself in a treatment program for adult children of dysfunctional families.

Today, I am 17 years sober and more than three years into recovery from codependency. I usually understand what I feel, as I feel it. I have self-esteem which, while fragile at times, is based on knowing my character assets and owning them. I accept my powerlessness over other people on a daily basis, and trust that my needs will be met through the grace of my Higher Power. I use therapy and frequent attendance at CoDA and other Twelve Step groups as a basis for ongoing inventory work and housecleaning. I try to make myself ready to have God remove my defects and defenses, knowing He will, in His way and time. I maintain a measure of serenity through meditation, often meditating on affirmations for my inner child. To whatever extent I have anything to give away, I'm willing to share myself with other recovering people. I have everything I need.

For me, codependency is a process of manipulating myself to meet others' expectations, in a futile attempt to control their thoughts and feelings so they'll not shame and abandon me. Behaving codependently involves being dishonest with myself and others about what I think, how I feel, what I believe—in short, who I am. I don't have to hide from you today. I can show you who I am, and I'm not in control of what you think of me.

I'm building a loving relationship with another recovering person. I'm not doing it "perfectly"—I don't have to—but I am succeeding reasonably well at being open about myself, accepting myself and my partner as we are, and avoiding controlling thoughts and behaviors. I also have other friends, and for the first time, I feel capable of being a friend. Human life is relationships, and one of my goals in recovery is to participate honestly in them. I have no alternative but to take the risks, feel the fears, and accept the consequences of being who I am.

Sometimes I revert to the old fear that if I'm not on guard, sooner or later I'll be judged and rejected. At these times I feel self-conscious, and my spontaneity deserts me. When I pray and admit these feelings to safe people, they pass. The Chameleon lurks outside my door, but I try not to let him in the house.

by Peter C.

CoDA COMES TO MARYLAND

My birthdate is 4-3-43 and I have always thought that date was somehow special and unique. However, only recently have I begun to feel that way about myself. On the date of my birth, my mother was 39, my father, 47, and I had two sisters who were 13 and 18.

My mother was planning to leave my father because in a few years both her daughters would be old enough to be on their own. Of course, my arrival changed her plans. My father was excited at the prospect of having the son he had always wanted. I was his last chance, and his hope died the day I was born. His own father had died when my father was only three or four years old, and he wanted to be the father he never had to a son. He reportedly said "Oh, shit!" when my arrival was announced. My sisters were excited about having a little baby sister and were given the privilege of picking out my name, Susan Colleen. My parents never slept together again after I was born.

My father was a tyrant. He was always right, and his word was law. I was taught there was only right or wrong, black or white—no gray. My father was never physically abusive, and for that I am grateful, but he was a master of mental and emotional torture. He never gave my mother or any of us any peace. I think he learned it from his mother. His mother never remarried and raised him, with the help of her mother. He knew she had thrown herself down a flight of steps while pregnant with him, hoping to cause a miscarriage. Emotional blackmail was the tool he used to get his way, and having become a master at it, he always won.

My mother, on the other hand, was very passive. A sickly person, she used illness as a way to protect herself from him. She never crossed my father in anything. She took his constant nitpicking and belittling until the day she died.

I learned to stay out of the way while growing up, and to say and do the right things most of the time. It was wonderful when I learned how to read. Books provided a pleasant escape from my bad feelings, as well as the bitterness and reality of living in a home devoid of loving, caring and nurturing support. All my "coping mechanisms" worked fairly well for me until I reached my teenage years. While trying to mature and become an individual, I had many slips. When I spoke up for myself or tried to explain my point of view, the consequences were horrible for me and my mother. My sisters had escaped by then. I kept hoping, from time to time, to elicit some support from my mother because I thought she could understand me better than my father. But eventually I gave up. I told my father exactly what he wanted to hear even if it was a lie. I couldn't confide in my mother; she told me not to tell her anything I didn't want my father to know, because she couldn't lie to him.

I can never remember my father having any friends or close associates. It seemed to me that he devoted his time to controlling the family, even my sisters and their families. My mother had friends in her church, and later when she worked at the local Y.W.C.A. She went to work when I was 14. I had friends away from home in school, church and the Y.W.C.A. whom I rarely brought home.

In late adolescence, I was looking for a way out. I expected my prince to come and take me away from all this. He would love me and cherish me. He would protect me and take care of me, and we would live happily ever after. At 16, I met a lonely sailor whose home life hadn't been the best either, and of course we fell in love. By 17, I was pregnant, and we ran away and got married. "Free at last," or so I thought. After apologies for our rash actions, we were admitted back in the family. Now my father had two more lives to control, my husband's and my son's. My first marriage lasted 16 years.

I only knew two roles to play, and although I said I'd never be like my father, that's exactly what I became. I was an expert at control and manipulation. I used emotional blackmail, fear of rejection and withdrawal of love and affection to get my way. During those years, I told myself that what I was doing was in the best interests of my husband and son. I lost all sight of self on a conscious level. I was somebody's daughter, somebody's wife, and somebody's mother. I focused all my attention on my husband and son and drove them to the brink. I used every trick I could think of to keep them in line. I sacrificed everything for them and the result was that I was filled with anger, resentment and hatred when they didn't conform to my wishes.

I earnestly tried to be a model wife and mother, and when the marriage ended it felt like my life was over. I remember telling one of my friends in a drunken, sobbing stupor that I felt like a nothing, a zero. Actually, I think the marriage ended because I got tired of trying to control everything to keep it together. It took an enormous amount of time and energy. And naturally, I was already looking for another prince to set me free. I didn't have the courage to be the one to leave the marriage. I would have had to admit defeat, and I wasn't ready for that. I was willing to hang on until the bitter end. My husband had met a woman who was looking for a way out of her mess—an unhappy, abusive marriage, complete with three children. She was able to give him love and support during one of our extremely bad times when I was on a tirade. She made him feel wanted and needed, which he certainly wasn't getting in our home, and he left our marriage for her.

The next five years of my life were probably the most insane. At 33, I was single. By this time, both my parents were deceased and I had no one to tell me what to do, no one to be responsible for except my son and I figured he was old enough to take care of himself. Hadn't I done without and given him and his father the best years of my life? It was my turn, and I didn't waste any time trying to make it up to myself. I met my son's physical needs, but abandoned him emotionally.

I became a real swinger, and when any pain came up, alcohol was the easiest and quickest solution. I was terrified of being alone, so I didn't spend much time at home. There were always parties to go to, singles' bars to frequent, and if all else failed, I had my bottle for comfort, warmth and understanding. During this time my ex-husband remarried, my son left home and eventually joined the Navy. The search for the prince went on.

I don't know if there is any significance or not but on the Ides of March, 1981, I met Prince Number Two. I was in a nightclub with two of my girlfriends discussing how the singles' scene was getting old. The fast lane had turned into a rat race, and I was telling my friends of the plans I was working on to start a new life. I wanted to be in a stable, solid relationship, to gain respectability, to be part of a family and a community. I knew I needed to make some drastic changes. I had just ended a relationship with a man who was definitely not marriage material, and I wanted to sell my house, quit my job and move to Florida. There, I thought, I could start over, meet new people and eventually find a prince.

Prince Number Two came over at that point and asked me to dance; that was the start of my second marriage, which lasted five years. He was a dashing man with charm and wit. Within six months we were married, and I scrapped my plans for starting a new life on my own in Florida.

At first we talked endlessly. He couldn't give me enough compliments or do enough for me. He wanted to spend all his time with me. His family seemed very warm and friendly. He wanted a family life and a community life. It all seemed too good to be true.

The first year was a flurry of activity. We partied a lot. We were always going someplace, doing something, and we seemed to have plenty of family and friends around. Sometime into the second year, reality set in. We had gone through my life's savings and bills were starting to become a problem. He couldn't get settled into a job that was right for him, and I was working a lot of extra hours to keep our heads above water. As money became tight, I began to realize just how much money was being spent on alcohol. Our weekly trips to the grocery store were followed by trips to the liquor store or vice versa.

This dashing man had become smug and self-righteous. I was starting to see through his charm and wit for what lay beneath them—intense satire, a master con job. Our talks were mostly arguments with a lot of mud-slinging. The compliments I got from him now were left-handed. He couldn't do enough to me to make me feel useless and worthless. He was around me and on my back so much I felt smothered. I had no space—I couldn't breathe. He wanted me to spend all my time with him, and I became the butt of his jokes around his family and friends.

His family was still warm and friendly but I also detected fear in them. They told me how much he had changed for the better since we were married and what a great influence I was on him. I think their fear was that if I stopped carrying the ball and being his caretaker, they were going to get the job back.

Family and social gatherings became a nightmare. Just as I had said I would never be like my father, I had also said I would never be like my mother, but that's what I became at this point. It was a very painful time for me. I allowed myself to be belittled, degraded and humiliated in front of his family and mine, as well as in front of our friends. It was almost like I was back at home with my father again, but this time as my mother. This hell continued for three more years. I stayed in the marriage for several reasons. My son had been given an appointment to the U.S. Naval Academy, and he was back here in Maryland. I was very proud and happy for him. The time and space apart had helped our strained relationship to become better, and I wanted to do what I could for him while he was at the Academy. I didn't want to admit defeat in a second marriage, and my husband's family kept telling me that I was an intelligent woman who could use psychology on him to make the marriage work. Finally, the time for my son to graduate was getting close. If I could just hang on. The situation in our home had escalated over the years. I had become a passive victim and the martyr role was beginning to fit. One of the frequent times when I thought I just couldn't live through another day, that my life wasn't worth living, my mother-in-law suggested I call and talk to my pastor. I did so and I poured out my heart to him. He was caring, supportive and recommended I go to Al-Anon, which I had never heard of before.

On March 20, 1986, I attended my first Twelve Step meeting—Al-Anon. I can still remember that day. My appearance and demeanor then reminds me of pictures I have seen of people arriving at Ellis Island. I looked like I just got off the boat. I was haggard, weary, frightened, lost, depressed—utterly hopeless. My life was a mess, and I knew I needed help. The people there assured me I was not alone in my suffering, that things could get better if I kept coming to meetings and gave myself a chance. In May, my son graduated from the Naval Academy and left for his first duty station in Monterey, Calif. My friends in Al-Anon helped me get through some tough situations during graduation week. On June 10th of that same year I joined my second Twelve Step program—Alcoholics Anonymous. The three months I had spent in Al-Anon had helped me to get honest with myself. I had found a Higher Power I could rely on, and I knew what I had to do. While I had focused on my husband's drinking I couldn't see my own. Although still plagued with some fear and anxiety, I could plainly see there were many others in the same boat. By learning to use the tools of the program, my paranoia subsided. I began to have hope that my life could and would improve with my Higher Power's help. By using prayer and meditation I started getting moments of peace and serenity, and I wanted more. I came to believe that no matter what happened, everything would be OK, and most importantly, that I would be OK.

That first year in AA was tough. After five months of constantly battling to stay sober, living with my husband who was still drinking, I had the courage to go through an intervention for him with his family. When he refused to go into treatment, I moved out. I rented a room and still managed to maintain the expenses on a house I couldn't live in. After six months, my husband joined AA, signed separation papers and moved out of the house. I moved back into my house and started to rebuild my life, this time on my own—no longer looking for a prince, but relying on my Higher Power.

One month prior to celebrating my first anniversary in AA, I read a book about codependence. At first, I was devastated. I had worked so hard and come so far, yet I felt like I was back to Square One. I slowly and painfully reread the book, and I started seeing myself for the first time. I broke through the delusion and denial I had been living with for so long. I not only recognized my own codependence, but I began to observe it in others, both in and out of the program. Externally, a lot of their problems were different than mine, but intuitively I knew that on the inside, our problems were the same. I just didn't know what to do about it. I was willing to do anything, even become a therapist to help other codependents. I was angry that there didn't seem to be anyone doing anything for codependents unless they happened to have a friend or family member in treatment for drug and alcohol abuse. I sensed there were a lot of us out there not getting help, and I wanted somebody to do something about it.

I was earnestly trying to work Steps Six and Seven and getting nowhere. I went to a lot of meetings, talked to anyone who would listen and prayed. No help seemed to be forthcoming. Meanwhile, my son had married a girl in California, and they were expecting their first child.

In September 1987, I went to Monterey, Calif. to see my new grandson and visit my son and daughter-in-law. While attending a meeting in a treatment center in Pacific Grove, I saw a notice on a bulletin board for a CoDA meeting. There was only one meeting a week then, and I felt badly because I had missed it. People at the center gave me some literature about the program and told me they would have someone from the group contact me before I had to leave for home. A lovely woman named Janet called to give me information and told me that coincidentally she was coming to Washington, D.C., the next month to help a woman named Christine get a CoDA meeting started. I told her I'd be there!

Before I came home, my son took me to several bookstores where I was able to pick up books on codependence that were on the CoDA recommended reading list. These books were not yet available here in Maryland. I was hungry for the information—I knew that for me it was the part that had been missing from the Sixth and Seventh Steps.

On October 9, 1987, Cheryl and Walk, a couple who sponsor me, took me to that first meeting in Washington, D.C. I got to meet Janet and Christine in person. It was wonderful that somebody was doing something about codependence, and it looked as though Washington, D.C. would have regular meetings soon. There were also some people there from Virginia interested in starting a group. I was hopeful that Maryland would have CoDA, too, but no one from there was ready to get involved. It hadn't even occurred to me to start a group myself. I wanted someone else to do that so I could go to it and get better. Then I remembered the words from a book I'd read recently, which are paraphrased here: "Remember, you cannot recover from codependence alone! You must find a therapist or a support group that deals with codependence, and if you can't find one, start one!" For the next couple of weeks I drove my friends crazy. I read all I could about codependence. I talked 'til I was hoarse. I typed and copied material which I handed out, and finally two people who were to become my dearest friends emerged, Stu and Judy. They knew what I was talking about, and they understood.

On October 23, 1987, Stu, Judy and I drove to Falls Church, Va. to attend their first meeting. The three of us worked very hard over the next couple of months and finally on January 21, 1988, with the help of some of our friends, the first meeting of the Metamorphosis group of Co-Dependents Anonymous in Maryland, group MD001 was held! We were happy and excited because we knew our recovery was beginning, and we could share it with others.

Judy went on to become one of the first state delegates to ISO from the state of Maryland. She is married now to another CoDA member and is still an active member of the Metamorphosis group.

Stu went on to become the first chairperson of the Maryland State Assembly of CoDA. Then he became a state delegate. He is also my significant other. Our relationship blossomed as we became involved in the program.

As for me, I served as the first secretary of the Maryland State Assembly for CoDA. I have also realized a dream come true. I started a book business specializing in recovery material. Books played a large part in my recovery, and now I am able to offer a service to others which I wish had been there for me when I needed it.

Today I am becoming happily and usefully whole. Twelve Step programs have saved my life, and CoDA, in particular, has brought out the best in me by continually helping me become the person God always intended for me to be. I wish the same for you.

by Susan S.

GAY, CATHOLIC, AND CODEPENDENT

"Codependent, what does that mean?" I asked my therapist about eight years ago.

I'd heard that word before but never understood it. I forgot what he answered, but whatever he said didn't apply to me, I thought. Little did I know that the word "codependency" would mean a lot to me as time went on. I've also learned that codependency can mean a dozen different things to a dozen different people, and each person is right in their interpretation.

The next time I heard about codependency was a few years later in a magazine for adult children. I had been attending ACoA meetings for a few years. Now I read about a new meeting called "Co-Dependents Anonymous."

In the early Autumn of 1988, I was in Manhattan in the Gay Community Center. I often traveled into

Greenwich Village from my suburban home to attend a Dignity Mass in St. Johns Church. The next time I saw that word again was on a poster announcing that new Co-Dependents Anonymous meetings were being held in the center. The Dignity Mass was scheduled for 7 p.m., and the meeting was to start at 8:30; I was able to make both.

I attended my first CoDA meeting the second Sunday of October 1988. I had been going to AA, NA and other Twelve Step programs for about a year. CoDA meetings had been in existence for only a few months and fewer than half a dozen existed in all of New York City at the time.

After attending my first CoDA meeting, I went back several Sunday evenings to learn more. We met on the third floor while a wrestling team was practicing upstairs. Many of us cringed as the gay wrestlers slammed each other on the floor above us. For some adult children, I'm sure it reminded them of home with Mom and Dad battling.

During the next few weeks I brought some recovering friends with me to the CoDA meetings, and we started our own meeting in the suburbs the next month.

My own personal recovery from drug and alcohol addiction began a year before. My own little world of sex and drugs came apart and was about to be exposed. The summer before, I had been smoking crack with a young man who decided to kill his roommate and use me as his alibi. To me, that night was just an ordinary getting-high night. I didn't know that the guy with whom I was sharing my crack pipe had just killed someone.

On Monday, October 19, 1987, his lawyer came to my office and told me that there was going to be a murder trial, and I was the alibi for his client. That night I thought I was going to kill myself by jumping off a roof.

Two days later, I surrendered and went to my first Narcotics Anonymous meeting. I was stoned from pot which gave me the courage to go to the meeting. I had a bag of pot in my pocket at my first NA meeting and I didn't know what to expect. I was willing to give up cocaine, but these bastards told me I shouldn't smoke pot or drink either.

I did the dance of denial for a month or so, yet by the new year I was alcohol and drug free. I participated in AA and NA more and more; I greeted 1988 in at an AA Dry Dance.

By attending NA, AA or Cocaine Anonymous meetings almost daily, I was finding a new life for myself. Looking back five years later, the alcohol was simple and the cocaine was a piece of cake compared to my codependency. Today I still attend both AA and CoDA meetings; I need both for my recovery.

I grew up the oldest child in an alcoholic family. My first memory is fear—all of my memories contain fear. CoDA has given me a safe place to share these early memories. The old timers in AA complain, "This is only about alcohol." I don't like feeling rejected at meetings. Many of the people in CoDA don't ever realize I go to AA. When I share in CoDA, people just nod their heads and I know they understand.

My first memory is about an incident that

happened 50 years ago, and if I close my eyes I can recall it vividly.

I was 16 months old and my mother had left me. I know now where she went, but at that age I didn't. I felt abandoned by God. I was being held by my grandmother in her arms, and we were on the roof of our apartment building. The year is 1942, and I'm holding a blue balloon in my hand. Across the roof is my father with my uncle. As he approaches me, I sense he is "different" and I am scared. He tries to take me out of the security of my grandmother's arms, and I struggle to cling to her for safety. I lose the balloon and when I now close my eyes I can still see it drifting away. It was a brief struggle—a 16-month-old baby afraid that his drinking father would drop him off the roof. Later in life, whenever I thought of suicide, I considered jumping off a roof; I would never shoot or hang myself.

People are amazed that I can remember that far back. I guess I started burying feelings long ago. I don't remember my mother coming back home, but she did a few days later with a new baby. In the early 1940's, woman were hospitalized 10 days for maternity. Ten days is a long time for a 16-month-old boy, especially in the hands of a drunk.

My second memory was a few years later. I was about five, and I walked into my parent's bedroom. My mother was lying in bed nursing another new baby. He was the fourth child.

My third memory is of my first day of school. I was still five and my parents drove me to this big building where there were a number of women wearing long black dresses. My parents left me there and returned to bring me home for lunch. When they drove me back, I wouldn't get out of the car. How did I know they would come back again? There were three siblings in the car, and I especially remember the baby laying in the car seat. He was the one my mother was nursing. I never completed my first day of school, and the nuns in their long black dresses never knew why.

All of these events have manifested feelings of emotional abandonment I've experienced all my life. The only time I remember hugging my father was seven years ago. I was 45 years old, and he was in his coffin. I knew it would be my last chance.

At CoDA meetings, I'm able to talk about the many defenses I've used over the years to avoid the emptiness I feel inside. In my lifetime I've used alcohol and drugs, but also food, sex, grandiosity and my old favorite, anger.

I spent the first years of CoDA and ACoA talking about the anger I felt over my father's drinking. When I went to the cemetery this year on the anniversary of his death, the tears stung as they rolled down my cheeks. I could feel the pain as I cried, and I gasped for air. My pain comes from deep inside and it hurts so much. It was much easier to be angry in destructive ways to myself.

I started visiting my father's grave seven years ago. I used to throw rocks and my empty beer cans at his tombstone. Every Christmas Eve he would come home drunk and fight with my mother. Every holiday I wished him dead. One of my worst visits to his grave was Christmas Eve of 1985 when he had been dead for only a few months. I realized that year that I got my wish, and it was one of the most painful days of my life. I still visit the grave every Christmas Eve, and I can still feel the pain. It comes from the belly. It's the same pain I swallowed over the years as I watched my parents fight.

I was about 21 years old the year I threw him over the Christmas tree. He had been attacking my mother as she was decorating the tree. What a shocked look he had on his face when he wound up on the floor with the tree and tinsel. I always had to protect my mother. If she died, I knew I wouldn't survive.

When I think about those violent episodes and envision anyone else but my father hitting my mother, I'd kill that man with my own hands. When that man is your father you just bury the pain. What always confused me as a child was the next morning after these fights. They behaved like nothing happened; my mother would be making my father breakfast. I had to look carefully to make sure it was jelly and not blood on the knife for his toast with coffee. When I qualify these events in a CoDA meeting, heads just nod.

My greatest childhood dilemma as the oldest sibling was to try to find a way to "fix" this situation. I thought the reason my father drank was me; it was all my fault. I could never pinpoint why. I recall one day when I was about nine or ten and my aunt brought my father home drunk. As she was driving past a local park, she saw her brother sleeping on a bench. "Look what you did to your father!" she yelled at me later. It was bad enough living with it, now I caused it, too. Nice little combination of shame and guilt for a 10-year-old to deal with.

I use to be mortified when my father would stagger up the street drunk in broad daylight—a sight to behold for all the neighbors to see. I didn't believe what was happening to me and my family. When he got home, he would close all the windows so that the neighbors didn't hear him fight with my mother. I was always there—the faithful watchdog to take care of my mother. I could never leave her. My biggest fear was that in a drunken rage he'd kill her and us, too. Most of their arguments were verbal, and occasionally he would throw a punch.

"What are we going to do with your father?" my mother once asked me. What a tough decision for a 10-year-old to make. My father was a binge drinker and after a few weeks, he wouldn't drink for a few months. His nondrinking times were as scary as the times he drank. I always feared he'd start to drink, and he always did. I always felt like I was walking on eggshells. One day when I was 12, he brought home a rifle to kill my mother and "her boyfriend" who was a figment of his imagination. "How can I fix this?" I kept thinking. "How can I stop this before we all die?"

One time I stopped him from coming after my mother with a carving knife by yelling at him. Then he turned on me. Do you know what it's like to stand paralyzed in the corner with your father waving a carving knife at you? "You'll never amount to anything," he screamed. It was one of the saddest memories of my teenage years. It was like a horror movie. Most teenage boys had a hero in their father; I had a terrorist. Survival was the name of the game.

In my early teen years, I found comfort in masturbation. That would take my mind off anything. In my sophomore year of high school, I found a few classmates who also liked to masturbate. Occasionally we told our parents we were going to our friend's house after school to do homework. No adults were home at his house. We never opened a book; we were learning to open the closets of our own homosexuality. I really don't know why I'm homosexual. It's just been a part of my life. When people ask me, "Why are you gay?" I honestly answer, "I don't know ... why are you straight?"

I started discovering my sexuality in the mid '50s. Gay Rights hadn't occurred then. In fact, the word "gay" wasn't even a term used at that time. I was totally confused. I needed to look up the word "homosexual" in the dictionary. It said, "sexual desire for others of one's own sex." That sounded right. Now I was a homosexual and I was going straight to hell said my church. There was no mention of homosexuals on radio or TV. Nothing was written about us except bad things. I remember watching Milton Berle dress up like a woman on his TV programs, and I feared this was my fate. Uncle Miltie was an ugly woman on black-and-white TV. Jack Benny would swish and make fun of queers on his show, and homosexuals were always ridiculed. I never recall hearing one good thing about a homosexual growing up. I thought I was the only one.

My greatest internal conflict was being gay and Catholic. I spoke to a priest about my homosexuality when I was dating a girl in my early 20s. He told me to pray and it "would go away." I prayed and the only thing that went away was the girl. I was going to Hell for sure. When the Guy who is supposed to love everybody doesn't love you, you're in real trouble. Talk about emotional abandonment!

I went into the service and met a few other guys like myself. When I was on leave, I wore my uniform around town, and eventually some man would start looking at me and smile. I remember going into my first gay bar. I was shocked to see so many other guys. They were all normal-looking; no one looked like Milton Berle in drag.

"This was more like it," I thought, and I became sexually active. Back then, I called it love—now I call it validation. In the 1950s and '60s, the only person who would validate a homosexual was another homosexual, and we usually did it in bed. I could never validate myself. I didn't share my secret life with my family. I was able to develop a small circle of gay friends in my early-to-mid-20s. Today, only two of us are still alive. When Frank called me last March to tell me that Sal had died of AIDS, he cried, "I'm looking at a picture of Sal's 40th birthday party and everyone in the picture is dead." AIDS has taken its toll. A few died of alcohol or drugs. All died trying to find validation.

We all had some good laughs together and partied a lot. Now it is like musical chairs with Frank and I. I've tested negative for HIV, and he won't take the test. "I don't want to know," he told me.

"AIDS is God's way of weeding out His garden," said a Reverend of the Moral Majority. My own Catholic church seemed to echo that message. I grew up feeling emotionally abandoned from my parents and now the granddaddy of them all—God—had abandoned me, too. For me to survive, I had to become a mere shell of a man. I had to shut down even more emotionally. This was a survival technique I was not consciously aware of at the time.

Through the rooms of CoDA, I can walk back over the eggshell path of my life. When I tell people in a CoDA meeting that I'm gay, I feel safe. When I was younger, I learned people were killed for just being gay. I know gay people who have killed themselves because of the emotional emptiness and the rejection of family, society, church and God.

I survived because I shut down. Things started to change for the gay community in 1969. Today's Gay Rights Movement started at an inn in Manhattan's Greenwich Village. I remember watching news of the Movement on TV and reading about it in the newspaper. The police would regularly raid gay bars in Manhattan to harass the patrons. On the night of Judy Garland's funeral, we fought back the police. I recall watching newscasts showing police on horseback beating gay patrons outside the bar. Every time I saw someone get hit, I felt the pain. How can people validate themselves when they're being beaten by the heroes of law and order?

Through those beatings and the pain, members of the gay community were able to find their own strength and validation. Every year I march down Fifth Avenue in Manhattan's Gay Pride Parade. When I march on to Christopher Street and past the inn, I feel a sense of pride. Before that part of the march, I walk past the seat of the Roman Catholic Church in New York City. Every year the cathedral is surrounded by police barricades. Those barricades symbolize the church's attitude toward homosexuals—"Not only can't you come in, but God isn't coming out!"

With that strong message, it's no wonder I was going to kill myself. My secret life of drugs and sex had became public. I had read about myself in the newspaper: "the homosexual lover of a convicted murderer." In the beginning, drugs gave me courage; they killed my fears. Now, CoDA does the same thing; it calms my fears. I was able to deal with my drug addiction and alcoholism in the designated Twelve Step programs. What I did not realize in the beginning of recovery was that I was destroying my defenses, and eventually my buried feelings would emerge.

Just as I say in AA that I am powerless over alcohol, in CoDA I share that I'm powerless over my fears. By listening to other people at meetings, I can relate to their fears and emptiness. I heard once in a Manhattan CoDA meeting that getting rid of your fears is like "tearing the meat from the bone."

Today at CoDA meetings and through the Steps, I can verbalize my fears. Many people suffer from homophobia, the fear of homosexuality. I suffer from internal homophobia; I fear me. I'm afraid of who I am. I need another person to tell me it is OK to be me. I'm dependent on other people's validation. In CoDA meetings, no one cares if I'm gay. Their love, acceptance and validation help me greatly. I never felt validated as a child. I was a "good boy" if I did something or if I took care of a younger brother or sister. I work today as a care giver, and I had many,

many years of experience before I started my job. For our family to survive, I felt I had to take care of them. I became the surrogate spouse to my mother and the surrogate parent of my siblings. I was almost 40 when I felt it was safe for me to move out on my own. I was never a human being; I was a human doing, always doing for others.

Today in CoDA I'm doing for myself. The recovery process is very painful. I feel my fears today, and it's an actual feeling in my stomach, but it's so scary. I know it will pass, and that is my saving grace. I've learned to give back to the Catholic Church all the shame and guilt they have given me. They are condemning me for something I have no control over—my sexuality. I invite them to look into their own closets and accept the large number of gay priests. When they learn to accept themselves, they can learn to accept me. I always feel so sad when I hear of a priest who sexually molests a young boy.

Through the Steps of CoDA, I can share 50 years of fear. Under the fear I hope to find faith in myself. Before that, I had to feel the emptiness. Sometimes the emptiness scares me; it can be so paralyzing. In times like these, I rush to a CoDA meeting.

When the pain gets bad enough, I become entirely ready, then I humbly ask God to remove my old belief systems that are causing me so much pain. I'm talking about feelings in me so ingrained that they have become part of my being. I can't change them alone; I can't wish them away. For me, the first three Steps are simply: I can't, He can, I'll let Him.

I compare codependents to those beautiful toys you see in store windows at Christmas time. Trucks, dolls, soldiers and games—all beautiful in the window but unable to work the minute you bring them home. They don't have batteries. Sometimes we don't have batteries and look to others to supply our needs.

I'm not dependent on myself, yet. I'm still working on it. I realize that no one can give me anything to make me work. I know deep down I have the ability to make myself work. It is deep inside me, but I must discover it in myself and through my Higher Power. All I ask in CoDA is for someone to listen while I dump the pain I have carried all these years.

I know I'm a child of God. I know that God is not Catholic. I thank God, that God is not Catholic. That is my Third Step working.

Outwardly I look great. Inside I am damaged goods. CoDA has given me the hope that emotionally I can heal, if I'm willing to go through the pain, even the hurt when I visit my father's grave. I was not able to cry when my father died—now I can. I grieve him and I grieve what I did not have. I wish he was still around. Today, I know what he went through, and I forgive him. It is tough being an alcoholic; it is no bed of roses. I know he did his best and provided our family with all the material things. He wasn't perfect with emotional needs. Who among us is perfect? I would not have traded him for the world.

If I accept my parents as they are I do not have to seek them in other people. I think we work out issues with our parents in our current relationships. It's amazing how we can find them in others. I've been pursuing a relationship for a dozen years because of this reason. He is the perfect combination of both my mother and father to create the feelings I think

I need. My thought patterns still resort to: "All he needs is a little 'fixing.'" I met him 12 years ago. He lives in Chicago and was in New York visiting his family. He was born and raised in Manhattan. We met under a full moon on a summer night on the street near a gay pick-up area. We had a few drinks, a joint or two and made love on the beach.

That night was one of the greatest moments in my life. They make movies about nights like these. I was in "love," and I didn't even know his last name. He validated me like I hadn't been validated in years. I was going to love enough for both of us. His relationship in Chicago was fading, and he wanted to move back with his family in New York. He was fun—one hell of a guy—and I enjoyed him. He had a great sense of humor and we got along very well together. He was the closest thing I've ever known to love. (With my background, the competition was not tough. Blow in my ear and I'll follow you anywhere.)

The first night on the beach we talked until daybreak. One of the things he told me was that he grew up in an orphanage. When he told me that, I thought, poor baby, I will never leave you. He didn't even have to ask, I was that good.

A year later, he decided he couldn't leave Chicago. He's still there. The distance between New York City and Chicago recreates in me the emotional distance of my childhood. If distance is love, I'm a good learner. I was afraid to love him because I'd go to Hell, via the Vatican. I was afraid to leave him because I would be alone. I am caught again in the middle of fear. I was afraid to go to school and leave my mother, and I was afraid to come home and find out what happened. In grammar school, I use to just stare out the classroom windows and wonder if she was alive.

I haven't seen my Chicago friend in five years. He's having a relationship with another man, but that doesn't matter. He just needs more time. His lover is an active alcoholic, just like my mother was. I want to "fix" him and make him come back to New York so that we can live happily ever after. Neither he nor my mother would ever come to their senses. I just don't know what is wrong with people who won't listen to me.

In the Spring of 1989, I attended the first CoDA conference in Manhattan. The guest speakers were Ken and Mary R., the founders of CoDA. The thing I remember most was Ken saying of his past marriages: "I always thought I chose my wives. Now I know it was my child within who picked them."

My child within still searches for the perfect parent. Recovery in CoDA is teaching me to be my own parent. No one but me knows what I need. If I become codependent on you to validate me and give me what I need, I will always come up short.

I started attending CoDA meetings in October 1988. I celebrated four years of recovery during the Columbus Day weekend of 1992. This was the quincentennial celebration of Christopher Columbus discovering a new world. CoDA also has given me that same discovery in myself.

by Jim S.

PAINFUL JOURNEYS

Jake's Story

"Be a man... Suck it in... Men don't cry..." As far back as I can remember those were the messages I received from my family. My father, mother and grandmother also used to say: "Don't cry; it doesn't hurt; it'll be OK; always make sure you don't say the wrong thing; keep the secrets in the house; don't let them out; you might hurt someone's feelings."

I can see a picture of my sister and I when we were four or five years old, sitting on the front porch of our house. I'm the older brother who was never there for her. The picture is one of fear and no trust. Looking back, I feel I'm looking at two kids in a prison camp. I feel very sad; it's something I thought I had blocked out.

The safest place to be was away from our father. When he was home, he was always in a rage; nothing we ever did could please him. As the years went by, the I safest thing to do was to say nothing, in hope that he wouldn't say anything to us. He was an alcoholic tyrant; an abusive, lazy man who could not love. The only time he hugged us was when he was drunk. Have you ever been hugged by a drunk? It hurts.

The family pictures were all sad. The only pictures that show us happy were ones not with the family, but with friends.

And many of the messages I heard while growing up told me that I wasn't good enough, I was dumb, or that I should try harder. I wish I could be a kid again!

We never had friends over to our house because either Mom or Dad would be drunk; it was just too embarrassing.

My greatest fear was the strap. What great tools my family had: fear, anger, hate and prejudices. I thought we had a normal family then. I knew I would make it better than my sister and I had endured.

The only real happiness I felt as a child was when I was away from my home and played with my friends. I carried that into my marriage, always thinking this was normal behavior. I would work long hours at the beginning, but always found time to play, and play I did.

I found that when my children were growing up they didn't want to be with me and do things with me. If they did, it was always at my convenience; I thought I was doing the "fatherly duty—the right thing."

Normal to me was to drink, play, have fun, but never with my family. I had to take care of myself, just as when I was a child.

There were affairs with other women through the years, which I always justified; it was never a problem with me—it was my wife's fault. I enjoyed living in a man's world full of double standards that almost all the men I knew followed.

I always felt that I was leading a triple life. In my mind I thought I was a great father. I tried to be with the kids, but there was always work, golfing, bowling and clubs which I put before my kids.

When I was with them, they had to perform or else I would rage or find a way to leave. They could never be good enough or do the right thing. I repeated what I had learned!

What a joke my years of marriage were, of not being there, living a continuous lie, totally unavailable for my wife or family.

It finally happened: my drinking, whoring, partying and stress led to a heart attack. Did that stop me? Some, but finally divorce proceedings made me stop and take notice, but it was too late.

A decision was made to move to another state and start a new life as an unmarried man. I wanted to start that new life by telling my wife the truth about my infidelity during our marriage, which I had denied all through counseling. The man's code—lie, lie, lie, and I was so tired of living a lie. I wanted truth. I believe from that day on, I was in recovery not knowing what the program was about.

The move to the Southwest brought me to a Twelve Step group that became my family for three years, and another move brought me into CoDA and a men's focus group. These groups have brought me a belief in myself and a Higher Power.

My relationship with my family continues to improve on a daily basis. I now have a relationship with my son whom I love very much. We're working on a friendship, truth and forgiveness. I'm able to say, "I'm wrong, I made a mistake; I'm sorry, please forgive me"—all new words for me!

I love my daughters very much and struggle to find ways to let them know that, but the relationships are just starting. Being there for them unconditionally is hard for them to accept, but I won't give up. This recovery work is not easy; there is a lot of rejection and mistrust, but not nearly as much as there was in the beginning. I take it one day at a time, and the rewards are great with my whole family.

My wife and family are everything to me. Keep coming back, it works!

Kara's Story

My codependence began in childhood when I learned to take care of "big people"—a severely alcoholic father and a fear-based, codependent mother.

My father died when I was seven years old, and I did not grieve his death, nor deal with my anger toward him until I was 40.

Mom remarried and that marriage brought stability and validation to my teenage years. Dad died when I was 20 years old. There is still collective abandonment around these men; they greatly influenced my life in both negative and positive ways.

Magnetism, attraction, then love led to marriage at the age of 21. Only on the honeymoon did I realize that there was something very wrong with the relationship, and it remained that way for decades.

I can't begin to explain the pain of learning you are married to a sex addict. How could someone live with another human being for decades and not know that? That question has been a complex challenge to understand, accept and let go of.

As a co-sex addict, I expended enormous energy to avoid the truth about sex addiction. To stay in my marriage to Jake, I had to deny three addictive fears: 1) that I would lose my identity in the relationship; 2) that I would have to deny what I knew to be true; and 3) that meeting his needs would have a price.

To tell these fears would guarantee abandonment; and for me, abandonment meant death. I held myself responsible for all the pain in the person I loved. Outwardly, I appeared to be unaffected by any problems, and great intense energy was expended to conceal problems. There was always the vacillation between domination and nurturing so that I felt some intimacy with minimum risk.

Yes, I didn't want to know it; a better choice for me was to accept that I was married to an alcoholic and a gambler. Our home was like a hotel, each person going his or her own way. I picked up the pieces, especially as the degrees of powerlessness and unmanageability increased; being overly responsible—that was my forte. He did less, I did more, and criticism escalated, especially when I was busy nurturing the children. My expectations increased as I took on more. My involvements seemed to further his justification for his compulsiveness, partying and drinking.

My desperate need for love and nurturing exceeded any one person's ability to respond. I made perfectionistic demands on all aspects of his behavior in a misdirected attempt to satisfy my needs. When my needs were then not met, I internalized rage which resulted in self-pity, despair and resentment. These low times alternated with periodic hope that things would change. I guess I set such high standards to contrast the horrible role my father played in my life, that I must have believed that if my standards were met, I would be happy.

I never communicated a personal need, only the disappointment in unmet expectations not being filled.

My mother's role model of self-sufficiency, martyrdom and self-righteousness was what I knew. Sex became a trade-off for love and intimacy; it was the only time we touched each other. He was never home one entire day for the first four years of marriage, and then afterwards, only because of a short illness.

Years of emotional "family" abuse created apathy and separate lives—a horrible legacy for our children to resolve in their journeys. The rigid rules I learned in my family of origin were passed along with piano lessons and sports. They were:

1. Don't express feelings.
2. Don't get angry or upset. Internalize it.
3. Be good and nice. Wear a smiling mask.
4. Live to avoid conflict.

5. Be extremely protective of family. Never discuss the family outside.
6. Become needless. Only addicts' needs are met.
7. Everyone in the family must be an enabler.
8. Be in control; deal with it.
9. Remain loyal at all costs. Never leave.

These sick rules kept my eyes from seeing, ears from hearing and kept me from feeling anything.

Love without honesty is possessiveness. It affords no growth, no freedom and eventually no hope.

I carried the rigid rule of "never leave—remain loyal at all costs" for 20 years of marriage until one day I realized I had lost that hope.

Hope was the one thing that propelled me as a child. Things will be better.

I'll never forget the day I knew I had lost hope. I was visiting a friend who was dying of cancer. She was in the same type of business I was and her husband had just fathered a child with another woman. I stood looking at her pain-racked skeleton of a body and saw myself in a few years. At that instant I made a vow to change my life, and I had no idea what that meant! My recovery began.

Shortly after that day, my husband and I were on a planned cruise with four other couples. In the evening, I stood alone on the deck watching a beautiful sunset while my husband was drinking and playing cards. An elderly couple was next to me, and when the sun was at its brilliance and shimmered on the ocean they turned, embraced and kissed so lovingly that tears just streamed down my skin. I knew our old age together would never be like that.

I knew I needed to separate emotionally from my husband. It was unbearable to live in a relationship without any intimacy, love or even kindness anymore.

The next day on the cruise I became ill and was running a fever. I did not feel at all like going out of the cabin for dinner. Typically, my husband would pick a fight, rage at me, then storm out of the room. I would end up crying myself to sleep. This happened again, but for the first time I recognized the dynamic. The ship's doctor gave me some medication, and I felt better the next day.

I walked on the deck to get some sun and struck up a conversation with the woman next to me. She was telling me about the guy who hit on her all night and said, "There he is," pointing at a man. It was my husband! I asked for a separation the day we returned from the cruise, and he couldn't understand why.

He convinced me to go to a marriage counselor. The very first session provoked thoughts which led me to believe that our relationship had no hope. But I knew I needed to learn about this kind of sick relationship so that I wouldn't repeat the same mistakes again. Why did I still love that man but knew for my own sanity it needed to end?

Reading had been an obsession for me. The repeated notion that I should attend a Twelve Step group to deal with the alcohol in my family of origin seemed ridiculous to me. I thought I could just read a few hundred books and have this recovery thing down pat!

Finally, I agreed to go to a meeting when the therapist insisted. I'd never cried in front of outsiders before—after all, I was the "strong one." A deluge of tears streamed down my cheeks after the list of characteristics was read. This reaction continued for months. People in group became persons; persons became friends, friends begot a "best" friend and co-sponsor.

The desire to separate from my husband became stronger which provoked and escalated his rage and abuse. I filed for divorce after my husband tried to rape me. My children witnessed that, and it was as if I were seeing the event through their eyes. I saw that happen to my mother as a very young child. I told them to call the police and to never accept that kind of abuse from anyone.

There was no hope whatsoever for this marriage! On our 23rd anniversary, I saw my husband leaving to begin a new life in another state. Our divorce was almost final, and he chose that day to tell what he could never tell me during the 18 months of counseling. He had had affairs throughout our marriage from the very beginning until he had experienced his heart attack. There was nothing left but an empty shell of the marriage.

It was so shocking! That day was the first truthful day for us. Things now made sense. It was the day our story began.

Our Story

Kara: Living alone was not a real challenge for me because nothing really changed. I had become self-sufficient and independent throughout the marriage. Living alone for my husband, Jake, was dramatic and painful. He was thousands of miles away from family and friends, trying to develop a new business in which he faced rejections on a daily basis.

Jake: We began to talk on the phone; minutes stretched into hours, and intimacy and truth became the norm. We once again could hear and feel the good things about each other that we experienced as we fell in love years ago. These were the very areas of our personalities that we deliberately tried to change and sabotage in each other because of our dysfunctional programming and incomplete personalities. Our phone conversations became the start of facing and accepting our individual responsibilities for all those years of turmoil in our marriage and inadequate parenting to our children.

Separation taught Kara that she could be happy without being married, and it taught me that I really wanted to be married and to be a father.

Kara: The most important support systems in that transitional period were our Twelve Step groups. Jake had joined a group that explored alcoholism in the family of origin. He really began to work the Steps and found a Higher Power which guides him to this day. I not only kept up with a similar group where I lived, but also attended a Twelve Step group for couples trying to save their marriages where infidelity was the main issue. I would remain in the group until I began another relationship or got a divorce.

Jake started to fly in on a monthly basis, and we went to the couples group meetings together. The final divorce papers were never signed, and on one of those visits, we decided to give our marriage another try. Our counselor was also a minister who helped us to renew our vows with the most glorious smirk on his face! Our children who were in college kept their distance from us, and our daughter in high school seemed to carry the pain of our relationship and withdrew emotionally from us.

Jake: Kara moved to join me and to see if we could start a new life together. Since there weren't any couples groups available in our area we started one. We met every week for the next two years. It was a safe place to deal with pain, memories, lost dreams and more pain. We learned how to talk to each other about everyday traumas concerning infidelity, whether it was looking at a woman too long, sexualized conversation or a jealous overreaction.

If we have some type of regressive behavior or reach a crisis point in the relationship, we go to a couples recovery workshop and put resolution to the problem so that we can move on.

Kara and Jake: Today we go to CoDA and use that group to work on all our relationships. We have felt the pain from the past, and changed many messages that were formed from emotionally painful experiences. It is now our challenge to put the negative to work for us—not to rehash the past, but to move on by living consciously in the present.

We're grateful to CoDA and all the other groups which have laid out the plan, given us the words and modeled the behaviors when we could only hold on with our fingertips, knowing if we could just keep holding on we would make it!

by Jake and Kara

NO MORE SECRETS

Strong, controlling, calculating, perfectionistic, willful, serious, super-responsible, heroic, surviving.

These words pretty much describe who I've been and how I've functioned in my growing up to be a good codependent. That perfectionism still creeps up occasionally! I'm so grateful that I'm in recovery!

My family was what would probably be described as normal, middle-class, and hard-working. We moved around the country a lot as a result of my father's work. Because of this facet of family life and others that I will share later, I learned not to develop a whole lot of friendships. As soon as I did so, we would move and leave those friends behind. So, the family became the only ones that I could truly count on to be there. And, oh, how I relied on their attention and belief systems! Both my parents came from families that were not whole units. They learned the behaviors in each of their families that enabled them to survive. They carried these behaviors into a marriage and family. I realize now that they did their best in rearing their six children with their tools, behaviors and belief systems.

The first experience that I remember as a behavior of codependence came about when I was five years old. At the time, I was the oldest of four children, and my mother was about to give birth to the fifth. As the oldest, I was given the responsibility of helping to care for my siblings with their normal, day-to-day activities. I thought that it was great fun, and I felt so grown up! As the days went by, I started to develop a blinking problem as I would sit and watch cartoons on TV. My mother noticed this and, thinking that something was seriously wrong, took me to see the family doctor. Fortunately, the doctor asked the right questions, and came to the conclusion that I had taken on way too much responsibility in the family. My mother gently and slowly decreased my "load," and the blinking disappeared.

As I was growing up, I was given as much responsibility within the family as I could handle. But when my mother was seven months pregnant with my youngest sister, something happened that would affect my growing up like nothing else. My father was just getting started with a hotel company, and as a result, he spent many, many hours at work away from the family. My mother ended up in the hospital with a life-threatening condition, and we kids were left in the hands of an abusive housekeeper who would chase us around the dining room table when we misbehaved, exclaiming that if we weren't good, our mother would never come home. I was nine years old and just starting to develop some awareness about who I was, my autonomy and my sexual identity. I was molested by our housekeeper's husband—twice. The first time, I felt a lot of shame that I let it happen. The second time, I felt not only shame about letting it happen, but also a sense of excitement about this new part of me that was just starting to develop. And then I felt a lot of shame about the excitement! I knew that it was wrong, but I was being betrayed by my body! I was told by this man that if I ever told anyone about what happened, my mother would die. I kept that secret for 25 years. I believed I had total control of my mother's fate, and I never wanted to have my mother leave me as a result of something that I did. As a result of having been molested, I believed that making love was a dirty, vile act that was such a contradiction in terms!

After my youngest sister was born, my mother became progressively and finally heavily dependent on prescription drugs and alcohol. As that happened, I ended up taking on much more responsibility within the family. I was the surrogate spouse to my father (who was deep into workaholism) and the caretaker to my mother and the rest of the kids. I must admit that I took this responsibility very seriously and delighted in the admiration of all of my father's friends and business associates. I also believed that the six children of the family were responsible for the fact that our mother drank and our father stayed away from home a lot. There were times that I drew the kids together and made them promise, in writing, to be good, to behave and to do nothing that would make our parents drink or stay away. I even gave our parents a letter once with all of these promises spelled out. Once again, I really believed that we were the determiners of their fate. The problem was, no matter how hard we tried and no matter what we did, it never changed anything. I began to feel that I was bad because I couldn't change what was happening with our family. But I did keep trying. I didn't know what else to do!

We never really talked about what was going on with our family outside of the house. I remember the desperate feeling of doing everything possible to make the family look perfect. After all, everyone else looked like they were doing just fine, thank you.

I used to listen to baseball games on the transistor radio under my pillow every night. There was an announcer who called the games who had a very soft, nice way of talking, describing the plays and the players. I would fantasize about what it would be like to be his daughter, in his family. It would be idyllic.

As I went into high school, the family was deteriorating at such a rate that my only respite from the turmoil was school. I felt that I couldn't afford to develop close friendships, because I never wanted to have to ask friends home and see what was happening with our family. And I rarely told my parents about functions at school because I felt such shame for myself and them that I didn't want anyone else to see what I saw. I got involved in many extracurricular activities so I could stay at school longer each day. I did well in those activities because of the perfectionistic behavior that I had developed. I was OK at school. There was a girl in my class who could do everything: made straight A's, was captain of the cheerleaders, was voted president of Student Council, was cute, had the lead in the plays, was nice, could sing. I envied her and thought how neat it would be to be like her and be in her family. The school had a breakfast once a year in which one of the student's fathers would come and address the students. This girl's father came to speak during my freshman year. It turned out that he was the announcer I had listened to so many times on the radio! It all fit into my idea of the perfect family system!

During my junior year of high school, my parents reached a point where something had to give or they would split up. I was very afraid of that possibility and fought like a tiger to keep the family together. I didn't want them to go to a marriage counselor because I knew that he would tell them that the marriage was hopeless. I believed we could handle it ourselves and I would re-double my efforts to make the kids stay in line. It felt like I was treading water and losing the battle. My mother, after much counseling, decided to stop drinking. I thought how wonderful it was that I would finally be able to get my mother back. But I soon discovered that although, at first, I had lost my mother to alcoholism—I then lost her to AA. I recognize now that what she was doing was for her and her sobriety. And as I've grown up, the results of what she did then have led to the wonderful relationship that we have today. My father supported her in her decision and attended "spouse and souse" groups with her. I noticed that as he went to these meetings, he started to spend more time at home with us. He was starting to take a look at his participation in the family dysfunction.

After I graduated from high school, I got into the perfect career for a caretaker. I became a nurse. It was so much easier to take care of other people. I didn't have to take care of me, and I got all that same admiration as I had before when I was helping others. It was only after I got into recovery that I realized there wasn't a day that went by that I didn't go to work deathly afraid of making that one mistake that would cost a life. I became a pretty good nurse as a result. But after nine years in the profession, I became tired of handling everyone else's problems.

I did, however, get into another service profession. The prospect of being able to travel, to "get-away-from-it-all" and to be able to tell others where to go seemed to be ideal. It was as a travel agent that the beginning of my bottom started to be realized. I began to drink more than was appropriate. I became isolated from others. I had such negative self-esteem that I had no regard for people who said they cared about me. The behaviors I had learned in order to survive were not working as well for me anymore. I really lost control of others. I couldn't make them do what I wanted them to do! I had always been a great listener and had a shoulder for anyone whom I could coerce to use it. Now, I was starting to ask, "Who listens to the listener when the listener has something to say?" Yet I couldn't believe that I had anything to share that was worth anyone's listening. I felt so alone.

A friend of mine, to whom I'll always be indebted, finally shared some of her concerns and observations about me. She told me she was afraid for me and hoped that I would get some help. That was all that

I needed to really look at what was happening. In the meantime, my parents had worked a lot on their recovery, so much so that my mother had gotten into the mental health profession. It felt OK for me to go to them and talk about what was going on with me and ask for their help and support. It was one of the most releasing experiences of my life, to finally be able to share my pain, to finally be able to admit that I had a problem that, no matter how hard I tried, I couldn't solve alone.

I was lucky enough to be able to participate in an inpatient codependence treatment program. There, I began my recovery. I learned it was OK to be just who I was, that I was a lovable, perfect being and that I needed to start to address some of the behaviors that I had learned. I had the opportunity to look at that secret I had carried for so many years. I got to tell my mother about what had happened with the housekeeper's husband; and, as of this writing, she is still alive. And she understands why I couldn't tell anyone. I learned it was OK not to have to fix everything and everyone. Here's an example: There was a lounge chair in the hospital that had a loose arm. It would have been totally understandable for me to reach under and tighten the screw. However, for 28 days, I made a choice not to do that. It was a silent triumph for me. I left treatment ready to put what I had learned to the test.

Returning home, I came to the realization that I could use my codependence to recover from it. I became a fanatic about recovery. I had gotten enough strokes and love in treatment that I wanted more. It seemed that the more I did for my recovery, the more

I received. I found out about Co-Dependents Anonymous within a month of my release from treatment. When I walked into that room, I felt that I was home. There were people talking about a lot of the same behaviors that I had learned, what they were doing to learn new behaviors to handle difficult situations, and the family of choice they were developing. These were all things that I needed and wanted to hear. I added CoDA as one of my recovery tools.

As I learned more about this recovery process, I became painfully aware of all of the aspects of my life that these old behaviors had handled. I realized that I had to grieve the loss of these behaviors. After all, they had helped me survive a lot of painful times. Some old behaviors were very easy to release. I believe they were those that were more on the surface. The tougher ones were those that were insidious—they would sneak up during the particularly stressful times. The control, perfection and judgment were the primary ones for me. I had believed that as long as I could control the situation, person or place, it would all be perfect and that everyone was off their rocker for managing it or them any other way! In recovery, I had to learn to let go of these traits because they never really materialized the way I dreamed. I still find myself kicking and screaming about that at times. As I said before, for the first few months I used my codependence to recover from it. I believed if I worked my program 24 hours a day— through writing, reading, therapy, service work and going to meetings—and if I did it perfectly, then I would be rid of my disease and I could go about the business of living, never having to worry about it again. Once again, I found myself becoming more isolated, lonely and burned out. About six months into my program, I reached a plateau on which I had no strength to move forward and I was deathly afraid of going backward—back to the way it used to be. Through meetings, I found the courage to realize I had not given myself permission to start to live life. And with my family of choice, I began to have fun. That was a new concept! I had heard quite a bit about this fun business, and I wanted to find out how to do it. I realized how much fun it was to laugh and let my little girl enjoy some of the good times she hadn't been able to experience earlier in life. One time, I got to go to an amusement park where I went on rides I wanted to ride, ate what I wanted when I wanted, and bought what I wanted to buy! That, in itself, was healing. So, without even realizing it, I was working my program without really working on it. And giving myself the rest that I deserved enabled me to tackle more pieces as time went on. I found out that it was OK to be me—whoever that was at the time—and that I didn't have to be anyone's perception of the perfect recovering codependent.

One of the misconceptions I had when I started my program of recovery was that the stresses of life would disappear. I was so ready to place the blame of all of the stresses in my life on this disease that I thought that as I recovered, they would vanish. To a degree, that was true. But it was more on the reactive side of the actual problems. The normal problems of life have still surfaced from time to time. However, I have learned new behaviors on how to deal with them that have prevented them from escalating into such extreme emotional nightmares. One of those behaviors is talking with people in CoDA about the problem and hearing them share their experience, strength and hope around how they have dealt with similar situations. I don't feel terminally unique anymore. I don't have to ride the roller coaster of emotions that stress causes anymore. I can let go a little easier of the old issues of control that kept me in stressful situations and their consequences. I realize that I have no control over all of those situations that caused me stress. I also realize that I can only be responsible for me and how I handle it in my recovery. I know that I can have feelings about life, its pitfalls and its accomplishments.

There are times that I get to other plateaus in my recovery. I have found that if I give myself permission to just experience them as resting times—times during which I can just become more aware of my strength and character defects—that I don't have to feel so compelled to do something about them. And I can trust that I will not be stuck forever in a state of awareness. And that, no matter what happens to me and my recovery, I will never go back to being the exact same person I used to be. That concept can be rather paradoxical and quite scary but also very freeing!

Each day brings new awareness about me and my life. Each CoDA meeting gives me an opportunity to share those awarenesses and to hear similar experiences of others. And each night before I go to sleep, I am more grateful. I am grateful to my Higher Power for trusting me enough to learn more about me and to do the best that I can with all that I've learned. I am grateful for the tools that I have to use in my recovery. And finally, I am grateful to me for being able and willing to love, nurture and grow; that it's OK to be: vulnerable, honest, trustworthy, fun, responsible, helpful, confident, precious and free!

by Karen R.

MEN DON'T CRY

As I began to write my story, I instantly hear a voice within informing me that I am doing something wrong. Growing up in my family, I had learned never to talk about our problems with others. This message kept me incredibly miserable for many years. However, I will begin this story at my bottom, a time in which I had felt more despair and hopelessness than I could ever remember.

This day began like most others I remember. I awoke feeling angry for no apparent reason, pushed everyone that loved me away, and headed for my 70 plus hour-a-week job.

Upon arrival at work, much to my dismay, I discovered that after almost one year as Treatment Director of an adolescent chemical dependency treatment program I was being laid-off. I was devastated and outraged at the same time. How could they do this to me?

I worked more hours than anyone there; I performed at least three jobs at one time for them; I had even quit my own business to come work for them; and after all, I was the most dedicated employee they had. How dare they do this to me!

In total despair, I went to get in my car to drive home. I only lived two miles from the facility, but this drive home seemed more like 20. What was I going to tell my wife and son? What would we do now? How could I possibly face them?

When I did arrive home, an eerie feeling came over me. As I entered the house, a coldness thickened the air. Seeing no one in the living room, I headed to the bedroom. There was my wife packing a suitcase. For the moment, I forgot about work and asked her, with fear lingering, what was it she was doing. She looked at me, unknowing of what had transpired at my work and said, "We're leaving you, and I want a divorce."

I believe at that point I went into shock. I was speechless for a time but soon began pleading and begging her to stay. I made all the same promises to her once again. None that she hadn't heard before. I even tried to make her feel guilty by telling her what had just happened at work. To no avail, she packed and left with our son.

This relationship was no different than the many previous relationships. They always began with an obsessive quality, the kind of obsession that disallows even the slightest distance between us. Every spare moment was spent together filling a deep craving indescribable to most, yet not to the codependent.

The obsessive dependency I had in these relationships always precluded the same pattern. I became less intimate and less sexual by the day. I became irritable and angry morning, noon, and night. Hopelessness and misery replaced all happiness. I wanted her as far away as I could have her, yet not out of reach. I couldn't blame my wife or any of the others for leaving.

I didn't realize it at the time, but my entire identity was my wife and job. In one day I was losing both. My insides felt ripped out; my identity was gone. It felt as though I was nothing without them.

The decision I made was to end my life that day. This wasn't new to me. I had thought about it many times and attempted it twice as a child. There would be no attempts this time; I was going to follow it through.

As I sat in my home alone, contemplating the surest, most painless way, a thought came to me. I began remembering a promise I had made to myself and son. My father had abandoned me at three years of age, never to return. I swore I would never do this to my son. At this realization, I began to cry. But men don't cry. I did for two weeks; I didn't stop.

When the crying was over, something had changed in me. I couldn't describe it, but I could feel it. I went to a Twelve Step meeting that I had been frequenting since I had stopped drinking. When I arrived, I shared my recent experience with an old friend. She suggested I see a therapist she had seen. With much hesitation, I went. What I discovered after seeing this therapist and following his suggestions was the beginning of an entirely new way of living.

I was introduced to codependence recovery. I had heard this word before in my own profession as a therapist. I believed, like many in my field, that these people met in meetings to blame their parents for their problems. But then again, no one ever accused me of being open-minded.

One thing was for certain, my way of living and having healthy relationships was not working. So I followed directions: I went to meetings of Co-Dependents Anonymous, I got a sponsor or two, and I pried open my closed mind through prayer.

I began discovering that I was stuck in my childhood, pretending to be an adult. Messages I had received about myself as a child were disallowing me healthy relationships as an adult. I found out that I had a disease called codependency, and that this was the root of my life's misery. Most importantly, I found a way to change my old belief system and develop a new one that would allow me to be free of my past and experience joy in my present.

No longer did I have to hate myself. No longer did I have to be ashamed of being me. People began to relate to me differently. People began to trust me more deeply. I was no longer stuck as a child, pretending to be all grown up.

Co-Dependents Anonymous has given me the opportunity to be the father I never had, the husband I always attempted to be, and the man I always believed I couldn't be.

I would hate to think that my story sounds like a frog turned prince because I still feel very green some days. However, the hope I have today is one that is deeper than ever before: the hope that allows me to be open to growth; the hope that allows me to give freely to others; and for those still searching for answers to problems and misery at home, I offer my hope discovered in codependence recovery.

by Chuck W.

TRIAL BY FIRE

Codependence didn't respect anything my family told me was important or valuable: money, power, prestige, education. None of the things we are often told and believe, that make up a good environment for children, protected me from codependence. I was raised in one of those "good homes." My parents were both attorneys, although my mother didn't work again after she married my father. There was an excess of material things for all of us. We were envied in the small town where we lived for all we had, for all we were able to do, for all we knew.

No one knew, however, that my father was an alcoholic; that he came home every night, drank a bottle of Scotch, raged at everyone, often became physically violent, and then passed out. No one knew that a horse whip was always packed along with the cooler and the bathing suits for those glamorous vacations we frequently took. No one knew my mother was so depressed she was incapable of protecting us from our father or taking care of us herself.

Everyone knew I was "hysterical," "too sensitive," "crazy," "wild," "weird." No one knew I had become accustomed to physical, emotional, spiritual abuse or that I had been emotionally abandoned by both parents or that I was the mother for my younger brother and sister. No one knew that I was "acting out" every time it looked like my father might hurt someone else in the family so that I would be the one abused.

All through the years of growing up, most people who knew me thought I was "messed up." What they didn't know was that I had survived beatings, incest, constant emotional battering, abandonment, and my father's alcoholism. I don't believe children are codependent; they are abused. As an adult, I was a codependent as a result of having to cope with my abusive childhood.

As I grew into adulthood, I was only attracted to the "dark side." It was where I thought I belonged— where I felt I fit in. And how I felt was absolutely worthless. I knew my parents didn't love me and that made me unlovable to the whole world. Kind, accepting men capable of loving were boring to me. I didn't know how to be in relationship with anyone who thought I was all right just the way I was. Again and again, I was involved with violent, raging, alcoholic men. I always believed the problems in the relationship were my fault, and if I could just change something about me, everything would be OK.

Although I didn't allow my children to be physically abused, I did remain married far too long to men who abused them emotionally. I had been an active alcoholic and drug addict since I was 15 and I felt at home with other alcoholics and addicts. We understood each other, it seemed. Today, I know we did, because we all had buried deep inside that pain that we numbed with chemicals.

I was filled with shame. I was ashamed that something was fundamentally wrong with me. I was ashamed that others seemed able to cope or to take action or to adjust, while I just became paralyzed by my life experiences, over and over again. I was so ashamed of who I was that I was always pretending to be how others wanted me to be. I was ashamed of the marriages I made. There were three of them; I was ashamed that I couldn't leave them when inappropriate things continued to happen—things like infidelity, alcoholism, raging, domestic violence. I felt "less than" everyone else. I felt I really didn't have the right to be alive. I was ashamed that I couldn't live a day without alcohol and drugs to numb the pain of my life and the pain of how I felt about myself.

As the years went on, the codependence became worse. At 40, I had been an alcoholic and drug addict for 25 years. I was clinically depressed, like my mother. I was finally leaving my third marriage, after eight years of constant emotional abuse of me and my children. I could barely work; I had my own business, and I was just letting it die. I felt so hopeless and worthless and terrified. Everyday, when I opened my eyes, I felt absolute terror, and then dread, of the day that faced me. My feelings were numbed by chemicals and depression. I was like a zombie. I was dying—truly. I had a spirit and a body, and both were dying.

When I look back on how I came into recovery, it's clear to me that my Higher Power—who I choose to call God—was with me, even in that time that appeared to me to be my death-in-progress. The stories about children being sexually abused in day care centers were all over the news. I was irresistibly attracted to them. Every story made me drop deeper into sadness, but I had to keep watching them on TV and reading about them in magazines and newspapers. Finally a good friend told me I needed to get some help and recommended a therapist.

I had been in therapy off and on for 10 years trying to figure out what was wrong with me. None of it had helped much. Still, I was desperate this time; I couldn't function anymore, and the sadness surrounded me like a fog.

In the first session with this new therapist, she asked me to get an image of the sadness. I closed my eyes and saw, for the first time, myself as a five-year-old child—a perfect, beautiful, sweet and intensely sad child. CoDA didn't exist at this time; the word codependent didn't exist either. But God had brought me to a person who would work with me on my codependency. For the next 18 months, we discovered together what happened to me when I was a child, how I had learned to cope, and what wasn't working in my adult life.

After she moved from my area, I continued to use the techniques she had taught me to try to heal. I had a lot of information, and I did feel better about myself, but I was still so alone and so different. No one else I knew had a history like mine or was dealing with the pain and the problems with living that I was.

I had stopped the use of chemicals through Twelve Step programs available for alcoholics and drug addicts, and the companionship of those programs along with the Steps and Traditions helped more than anything else. I soon learned that I couldn't talk about my "other" journey there—the one I was taking out of the pain of codependency. I needed a place to belong, a place to share with other people who understood that all the fixes I had used had to do with the pain of living life as a codependent.

After a few years, CoDA arrived—at last, a spiritual program built around those Twelve Steps and Twelve Traditions I had come to love and to believe were divinely inspired. CoDA gave me a place to share with others the work I had continued doing on my own. Even though I had struggled to work on recovery for years, I had continued to feel very different—"less than" others—because I didn't know anyone else going through this process. CoDA gave me a place to belong, where I discovered others who were like me: men and women who had lost any sense of themselves, who had sacrificed personal ethics and values to be loved, who felt worthless and despairing. And, men and women going through the pain—yes, pain—of recovery, because recovery in the beginning is a painful journey of remembering and having feelings return—all feelings.

Today, six years from the time I first saw the image of myself at five, my life is better than any dream I could have dreamed. I have a job I love. My children are in recovery from their own abusive histories and we talk about it together. I have remarried—to a man in recovery himself—and I feel loved, nurtured, accepted and supported for the first time in my life. I wake up every day ready for that day, knowing whatever it brings is God's will, and that God only wants the best. I fall asleep every night thanking God for his loving protection. Recognizing my own codependence and how powerless I sometimes am over my behavior has helped me love and accept others in a special way. We know each other on the deepest levels because all of us have survived life through trial-by-fire. When we talk from our truth, we hear the same pain, fear, anger and shame.

I work those Twelve Steps and I pay attention to those Twelve Traditions. I know that going to meetings, working the Steps, staying as honest with myself and others as I possibly can, and doing service work for CoDA are the things that will keep me recovering. I want to heal. I want the pain and shame and fear and anger to stop running me. I would do anything today to continue to receive the gifts of recovery.

When I go to meetings, I'm able to say with joy and gratitude, "My name is Candace and I am codependent."

by Candace S.

OFF THE ROLLER COASTER

For the first 38 years of my life, I felt like nothing. Despite excellent academic achievements in high school and college and my musical ability as a church organist, I was convinced I had no marketable skills. Even getting my master's degree and serving as the president of the local League of Women Voters didn't increase my self-confidence. I denied my codependence through cycles of overeating and dieting as well as long periods of depression.

Ironically, my recovery began with the "acting out" behavior of my daughter. By the time she was 13, she had a serious drug and behavior problem. She was arrested on January 31, 1982, at 2:00 in the morning with 38 grams of marijuana in her pocket.

The next few years I would experience dramatic plunges followed by valiant efforts to soar into self-transcendence. Whether it was plunging or soaring, it was part of the same disease, codependence.

To be totally honest, there were times when I liked the roller coaster ride. It made me feel intensely alive and aware. The fear of boredom was a symptom of my chronic state of anxiety. I myself was hooked—not on an external drug, but on the almost constant rush of adrenaline released by my own body in its response to the high levels of stress in my life. Eventually I bottomed out enough to suspect the roller coaster ride might not be that much fun. Then, and only then, did I decide I might like to get off. Then and only then did I begin to learn how much better, how infinitely better serenity is.

I had to become a lot sicker before I could get better. In October of 1981, I had gotten a part-time job which added sexual addiction and workaholism to my growing insanity. Prior to my daughter's arrest, I had felt as if I were on top of the world. Finally, I had thought it was my turn to live.

My husband and I were devastated by our daughter's behavior. Both his parents and mine had rigid attitudes toward drugs and alcohol. I felt like a butterfly being stuffed back into its cocoon. The roller coaster was plunging earthward, swallowing me. I felt as if I couldn't breathe.

My husband and I were locked into a fantasy world of denial and "people-pleasing," each locked in a solitary cell of pain, guilt, and growing hopelessness. We bumped in the night like snarling, starving beasts. Misery permeated the house like a poison gas. There was the moment when we looked back, after the worst had passed, and fantasized about taking a match to the house and gleefully watching it burn to the ground. With it might go all the bad memories.

I had no friends with whom I could talk. I felt as paralyzed as a rat stuck in an electrically-charged cage, "shitting all over the place" in fear. On the other hand, I felt hopelessly constipated. I held in every "negative" (honest) thought and emotion, poisoning myself with self-hatred and self-deception.

My recovery began in the summer of 1983 when a friend, who was herself a recovering alcoholic, invited me to a Saturday morning open meeting of another Twelve Step program. Through that Fellowship, I learned the "laxative" qualities of human speech. For the first time in my life, I had an opportunity to say whatever I needed to say without being judged or fixed. I learned honesty, humility, and gratitude by their example. I learned a better way to live.

I found that writing helped. I didn't feel so alone. The words were comforting. They gave me the sense that I still existed. I could think and function. I grabbed onto words like a drowning man grabs onto a life raft. I found a way of stepping outside myself to put into words my own silent scream. A spider holds itself in space by spinning webs. I held myself together by spinning poetry. My Higher Power still speaks to me through my writing.

In taking a Fourth Step, I discovered I was a very angry lady with strong sexual needs. I was a very angry lady. I resented authority figures because I felt I gave in to them too easily at the cost of my own needs and my own desires, at the expense of my own life force. I wanted to live in a "never-never land" without trouble. I wanted to be "good" all the time. I expected the world to like me always and to take good care of me in return. I wanted to achieve success in a career and feared it at the same time. I felt helpless to achieve.

I was an impatient person pretending to be patient, a tense person pretending to be calm, an arrogant person pretending to be humble. The solution wasn't a total rejection of self because I couldn't be perfect, nor a total rejection of life because it couldn't be perfect either.

Gradually, I worked the Twelve Step program, as taught by my adopted brothers and sisters, and it began to work for me. I realized I was unhappy because my own emotional well-being was dependent on everyone but myself. I believed I needed a divorce from my daughter and my husband. When my friend pointed out the possibility that neither one might ever change, my choices became clear. I could continue my obsessive focusing on how to change them. I could continue to be miserable with the current situation. I could physically withdraw from them both. I could detach emotionally with indifference or resentment. Or, I could "detach with love" by learning how to be happy within myself and by accepting them and myself as we were. That became my goal. It was a tall order and a revolutionary concept for me, but one that was challenging and liberating. By releasing the members of my family from being solely responsible for my happiness and well-being, I freed myself and them. I had to learn how to hand back to them the responsibility for their happiness. We needed to learn how "to live and let each other live."

As I stopped focusing on what I saw as my husband's negativity and reluctance to discuss feelings, some of the pressure was removed from him. He began to respond positively and feel less hopeless.

During marriage counseling, I became aware of how scared both he and I were of displeasing the other. We are two very different people. Instead of appreciating the difference, we were ashamed of it.

I thought, "If only I were more like him and less like myself, he would love me more. I'd be a better wife and more contented with my life."

He thought, "If only I were more like her and less like myself, she would love me more. I'd be a better husband and she'd be more contented with her life."

The truth is that we needed to be contented with who we were. By observing him, I could learn patience, steadiness, loyalty, the limitations of words, the value of silence, and the beauty of the concrete and the ordinary. From observing me, he could learn humor, exuberance, the value of vulnerability and feeling, the adventurous spirit, and the glory beyond the surface.

I am the kite he holds securely so I won't get carried away and lost in space. He is the earthbound basket stuck in the dirt which my balloon lifts up into the atmosphere. I am the bell that gladdens his silence. He is the hush that quiets my noise.

In September of 1989, I attended a weekend retreat on CoDA. The concepts of codependence put into words what I had previously sensed about myself and my life. I have learned that my difficulty saying, "no," my not being responsible for my needs, my caretaking of other people's feelings, my lack of boundaries, and shame are important issues to me.

In Co-Dependents Anonymous, I have come home at last.

I am a person of extremes—an all or nothing kind of person. By working the Twelve Steps and attending meetings, I am moving closer toward a harmonious balance. I recognize that one person's Golden Mean may be another's extreme. There will always be someone who considers me too emotional, too moody, too intellectual, too aloof, too exuberant, too analytical, too other-worldly, and just plain too, too much. That's OK. Since I'm the one who has to live in my skin, it is my Higher Power and me who know when I'm "just right." That feelings of "all rightness" happen more and more frequently the longer I work the program.

Of course, I must extend the same courtesy to others. Sometimes I judge people as too superficial, too unfeeling, too materialistic, too self-deceptive and too negative, when in reality, they may be just right, too. A maple tree is not an oak tree is not an elm. A rose is not a violet is not a lily-of-the-valley. How wonderful!

Life is not perfect and neither am I. I have a challenging career and I'm not obsessed with making up for lost time. I have a family in which we can say what we need to say and be who we really are. I have good friends, and I'm also learning how to be my own best friend. Higher Power has become my best friend, too. Just for today I know that I have enough. I am enough!

by Janet K.

BOBBY'S HOPE

I found myself in my mid-forties full of fear and not knowing why, full of anger and not knowing why, not able to have a meaningful relationship and not knowing why. I was afraid to discuss it with someone else because somehow I knew it was my fault. I felt that I didn't fit in, that I was "less than" everybody else. I had been working the program of Alcoholics Anonymous for a number of years and had been successful in stopping the addictive behavior, but I wasn't enjoying life; I wasn't happy. A friend who had joined CoDA mentioned to me that I might find something there for me. At the time I was in one of my periodic bouts with, "What good is it? I've done everything they've told me to do and I just don't seem to make any progress. I'm depressed about life and I don't know why." So I followed my friend's advice and I went to three CoDA meetings that summer. I know today that I wasn't hurting enough then because I was very judgmental about the meetings. I said, "There's too much blame here and not enough ownership of one's own stuff," so I didn't go to any more meetings.

Later in the fall of that year, I began a relationship that only lasted a few weeks, yet it was incredibly painful when we broke up. I began blaming myself for its demise and projecting on how, "If only I had been a better person, or if only..." It went on ad infinitum. I hurt and I didn't know why. Worse yet, I didn't know how to deal with the hurt. So on the Friday after Thanksgiving, I went to my first CoDA meeting for me. That was the start of my recovery.

The first thing I did was learn the truths of my history. I began the talk of my family of origin. I'm the fourth son of my parents and was always called the baby in the family. My older brothers and I were each born about two years apart. My family was Irish Catholic, and both my parents had emigrated from Ireland at an early age. The only other relatives we had in the United States were an aunt and uncle who also had four children—three boys and a girl. My aunt was my mother's older sister. Both my parents came from very large families, most of which stayed in the British Isles. Thus, during my lifetime, I met none of my grandparents. I have subsequently met my aunts and uncles on my father's side on only one occasion.

My upbringing can be characterized as one of heavy physical, sexual, and spiritual abuse. My household had extremely strict rules, and any deviation from the rules was met with physical beatings as the punishment for stepping out of line. Hair brushes, broom handles, and belts were some of the weapons. Face slaps and bare rear-end punishments were common. I learned quickly, in watching and hearing my brothers being slapped and beaten, how to avoid the same fate. And, I wasn't always successful at avoiding the punishment. I learned to watch adults and pick up signs that told me how to act. I was taught not to cry. If I did cry, my mother would tell me she'd really give me a reason to cry. I learned not to feel, because whenever one of my brothers had feelings, he would be punished for them. I learned to look outside myself to see how "you" wanted me to behave. I learned to hate conflict and fear confrontation, because in my experience whenever either was present, the result was always punishment. Crying meant punishment. The only proper feelings were joy or happiness. Thus, I came to believe that if I wasn't joyful or happy, something was wrong! My mother was the main offender as punisher; my father only became involved when a beating with a belt was "warranted." My mother would say the classic line, "Wait until your father gets home!"

I was raised as a practicing Catholic. My family went to church every Sunday morning from as early an age as I can remember. Absolutely no noise or nonsense was tolerated. If I made any noise in church, I was slapped. I went to Catholic schools and was taught by nuns. Any conflict or problem at school always came out in the nun's favor. I knew that from watching my brothers where one time, one of them was forced to get down on his hands and knees and apologize for something he had said. So when the time came for me to go to school, I went afraid to do anything because I would always be judged to be in the wrong with a stiff punishment as the ultimate result. Early on in school, I remember not wanting to answer questions because I might have the wrong answer, and I was afraid of what they would think of me. I eventually became afraid of what "you" would think of me, so I worked at trying to please you and be who I thought you wanted me to be rather than to just be who I am.

My mother tried to get each of my older brothers, and eventually even me, to become priests. My oldest brother fought and fought and finally got out of entering the seminary. My next two brothers went to the seminary; one of them did become a priest. I believe today that my mother had severe childhood trauma and her way of cleansing the guilt she carried was to offer her sons to God. By the time I got out of grammar school, I was bound and determined I absolutely would not go to the seminary. Looking back, this was truly the first time in my life that I stood up for me. I made a decision that I would not do what my mother told me to do. My stubbornness and the rebel in me came out for the first time. There was, of course, a price to be paid for that. My brother the seminarian/priest became the favorite. The issue of fairness became big, but I hadn't yet figured out why.

My father was a heavy drinker who quit about the time I entered grammar school. He did not join Alcoholics Anonymous, but instead joined an Irish religious group called the Pioneers. Throughout my childhood years, he worked to support the family. He generally worked shift work, being gone all afternoon and evening or at night. Then he would come home and sleep all day. I really only saw him a couple of days a week for any length of time. On the days he was sleeping, it was another reason to be punished if I made any noise in the house. To expect four young boys not to make noise was of course absurd, but that's the way it was. My father had chances to move from shift work to straight days, but he chose to not be in the house and in conflict with my mother's iron-handed rule. He wasn't there for me when I needed him.

When I was in grammar school, I became a latch-key child when my mother joined the work force. My brothers were allowed to go out after school, but I had to come home and stay there. I developed a baseball game on the living room rug where I used encyclopedia books with the binding side up as the outfield fences. I used baseball playing cards with a marble as the ball and a pencil as the bat. In fifth grade, I started selling newspapers on the corner newsstand on Saturdays. In seventh grade, I started working on Fridays after school; and on Saturdays I worked in a grocery store as a bag boy. In eighth grade and all through high school, I worked this job full-time after school and on Saturdays.

In my family, with two brothers in the seminary, dating was not encouraged. I went to a Catholic boys high school and attended a Catholic men's university. I didn't learn to drive until I was 20. I didn't like to bring friends to my house when my parents were there, and didn't know why I had anxiety attacks (starting in college) on a regular basis. Most of what I learned to do or not do I had learned from watching my brothers.

Worst of all, I had developed a relationship with God that was totally based in fear. My God was a punishing God who kept a record book on me. He made entries in it whenever I did anything wrong. The only way to live life was to do everything right. Growing up, I was so afraid to do anything wrong that I had to make up "sins" to tell to the priest when I made my first communion and first confession. That continued for some time since we were supposed to go to confession every two weeks.

After college, I joined the service for a couple of years, then came back and got a job very quickly. I remember my mother pushing me to go to work and I didn't understand the real ramifications of her actions. I moved back into my parents' house after the service. In the next few years, my brother the priest left the priesthood. Shortly thereafter, my father died. When I was 31, I moved out of my parents' house to a different city to take a job offer. I believe it was then that my recovery really started. It took me five more years to get to my first Twelve Step program. That was the move that started my break from the family disease. I had finally done something that was for me.

It was in getting my family of origin work started that I began to see the role I had played in my family. I had been a scapegoat, and the lost child. I had bonded to my mother. I had been extremely codependent, using other people's values, looking to them for my validation, looking to see if I could figure out what you needed me to do for you to like me. I had carried a great deal of fear and shame that actually had been my mother's. It had been passed on from generation to generation in my family. Likewise, I had also carried a great deal of fear that was my father's.

I had always claimed that I was in control of my emotions, but the truth was I was filled with anger that I had stuffed down inside me for years. This anger would periodically erupt sideways when the holder was full. I skipped through my other emotions very quickly and always landed in my anger, then denied that I was angry. "Who me? Angry? Not me!"

I was lonely but I didn't own the loneliness. I couldn't do relationships but didn't know why. I had a lot of fear of judgment and shame. I finally started to own my fear. I had a lot of fantasy about life, very similar to when I was that little boy on the rug playing a baseball game in the living room.

Suddenly, it all started to fall into place. I began to see how my history was controlling my life. I began to see I was repeating my parents' behaviors which were similar to their parents. I began to see how I ran from feelings because they were "bad," just as I had learned in my childhood. I began to see how fearful I became if you ignored me, how I feared a negative judgment on your part, how needy I was for your approval and love because I didn't love myself.

I began to see what had happened to that little boy inside me, Bobby. I began to see how afraid he was, that together we had skipped the childhood and adolescent years and become an adult. We missed the joys of being a child, the safe testing grounds of making mistakes, the adolescent pushing at the boundaries in the process of becoming an independent thinking, whole person. We missed the teenage years of finding our independence and our sexuality, of learning the social skills of interdependence. I came to see that the true secret to my continued recovery was the healing of my inner child.

The grieving process for all that never was began for much of the physical, emotion, sexual, and spiritual pain that had occurred. Somehow, here on paper, it seems so simple and straightforward. But it wasn't. It was the most painful period of my adult life. Physical body pain memories came back. The black pain of the past came back and lasted for weeks. The tears came when I saw a movie where someone was there for another person—for no other reason than for who that person was. I know that I am nowhere near done in this area, but the pain doesn't seem as bad anymore, and it doesn't seem to last as long as it first did.

I began to make contact with Bobby, and as his trust in me started to grow, so did the frequency of contact. His stuffed lion, Ozzie, has a more prominent place in our house today as one of the family. We write down our positions on the day's happenings on an almost daily basis. We sit down and just talk on an ever increasing frequency. We dance, sing and play like we've never done before.

And there's a teenager who has only recently come out. He's an angry dude who will tell you exactly who he is. He's very powerful and very independent.

The word love is used often and openly in our household today, in stark contrast to the one I grew up in where that word was noticeably absent.

Finally, understanding my history and how much it has affected everything I have done in my life, the real change came for me when I began to work the Steps of CoDA. I saw how powerless I really was over others. I went through my own history year by year and saw the unmanageability of my life in relationships.

I began to trust my Higher Power, whom I choose to call God, to take me where I need to be. I believe today that God gives me the wisdom and strength on a daily basis, and that my part of it is to be willing. I believe that the Second Step is the hope step, and it is the child within me who always has the hope that everything will work out for the best. It was the child who always wanted to stay there, and we will work it out because it was he who so wanted to be loved. Today he still has that hope, but now it is based on a trust in my Higher Power. My God today is a loving Higher Power who cares about me, loves me for who I am and for no other reason. He loves me no matter what I do or say. I'm not perfect nor will I ever be, but my God loves me unconditionally.

The CoDA Fourth Step inventory has been an eye opener for me. It has shown me what my part of all this has been. I was neglected when I was growing up, and I picked up on that neglect in taking care of myself. In my relationship with others, and most of all in my relationship with myself, I neglected my physical, emotional, sexual, intellectual, and spiritual needs. I have finally taken responsibility for me and have stopped blaming my past for what I do today. I still hold those accountable for what they did or didn't do, but my life is no longer controlled by my past. Things still come up, but now I work to separate what's about my past and what is about today. I don't have to take my past out on someone else today, and I thank my Higher Power for putting people in my life who lovingly helped me to see these things. I bring the willingness, He gives the wisdom and the strength.

Finally, the real joy in life has been the reparenting of that little boy, my inner child, Bobby. Every day marks a growth where he shares a new experience and emerges as a more confident, more loved child. There's a teenager there today, too! In my giving up the control that I have used as a mechanism to stay stuck, the originality and spontaneity of my inner child has started to come out. The obsessive self-reliance has started to go away. The energy has changed; new and wonderful people are entering my life. Every day something happens that involves my inner child that is new, fun, sometimes scary, but always different. From today on, I look forward with the renewed hope of that little boy.

by Bob H.

FINDING MY CHILD WITHIN

I learned to be codependent from a lot of people and for several reasons. Among these reasons was one big one: to survive. I was afraid that if I didn't "behave," "do things right" or comply, people would reject, shame or leave me in some way. If they did, I might not survive. I learned that from an early age.

All I ever wanted was for my parents to love and accept me, and I wanted to love and accept them, but something seemed to block that from happening very often. While it took me" a long time to find out, I know now that both my parents were wounded and unrecovered adult children of dysfunctional families, and it showed up in each of them as active codependence. Growing up in that environment, how could I possibly learn to be healthy and happy? How could I expect to have fulfilling relationships?

In addition to my family, I grew up in a dysfunctional, middle-class neighborhood. In fact, looking back, most of my whole culture was unhealthy: the schools I attended, churches, political system—nearly everything. It taught me that the answer to functioning and being happy was always outside of me, and to get it, I had to be "nice," yet aggressive and smart, but not boastful.

I remember being shamed a lot, especially by my parents, especially when he was there—my father. In their eyes I just never seemed to do things "right." I was repeatedly stifled for my natural inquisitiveness about things such as rules, relationships, and sex. And no one dealt with my questions about the relevancy of what the schools and churches taught.

Even though I've done a lot of healing and recovery over the years, it's still painful for me to write this. In addition to a lot of shame, the most prominent emotions I remember feeling while growing up were sadness, anger and confusion.

I was the oldest of three kids. My parents always put the burden on me to "set a good example" for my younger sister and brother, but they were never clear with me just how I was supposed to do that. And all the while, who was setting a good example for me? How was I to learn? Since I never seemed to do it "right" and didn't seem to get their acceptance and love, I thought there was something wrong with me. I thought I was the problem.

Inside of me, countering all of this, was a spark of energy, creativity and joy. When the pain wasn't too overwhelming, that part of me which I now experience as Me, that little boy, would come out and relate, create, celebrate and be. I had a few people, who at times, loved and accepted him—my mother, grandmother and step-uncle. But most of the time, he didn't feel accepted and loved, and so he went back into hiding. Many people, especially my father, couldn't allow him to be. They would shame, reject or criticize him in some way.

I was usually shorter in height than my peers, and felt less-than and somehow inferior to others. Sometimes I was a slow learner. So for this and all the above, I tried to overcompensate by achieving in other areas of my life. And in that achieving, I got into overachieving. I received diplomas, degrees, fellowships and specialty board training and examinations. I tried marriage and a child. I tried to make a good income, and have nice "things." But all this never worked; they never filled my emptiness because all I wanted was to be loved and accepted for who I really was.

At the same time, I went through a "religious" codependence. I had relied on others to tell me how I should know and relate to God. I remember being forced to go to services in all but my eleventh and twelfth years. At that time I went on my own. Looking back now, I know why I was so motivated; I was looking for healthy fathering, and I found it in a Sunday school teacher. Before that, I had found it in my step-uncle and later in a neighbor. (While both of these men were active alcoholics, they seemed to give me some love and acceptance that I consistently missed from my father.) But about age 17—when I began college—I stopped going to church.

What I learned over the next 30 years was that I had to find my own spirituality, not someone else's. That took a long time. I was an agnostic and an atheist for about 16 years—and unhappy. Then I found the Twelve Steps and began wrestling with them. And I began to meditate once or twice daily.

I remember a meditation teacher trying to explain what "cosmic consciousness" was; I didn't know what he meant, probably because I had never experienced it. I now know it's what we call serenity, fulfillment, inner peace. He said that many people began to realize cosmic consciousness after several years of meditating daily, often after about seven years. I began meditating in 1973 and realized the start of my own serenity in about 1979. At that time, I didn't need to "believe" in God because I knew God in my heart, and I have gotten to know the God of my understanding more deeply over the years.

But something was still missing. It was my child within—who I really was. I looked for him from 1977 to 1988. It was slow and painful. And letting go of my false self, my codependent self, was also painful because I was so accustomed to it. My codependent self had protected my child, while at the same time stifling him.

I had to learn who I really was and who I wasn't. I had to learn about my healthy human needs and about healthy boundaries to protect my child within. I learned about feelings, what they meant and how they could help, as well as what they didn't mean and how they couldn't help.

My healing began when I started using daily meditation at the age of 35 and the Twelve Steps two years later. Several other things have helped me, too, including individual and group psychotherapy, reading, and attending meetings of the Fellowship of Co-Dependents Anonymous. Each of these added an important dimension to my recovery.

I got involved in the Adult Child movement about the time it started in the early 1980s. Before that, I was a helping professional (without codependence recovery) and felt I should know how to help other people perfectly. I couldn't do it. So I tried to control them and anyone else who was involved with them. I manipulated and denied a lot of my pain. I was frustrated with my job teaching at a medical school, where all of what I'd learned in recovery was subtly rejected by a majority of my colleagues. After over 12 years of attempting to control and fix two systemically codependent medical schools, I gave up. This was probably my bottom.

It turned out that private practice as a helping professional was so much better for me that I thrived in it. At that time, I went to some of the first CoDA meetings in existence and found a lot of psychological and spiritual nourishment there.

As I continued to heal, doing all of the above and with the help of my work in CoDA, I found out how powerless I was as I tried to control or to fix my "family-of-origin." I'm still learning how my father mistreated me from the time I first came into this world. Even now, when I try to express myself strongly or creatively around him, he still refutes, negates, invalidates, shames, or patronizes me. He's done that all my life to me and to others in my family, but bring in someone from outside the family, and he turns on his people-pleasing charm. So at the age of 52, I have an 82-year-old dad with whom I am still trying to communicate. I've learned not to expect much.

I am so grateful that the rest of my "family-of-origin" is in some kind of recovery, because we validate and support one another and have healthier relationships. And I didn't have to fix them; they did it on their own. My mother loves attending CoDA, and my sister and brother enjoy it, too, although they seldom go. Since we've been in recovery and attending meetings, I've seen a big difference in how we appreciate one another's company. My sister's first husband was a violent alcoholic and her second, a sex addict. My brother's two wives were both alcoholic.

While I choose to stay away from my father, I enjoy my relationship with my brother, sister, mother, and daughter, and I have a long term, fulfilling relationship with a woman. I also have a loving and nourishing relationship with my Higher Power. Life is a joy now as I continue to learn and grow. I owe most of this to my recovery and to the Fellowship of Co-Dependents Anonymous.

by Charlie W.

LISTEN TO THE WIND

The pain I felt was stronger and deeper than any I could remember before. My wife had just told me she was leaving me. I couldn't believe she would actually go. We had separated before, but we had always gotten back together. This time was clearly different. She was leaving for good.

I begged her to stay. I promised I would change. For real, this time, not like the broken promises I had made in the past. She was not to be dissuaded, however. She moved out by the end of the day.

During the next few days, I cried like I had never cried before. At work I couldn't concentrate. I held back my tears and pretended to be OK. When I came home and noticed that she was gone, I cried my eyes out. Sometimes, I just laid on the floor and sobbed into the rug. I thought I would surely die from the pain.

A few days after she left, I was crying and feeling great fear when I suddenly recalled that I had been in an orphanage as an infant. My parents told me about this long ago, but I had completely forgotten. They told me that my mother had had a "nervous breakdown" a few months after I was born, and she had had to go to a hospital for a long time. My father put me into an orphanage so that I'd be "taken care of" while my mother was gone. Suddenly, I was recalling sights and feelings I had while in that orphanage. These memories brought new floods of pain and tears.

In an effort to win my wife back, I started going to a CoDA meeting I had heard her mention. I thought I could change enough to make her want me again. I hoped I would learn how to deal with her and keep her happy. I never saw her at the meeting, but I kept going with the hope we would meet there someday.

The meetings seemed strange at first, but I soon began to realize that these people were like me, and some had experiences very similar to my own. I began to feel some relief by talking about my pain.

After a while, I asked a woman to whom I was attracted to sponsor me. She wisely declined and suggested I ask a man. I did, and he directed me to begin working the Twelve Steps.

The First Step seemed easy. I knew that I couldn't force my wife to come back and that I was absolutely miserable without her.

The Second Step seemed impossible, however, because I had trouble believing in a power greater than myself. I was raised to believe in a particular church's philosophy, but my parents seemed to be hypocrites and I had thrown God out the window when I went to a public high school.

One day a bookmark crossed my desk. It bore an "Indian Prayer" that began:

O Great Spirit

Whose voice I hear in the Wind

and Whose breath gives life to all the Earth,

Hear me

I am one of your children

I need your guidance and support.

As I read this prayer, my hair began to stand on end and I felt chills all over. All my life I had marveled at the wondrous complexity of nature. My most peaceful and rejuvenating experiences had occurred in the great outdoors. This prayer tapped into these experiences. I could say these words and believe them, I could really feel them. This was the breakthrough that enabled me to work the Second and Third Steps.

When facing the Fourth Step, I was driven by a desire to make amends to my wife so she would take me back. With help from my sponsor and others, I searched my relationship history for my misdeeds. I rushed through the Fifth through Eighth Steps within a few weeks so I could make amends to my wife and win her back.

But my wife didn't take me back. To my surprise, she said she was involved with another man and would never come back. I sank into a deep well of pain once again.

By this time, however, I had experienced enough relief by going to meetings that I kept going and kept talking about my feelings. Working the Third

Step on a daily basis, often many times a day, and the support I received from others in CoDA, helped me to let my wife go. We got divorced and agreed on a property settlement in a fairly peaceful fashion.

Afterwards, I learned how to live as a single person. It had been 15 years since I had lived as an unattached person; I was 17 at the time. I learned a lot about what I really needed and how to get it. Eventually, I didn't feel incomplete just because I was single. With this new perspective, I made a new and more comprehensive Fourth Step inventory.

Doing the Ninth Step amends based on my new inventory was much harder than before, but it was also very rewarding. I was afraid that if I went to department stores and paid for what I had stolen, I'd be thrown in jail. If I repaid an insurance company I had defrauded, I was sure I would lose my job as a result. And I was convinced that some of the persons whom I had mistreated in the past would verbally abuse me and use my admissions to damage my reputation. My sponsor urged me to have faith in the healing power of working the Steps, however, and I prayed for the willingness to continue. The willingness came, and my fears turned out to be, as usual, exaggerated.

Without realizing it, I believed that I'd always be happy after I made thorough amends. But of course, that didn't come true. While I certainly did feel more joy, I wasn't freed from the nagging self-doubt and criticisms that dominated my thoughts. As I began to hear these doubts and criticism in my head more consciously, I was dismayed that making thorough amends hadn't ended them.

That was when I realized I had learned the difference between guilt and shame. It dawned on me that what I was experiencing wasn't guilt, because I had made amends for everything I could recall doing. My inventory had been "searching and fearless." The facts were discovered and faced and thorough amends had been made. The doubts and criticism I heard inside, therefore, were not about my behavior. They were about me and my worth as a person. They were echoes of other people's voices from my past.

As I explored the connection between my feelings of shame and my upbringing as a child, I learned much about the reasons behind my adult behavior. I came to understand that the pain I felt at my separation from my wife was connected to the pain I felt as an infant, being abandoned to an orphanage. Healing the painful experiences of my childhood and replacing many negative and abusive messages I received as a child became important processes for me. Working the Steps brought me to this healing and the new life made possible by it.

Reading about child abuse and healthy parenting helped me find and begin healing my childhood scars. At first, it was my intellectual understanding of what happened to me that led me to my feelings. Later, I learned to identify and express my feelings. Lately I have begun to let the feelings come first. By acknowledging and experiencing the feelings, I am led to new understandings. I don't need to wait for the right book. I need only to let the feelings flow in a natural way. Those feelings bring the healing I need: gifts from my Higher Power.

The Steps have become a very important part of my life. Every morning, I refresh the truth of Steps One and Two in my life and say a Third and Seventh Step prayer. My Third Step prayer begins with the Indian Prayer I learned in my early recovery. Throughout the day, I try to listen for God's guidance. I often hear it, though I sometimes seem unable to follow through and act on it. I make Tenth Step amends throughout the day as needed; but if I'm not ready I'll put it on a list for another day and pray for willingness. Every evening, I review my day. I pay special attention to recalling the guidance I received from my Higher Power during the day. I thank H.P. for the lessons learned and ask for support in incorporating the lessons into my life.

Service work is an especially important part of my life. It reminds me of where I've been and how I got to where I am. It reminds me to appreciate the journey. It helps me to be gentle with myself.

My relationships have changed dramatically.

My father lives near me and depends on me to handle his bills, dispense his medicine and direct his housekeeper. Dad is elderly and ill and can't do these things for himself. Before recovery, I used to chastise him for his inabilities. I would badger and cajole him into taking more care of himself. I usually turned a deaf or scornful ear to his tales of woe. I even threatened to stop helping him when he wouldn't follow my advice.

Through recovery I am becoming able to accept him as he is. I'm learning to give what he truly needs, without resentment or neglect of my self. I can see his efforts to manipulate me, and I protect myself without abusing him. And when I lapse into old behaviors, I apologize. Most importantly, I have come to accept that he never will be the dashing, courageous, heroic and loving man I wanted him to be when I was a child. I have grieved a great deal. I still cry about it sometimes. It's no one's fault, and I am healing.

My mother is in a nursing home. She often blames me bitterly for having put her there. She forgets that she asked me to do it. I call her now and then. She claims to be a victim of the nursing home administration and other patients. She rejects the suggestions I make about how she can have an impact on her conditions, and I refuse unreasonable requests. As with my father, I have learned to let her make her own choices. I can let it be, knowing that it's not my job to save her or run her life. I support her in a healthy way.

I've married again. It's very different from my first marriage. There is much more communication of feelings, needs and wants. I express myself more clearly and I have a far greater understanding of what I really need and want from my wife. I treat my wife with far more respect and compassion, as I've learned to treat myself that way.

My wife recently had a minor medical emergency. I stood by her and listened to her feelings. I consoled her and helped her make choices. I held her and encouraged her. She later told me that she appreciated how I had supported her. She said that she never doubted I would be there for her. I cried at hearing this. I have changed a great deal since my first wife left three years ago.

I have a new sponsor now. I have new needs that my previous sponsor couldn't help me with. And I know that the next three years will bring more changes. Most importantly, I know and can feel in my heart that I'm being guided and nurtured every step of the way. I'll never be truly alone, no matter who is or isn't with me. My Higher Power will never abandon me. H.P. never has. I've been hearing his voice in the wind all my life.

by Wes M.

FINALLY STOPPED THE ABUSE

The family had all gathered at the funeral home. We had come to pay our last respects to the man who had died only a few days before. It was a cold December evening. The next day, this man would be buried, and we each would go on and continue with our lives.

The person in the casket looked peaceful. He looked as if he were in a deep sleep. I had to pinch myself to keep all of this in perspective. That man would never wake up. He had gone from this earth, and from this point forward all I would have are memories of this man.

Standing there, looking at him, no one would ever know or even suspect all the abuses, conflicts and turmoil that were such a large part of this man's life. I couldn't be with him when friends and other relatives came to pay their last respects. I knew I would lose my composure, and being the recovering codependent I am, I couldn't let anyone see me cry.

The "don't cry rule" had long been established in our family. Heaven help any man who dared break it.

They left, thank heavens, and then it was my turn. Finally the tears just rolled down my cheeks. I was sobbing out of control; thank God no one but my closest sisters were there to see this. I cried for the loss of a life we could have had together, and I cried for the life the two of us could never share. This man was my father.

Two weeks prior, God was good to the both of us. For the first time in his life, my Dad knew I loved him. I always have loved him. This message—the message of unconditional love—is the greatest gift an abused person can share with the abuser. It is a gift which says, "I love you as you are. I forgive everything which has ever happened to me."

In some rare cases, this gift of unconditional love can take a lifetime to realize. In far too many other cases, this gift never gets a chance to be presented.

God had truly smiled on the both of us with that most important gift. *"Daddy, I love you and I always have loved you,"* was finally given by my "little child" to my dad's "little child." Now the abuse could finally stop for both of us.

My dad is at peace and so am I.

But, it wasn't always this way, and here is where my story begins.

My name is Bob, and I am a gratefully recovering codependent. I am the oldest of six children. I am legally blind; however, this hasn't stopped me from working in a professional career and having a family of my own.

Before I go any further, let me say that I feel my parents did the best they could. They made many mistakes which took the form of continuing abuses. They were also quite loving. My recovery from codependence is as much a part of my parents' love for me, as it is acknowledging their abuses of me.

The truth is, I love both of my parents. They tried as best they could to provide me with a good life. For the most part, I think they did.

To start, I must state that my parents were hardy, "pioneering" people. My mother told the story that she and Dad spent part of their honeymoon putting the cabin they were living in on house jacks. At that time, their plans were to build the house of their dreams where this little cabin was now standing.

My mother was an electronic engineer, and my father was a printer. I often marvel at my Mom's accomplishments. She entered the field of electronic engineering during the mid-1940s. It was no small task for a woman to become anything other than that of the expected traditional homemaker during that time. My mother had entered "a man's world" and had done so successfully.

For the first few months of their marriage, everything was going according to plan; they were building their dream house and, then, I was born. To accomplish the goal of building the house, both my parents had to work. This meant they had to place me into a "day care" setting. One day, the day care owner discovered I could not see. At this point, my parents' lives changed dramatically.

I was small, then, and certainly unable to care for myself. I can only reveal here what my parents have told me. I can also add some additional knowledge on my parents' feelings about my blindness from an article on the front page of the Dayton, Ohio newspaper. My parents reacted to the situation as most parents would—first with shock and disbelief, then, with a plan of action.

I have always wondered how they each came to grips with the fact their firstborn son was blind. I guess the answer to the question really doesn't matter; what really matters is that they acted at the time to give me the best life they could. In reality, I suppose, that's what being a parent is all about. This is how I feel about my own children.

In the newspaper article, my mother spoke of the immense fear she and my father had about my future. They spoke of the callousness of some well-meaning professionals when they advised my parents to pack me off to an institution. My parents had the presence of mind to see beyond this advice and follow their hearts.

In all honesty, I believe I wouldn't be sharing this story with you if my parents had sent me off to Ohio State School for the Blind. My parents did what they had to do. Through their efforts and those of a skilled surgeon, I managed to get the limited vision I now have.

Life was not finished dealing its lethal blows to my family. In succession, my next younger sister was hearing impaired; the sister next to her almost died of spinal meningitis. And if these catastrophes weren't enough, a devastating blow occurred when my mother was burned seriously with radiation from radio tubes which exploded in her work area.

The result of all of this tragedy is predictable. Each family member became extremely codependent and dysfunctional. My father did what he did best, which was to financially provide for his young family. Meanwhile, the extreme dysfunction in our family took its tragic toll. We children lost a father and gained a "robot." Dad did what he had to do for us all in order to survive. Beyond that basic skill, which was compounded by our various afflictions, he couldn't do anything more. This "forced survival" brought with it the extreme abuse we all suffered.

To be sure, my father was the perpetrator of immense physical abuse on us children. However, I believe it fair to say he was only responding to the massive abuses hurled upon him at that time. I remember a time in my younger life when my father took on the role of being "my Daddy." I remember going to church with him and the way he tried to teach me about loving Jesus, who is my Higher Power.

I also remember our first discussion of sex. Both my parents sat me down and talked to me about the issues of sex. Dad said everything God created is beautiful. He spoke about the sexual relationship between a husband and wife as being loving and beautiful. This is the approach I want to take with my young son.

My parents spoke openly about racial issues. Dad made it clear he would not tolerate the term "nigger" to be used by any of his children. My parents taught us respect for everyone. Everyone was equal in their eyes.

Then something happened. My parents changed. The loving Daddy became the abusive father, and my mother suddenly was not available for us children. There was no warning to any of us about this change. It seemed to happen overnight.

I need to be clear here. Dad did not suddenly become an abusive parent. Before the noticeable change, there were times in my life when my father was extremely abusive. However, I am saying these times were infrequent compared to future abusive episodes.

For sure, there was abuse. I remember when I was about three years old, my father beat me with his belt. This was the first of many such beatings. The issue which triggered this first abuse was as follows: I had given a model railroad car to my best friend. That's it, nothing more. I still can't comprehend how a grown man could beat a little boy over a little issue as giving a toy away. There was another time I apparently misbehaved. My father came home from work and put me in the car. I was given to understand from the beginning of the ride that he was taking me to an orphanage. I was scared, and we talked about what would happen to me there. We finally arrived. My father stopped the car. He made me get out of the car and walk up the hill to the big wire fence ahead. He told me to look into the yard beyond the fence. I had to press my nose up to the wire fence and look in. I was scared. I didn't know what to do. Then he told me to come back to the car. I looked down the hill. That car was so small. My father told me that an orphanage is a place where bad boys and girls go. If I didn't start to behave, he would put me there.

I am aware that parents disciplined children in

these days with the current knowledge available to them. I am hard pressed to understand how *any parent* could openly threaten his child with the chance of abandonment if he didn't behave.

School proved to be an interesting situation for me. In my early grades, my parents had to transport me to a special "sight-saving" school. My day started around 5:30 each morning. Dad would have to drive me to school, because the school wasn't in our district. He had to be at work by 7:00 and that meant I would arrive at school at 6:30. I would sit inside the building for two hours until classes started at 8:30. I couldn't go to school in my district because the district wasn't equipped to teach a legally blind child.

My parents understood that this school was holding me back. They also understood that associating with blind people made me act like a blind person. They realized I would have to function in society as a normal individual who had a limiting condition rather than a blind man—limited totally by his lack of physical sight.

My mother did extensive research at the Aero Medical laboratory at Wright-Patterson Air Force Base. Through her unrelenting efforts, I could attend my regular school in the fourth grade. This was no small accomplishment. I wanted to be treated "normally" as much as my parents wanted that treatment for me.

Fourth grade was quite possibly the best grade of my life. I made friends rather easily and loved school. Ours was a small township school, and in those days, classes were small and all the children knew each other. However, with the massive expansion of activities at the air base in the late '50s and early '60s, all this was to change.

There was no way for any community to adequately prepare for the massive expansion taking place within its boundaries during this period of time. Wayne Township was no exception. The result was that our small classes boomed into larger classes almost overnight. The rural community of Wayne Township had instantly become (for want of better words) "a small city which was bursting at the seams." Somewhere in all of this, I managed to get lost in the shuffle.

I didn't fit in. It was harder to make and keep friends. My lifestyle was different from the lifestyles of the new kids coming into the community. The differences between me and the other children were noticeable during the earlier grades. However, as children, we all managed to cope rather well. But as we grew older and entered our teenage years, differences became unacceptable. I was definitely different. I had a disability. To some students, this meant that I was unacceptable.

The problem was I was becoming unacceptable to my parents, too. Nothing I did was "right." My father's abuses were becoming most frequent now. I also learned that I couldn't trust my father when he made a promise because he would always try to find a way to get out of keeping it.

Yet, in spite of all this, he understood some of my feelings.

I was a freshman in high school. Dad somehow

managed to learn of new advancements made in contact lenses. He managed to sense the immense humiliation I was undergoing because of the thick cataract lenses I had to wear. I recall him telling me that contact lenses may help the situation. I remember the day I got them. It hurt me to wear them, but I wasn't going to complain. I was 14 at the time, and even I knew that wearing contacts could help with the "ribbing" I was taking. The contact lenses would make me feel normal, I hoped.

I couldn't understand, then, that the problem wasn't mine. It belonged to those few students who were having their fun at my expense. This lesson would be learned many, many years later. But on this day, I would enjoy true liberation. From now on, I wouldn't have to wear those thick heavy glasses. I came home that afternoon and Mom had made my favorite pie, lemon meringue, to celebrate the occasion.

Beyond this, situations went from bad to worse. Having the contact lenses wouldn't stop the pain I would feel through the abuses from my father. The contacts wouldn't stop the pain I would feel as my mother just stood by and watched it all happen. The contact lenses wouldn't help me justify my need to communicate to my parents my love for them. I was hoping that if I was successful in doing this, the abuses would finally stop. There was nothing I could do to stop the abuses at home and from the few students at school.

Through all of this, God was good to me. During my high school days, God gave me the special friendships of three people who provided valuable lessons that would help me tremendously in later life. These people were three female students; Paula G., Kathy P., and Kathy L.

Now, before I share the good times I had during my high school days with you, let me first share with you an observation.

All of the ridicule and the trauma I had to face seemed to be at the hands of men and teenage boys. Rarely can I point to the time when a young girl or a young woman actually tried to harm me. I think my survival instincts have led me to believe that my life would be much safer if I shied away from men and boys and shared more of my life with girls and women.

One of these students was Paula G. I have admired her courage for these past 25 years. In high school, she came to me one day and told me that I had something of worth to share with people. Both of us took the same speech course. On a Saturday outing at a host high school, Paula told me, "Bob, you have fabulous extempt (extemporaneous) qualities and you really should develop them." As you can see, I have carried this message of encouragement for the better part of a lifetime. Paula was the only person in my class who took the time to tell me of one quality that I had to share. This compliment has always been important to me. In a life so consumed with continuing abuses and neglect, this bright spot shared by Paula gave me something of worth to hope for.

Life in high school was taking its toll. No matter how hard I tried, I couldn't keep up with the rigorous pace set by all my teachers. It was difficult for me to read. I have to say that the school tried as best it could. My guidance counselor got me large print textbooks, but the material in them was obsolete long before I ever started to read them.

There was a second bright spot in my life, then. A young lady named Kathy P. took it upon herself to start reading to me and tutoring me in high school. The idea of having a reader and tutor wasn't new. This idea had been around for many years, with very successful results. However, having a student read to me and tutor me, someone who was my peer, was a new idea. And during this time, Kathy never put me down. She gave me respect as a person, which until this time had been lacking in my life.

The idea that I would not be rejected for any reason was new to me. To be honest, I was afraid that at any time, Kathy would reject me as other students had done in the past. Much to her credit, she never did. Her acceptance of me for who I was carried me though many situations later in my life.

Then the third bright spot was Kathy L. She was my first love. She treated me with respect and dignity. These were feelings foreign to me prior to meeting her. This was a special time for me. Through loving Kathy, I learned I could give of myself. The feeling of giving to another human being felt good. I also learned I could share my life with Kathy and she could share hers with me. The idea of mutually sharing with one another felt good.

While I tell you of the good side of this relationship, I must also tell you of the addictive side. For me, my first love was addictive. I am speaking only for me, not for Kathy. This relationship provided me with a means of escape. With Kathy in my life, I could temporarily numb the pain of the extensive abuse I was suffering. This relationship also brought with it the intense feelings of shame for who I was, the family that was mine, and the life I was living at the time. I was in a constant state of fear. My fear told me if Kathy ever found out I was abused, or if she ever found out how bad my family really was, then the only option left for her would be to abandon me.

Along with the fear and the joy of this first love came the pain I felt when life dictated that we each had to move on. The pain of the breakup was awesome. I can't describe how badly I felt. I loved Kathy, and I didn't want to lose her. That was my unselfish thought, or so it seemed. Then, there was the selfish side of me. Loving Kathy was my "ticket out of hell." As long as the two of us had a relationship, the hope ran high for me that I could one day escape from the hell I was living in.

Fortunately, Kathy was much smarter than I was. I don't remember why we broke up, but I can thank her now for having the wisdom to see past the present situation and into her future. That future could never include me.

The loss of a first love is a traumatic time for anyone. This is a time when the need for a true friend becomes paramount in your life. Now, the parent of a teenager may have to become that friend to help the teen through the grief he is feeling. Sadly, this never happened for me.

My parents never had the time I needed for them to share with me and help me grieve this loss. Now that I look back on it, I was not permitted to grieve over it. No grownup ever told me that he or she understood how I was feeling at the time. No grownup ever took the time to just listen.

These issues help you see the basis for my life heading into adulthood. These were issues which I could never really deal with. Frankly, I doubt anyone knew how to deal with them back in the late '60s and '70s.

These unresolved issues of physical and mental abuse, the lack of trust of my parents and my overwhelming fear of abandonment by everyone were issues that propelled me in and out of relationships for the next 25 years. Something needed to be resolved, but at the time, I didn't know what it was.

Well, that is my story. Here I am, years later, reviewing the lessons I have learned. A very practical lesson I've learned is that I can stop the cycle of abuse which has plagued my family for generations. If I were asked to state the most important lesson in life for me, this would be the one.

Unlike my parents, I can promise my children a brighter future with the wisdom I've learned and with the love of my "Higher Power" (which, by the way, is Jesus Christ). I can deliver this promise. I can really give my children a brighter future.

Last, but not least, there are my children, Christopher and Jennifer. When there was no other reason, Chris and Jen provided the reason for me to seek recovery. My journey back through my childhood and my desire to face and conquer the fears and the abuses of my past, was inspired by my desire to provide a better life for these children. Chris and Jen will always hold a special place in my life for their contribution to it. Truly, these children are a precious gift from a loving Higher Power. I can say without question that Jesus has blessed me with two beautiful expressions of His love.

All of this has taught me to look at life as a precious gift. This certainly is in contrast to the way my parents viewed life and their children. My parents viewed us as "property." That doesn't leave a good feeling in the heart and the soul of a child. I view my children as precious gifts. I feel I love my children in much the same way I feel Jesus loves me.

It has taken much time, love and patience for my family and me to get to the place we are. I am at a good point in my recovery, yet, there is much more recovery work I must do to arrive at the point I need to be for a normal, healthy and happy life.

Through CoDA, and the love of Jesus and all the people He has put into my life, this is only the beginning. The best is yet to come!

by Bob H.

KEN'S STORY

Mary called me at work and said she couldn't take the raging and other problems in our marriage. She was leaving. The panic, pain, shame and rage I felt were so great that I immediately left work and went to a hotel. In great pain and fear of abandonment, I thought, "Something must be fundamentally wrong with me." I'm not able to have relationships, a home, a family or a marriage like other people. I'd tried so many times to be a loving man. It was my fourth marriage; I was failing once again. I hurt more than I had ever hurt in my life. I raged; I cried. Finally, in despair, I considered committing suicide, the only way to end the painful, burning emptiness inside.

"I don't want to die, but I don't want to live in this kind of pain anymore. I'm 37; I've failed at trying to make love and marriage work since I was 17. I'm nine years sober in AA. I've been a therapist in the recovery field almost nine years. I am knowledgeable about addictions, codependence, family systems and recovery. I supervise a clinical staff of 20 people in a residential program for addictions treatment. Why the hell can't I live in peace with another person? I must be really defective." I raged and cried more.

For two days I was in that room. I finally decided to divorce Mary, to give up my son to his mother and to move where no one knew me. The pain, shame and fear subsided somewhat, and I finally fell asleep for the first time. When I awoke, I decided to see our marriage therapist. I was certain she must have talked Mary into leaving. I would tell her what I thought of her and Mary and about my decision to divorce and move away.

The therapist had supported Mary's decision for a temporary separation because we were so engulfed and obsessed with one another. She suggested I begin recovery from codependence. If Mary was also willing, we might be able to save our marriage. Our therapist suggested that if we wanted to make our marriage work, we would have to commit to do whatever was necessary, individually and together, to make our marriage healthy, mature, loving and safe. We both agreed.

For the first time, I began to feel real hope that it was possible to have a loving marriage that held within it a healthy degree of trust, respect, joy and serenity—one in which fighting wasn't the norm, and fear, anger and shame weren't constants. My relief was overwhelming. I had finally hit bottom and was ready for change. I had been clean and sober for almost nine years, but I still used passive and aggressive rage and sex addiction to medicate the overwhelming feelings of my codependence. I had to begin recovery from these problems with the help of the Twelve Steps, sponsors, friends and our therapist. Otherwise, they would have hindered and blocked my codependence recovery. I began the work of dealing with these issues and soon began to work on my codependence as well. I began to work the Steps with our therapist as there was no Twelve Step program that addressed codependence.

My codependence First Step covered relationships with family members, friends, mates, children, myself and other significant people. It took about nine months to complete. I began to see how codependence developed in me, and how friendships, family and work relationships and my marriages had progressively become unmanageable and been destroyed.

My codependence began when I was born. My father had been a good man; but, consumed by his alcoholism, had become a raging, violent, sexually addicted drunk. He died from alcoholism at 42— just 15 months after my birth. I don't remember him at all. My mother was a caring woman who suffered from a severe eating disorder. She passed away at 72, weighing over 340 pounds. She was addicted to prescription drugs and passive fantasy sex addiction. She was nurturing, but more often smothering, angry, or unavailable.

After raising two daughters, my mother desperately hoped that having a son would make my father quit drinking, bond with me, be her husband and help raise our family. I was to be the hero and savior of her marriage. When my father died, I became the surrogate spouse and scapegoat for my mother. I had little male influence to learn from and was treated like the baby of the family by both my mother and older sisters. My mother alternated between spoiling me, raging at me or threatening to send me away.

She desperately needed to maintain a social image of togetherness, warmth and lovingness which hid our many family wounds and secrets.

The only feelings allowed in our family were happiness and, occasionally, fear or pain. I learned from my mother that rage was the way to express not only my own feelings, but my family's as well. I acted out the anger for all my family members. As I moved into young adolescence, the scapegoat role continued. I became the family's designated emotional problem. Throughout school, in the neighborhood and social groups, I didn't fit in. I was most often an outsider, a loner, and my ideas were often shamed as being dumb or stupid. I had little self-esteem and was overweight by 20 to 40 pounds until I was 13. I was teased a great deal and not included in groups and activities. Neither my mother nor my family encouraged me to participate in sports.

To gain attention, I would clown, act out or rage. I lied to the kids, started fights or isolated. I was gullible and used a lot by friends. I felt lonely, ashamed, scared and angry most of the time. Usually no one knew. Due to my lying, acting out, fighting and thefts, I was thrown out of grade school at eight years old. I was sent off to military school. My mother remarried at that time. My stepfather, a bartender, was rarely home and showed little interest in me. Four years later, he, too, died from alcoholism.

By this time I had given up believing in myself. Life was not safe or fair. In order to survive, I abandoned the little boy in me, named Tim, who carried my hopes and dreams. I became very angry, fearful, guarded, controlling and rageful. I remained in military school for six years, except for a brief attempt at public junior high school. I was asked to leave for fighting and for scaring a girl by asking her to be my girlfriend. No one explained what I had done wrong. They simply sent me back to military school where I was periodically physically and sexually abused. I was also verbally and emotionally shamed, often in the name of discipline. My scapegoat role continued.

I was labeled gay, but I was simply confused with no one to help me understand my developing sexuality. I was asked to leave school for fighting, smoking and being sexually inappropriate with another student. I felt both relieved and terrified. I was sent to a school for court-ordered and emotionally disturbed kids where I was thrown out after a year for violently attacking a gay student who sexually approached me. I was sent to a minimum/maximum security school in Texas. At both schools I was abused and neglected. I was abandoned for up to four or five days at a time, in total isolation. In Texas, I was befriended by a psychologist who seemed genuinely interested in me. With his help, I developed enough self-esteem to return home and complete my senior year in public high school.

I had changed, but my mother had not. I soon returned to my roles of surrogate spouse, scapegoat and family problem. My small degree of confidence and self-esteem were soon replaced by my old, familiar behaviors to cope with the pain, loneliness, fear and shame. At school, once again I was an outsider and a loner. My girlfriend from Texas came to Santa Monica while I completed my senior year. When she became pregnant, we were married, with much shame, by both families pressuring us not to marry and to abort the baby. We moved to Phoenix. I was an "adult." I was married, expecting a child and living with my wife on our own. Marriage meant freedom—a way out of the insanity at home.

In truth, I was in as great a prison as could be. I was 17 and a victim of emotional/physical/sexual abuse, spiritual neglect, enmeshment with my mother and severe abandonment. I was an alcoholic, drug addict, rager, smoker, sex addict and codependent. I had little emotional communication or parenting skills or boundaries. I was a high school dropout, and I had no idea how to fulfill my needs or those of others. But, I was ready for marriage, fatherhood and life's challenges.

My first marriage lasted almost six years; my second marriage lasted four. Though I loved and wanted each of my sons, both marriages began through unplanned pregnancies. In my eyes, I would be the hero and savior once again. I would create a home and family and finally, I would belong. However, in both marriages I became what I had been trained to be since childhood—first the hero and savior, then the problem, the bad guy.

Throughout these marriages, I lived all over the Southwest and West Coast, always looking for a new start. I moved from job to job, bought and sold drugs, raced cars, tried to be a biker, had a psychotic break due to L.S.D., created and failed three businesses, obtained a G.E.D., quit college, attempted numerous career changes, wore my hair long, then short and tried to become various personalities with completely different lifestyles. I was always running away from myself to something else. Though often unintentional, I used, harmed and hurt many people in the process. Both marriages were consumed by my severe drinking, drug abuse, sexual affairs and irresponsibility. My raging and violence progressed. The deep pain, shame, fear and loneliness of my codependence were buried under it all.

I was afraid of abandonment, of being wrong and of being judged and criticized. I hated myself and how I felt "less than" others. I covered up my feelings with alcohol, drugs, sex and anger. When these failed, I pursued fantasies about the next job or the next sexual conquest. The things I feared most eventually became real. My body and spirit were slowly dying from the alcoholism and drugs. In my delusion, I thought I was just like everyone else.

My second wife left me after I violently attacked her during an alcoholic blackout. At 28, I went to AA, not to get sober, but to look good long enough so that my wife and my son would come back. A physician told me that had I not stopped drinking, I probably wouldn't have lived to be 29. Even though I had never known my father, I was living out his life pattern, progressing even more rapidly in my degeneration than he had. I became committed to working my AA recovery for myself. I also began therapy with a genuinely caring man. It was the first time in my life that I could recall anyone asking what

I thought, how I felt, what I needed or wanted. I was shocked. I had no idea how to respond to his questions. In therapy, I began to develop a relationship with myself by renewing my relationship with Tim, my child-self. I didn't mention this to anyone; this kind of thing wasn't generally accepted in recovery circles.

I returned to college to complete a degree in counseling. I was a recovering rager; my family was primarily women, and I was raised by therapists at the schools I attended. It comes as no surprise that I chose my first counseling work to be in a battered women's treatment facility. With the help of AA, my therapist, and recovery and professional friends, I began developing a more stable life in recovery—that is, unless I began an intimate relationship. I gained custody of my oldest son (due to difficulties his mother was having), and was able to be much more available for him. Yet, with few healthy role models from my past, my parenting skills left much to be desired.

Treatment and recovery from codependence did not exist then, yet it was the source of my deepest sorrow and greatest compulsion. I was developing enough self-esteem to look good on the outside, but I was still lonely, afraid, angry and ashamed on the inside. I spent a great deal of my first year clean and sober, trying in vain to get my wife and son to come home and fulfill my fantasy of home and family. They did not return, and we divorced at the end of that year.

About a year later I met the woman who would become my third wife. Out of constant fear of abandonment, I set out to become everything I thought she wanted. I abandoned many of my spiritual and philosophical beliefs to become a Christian. I became so involved in the church, I abandoned much of my AA program. Without the aid of alcohol, drugs and smoking to block out my feelings, I became more needy, fearful and dependent upon her. As a result, she would withdraw from me. Then I would rage and isolate. I felt threatened by her relationship with her children which took her away from me. I wanted her children to care for me as they cared for her and their father. I couldn't see how unrealistic my expectations were and how driven I was by my codependent feelings. Naturally, I was closer to my own sons, but due to my obsession with my wife and my fear of loss, I was once again unavailable for them.

In time, I withdrew from the marriage but was still obsessed with the church. I had a brief affair with a prominent church member and shared my feelings of guilt with the church pastors. As a result, I was no longer acceptable to teach in the church. I was now an outsider at home, church, and, as I believed, in AA, as well. Later I came to understand that the affair was my way of trying to get back at my wife and God for the way my life was going again. As I became more rageful and withdrawn, my wife separated from me. The marriage lasted less than three years. I pulled away from the church, moved to San Francisco to develop a treatment program, and re-established a strong AA program. My oldest son stayed in Phoenix with his mother.

During the divorce, on a visit to Phoenix, I met and began a relationship with Mary, my wife today.

It was instant love. More terrified of abandonment than ever, I was determined to make this relationship work, even if it killed me. It almost did. Soon after we met, Mary moved with her children to San Francisco.

We immediately set out to fulfill our old, familiar fantasies of a happy home, family, and marriage. But very quickly, the honeymoon was over. Again, I began raging and isolating more than ever, fulfilling my lifetime roles as caretaker, bad guy and problem. This time, I was competing with Mary for the same roles, which made things worse for me. Without my roles, I knew no way to be part of a family or relationship. My fear of abandonment grew even worse. I saw Mary's relationships with her children as a threat to our closeness. I tried at times to sabotage these. I depended on her children to tell me I was a worthwhile parent, and when they wouldn't, I either punished them with anger or isolated from them. I didn't know how to just be their friend.

The treatment center closed for financial reasons, and I was unable to find work in San Francisco. We returned to Phoenix to live with Mary's parents. Our children were living with their other parents. As I was unable to find work in my field in Phoenix, we lived on Mary's parents' support, my unemployment checks, and Mary's minimum salary. My family declined to provide any financial support for us, which felt like major abandonment to me. I was broke, couldn't get a job and saw myself as a failure. My self-esteem was at an all-time low, and I felt crazy most of the time.

We tried a brief geographic move to Prescott, but I could find no lasting work there. My neediness, fear of abandonment, declining self-esteem, isolation and rage were rapidly escalating. Our children came to live with us. My parenting skills, mostly developed in military school, were about control, perfectionism and "rightness." Our children were afraid of my unpredictability. They never knew how I would react to them.

At this time, Mary and I both determined that God would honor our relationship if we were married. However, marriage only made things worse for me. Now there was no escape from the insane drug Mary was to me in my codependence. A new job for me at a treatment center in Wickenburg brought us back to Phoenix. The job temporarily helped restore a sense of self-esteem, but the progressive insanity quickly returned. Soon after I began working, Mary's women's group therapist referred her to individual therapy. I am truly grateful, as my codependence recovery began with that referral.

Mary began her own therapy. The therapist suggested I join Mary for a few sessions. I agreed, thinking I would go to support Mary. My delusions soon began to crumble. It was only a short time later that I found myself in that hotel room, raging once again. Only this time, I wasn't raging at others or passive-aggressively dumping on others with a smile. I was turning the rage inward, considering suicide.

As I read my First Step over and over, I wondered how I, a therapist, was never able to see these things within myself. I felt scared about how deluded I was and how much denial I had been in most of my life.

I felt overwhelming sadness about the power of codependence and the great losses throughout my life.

I saw so clearly the abuses, neglect and profound abandonment by my father, mother and many other significant people from my childhood. I saw the shaming lies I was taught to believe about myself, like "I'm wrong," "I'm a problem," "I'm not good enough," "I'll never amount to much," and "I don't deserve good things." I saw that I was trained as a child through words, feelings, attitudes, behaviors and reinforcements to become a hero, savior, scapegoat, problem and caretaker for others. These roles were my identity. I had lived them over and over again in every significant relationship I had experienced as an adult.

The progressive powerlessness and utter unmanageability of my life and relationships were now so clear. The more I saw, the more hurt and angrier I became. I was a victim; I wanted to blame everyone else. Our therapist helped me to acknowledge my wounds, to release my past and to stop blaming. She helped me to express my true feelings rather than to rage. I will always be grateful for her guidance and care. I was relieved to discover I wasn't bad or defective and that Tim was not a bad kid. I could change and become a loving man. I could begin by parenting myself and teaching Tim that he was a loving creation of God. I was relieved to realize that my family members and others from my past were not bad people either. They, just like me, had done the best they could with the abilities they had. I was also grateful to acknowledge the many strengths and gifts they had given me. I no longer blamed anyone. And as God continues to reveal more insights to help me understand my past and present, I continue to work my First Step daily.

I began to work on my Second and Third Steps. I did believe God could restore me to sanity and I was willing to turn my life and will, my past, my childhood, Mary, our children and my recovery over to the care of God. However, would God be willing? In my shame, I believed that I had hurt too many people and done too many wrongs to deserve the gifts of loving relationships and God's healing. This belief had always stood between me and my relationship with God. I needed to forgive myself before God could significantly heal my codependence. If not, I would continue to sabotage my healing through self-inflicted punishments. My therapist suggested I include God and myself in my Fourth Step work and trust that God's healing would come in time. I wrote down all the codependent behaviors I could remember from all my important relationships. It took time, not only to remember, but to work through my shame, guilt and sadness for my wrongs.

In my marriages and many close relationships, I had abandoned myself and tried to become what I thought "they" wanted, often forcing them to become what I wanted. Love was usually buried under the obsessions and entanglements. I would create a fantasy, make it happen, then slide into my codependent childhood roles. The closer I became with someone, the more frightened I was to be honest about my feelings. Afraid of their shaming judgments and possible abandonment, I denied myself and my feelings. As a result, my fears increased.

I also tried to control and change my mates, children and friends so these feelings, fears and pain would go away. I tried to manipulate others to make me feel worthwhile, special or important. These were responsibilities that no others should or could fulfill, although I was unable to fulfill them for myself. I expected others to treat me differently than people in the past had, but how could they? Not only hadn't I changed, but it wasn't their job. With God's help, it was my job. It was extremely painful and humbling to review these specific examples.

I was determined not to punish myself. There was Tim, my inner child. I had hated this little boy and punished him long enough. I was finally ready to love Tim and trust that God would heal me.

Though afraid of her judgment, I asked our therapist to hear my Fifth Step. I was learning to trust her, and she was teaching me to trust myself, Mary and others. She was compassionate and could accept me as I was, unafraid to challenge me head-on when I wanted to react. I know God worked through her and was present during my Fifth Step. An incredible burden was removed from my life. There was something spiritual, magical and healing about sharing my Fifth Step. When finished, though emotionally drained, I had a sense of hope about my ability to be a loving man with my wife, children, and others.

The healthy shame, guilt, humility and hope from my Fourth and Fifth Steps pushed me through my

Sixth and Seventh Steps. I had been working on some of my codependent character defects in therapy, but now I was ready to change whatever I needed to. I saw that my codependent defects of character were only a small part of me. I was and always had been so much more, but my shame and fear had not allowed me to see much of God's creation in me. By humbly asking God to remove my shortcomings, I committed to work on both my codependent habits and the emotional power of my history and to seek the help of God and others whenever I was unable to do it for myself. I was developing faith and trust in myself, and my goal became lifelong progress.

My Fourth Step inventory helped me prepare my Eighth Step list. The second part was more difficult. I wanted others to like me. If I told them of my wrongs and made amends, they might judge, hate, shame or abandon me. My codependence still had a hold on me in many ways. With the help of my therapist and recovery friends, I began to see that my Eighth and Ninth Steps had to be done for me alone. I needed to approach this as a responsible self-parent, not as a needy child. I needed to be present for me and my child-self with boundaries, no matter how others thought, felt or reacted. I had to let go of my deep desire for the approval of others. I had to accept that God approved of me as I was and that I was on the right track. In spite of Tim's fear, I had to approach this Step with courage and trust that the highest good would come from it all. Here I was facing the core issues of my codependence. Slowly, the willingness became stronger as Tim's trust in God and in me as a self-parent grew.

I began work on my Ninth Step. Some of my amends experiences were wonderful; some were scary and painful. Some—especially those I wrote—were not acknowledged. I realized I'd have to work hard to change myself so that similar problems didn't reoccur. But I was growing in strength and willing to do just that. As of this writing, I still have some amends to make. Timing, difficulties beyond my control and in some cases, my own growth, have been at play, but these amends will be made when opportunities present themselves and as I create them.

My Tenth Step is an ongoing, daily experience. With time, healing and growth, it became easier to be accountable for my wrongdoings. The fear and shame from my past began to lose its power which helped me to be more present for myself and others. At times, I saw the same behaviors repeat. These were behaviors I felt powerless over, and I had to formally work the Steps on them. The Tenth Step has kept me on my toes. In my codependence Step work, I began to see that in spite of my ignorance, God had carried me and others through so much in my life. My relationship with God became even more important to me, helping me gain an ever growing, truer sense of who I am and the power to be a loving man. Daily prayer and meditation became direct ways of continuing to develop that relationship. The simplicity of Step Eleven amazed me. At times my meditations, especially my prayers, became crowded with pleas for knowledge of God's will for Mary, my kids, finances, business situations, CoDA concerns and other outcomes and the power to change them.

I was once again praying in fear, trying to control outcomes rather than accepting God's will and presence in my life. A friend once said, "If I can control or manipulate God through my prayers, I better get another God as soon as possible." This Step has pushed my faith in God to greater heights and helped me align more closely with the power to carry out what I believe God's will and love to be.

Like Steps Ten and Eleven, Step Twelve became a daily practice. Each of these Steps had brought about profound spiritual awakenings which continue to be ongoing for me. In my enthusiasm about these and my desire to carry the message of hope and recovery, I tried to force-feed them to my children, family and friends. I tried to get them to talk about their histories, their feelings and their past with me. In doing so, I began to drive some of them away. I quickly learned that they simply wanted me to love and accept them as they were.

I learned to carry the message through the examples of my codependence recovery and God's healings within me. These attract those who want what God has given me. I also learned that if I want to keep what God has given me, I must be willing to give it away.

Today, I continue Step Twelve mostly through service work in CoDA and by being available to others. God moved through many others to me; my job is to pass it on. And I must stay vigilant for those times when my codependence is wreaking havoc in my life. Step Twelve always brings me back to Step One and that person or situation I feel powerless over or which is unmanageable to me.

As I completed these Steps for recovery from codependence, I began to believe for the first time that life was something I could cherish. But, as our therapist had pointed out, individual healing was only the beginning. With her help, Mary and I learned how to communicate in new ways that minimized defensiveness, discounting and abusiveness. We learned to negotiate our needs and wants, to compromise, to stay present with each other and to control our raging. We discovered the "escape hatches" in our marriage and agreed never to use them or the words "divorce" or "separation" as threats. Trust became easier. Mary became my dearest and closest friend. Together, we were like two children maturing at high speed in a marriage that seemed brand new.

We recognized the need to work the Steps on our marriage. This work helped clear the past and build a spiritual foundation for our future. After two years, we felt a strong need for more support than a therapy session could provide. The idea for a Twelve Step support group for recovering codependents emerged. We saw it as a way to meet our needs and to carry the message to others. We talked with other recovery friends who were working on codependence recovery as well; their responses were positive. Together, we held the first CoDA meeting. As I shared my codependence story that first night and listened to others share, it was as if God had opened the flood gates and finally, there was a place to pour out and share our codependent and recovery experiences. I went home with an overwhelming gratitude to God for the great relief I felt in now having others to share recovery with. From that first meeting, CoDA grew at a phenomenal rate nationally and even internationally. I was elected chairperson of the first Board of Trustees and CoDA held its first National Conference just prior to CoDA's first anniversary. It was an incredible experience to see and feel the presence and loving power of God throughout that conference and so many since.

Service work provided me with a mirror of many areas for me to continue my recovery in relationships with others—especially in the areas of acceptance and letting go of approval and outcomes. I gained a deep respect for the spiritual wisdom of the Twelve Traditions as they guided me through my service work. I learned I was never alone. I had never known how full and rich my life could be, nor how grateful I could be to so many for their love and care.

I am finally at home in my heart, and am a part of and at home in my family. One at a time, I have worked to let go of our children. I'm grateful that "God has no grandchildren" and for the relief and joy I feel from working to see our children as equals. Mary continues to teach me much about myself and loving.

Her presence, thoughtfulness and care are a great source of love for me. Our child-selves delight in each other's company. We continue to honor our commitments to each other, and our friendship grows stronger every day. Life has become a very precious gift.

The number twelve has always held spiritual significance for me. Twelve years ago, Mary and I saw the movie "Ghandi" and were deeply moved and began then to talk about how spiritually important it seemed to somehow make a positive difference in the quality of life on earth. We had no idea this was God's beginning inspiration for what would become CoDA four years later. We also had no idea of the work that we both, separately and together, would have to do to make a positive difference in our own lives first.

Now, twelve years later, the writing of this story marks the completion of a significant milestone in my life. Just as we come full circle in completing the Twelve Steps and again in applying the Twelve Traditions, Mary and I have come full circle in these twelve years. We had the opportunity to once again watch "Ghandi" during the writing of this story. Again we were moved to tears, but with a much greater understanding of that quiet man's spiritual strength, humility and empowerment. This time it was with a deep appreciation for God's inspiration and creation of CoDA and an overwhelming gratitude for being part of that creation. My heart was overflowing with emotion for prayers asked so long ago and answered throughout these twelve years.

"Gratitude" seems somewhat a shallow word for what I feel for God's gift of CoDA, God's love, healing, goodness and my codependence recovery. Nor does it encompass my feelings for the precious gifts and love I've received from the CoDA Fellowship, especially when I was unable to love myself. But gratitude is the word that comes closest to describing the feelings of my heart for all that has been given to me. I look forward with anticipation and hope to the continuing magic, mysteries and miracles of recovery in CoDA.

By Ken R.

BILL'S STORY

I think my story starts at the age of about two years, which is longer ago than I care to remember. So I didn't—for a long time.

My history of abandonment was something I never really looked at. Abandonment to me was an unwanted child, left on a church doorstep or some stranger's front porch. But, the word didn't apply to me. My parents were good, upper middle-class folks. My sister and I were always fed well. We were dressed in the current children's fashions. We always lived in a well-heated, large house. We only had one car at a time, but that was because my father hated driving. All things taken into consideration, we seemed like a perfect family except for a couple of unseen factors. Perhaps "unnoticed" would be a better word— unnoticed by those on the outside of the family.

The fact of the matter is that both Mom and Dad drank—a whole lot! Even though the early part of my life extended through The Great Depression, which was made even more depressing to many people because of Prohibition, my mother and father always seemed to have cocktail parties and there was always liquor in the house. Dad told me once that they even made the proverbial "bathtub gin."

At the start of this story, I mentioned that my earliest memory was at the age of two. I was on the boardwalk in West Hampton, Long Island. I was looking for my parents who had left me with the cook/nursemaid. Somehow I had evaded her and gone on a search. I was in tears, wailing is more appropriate, because I couldn't find my mother and father. They were out on the beach at a party. I have the memory, but the details were supplied by my father years later at another cocktail party as an amusing anecdote of my baby years. I didn't laugh.

I contracted infantile paralysis, polio as it's now called, when I was six. I was bedridden for about six months. When I was first allowed to walk, I dragged my right leg slightly (still do when I'm very tired) and was put back to bed for another six weeks. It was during this time that I sensed a major change in my father's attitude toward me. I felt a withdrawal, a closing off of feelings in him. Today I think he must have been saying to himself that the son he had was no longer the son he wanted. In all likelihood, this boy in the bed would not be a star athlete, runner, football player or first baseman; he might possibly be a cripple! Whatever his thoughts were, our relationship changed after that. On the other hand, my mother was always at my beck and call, the beginning of an enmeshment that eventually became very dangerous.

I did not become a cripple physically. However, I did develop severe asthma. My parents tried every cure that was known in those days, including recovering every piece of furniture in our home with something called Egyptian cloth. They sought help from every quack with a promised cure for asthma, every "legitimate" allergist on the east coast. Finally they heeded our local general practitioner and decided to send me to Arizona, where the climate was said to alleviate allergies of all kinds.

And so I was sent to Tucson in 1936 to a boarding school. My mother came to Arizona with me and saw me settled in school, then returned East. The press of work and, I realize now, the expense, kept my father from coming with us. But, when my mother left, even had I understood, it would not have changed the fact that I was 10 years old and alone in a new, scary atmosphere with people I didn't know or trust. I still heard my dad's admonition to, "Be a good little soldier." At 10, most children are adaptable, and gradually I became accustomed to the new life that had been forced on me. Not surprisingly, from the time I arrived in Arizona, my asthma symptoms disappeared. I learned to ride a horse and play tennis and softball. It was a coed school, and eventually I developed crushes on girls. By my second year at the school, my grades had even begun to pick up.

In the next two years, a number of things happened that really began to set some of the patterns of my codependency. When I had realized that my father was not going to be there for me— either emotionally or physically—I transferred my feelings to my mother's youngest brother. David was nine years older than me and became my champion, teacher, protector and mentor. He did things with me for which my dad had neither time nor interest.

In the fall of my second year in Arizona, I received a letter from my mother telling me that David was dead. I'm not sure whether she told me in that letter that my uncle had committed suicide. He had married a beautiful girl who almost immediately started being unfaithful to him. My guess is that she married him for the money that my grandfather would bequeath to him. At any rate, David couldn't take the betrayal and took his life. I later learned that he, too, was an alcoholic; it ran in Mom's family.

I was devastated by the loss and couldn't understand it. I cried and isolated until one of the masters at the school took me under his wing. As I said earlier, kids are adaptable, and Bob J. replaced my uncle. He did the same things for me that David had. He listened to my hurts and my happiness, helped me with my studies, and was in my corner when I needed a man there. That next summer, I went home for the only time during my stay in Arizona. Returning to school in the fall, I couldn't find Bob. When I asked where he was, I was told that he had been killed in an auto accident during the summer.

I didn't cry as much that time, nor isolate as long. I simply followed my pattern and replaced Bob with another master at the school who did most of the things for me that Bob had—with one addition. That spring, when it became warm enough for us to swim, I was the last one into the boys' dressing room one day, and Mr. W. was waiting for me. He had a large erection that he wanted me to "help him with." To this day I don't know how I got out of there, but I did. I made sure that I was never alone with him for the rest of the year or the next. I was afraid to tell anyone what had happened. I thought that somehow it was my fault.

Today I know that my distrust of men in general and older men in particular became locked in that spring afternoon. I was 12 years old. Whatever childhood I had was over that day. There have been men throughout my life who've wanted to help or mentor me in healthy ways, but I rejected or undermined all those who offered aid out of the fear that they would either abandon or abuse me.

In 1939, I moved to another school. It was a working ranch and an excellent school. My grades went to hell that year, but I had a pretty good time. It was the start of my defiance of adult-made rules. We sneaked out for moonlight rides through the desert. I learned to smoke. I defied authority whenever I could get away with it and often when I couldn't, I just didn't seem to give a damn.

On the positive side, I participated in fall and spring roundups. The school had its own spring rodeo, and I won prizes for horsemanship and specialty riding (so much for being a cripple)! In other words, I did most of the things boys do in their early teens. I remember it as the best time of my early years. Those memories stayed with me for 25 years until I could get back to Arizona.

In the spring of 1940, I returned to Scarsdale. I was told that because of the war that was raging in Europe, I wouldn't be able to return to Arizona in the fall. To assuage the loss, I was allowed to go to Martha's Vineyard that summer with my older cousin, Arthur. That summer I learned that alcohol could work wonders on fear of strangers, girls, strange places, and home. That first drink my cousin gave me transformed the shy, frightened little boy into a man of the world! I got violently ill the first time I drank with Arthur and his friends, but I went back and did it the next night! I was on my way to becoming an alcoholic.

Readjusting to life in the "East" was not easy, but adaptability came into play again and I managed. Though Arizona was never far from my mind. I wasn't the greatest student to hit public school in my generation, not from lack of ability but from lack of interest. The drinking that I had begun the summer of my return was not really in evidence, except on occasion. I went through the ups and downs of high school romance. The pains and fears, the successes and rejections, were all there. My first high school love is still in my memory. I have been unwilling to let her go. It ended badly through my absolute need to be right, aided and abetted by more than a few drinks.

Anything I ever learned about male/female relationships came from friends and books. My parents studiously avoided telling me anything worthwhile. My mother did leave a book on "sexual knowledge" lying about for me to find. Dad didn't have anything to say on the subject. They did, however, manage to introduce me to the warm-blooded daughter of friends, thus passing my education on to a teenager with advanced degrees! I made a willing pupil. I suppose I should be grateful, but I'm not sure to whom.

The enmeshment with my mother had started with my early illness and was becoming stronger. My mother would often model her latest gown or lingerie for me. Whenever my father was unavailable, I became Mom's designated escort. It felt uncomfortable, but I wasn't sure why. People became used to seeing us together as a couple. I also became her confidant. There was fear, shame, anger, and arousal all mixed in these roles I was given. Through the recovery process, I have come to realize that I was being emotionally incested. At the time, it was terribly confusing.

In 1944, I was ready to go into the service, only to find that I couldn't pass any of the physicals. All my friends were in the war. I've been told by those who were in combat that I was very fortunate. Perhaps, but I don't think so. Those who were in that war came out with a maturity that I never managed to achieve. While they were overseas, I continued in school, including a postgraduate year to make up for my lack of enthusiasm in high school. My drinking had begun to take on more serious proportions by my senior year. I always had at least a beer handy. I graduated from the postgraduate prep school with honors, just to show I could do it, and went directly to one of the top Ivy League colleges. Since there was nothing to do in the New Hampshire hills on weekends, we drank a great deal. I didn't want to be there; I wanted to be at the University of Arizona. But Dad was footing the bills, so there I was. I managed to drink my way out of college by the middle of my sophomore year. I believe it was a massive peeve at my father for not letting me attend the school of my choice. I also believe, now, that it wouldn't have made any difference.

From college, I went to work at an advertising agency in New York, in the radio and television department. But, probably because of my father's influence, I was transferred to other departments as an executive trainee. I really liked the radio and TV business and resisted these changes as much as I could.

My mother and father's relationship had been degenerating steadily over the years. Their fights were getting louder and more physical. Tension in the house was almost unbearable. My sister and I had always been careful not to bring friends over when the fights were on; now we never did. During the summer of '49, a friend and I decided to take our vacation together on Nantucket. We took off for our vacation one Friday in July. My mother saw me off, making sure we had enough beer for the drive. She looked lovely that morning. That Sunday on the beach, I heard my name being paged on the loud speaker. As I went to take that call, I already knew what had happened. My mother had died that morning. A suicide.

I went home immediately with the help of some friends on Nantucket. I took care of most of the social amenities entailed in the funeral. My dad was almost incapacitated. My mother had left a note blaming him, and I did too. I also blamed myself. I couldn't cry, nor could I grieve for her. It was to be 38 years before I could grieve and put closure on her death. I stayed functionally drunk for the whole week.

When the funeral was over, I took leave from my job and went to stay with friends on my other refuge, Martha's Vineyard. For eight weeks, my friends enabled me to stay pleasantly smashed. My mother's family was also on the Vineyard at the time, and one of my cousins and I became very close. She was having a bad time with her boyfriend, and I had a convenient shoulder. We didn't become lovers, but it was a close call. Two years later, she committed suicide over an affair, and for a long time, I blamed myself for her death, too. That stay on the island was the beginning of my real dive into alcoholism.

By April of 1950, I was married. Gloria was someone I worked with and I used that as an excuse to leave the agency and go to work at one of the major networks as a producer/director. I feel that originally when we married both Gloria and I were escaping from the pain of intolerable family situations—not the best foundation for a marriage. I know now that Gloria really loved me deeply, but since I had no real love for myself, I didn't believe it then. In the meantime, my drinking had not improved, except in quantity.

By 1954, Gloria and I had three lovely daughters, and Gloria also had a petulant little boy—me! By 1956, our marriage had gotten to the point of no return, at least for me. My lack of self-esteem, my drinking and finally my turning to other women made Gloria and I strangers to each other. My guilt and shame had reached a point where I could not communicate at all with her. I could not hear her at all any more. ABC had had enough of me by 1960, and I was fired from the only place I felt at home. In '61, I hit my first terrifying alcoholic bottom. With the help of another of my mother's brothers I admitted myself to a sanitarium to quit drinking. I was not to have another drink for 15 years. I had no knowledge of AA, and went through those years with a kind of warped pride in my strength of character. I now realize I was on an extended dry drunk. I could not find work in my profession in New York, so in 1964, I returned to Arizona.

In 1965, two things happened. Gloria and I were divorced. She had stuck with me through the worst, but was unwilling to leave New York for the total uncertainty of me and Arizona. And, that same summer Dad died. From the time of my mother's death, his drinking had gotten more and more destructive. He was in and out of hospitals, either from injuring himself or to dry out from the alcohol. I tried to get back to New York in time to see him one last time, but I was too late. In the end he died— an unrecovered alcoholic. Another abandonment, and I could find no feelings about it.

I worked in a variety of jobs, mostly radio, during the next few years, always with a vague feeling of desperation. I really didn't know who I was or wanted to be. I married twice between 1965 and 1974, both times out of loneliness and the hope that the relationships would fill the vast emptiness in me. In 1976, in an effort to hold the last marriage together and to be able to communicate with my wife, I drank again. At first a little wine lubricated my inhibitions enough to tell her how I felt. We talked of ending our separation and doing the things happily married folks are supposed to do. The few glasses of wine quickly became a few bottles and then I was into the hard liquor, and before I knew it, I was back where I had been 15 years before. Then I was far beyond that. I wanted desperately to stop and couldn't. The terror of those last few months will always remind me of my powerlessness and unmanageability. It only took 11 months, but I was farther down than I had ever been. I was divorced again, I had no job and few prospects. In sheer terror I went to a local alcohol recovery unit.

It was January 1977. Fourteen days later, when I left, I knew I never had to drink again! I finally was doing it for myself. I had surrendered to a Higher Power who didn't want me to die a drunk. This time, I joined a Twelve Step program and worked at it. Things began to turn my way again. I got my job back. I felt comfortable with other people. For the next six years or so, I proceeded somewhat merrily down the road to recovery. But, the enjoyment started to flatten out. My depressions became deeper and longer. Relationships kept falling apart. Talking did no good. More meetings did no good. More reading did no good. Three years, twice a week, at a psychologist didn't help. By my ninth year in AA I felt that if this was all there was to life, I didn't want to be here. Drinking was not an option. Death was!

Fortunately, a friend caught me one day and said, "I have been watching you die for the past few months, Bill, and I won't lose another friend to codependency! Let's talk." Our talk that afternoon started me on the path to my real recovery. I cried for the first time since my mother died. We talked of things I had never mentioned before. We told each other some of our history, and suddenly I was no longer alone. Someone really did understand me.

In one short week at a family workshop, I began to understand that through many of my childhood events and my adult choices, I had become a codependent. I began to get my family history in order and find some answers to questions I had pondered my entire life. In the fall of 1986, some of my friends gathered to share their stories and histories at what turned out to be the first meeting of Co-Dependents Anonymous. (Our Fellowship became official the following February.)

In the ensuing years, my recovery has taken on new life and so have I. As time has passed, I have managed to deal with many of my losses and abandonments of the past. I have resolved my relationship with my father, which had never been better than adversarial. I finally realized that while he had to be held accountable for the misinformation he gave me, I had to accept responsibility for my reactions, which ranged from being surly to acting physically violent. I spent many years blaming my father for most of the "if onlys" in my life; that blame made it OK to fuel the anger and rage that had been my constant companions through the years.

I have put closure on my mother's suicide and the emotional incest she visited on me in the form of veiled suggestions and open invitations. The latter was hard to accept and has affected my relationships with women all of my life. I don't excuse her behavior, but now I understand it. Along with the understanding, has come forgiveness of them and myself.

Through all of the healing I have gained in these years, my Higher Power has been very much in evidence. Years ago I had abandoned Him/Her/Whatever through my guilt and shame over the things I had done, thought and felt. Today I know that even though I left my Higher Power, He never left me. Through the Twelve Steps of CoDA and my other program, I am beginning to feel the spirituality I didn't think existed. I have come to like myself, (admire is a little strong), most of the time. I have male friends whom I trust and I even have some trusted female friends. I think a lot of that trust has come from an increasing ability to trust myself.

In five short/long years, I have come from a point where, while drinking was not an option, dying definitely was, to the point where today living is the only option. I still have bad days, now and again, but they are just that—bad days. I realize there are no big deals! As a very dear friend of mine has said, "Tell the truth about yourself at all times and be present at all times, then your relationship with yourself and others will work." If I hadn't been in recovery from codependency, I might never have heard those words. I also know it ain't over 'til it's over!

by Bill S.

CODEPENDENCE MANIFESTED AS MULTIPLE ADDICTIONS

Codependence manifested itself in my life in the form of many addictions and self-destructive behaviors, and it nearly killed me. Because of my misunderstanding of what codependence is, it took me a long time to find my way to CoDA. Today I know that codependence is the root of all my addictions.

As a child, I was beaten, burned, molested, and humiliated by the two people I needed most, and whose job it was to protect and nurture me. I was taught by my mother that I was bad, and by my father that I was stupid. I learned to hate myself as a result of growing up in this toxic environment. I felt inadequate in every way.

I never thought of myself as an abused child until I got into recovery at the age of 27. I always felt there was something "different" about my family, but never thought much about it before recovery.

My mother held me down and burned me with matches at the age of five. It was her way of teaching me not to play with fire. I screamed and pleaded for mercy with every ounce of breath I had, but to no avail. I never experienced such terror and pain, either before or since, and from it I drew the following conclusions: A) I must be a very bad person to make her do something so horrible to me; B) It was useless to assert myself, so I rarely did after that; and C) I decided if my own mother could hurt me so badly, I'd never trust anyone ever again.

At a very young age I started finding ways to escape. I became a fantasy addict, and my first "drug" was television. It took me out of my painful life into safer, happier worlds. I was so caught up in my fantasy world, I couldn't function and found it hard to do my school work. If the lessons were difficult, I'd slip into my fantasy world. My report cards always contained comments from my teachers: Jack is very bright, but doesn't finish his work/doesn't try/doesn't pay attention/needs to learn discipline, etc. I spent the rest of my life trying to learn discipline. It never worked, and the more I failed, the more convinced I became that I was worthless. Consequently, I hated myself all the more.

I learned to survive in school by being class clown. When I look at pictures of myself from that time, I can plainly see from my pained expression that I was a sad, lonely, frightened little boy. I often ask myself, "Couldn't anyone see how badly I was hurting? Couldn't someone have done something to help me?"

The next development in my disease was food addiction. I found comfort in eating. It seemed to fill the emptiness inside me. I started eating compulsively around the time I was being incested. I started putting on weight, decided I was ugly, and therefore had one more reason to hate myself. Through the rest of my life, even at times when I was thin, the belief that I was ugly remained.

Next came sexual addiction. My parents had pornography stashed everywhere in our house. The pornography ranged from the topics of heterosexual sex, gay sex, rape, torture, child molestation, incest, and bestiality. Because it belonged to my parents, I assumed these things were all normal. When I reached puberty, discovered masturbation, and became curious about sex, I found answers to all my sexual questions in the pornography. At the age of 11, I read my first epic porno novel about rape, torture, and mutilation.

My fantasy addiction became fused with my sexuality, and I became a sexual fantasy addict. Obviously, I grew up with some very twisted ideas about love, sex, and women. For the next 15 years, the pursuit of sexual thrills took precedence over all else in my life.

Shortly after this, as a teenager, I became both alcohol and drug addicted. By taking chemicals, it was much easier to live in a fantasy world. In high school, I became one of the "burnouts," and for the first time in my life, I found a place where I belonged. I hung around with others who were looking to escape and trying to numb their pain. We took drugs, cut school, and got into trouble. Three of these people died in car crashes, two others were crippled, one committed suicide, and another had his face shot off during a drug deal.

There were a lot of missed opportunities in my life, especially in high school. Many times I wanted to get involved with some project or club, but never felt I fit in. I was always stopped by thinking those things were for good kids, smart kids, nice kids, other kids, not kids like me. I was talented in art, and even won first place in an art show, but never allowed myself to pursue it. I wrote poetry, but dreams of getting a book of poems published, like any other dreams I had, fell by the wayside. My teenage years went by in a blur. I dropped out of high school, and got my diploma several years later.

As an adult, I found myself out in the world with no goals or skills to cope. I could never hold a job for more than a few months, and several attempts at going to school were equally futile. I bounced around between my parents', grandparents', and friends' homes.

Besides my addictions, I also tried everything from meditation and various religions, to self-help groups and health food diets. I was also getting into relationship after relationship, always looking for someone to fill the hole inside me the same way I tried to fill it with food, drugs and sex. I was so needy, and at the same time completely unable to give anything in a relationship that they never lasted long. I chose partners just as sick as I was. Not only were they emotionally unavailable, but were oftentimes abusive as well. What little self-esteem I had was whittled away with each failed relationship.

The final phase of my disease was the three years that included my marriage and my divorce. I was 23, and she was 19 when we met. She came from a background similar to mine, and our relationship was turbulent and passionate from the beginning. I thought I'd finally found "true love." What I realize now is that a lifetime of addictive needs became focused on this one person. She was everything I ever wanted in a woman. She was beautiful, and quickly adapted to my sexual addiction. In turn, I adapted to her need for conflict and violence. I instinctively understood that she needed me as much as I needed her, and I believed she would never leave me.

The relationship became more manipulative, abusive and violent as time went on. After dating for two years, we married and divorced in the same year. I was devastated.

I had been seeing a counselor for over a year at that time. I was there trying to find a way to first fix, then save my marriage. When the marriage inevitably failed, I had to start looking at my own life.

I earnestly tried to start a new life for myself. I quit drinking, and threw myself into a new career. I was successful for a short period of time, but eventually started drinking again. I was at the lowest point of my life with the loss of my marriage, and all my addictions were out of control and worse than ever. I became suicidal, and there wasn't a day that went by for a period of six months I didn't think about killing myself. I think of that time as my own personal hell.

I woke up one morning after a night of drinking and knew something had to change. I didn't know if I was an alcoholic, and didn't care. I knew I had to stop, and realized I couldn't do it on my own. I'd tried often enough.

I had a friend I hadn't seen too much for a few years. He'd gotten sober and was working a program.

When I did bump into him here and there, it was obvious something in his life had changed for the better. I called him and asked him to take me to a meeting.

I took to Twelve Step recovery immediately. Even though I was skeptical and rebellious, wanting to do everything my way, I also sensed deep inside that I'd finally found what I'd been searching for all my life. If nothing else, it was clear to me I'd finally found others like myself—wounded and hopeless—who, through some miracle, had found a way to live healthy, happy lives.

I stayed sober from that first phone call, and also got into a program to deal with my sex and relationship addictions. My recovery moved along slow but sure for a couple of years, and for the most part I was happy with the new life I'd found. However, there always seemed to be something missing.

A year and a half into recovery I had my first sober relationship. It ended painfully after six months, but I walked away from it with many gifts. We both had put a lot of work into the relationship, dealt with a lot of issues, and were very honest. It was a huge step forward in my development. It was also the thing that pushed me into the next phase of my recovery.

When the relationship ended, I was overwhelmed with grief. For the first time in my life I was able to feel. Not only was I feeling the grief and loss of this relationship, unsedated, but also a lifetime of stuffed-away pain came bubbling up, demanding to be dealt with. Sometimes the feelings were so intense that I thought I would shake apart or explode.

I went to meetings almost every day. It was the only thing I knew to do. I shared my feelings, and begged for help in dealing with them. Many people supported me, and gave me words of wisdom and comfort. One man suggested codependence treatment.

I'd heard about codependence, but always thought that a codependent was someone who didn't have an addiction of their own, but rather got involved with addicts. I had plenty of my own addictions, and I thought any problems I had with relationships were a result of my love addiction and would be dealt with in that program. What I didn't understand is that codependence is much more than enabling, people-pleasing, or relationship addiction.

However, being in severe pain, I was willing to listen to something new. I took my friend's advice and went to a week of outpatient codependence treatment. The week went by fast, but I came away with some very important information, insights, and coping strategies. Most importantly, I met my inner child through a guided meditation.

This was important because it helped me understand the magnitude of the abuse I had suffered. Because of my denial and damaged self-esteem, it was very hard for me to imagine, on anything other than a purely intellectual level, that my abuse was all that bad. I had a hard time feeling like I'd been abused. But when I got in touch with my inner child and saw what had been done to "him," I was outraged. I began collecting pictures of myself as a child at different ages, and it has helped me heal my distorted self-image. I look at the pictures and can clearly see how precious and adorable I was, and am, and that nothing I did could ever justify the torture I suffered.

In treatment, I also got a very clear picture for the first time of just how sick my family was. I did my "genealogy," and it was all there in black and white: my father's sex, food and work addictions; my mother's food and rage addictions; and all the alcoholism and sexual dysfunction in the extended family.

I also discovered what a serious problem my suppressed rage was. I was the only person in my group that couldn't do the rage work. My counselors worked with me for a long time, and I really tried, but just couldn't do it. I finally got sick, and had to leave treatment for the rest of the day. The inner struggle I went through trying to tap into my rage was so physically stressful that the next day I felt like I'd been beaten over my whole body, and I could barely walk.

After treatment, I started going to CoDA. It didn't take long for me to start to feel at home there. The biggest problem for me was coming to an understanding of codependence that worked for me. Then, something was read during the opening format of a meeting that made sense to me: "Codependence is an inability to maintain functional relationships." Of all the definitions of codependency I've heard, this is the one I like best because it fits in with some other things I believe.

A spiritual idea I believe in (which is also a law of physics) is that the very nature of existence is relationships. I have relationships with my family, friends, lovers, myself, my Higher Powers; with my sexuality, jobs, environment, and my possessions. Take the old adage "money can't buy happiness." It's very true that I can be quite wealthy and still miserable. The reverse is also true. I can be broke and happy. If I have a healthy relationship with money, then I can use it as a tool, rather than a source of happiness.

Since the very nature of existence is relationships, and I had a disease that precluded my ability to maintain healthy relationships, I began to see that I was pretty well screwed.

I think of the disease of codependence as a tree. The roots of the tree are my childhood abuse and neglect. The branches are my acting-out behaviors I developed to cope with life. Both the roots and the branches have to be healed. I cannot stop the acting-out without healing the damage that spawned the behavior, and likewise, I cannot work on the roots if I'm still medicating myself with my addictions.

I've had to learn to be very gentle with myself. When I came into the program I was overwhelmed with the magnitude of my disease. I've had to learn to take it one Step at a time and one disease at a time. It took me 27 years to get this sick—I'm not going to heal overnight. Whenever I feel the need to measure my progress, I always look back at least a year to see how far I've come. That way I'm always sure to see some progress.

In CoDA I'm learning to love myself. I'm learning to stop the self-loathing and the self-defeating behaviors. I'm learning to have boundaries. To use my anger to protect myself. I'm learning to believe in myself, to know myself. To decide what's important to me, and to go after it with a passion.

There are two things I've done consistently since I came into recovery that I believe have saved me. I've been painstakingly honest, and I've had the willingness to do whatever it takes to get well.

I consider my CoDA meeting my home group for all the programs I'm in. If I could only get to one meeting a week, it's the one I'd go to. In CoDA, I can talk about anything. In other programs, people sometimes feel threatened if I talk about an aspect of my disease or recovery that doesn't fit neatly into that program.

In CoDA, more than anywhere else, I find that no matter what my particular abuse was like, or the specifics of my acting-out, I see we are much more alike than we are different. And it is in these common bonds that we find healing.

by Jack C.

I COULDN'T STAY AND I COULDN'T LEAVE!

My codependence began before birth. I was a "mistake." My arrival was an unplanned event that I often heard referred to later as "the best mistake we ever made!" So at a very subtle level, even deeper than consciousness, part of me knew that I had to be very good to earn the space I took up and the very breath I breathed. And yet, another part of me had a strong voice that cried out for the love and connection so necessary for my growth and healthy unfoldment. In fact, I screamed so loudly whenever I was put in another room that my parents relented and took me back to their room and their bed— until I was almost nine years old! For all those years, I spent every night sleeping between an often angry and resentful mother and an exhausted, workaholic father.

As a result of being engulfed energetically by those two very important people in my life, I developed very little awareness of my own self, my own boundaries, and my own needs and wants. In a sense, I was in training to be a human chameleon. I could (and still can) merge with others effortlessly and didn't know for years that many of the feelings I experienced were not mine but were actually the emotional responses of others. I was the moody one. At times, I felt like a tightly strung violin string that resonated with any nearby feeling. I was intuitive about what others were thinking, too, and could often pick up on their wants and needs, even before they were aware of them.

Because I was so ready to please, to assure receiving the love and continued connection that was so vital to my well-being, I was a very good girl, doing as I was told both at home and at school. I clung to my mother, in particular, as a safe haven from the world that she taught me to fear. How many times was I warned about all the scary things—out there? My only attempt to leave home and be on my own was a short two-week stay at camp when I was 12. I was intensely homesick and cried and wrote pitiful letters home for 12 of the 14 days I was away.

My father, whom I adored, became more and more successful in his profession and in his community commitments. He was a highly regarded civic leader who did an enormous amount of work, both for pay and out of his need to be of service to others. On the other hand, my mother had less and less to occupy herself with when my brother went away to college and my older sister got married. There was just me left at home to focus on, and the bond between us grew tighter.

Enmeshment, not intimacy, was a way of life in our family for several generations. My parents had lived next door to my father's parents for the first 25 years of their marriage, a fact my mother resented deeply. My aunt and her husband lived with my grandparents in the same house all their married life. Even though the family was so tightly bound together physically, we were continents apart in intimacy and honest emotional connection.

I graduated from high school and was accepted for enrollment at a women's college in the east. I left home filled with excitement, only to discover how desperately I missed being at home where I thought I was safe. To deal with the loneliness and depression I was feeling, I turned to food to fill the void and managed to gain 25 pounds between September and the following May. My grades, which had been excellent while at home, began to slump. I had already made up my mind to transfer to a college in my hometown even before the school year ended, when "fate" intervened.

During summer vacation, I suffered a spinal injury in a diving accident which required surgery. And my interest in the new intern on the surgical service, along with the injury itself, gave me "just cause" to remain at home that following school year. The next fall I was pregnant, and we were married a month later. Although we had our own apartment, it was not as though I married and left home, but more like my new husband moved into the family with me.

I remember summoning up all my courage to tell my mother I was pregnant so soon! And her response was, "How do you think you are going to take care of a baby when you don't even know how to take care of yourself?" I was terrified to talk back to her, but I managed to meekly reply, "Well, I didn't do that to myself, did I?" (meaning I didn't create my own incompetence). For years afterward, I was "helped" in so many ways by my parents that I remained dependent and unsure of my own abilities.

I tried to learn how to be a good mother by reading all that I could. My daughter was a delightful baby who was cheerful and easy to raise. My son, however, came into the world with an indomitable sense of self that *no one* could bend or mold. He was as willful as I was compliant. Over the years, his behavior became a problem I was no longer able to deal with (nor could school counselors, principals, local police, irate parents and the authorities of three successive high schools). It was only one of the stresses that eroded my marriage. My husband and I divorced after 16 years of marriage. Much to my shock and surprise, I had found out that he was bisexual and was involved with a handsome artist, a man who had also been flirting with me to throw me off track so he could be near my husband. I felt humiliated, hurt and incredulous!

I vowed to myself not to make the same mistake twice, so I began a relationship with a beer-drinking, sports-oriented advertising executive who was definitely attracted to women. Little did I realize how accurate that was! He was, most definitely, attracted to women, plural.

After I married him, I discovered he drank a good bit more than I had been aware of while we were dating. I moved away from "home and family" to

412

live across the country with him. Leaving my familiar surroundings was like taking a hot-house plant and setting it out in the snow in the midst of winter. I was certainly not equipped to handle what came next. All my dependence on my mother was transferred to my husband. My codependence came into full flower in that marriage.

As our problems with money, step-parenting and his attraction to other women increased, so did his drinking. I became frantic to keep him connected to me, so I became more and more responsible and capable to convince him that I was smart enough, pretty enough, sexy enough, etc. Anything he wanted, I tried to become. I turned into the chameleon that my early approval-seeking had trained me to be. If I was near red, I became red; near green, I became green. And living with a drinking alcoholic womanizer was like a plaid cloth. I went crazy trying to be all colors at once. I had placed my safety in the hands of a man who was chemically unpredictable and made him my Higher Power. Inconsistency was what I began to expect every day.

I had cut my ties to my family and moved thousands of miles away only to lose myself again by merging with an erratic, alcoholic, sex addict and the stress was driving me crazy. Because of his addictive behavior, I couldn't stay with him, and because of my total dependence on him, I couldn't leave. Finally, at an all time low point physically, emotionally, mentally, and spiritually, I hit bottom and took a whole handful of pills, one by one as though they symbolized candles on a birthday cake, and one to grow on!! This break with sanity was the macabre celebration of what could have been my death-day, but instead became my "re-birth day." And grow, I did!!!

It was in the hospital following my overdose that I was introduced to a Twelve Step recovery program. Although I didn't attend my first real meeting until several months after leaving the hospital, I became a "good kid" once again. Only this time my compliance served me well. I was so desperately afraid that I would be self-destructive again because I was still unable to leave my husband that I did everything that program people suggested:

"Go to meetings!" (I went to nine a week. It was the only place I felt safe.)

"Read the literature!" (I read all the pamphlets the first night. It took me until 2 a.m., locked in the bathroom.)

"Make phone calls!" (I'm sure some people were sorry about how literally I took that suggestion.)

"Get a sponsor!" (I was willing to do whatever my sponsor required of me, and she was very service-oriented.)

I was told never to say no to a program request. This wasn't hard for me to do since I had never learned to say no to anyone. Boundaries were nonexistent for someone like me who had such a blurred sense of self.

Little by little, I began to let go of my fearful dependence on my husband. I learned slogans like "Let Go and Let God," "Live and Let Live," "One Day At A Time," and "Detach With Love."

Miraculously, my frantic, clutching efforts to control everything around me began to lessen. The outer rigidity and compulsive structure I had tried to create around myself were my attempt to counteract the inner emptiness and terror I experienced when I felt alone in the world. It seemed like when I was born, the doctor cut the umbilical cord, and I had picked it up, endlessly trying to plug it back into someone or something to feel safe and connected again.

By beginning to work the Steps, I started to learn that I could feel a sense of love and belonging in the tentative bond I was beginning to form with God, my spiritual Father-Mother. All my fears had come from my belief in my separation from my real Higher Power.

I remember seeing a bumper sticker once that said, "We'll get along just fine as long as you remember I'm God!" At first this could have been me talking to others as I tried to cover up my feelings of unworthiness and inadequacy with grandiosity. But as I learned more about recovery, a change occurred in me, and instead, this became God's message to me. I had begun to surrender.

I finally said no to someone, my sponsor, when she told me it was time to write a personal inventory of myself. I managed to stall for a full three years before I reluctantly wrote my Fourth Step, but all the while the part of me that could say no was getting stronger.

As I developed more and more of a relationship with my Father-Mother God, I began to take risks that previously would have terrified me. I didn't feel so alone all the time because I felt like my Higher

Power was no longer separate from me, but was actually within my very being. In fact, I imagined that God was breathing me with each breath I took (sort of like celestial CPR). I discovered that the word "spiritees" was the Greek word for breath. Meditation for me was a practice of inhaling and saying to myself, "The Spirit of God is within me," and while I exhaled I would say, "The Grace of God surrounds me!" In a way, I was creating my spiritual womb of love and protection that I lived in as often as I could remind myself to do this. This has worked for me over the years, whenever I am consistent in my practice. Sometimes, even today, when I forget my connection, I "slip" and get scared again; however, with practice, I soon remember and am safe in my Higher Power's loving care once again. This is what I call my "conscious contact."

As I learned more about detaching from others, I began to respect their differences, and their right to make their own choices and experience their own consequences without my getting involved in their processes. As a result, I found that I had a great deal of time and energy available for use in my own life. Actually, it was more than enough to allow me to learn new job skills, complete an education and embark on a professional career of my own—as, of course, a therapist and counselor. All my program training made it very clear to me that I must be as hypervigilant about my own inner issues as I used to be about other peoples' affairs. The wounds of blurred boundaries, enmeshment and an undeveloped sense of myself in the past have turned into the gifts that, today, make me a very intuitive and talented counselor who continuously seeks spiritual guidance from my Higher Power in maintaining a healthy balance of care for myself and others.

My sponsor was wise in guiding me toward reliance on my permanent sponsor, God, to whom I rededicate my life and will each morning upon awakening. With much regret, I made the decision to divorce my second husband, knowing that in order to develop a relationship first with the God of my understanding and then with myself, I must face what I feared the most—my aloneness! My recovery definition of "fear" is that it stands for: "Face Everything And Recover!"

I moved to a new city in another state in order to make a life of my own, on my own. For a while, I went to the other extreme and developed what I called my "little red hen syndrome" of counterdependence, asking no one for any help and shutting down my vulnerability for fear of encroachment and enmeshment again. I am finally feeling secure in my sense of my own self and use my intuition as my guide.

As the CoDA logo states, this journey to the Real Me has been one of "Discovery, Recovery, Self and Respect." Because I am now aware of who I am, what I want and need and how to protect myself, I am able to share real intimacy with others, and perhaps, with a loving, respectful partner when God feels the time is right.

Although recovery began for me in another Twelve Step program where I learned a great deal about detachment from others whom I had made my Gods, my relationship with my Higher Power and my true self began in earnest when I started to apply the

Twelve Steps of Co-Dependents Anonymous to my daily life. I am eternally grateful that I will not go to my death never having known myself for who I am— God's perfect child, precious and free!!

by Mary J.

MARY R'S STORY

Here I was, over a year and a half clean and sober, yet crazier than I had felt my whole life. I was contemplating drinking again, divorce and another attempt at suicide. I felt trapped and hopeless with nowhere to turn. For years, I had convinced myself that all I had to do was to stop drinking and using drugs, and my life would be fine. After three tries, I was finally able to maintain a period of sobriety within Alcoholics Anonymous. I was proud of myself. Not since I was 11 years old when I was sneaking drinks, stealing my mother's diet pills and taking prescribed pain medication for menstrual cramps had I succeeded in living my life free of chemicals.

I had attempted periods of sobriety many times, but a feeling of dread would surface—a feeling of fear and shame. Without chemicals, I had no defense against it. I had tried sex, work, religion and starving myself, but I hadn't been able to make the feelings go away. Here I was at age 30, trying to stay sober and somewhat sane, but feeling completely hopeless.

During this time, my husband Ken worked at a treatment center that dealt with alcoholism, addictions and some "thing" called codependence. He shared the new information he learned about family systems, shame and addictions. The more he shared, the more soared and dysfunctional I became. After a few weeks, Ken's boss offered us a chance to attend the center's aftercare group. Whether he suspected the difficulties we were having, I don't know. But the result of his invitation was a gift—the beginning of my recovery as I know it today. I walked into the aftercare room, feeling terrified, like a little girl who hadn't gotten it right, again. I was full of shame. When it was my turn, I fell apart. I could barely talk. Everyone just listened. When I finished talking, I felt so self-conscious. I still remember the facilitator's words. She gave me the name of someone who could help me. On April 23, 1984, I walked into my therapist's office, full of the ever present dread. But, through God's grace and this woman's loving presence, I was able to share with her some of my story; I was scared to share it all. By the end of the session, for the first time, I felt a ray of hope.

Later, I realized that I had begun work on my First Step that day.

At the time, there was no Twelve Step program that dealt with codependence, so most of my initial Step work was completed in my therapist's office. My First Step took over a year to look at the effects my childhood had on me and how I had integrated so many destructive behaviors in order to survive. I didn't want to feel those feelings I had locked away for so many years. I felt that by looking at my past, I would be disloyal to my parents. It took some time to realize this work was not about blaming my parents, but about holding them accountable for their behaviors. I learned that codependence is intergenerational, and that my parents were doing what was taught them. Their dysfunction had been handed down to them, just as they had handed it down to me, and as I had passed it on to my children. This work was simply about stopping the cycle.

I could admit my life was unmanageable, but I was convinced that I still had power over my codependence. Somehow I could make myself change and control my feelings and behaviors. Fourteen months later, my surrender of the illusion of power finally came; it was both relieving and painful. I was able to look honestly at my family system and pursue the dysfunctional legacy without blame or vengeance. My surrendering helped me acknowledge the wounded little girl inside of me I call Mary Lou. She was full of fear, shame and pain, and I had been treating her the same way I had been treated. It was time for me to take responsibility and change the crazy cycle. This was strictly an "inside job," and with God's help and assistance, I would overcome. I began the arduous task of writing out my family history. As I did, I saw how many unhealthy messages and behaviors I had incorporated into my relationships with myself, God and others.

October 4, 1953, was the day of my birth. My arrival on this planet was not a joyous occasion for my parents. I was the last chance my mother had of producing a son. My grandmother told me that after hearing I was a girl, my father went into a depression. From the beginning, I was a disappointment. I felt it from as early as I can remember, and it was one of the most powerful roles I would deal with in recovery. I was the third and youngest girl in my family; my sisters were four and five years older than me. I took on the job of becoming the "boy" of the family. It became clear that my sisters were my mother's children, and I was my father's child. By the time I was three years old, my father began to incest me. To date, he says he has no memories of this, but my memories are clear and no longer clouded by drugs and alcohol. Prior to stopping the drugs and alcohol, I had remembered parts of the abuse. But, I had a difficult time honoring the forgotten memories as they surfaced in my sobriety. For a long time I believed I was making them up.

When I was five years old, my family moved to Arizona with another family from Kansas. For a short period, we all lived together in one house while our two houses were being built. We had cookouts, played games and celebrated all the holidays together. I felt more accepted by them than I did with my own family, but I wouldn't let myself get close to them. I already knew that, for the most part, relationships were not safe.

As I was growing up, I was confused about how my mother felt about me. She often appeared distant, angry, frustrated, opinionated and extremely unhappy. One of the things I heard from her over and over was, "Your husband comes first, then your children, then yourself." I learned that men got to do what they wanted, and the women would do the work. Women had to put up with whatever the man wanted and not complain. Women were martyrs; they had to keep the husband happy and the family together. I held these beliefs through three marriages. I kept my mouth shut, denied myself and stayed resentful.

I was very afraid of my mother. She was a rager and was violent.

I learned to stay out of her way, a behavior I continued into my adult years when anyone around me became angry. My sisters shared a room; I had one of my own. My sisters resented me for having my own room, and I felt alone and isolated. Most often, my mother focused her rage and violence on them. Then, they would become rageful and violent with each other. Each time these incidents happened, I was terrified and would hide or leave the house—a pattern I used in my adult relationships.

Both parents worked, so my sisters and I were unchaperoned a lot.

Many times, they would gang up on me, hold me down and tickle me until I wet my pants. They thought it was funny; I was scared and humiliated. A couple of times, they threatened to do this in front of my friends to embarrass me. To this date, I still have panic attacks if I'm physically restrained in any way, whether I'm at the dentist or playing with my husband.

My oldest sister and I spent more time together, but much of that time resulted in my people-pleasing or in pain. There were incidents of sexual abuse; and as I got older, she'd show me off to her friends as her sexy little sister. Sometimes she'd ask what I was doing, then she'd tell on me in order to get on our mother's good side. The betrayal was devastating, but I kept going back, until the pain of the betrayal was greater than my need to have someone to talk to.

My middle sister and I never had much of a relationship. I attempted to connect with her through teasing. I thought if I communicated as she did, we'd have something in common. All I did was to create painful and embarrassing situations for her which distanced us even more. I didn't try again until adulthood when, for a short time, we played softball together. After softball was over, we once again reverted to our old ways.

Most of my relationships with girlfriends or women friends resembled one of the relationships I had with my family. Either I was scared of the relationship (as with my mother), felt betrayed (as with my oldest sister) or was unable to connect (as with my middle sister). The relationship I had with myself followed this same course.

Being raised as the boy of the family, I had no idea how to relate to myself as female. I was confused as to what gender I was and what gender I wanted to be. It took me years in therapy to understand who and what I was. I was my father's female son. Dad was my hero, the one person in my family I needed approval from. He was a funny and charming man— very athletic. He told wonderful stories and sang songs to us. I admired him and wanted to be like him. Yet, he was my main sexual offender, and I was unacceptable to him as a daughter. We had a sick, damaging bond which was very confusing to me. I questioned myself all the time. If I did more sports, would he approve of me then? If I let him know I would rather dance than play sports, would he totally abandon me? If I acted or dressed seductively, would he like me then? My father was obsessed with sports, and eventually, I became just as obsessed. I could outrun, outthrow and outperform most boys. My illusion was that if I was as good as they were, then I'd be acceptable to my father. The loneliness I felt for his approval was overwhelming.

By the time I was almost 10, both the sexual abuse by my father and my mother's violence stopped. I began to menstruate. I started to rebel and act out in school. I was constantly told to leave my fifth grade class and work off my anger at the tetherball court. I showed up at school with black eye make-up and outrageously teased hair and was made to wash my face and fix my hair. I began to act out sexually with boys. The message from my childhood was to never say no to any male. I believed my true purpose was to be in service to men, to fix their pain and loneliness. The lonelier, angrier and more frightened I felt, the more I acted out. During the summer before sixth grade, I dropped my old friends and began relationships with the "wilder" kids in school. I began smoking, drinking and taking my mother's diet pills. I stayed away from home as much as possible. I stole, lied and isolated. How I was able to focus and perform in sports, I do not know.

From ages nine to fourteen, I became obsessed with the TV show about a witch named Samantha. If only I could wiggle my nose and change, I thought, then I could be all the things my dad wanted me to be. I would finally be acceptable to him. I was convinced I was too "bad" for God to be there for me and instead I began praying to Satan. For years I put myself to sleep by asking Satan to make me into a witch like Samantha. I told Satan all the ways I wanted to change. By the time I was 14, my room was filled with altars and objects. I realize now how great my sense of worthlessness was, for me to pursue this darkness. Satan seemed my only way out. I truly believed God didn't want anything to do with me. By the time I was 14 and a daily drug user, various events occurred that frightened me more than my sense of worthlessness. I stopped praying to Satan. Stopping my "fix" left me once again with an overwhelming loneliness, hopelessness and shame. My solution was to increase my use of drugs and alcohol.

I convinced myself there was no point in trying to gain my father's acceptance, so I dropped out of sports and began taking dance lessons. For years I had danced, sang and written poetry in secret because I never felt they would be acceptable to my father. Because I no longer desired my father's approval, it was not a problem anymore. I also became interested in acting and clothes design. I had inherited my mother's creative talent, but did not do very well at school. I had difficulty with comprehension, math, science and logic. I was put in remedial reading classes to help but it wasn't until recovery that I found out how severe my learning disorder was and still is.

My approval and acceptance began coming from the boys at school. During my sophomore year of high school, I met the first boy with whom I was totally obsessed. He had his own apartment. I thought it was "cool" that he wanted me. I believed I was truly in love. I spent a lot of time there doing drugs. He was the first person I was willing to be sexual with. This was a big deal because I had told myself I would only be sexual with the man who would one day be my husband.

One night we were smoking pot. Unbeknownst to me, my boyfriend had set me up to be gang raped by his biker friends. I was so hurt and confused. What had I done that had made him mad? How could I get him to care for me again? I walked home hurt and scared. No one knew, neither my friends nor my family. I was so ashamed. I excused my boyfriend. We had been loaded; he probably hadn't known what he was doing. His friends forced him into it. I convinced myself it was my fault; I shouldn't have been there. The next day I tried to convince him to love me again. The relationship ended shortly after this because he went back to his old girlfriend. I was devastated. I decided that I would never love anyone or let anyone get that close to me again.

For the next couple of years, my drinking and drugging increased.

I didn't attend school without some form of chemicals in me. I began shooting speed and smoking pot daily, taking L.S.D. regularly and taking downers and drinking constantly. I have few memories of high school and no idea how I made it through my classes.

When I was 16, my best friend's minister convinced me to stop my chemical use and to ask my parents for help. It was the first time someone really cared about my well-being. He didn't shame me or say I was bad; he just listened and shared his truth. I was so touched that I went right home and talked with my parents, but they didn't believe I was taking drugs and drinking on a regular basis. They took me to their minister who had no difficulty believing what I said. He was part of a group that investigated school drug users and I had been on their list. However, his manner of counseling was far from helpful.

A few months later, my illegal drug use came to a halt because I became pregnant. I thought it would be cool to be a married teenage hippie with a baby, so I hadn't used birth control. At 16 I was married, and on April 5, 1971, I had a beautiful baby boy. The gift of his birth began a chain of events that would change my life forever. I started to grow up.

My marriage ended when I was 18, and at 19, I married again. My alcoholism and drug addiction progressed at an alarming rate, only this time it was prescription drugs. My daughter was born a few years into the marriage. Her delivery was complicated by my alcoholism, and she was born at a low birth weight due to fetal alcohol syndrome. The marriage lasted seven years, filled with rage, violence and extreme control. Both my husband and I drank continuously which was the only way we could get along. Toward the end of the marriage, I became suicidal.

I saw a psychiatrist who thought I needed to be hospitalized, but I refused. I would do it on my own. I left my husband thinking everything would be OK if I was out of the marriage. It wasn't. There I was, a single mom, continuing my previous addictions: men, drinking, illegal and prescription drugs, an eating disorder and attempted suicides. I was still so out of control.

I tried many times to clean up, to be a better mother to my children. I tried joining churches. I studied the Bible and was even baptized twice. I tried Alcoholics Anonymous twice. Each time I stopped the chemicals or the men, the old familiar feelings would overwhelm me. My codependence and my addictions were my only refuge of sanity.

Then on July 8, 1982, I entered the program of AA for the last time. I had hit such an emotional bottom that I was finally willing to surrender my alcoholism, addictions and feelings to God. I was a mess; but by the grace of God, I haven't tasted a drink of alcohol or used drugs since that day. Each time I think of this, I'm reminded that miracles really do happen.

Two and a half months later Ken and I began dating. We had met previously the second time I attempted AA when he was dating a friend of mine. Something happened this time—something I have come to know as God's will and purpose. We broke all the rules: he was getting involved with a newcomer, and I was having a relationship during my first year of sobriety. In all reality, it shouldn't have worked, but today I realize our relationship was part of God's plan for us.

Ken was living in San Francisco, and within 30 days, I packed up my kids and moved there too. We became very intense very fast, experiencing extreme highs and lows. I was completely focused on Ken to the neglect of my children. I frantically tried to fix my familiar feelings with anything except drugs and alcohol. I was obsessed and out of control. I was in love.

In the midst of all the dysfunction, God planted a seed in Ken and me. We had seen the movie "Ghandi" and were both so moved by his story that we started talking about our own desire to be of service—to do something to make a difference in this world. Ken was the only person I had ever met who had as strong a desire to serve as I did.

Due to financial circumstances, we moved back to Phoenix to my parents' house. We were broke and broken. Ken was still finalizing a year-long divorce and business settlement. We stayed with my parents for four months while my children stayed with their father. I am grateful that my parents were willing to open up their home to Ken and me. It was the first time since I was 11 that I lived with my parents without using drugs or alcohol. I was emotionally reactive the entire time we were there and felt crazy. Ken and I were continually bouncing off each other and fighting often.

One time my father came up behind me and began rubbing my shoulders. I became overwhelmed with panic and immediately disassociated. Without the numbing effects of chemicals, the memories and feelings about the incest returned. Of course, I did and said nothing. Instead Ken picked up on my anger and became enraged with my father, but didn't know why. This was common when I was with my family. I wouldn't own my anger, and Ken would pick up on it. I kept thinking Ken was being unreasonable. Ken felt crazy; I felt scared.

Finally Ken was offered a job in Prescott, Arizona. I found a job in my field making a much lower wage than I had been paid in Phoenix. Ken's job didn't pan out and he went on unemployment. His oldest son came to live with us along with my two children. As in San Francisco, there were extremely good times and extremely bad times. The only thing that held me together was my Higher Power and some spiritual music.

We tried individual and couple's therapy. During my sessions, the therapist told me I should leave Ken, and during his sessions, she told Ken we should stay together. Needless to say, the therapy did not help us. We went to meetings and worked our programs; but it wasn't the alcoholism that was the problem, it was our codependence. We thought maybe God hadn't honored our relationship because we weren't married. Ken told me to let him know when I was ready. I bought him a card inviting him to be married on New Year's Eve of 1983.

Ken was offered a job as a primary therapist at a treatment center in Wickenburg, Arizona, so we moved nearby. I went to work at a local company. We were convinced that if we straightened out our financial situation, our lives would be easier. The first few months of Ken's employment were extremely difficult for me. The treatment center treated not only alcoholism and drug addiction, but something called "codependence." Ken was excited to learn about codependence and its effect on addictions and relationships. I became scared, thinking this treatment center would take my husband away. I had worked all my life to keep my feelings and memories down; I did not want to let them surface.

On April 23, 1984, after hitting my second severe emotional bottom, I saw the therapist who eventually helped me to understand my codependence. I was referred to her by the center director's wife. I will be forever grateful to these women for the help they provided me. I saw my therapist every week. Ken and I tried seeing her together, but my fearful reactiveness was so strong, that halfway through the session I would become silent and run out of the room.

Before I could finally surrender, I went through a suicide attempt, a brief separation and a program of drug therapy to medicate my L.S.D. flashbacks. Finally, during a five-day family systems workshop, I was able to see, understand and feel my powerlessness and unmanageability and to trust that God would restore me to sanity.

I began to heal. I was still focused on Ken and my kids, but not as intensely. I was learning to share my feelings and have some boundaries. My caretaking decreased and my caregiving increased.

I was learning to pray from my heart instead of from fear. I became focused on the college education I had begun in 1985. My self-esteem increased and I began to volunteer as a group facilitator at a local alcohol treatment center. People at my job began giving me more responsibility. Life was improving.

I began working on my Fourth Step. I had been unaccountable for most of my life, using everyone and everything to fix me and my hurts. I had become whatever I thought people around me wanted out of fear of displeasing or angering them. I was a rage-filled woman who looked nice.

I had told myself I would not raise my children as my parents had raised me, yet I had hurt and abused them just as severely. As a result of my addiction to men and sex, I had emotionally incested my children. As a result of my work addiction, I had neglected my children. As a result of my fear addiction, I had controlled and manipulated my children. As a result of my eating disorder, I had modeled unhealthy ways for my children to physically care for themselves.

I had used Ken's raging to remain in the victim role. I ignored him angrily or shut down passively every time he shared his anger. I attempted to control and manipulate him through jealousy, pity, sex and caretaking. I did it all while looking "nice." I had passionately avoided honesty by rationalizing, justifying or changing the subject. I wouldn't let Ken get close. I had projected the fear of my father's sexual abuse and my mother's rage into every interaction I had with Ken. Whenever we talked, I had another conversation going on in my head about the best way to avoid upsetting him. For years Ken did not receive my truth and honesty. I couldn't even tell him in person that I needed to separate. I called him at work to relay the news.

Looking at these issues was all very humbling to me and it gave me positive motivation to continue my recovery. I was determined to do whatever I needed to do to break this cycle. I did not want to abuse my children, Ken, myself or anyone anymore.

I shared my Fourth Step with my therapist and a

few friends in recovery and after many months, I finally completed my Fifth Step. It amazed me at the time, but after all of the uncovering from my Fourth Step inventory, I still struggled with my Sixth and Seventh Steps. I believed I was willing for God to help me change and earnestly and humbly prayed for Him to remove all my defects of character. But nothing was happening. I kept praying, I shared in my CoDA meeting, I talked with my recovery friends and therapist.

Then I became aware that I had tried to handle my behavior changes by myself. I wasn't risking new behaviors and leaving their outcome to God. I was doing them only when I thought the outcome would be favorable. I also realized I had conveniently forgotten to include my needlessness in my Fourth Step. I was needless with God, just as I was needless with Ken, our children and everyone else in my life. I began working on another Fourth and Fifth Step strictly on my issue of needlessness.

From that point my Sixth and Seventh Steps began to manifest in my life. I felt that I had truly given over all aspects of my life to God, including my needlessness. That's not to say I don't struggle with them today, but the struggle doesn't last as long and there are greater time periods between each bout.

God's grace continued to follow me throughout my Eighth and Ninth Steps. In the beginning I focused on the amends I needed to make to Ken, our children and myself. I put my effort into changing my abusive and hurtful behaviors. This felt like the greatest gift I could give any of them or myself. I practice my Tenth, Eleventh and Twelfth Steps each day to insure my recovery growth.

Keeping my behaviors as clean as possible, making amends right away, praying and meditating to God, sharing my experience with others and practicing these principles in all my affairs are the daily values I live by today.

Strengthening this new way of living was the motivation for my role in the birth of CoDA. So, when Ken shared his idea of starting CoDA, I was more than willing to do my part. The friends we shared with also responded positively; and, during September of 1986, we started the work of putting together the first meeting. I remember the night Ken wrote the Preamble and Welcome. After hours of writing, he emerged. As he read what he'd written, I felt an overwhelming spiritual presence. When Ken finished, we held each other and cried. It was an awesome experience.

There was an innocence about CoDA and all who attended that first year. CoDA grew fast and meetings started all over the country, even in Sweden. It wasn't long before we realized the need to incorporate the same way AA had. My recovery increased tremendously during that first year. Working on the Board of Trustees forced me out of my self-centeredness and into a more focused recovery. Less than one year after the first CoDA meeting began, we held the first National Conference. Never in my wildest dreams did I believe that five years after becoming clean and sober I would be involved in a program such as CoDA. One of the greatest messages I have received from my recovery is that God can use any person or situation as a positive healing force.

My service work in CoDA has been a mixture of wonderful and painful times. Over the years I have received personal and public attacks as well as praise and gratitude. I've not handled any of it perfectly, and at times I've not handled it very gracefully. My role as co-founder has been incredibly humbling and spiritually strengthening.

In all my relationships, whether with Ken, our children, family, friends or my relationship with myself, I would not change one person or event of my life—it's all a part of my personal and individual life tapestry.

I have risked and grown more with Ken than with any other human being. We have been each other's mirrors and teachers. Our marriage is filled with increasing compassion, fun, honesty and is more graceful than ever. Some of the richest times I have with Ken are during the presence of our child-selves, Timmy and Mary Lou, whether through playfulness or tears. I have never had a friend like Ken.

The miracles that have happened in the last 12 years have been the result of my letting go of the control of my life so God could work. When I think of my old belief that God was there for everyone else but me, I have to smile. How wrong I was. In my spiritual and religious studies, I have found a common thread about the need for a rebirthing of the soul. I know I have experienced that. And knowing what I know today, I would choose to embrace, all over again, the pain and agony of that long and arduous labor.

Gratitude only partially describes what I feel in my heart about the life and recovery my Higher Power has given me. I heard once that with recovery, we are no longer human beings trying to become spiritual, but rather spiritual beings trying to be human.

I pray that my human life continues to draw me closer to my true spiritual self, and that my human life honors and reflects the love of my Higher Power. This is what my life purpose is about.

by Mary R.

THE GIFT

I believe that God has given me one of His greatest gifts. That gift is my recovery program. The Twelve Steps of Co-Dependents Anonymous have enabled me to grow in a way I never thought possible. At times I even feel like a whole person.

I was a child of "the '50s," with rigid family values and a strong work ethic. My dad worked two jobs during much of my childhood. I was the second of six children. I believe we had a functional family until a catastrophe occurred in 1959. At the end of that year, my parents' firstborn child died of cancer at the age of 13. It was a slow and painful death. Our family was forever changed, forever different, and forever wounded. My "glad" family became a "sad" family. The brother I fought with, played with, imitated, needed, and loved was gone forever, except in my memories. At 11 years old, I didn't know how long "forever" was.

It seems I was able to block or numb out the painful, lonely, but much-needed feelings. Thirty years later, I believe that my four siblings reacted in much the same way. Someone said, "Children aren't allowed to grieve." I'm not sure all adults allow themselves to grieve in a healthy way, either.

Over the years, our family adopted a "no-talk rule" concerning my brother's illness and death. The no-talk rule meant no validation of the feelings, thus laying the groundwork for the denial of most of my negative feelings. I had no idea that this was only the beginning of my denying a part of me that so desperately needed to be let out.

I married at the age of 19 and thought I had chosen well. The man I married was a couple of years older that I was and was studying for the ministry. My church and faith had always been very important, especially after the death of my brother. A partnership for life with a person so devoted to God's work was no surprise to anyone. Having just graduated from nurses' training, I thought I had it all: my marriage, a new career, a different home, and in many ways, a different identity. I wanted desperately to be happy, and I believed wanting it would make it so.

My new identity was that of a minister's wife, an identity I was ill-prepared for, especially in rural Iowa. I was a "city girl," not accustomed to the constant scrutiny of everyone in town. But I adapted well and became what everyone wanted me to be. When I perceived that I was not measuring up to others' expectations, I tried harder, never asking myself what I wanted or needed at any given time. I wasn't happy, but I knew that someday I would be, if I just "did the right thing" by everyone else's standards.

I soon had another identity to adorn and perfect, that of being a mother. This was natural for me. Being the oldest girl from a large family, I had learned to be a caretaker early on. We had two children in less than two years, then another child four years later. This identity, I thought, would surely make me happy, and in many ways, it did. Being a good mother was my most important job, and at times I was consumed by it.

Since I didn't know how to live for myself, I lived through other people. When my husband succeeded at getting more education and a better job, I felt successful. When my children failed at a task, it was my failure. Through it all, I thought my life was pretty good, most of the time. There were painful times, but my denial of the painful feelings always won out, allowing me to stuff my pain. To be honest with myself or another human being about those painful feelings was impossible, so that meant they would have to stay buried awhile longer.

As the years passed, I focused more and more on the children and my work. My husband changed careers a couple of times, worked long hours and was home less and less. In 1985 he left, informing me he wanted a divorce and that he was in love with someone else. It was then I realized that his alcoholic behavior and my enabling behavior had destroyed the marriage we once had. The marriage was "dead and would never breathe again."

Once again I was numb. The pain of rejection and the feelings of worthlessness haunted me for months.

Didn't 17 years of trying to do the "right thing" count for anything? My whole identity was directly tied to my marriage and my family. Without the family intact, I felt as though I couldn't go on. To say the word "divorce" was impossible, let alone the vision of it really happening. The anger and hurt came almost immediately, and it seemed as if I cried for weeks. I truly believed that my three children were my only reason for living. I felt empty and very alone. I was a failure as a wife, and I wanted to hide from everyone.

It was during that time that I turned to a Twelve Step program. I was desperate, and the pain of my lost dream was all I could focus on. I don't remember much of those first few Al-Anon meetings, but I remember feeling safe there. I felt they knew, at least in part, some of my confusion and self-loathing. I heard about "living in the solution," and I wanted to know how to begin. I decided to concentrate on the first three Steps for as long as it took. I also decided to tap into my spiritual self and ask my Higher Power for strength and direction.

My closest friend was an AA member who helped me to understand about alcoholic behavior. The fog cleared, and I ever so slowly started learning how to live my own life and how to own my power. My friend and I read all the literature on codependency we could get our hands on and were in constant dialogue about what we had read. Today she is not only a friend, but my sponsor. She, more than anyone, has helped me to keep on track with my CoDA program. I am learning to feel my own feelings, and nothing has taken so much time and effort for me to do than that.

I've talked to a brother and sister about the trauma our family went through in 1959. I'm learning more about the little child in me, along with what it was like to grow up in my alcoholic family. My friend and I started the first CoDA group where we live because we knew we needed to be around other recovering people who were dealing with similar issues.

Today, my life is more my own than it ever was. I recently married a man who works his own Twelve Step program. I have found that our mutual dedication to this way of life is a real "plus" for our relationship. My boundaries are better defined, and some days I feel a true sense of serenity about my life. I still struggle for balance when it comes to caretaking and detachment. My "conscious contact" with God needs my daily attention; and I believe, more than ever, that He has given me one of His greatest gifts.

by Carol S.

JOHN'S STORY

The doctor had told Thelma he was indeed afraid she was pregnant. She overrode the fears this confirmation roused, idealizing her predicament.

Unmarried and alone, with the child's father in the deserts of northern Africa as the Australian Army fought Rommel, Thelma rationalized. Having her baby would be a patriotic act—Aussies were dying in the war against Hitler. She would do her bit and bring another into the world.

Hence I was born in January of 1941 in Sydney, fatherless, with a starry-eyed mother who took only half of reality into account much of the time. I would grow up discounting reality too, hoping for miracles, and often needing to imagine a rosy future to tolerate an uncomfortable or frightening present.

But my earliest memory, as of now, is one of an anguishing abandonment, not from any ill intent on my mother's part. I had turned two, and wartime work regulations required Mum to engage in full-time employment. I vividly recall being restrained, struggling with my whole being, by two strange women as Mum receded, trying to reassure me. Then she disappeared down the steps, behind a steel grille in the child-minding center. We had never been apart, and this was an unrehearsed and violent wrenching for an infant, nowadays understood to be extremely traumatic emotionally, but then it was thought to carry no ill effects beyond present tears.

Though I got used to the nursery routine, I often visualized the frightening eventuality of some strange woman coming to pick me up because she was my real mother and Mum had only been minding me for her. These ruminations terrified me, but I dared not voice them to Mum lest they materialize.

Quite possibly because of an early trauma in her own life, Mum experienced extreme anxiety regarding my bodily well-being. She'd go into an alarming panic at the slightest injury I sustained—be it a little cut or abrasion while playing. She restricted and supervised me to protect me from harming myself and her peace of mind. This fluttering control was deeply frustrating; her alarmist reactions made me fearful of revealing any injuries to her.

I was six, when, while walking to school one day, I ventured to pat a Blue Heeler cattle-dog and was bitten on the fingers. I panicked. What would I tell her? I couldn't hide the bleeding, stinging punctures. Shocked by this encounter with savagery, I ran tearfully homeward. Then I had a brilliant idea: I'd tell Mum that the teacher had caned me, then it would be OK. Mum cleaned my hand with antiseptic, then took me to confront the mystified teacher. What a stuff-up that was!

Mum's fretful controlling often filled me with an urge to escape and do my own thing; this seems to have established an impatience and wanderlust in me very early.

In one such incident, when I was five, Mum entrusted me with cash for the first time, when we ran out of breakfast cereal one morning. Overwhelmed by the power of the coins, I bypassed our shop and boarded a tramcar to town, where I knew a theater was playing a Tarzan movie. I was fascinated with the Weismuller character's unfettered jungle lifestyle. Arriving at the theater far too early, but still in the grip of my trip, I jumped a bus to Circular Quay, on Sydney Harbour, near where the Sydney Opera House now stands. Waiting there for the ferry to Manly Beach, I was queried by a wharf official, then escorted to the police station. The cops introduced me to a couple of press reporters and my captioned photograph made the front page of that afternoon's newspaper, I was in my pajamas! Mum's reaction was a mixture of chagrin, admiration and relief.

At her wit's end to curtail my erratic exploits and nerve-racking absences, Mum instituted a terrifying method of punishment; it was intended to teach me the meaning of death. She'd pin me to the bed with a pillow over my face, smothering me to near unconsciousness. This disillusioning regimen controlled me temporarily, but, since that time, whenever I've felt various physical or emotional threats, I've experienced a feeling of suffocation that has often caused me to flee, or to appease the source, at all cost.

Eventually Mum's anxieties, especially after I was hit by a car returning from school, caused her to put me into a church-funded home for boys when I was 10. Initially it was like a holiday camp for me and the other boys under the care of some kindly ladies and a single, grandfatherly school teacher. However, we were all transferred to another home, for an administrative reason.

The man in charge was an emotionally disturbed tyrant. On our first day he singled out our biggest boy who was 13, and on some pretext, broke a broom handle on him with the force of the blow. We were aghast. At his worst one day, he kicked an 11-year-old unconscious. I was too terrorized to relay any of this to Mum on her couple of visits, and the church wasn't aware of the situation.

A manageability, of sorts, allowed Mum to bring me home; she had a job and a boyfriend. He was a talented, fun sort of guy who cheered people up. I addressed him as Uncle Norman. Mum's new affluence buoyed me up too and I was on an ongoing "high" after the desolate church home experience. Gradually things soured.

Norman was a workaholic and an inveterate gambler. His addiction to the illegal game, "Two Up," (heading or tailing two pennies for stakes), brought the three of us, by painful degrees, to a penurious rock-bottom. Mum got "stressed-out" again as she attempted to control Norman by admonitions, which she in turn negated by enabling him with her money.

One night, he brought a gambler mate home to

stay the night in our cramped flat. Mum was such a compulsive pleaser that she cooked them breakfast. I used to work Saturdays with her, and we were an hour late. Mum was flustered and agitated. Her boss complained, and Mum exploded and told her to "shove" the job. Norman promised to pay his way, but for the next five weeks bedtime would come with no Norman on paynights.

He earned good money, and a week's pay would have cleared our debts, but he was on a losing streak and he'd arrive at daybreak, silent and grumpy at any queries, then we'd live on promises and assurances till the next paynight of fading hopes.

Norm left. Mum couldn't get work, and my small maintenance payment from my father stopped temporarily, just when it was needed most. Mum made up some bizarre meals from all the scant remnants in our cupboard. Then we just starved for four days; Mum's credit at our shop was gone. Defeated, she sent me in quiet desperation to ask for a tin of jam and loaf of bread at the opposition store. The understanding proprietress just handed me the food without blinking. She said not to hesitate if we needed more, and my shame evaporated with her kindly concern.

Mum regained a precarious solvency, but real fears of destitution were an ever present source of anxiety. These experiences of poverty in a "land of plenty," Australia, bred in me a deep hostility to the conservative elements in society and smug defenders of the status-quo. Fortunately today, progressive governments and humane people have instituted reasonable social welfare payments for the poor.

Depressions, with bouts of nausea, began to afflict Thelma at the time I began high school. We became more disorganized, and I was often late for school. I became so shamed and fearful of various teachers' gruff or ridiculing reactions that I began to play hooky. If I was running late and had to face an ordeal with one of the more abusive teachers, I would veer off my school route under the pressure of these fearful contemplations and experience "a high" or relief, but the price of this freedom was guilt and anxiety later. I missed so many days that I ended up second bottom of my A grade class, at the half-year exams. My grade teacher talked kindly with me and didn't demote me; I overcame my wagging and attended regularly. However, Mum's health deteriorated, and she put me into another boys' home.

I had encountered and engaged in sexually dysfunctional situations during my childhood in the chaotic neighborhood where I'd grown to the age of 13. I have some vague glimpses of being somehow involved in an erotic situation with a couple in their late teens, when I was four years of age or younger, with strong attendant feelings. Furthermore, a girl slightly older, who lived at our loose-knit flat, encouraged me in episodes of sexual experimentation from my seventh year onwards. I can understand her need now—her mother was emotionally cold and depressed and eventually abandoned her four children to her taciturn, workaholic husband. Children in such situations seek such warmth as they can. However, at 13, I longed after the tall attractive 15-year-old sister of my girlfriend, enduring exquisitely painful reveries of lust.

One day this elder sister brought a promiscuous friend to my best mate's flat when his parents were out. This friend allowed us boys to fondle her on the bed, but my "dream-girl" just watched and giggled without getting involved. These sorts of harrowing dysfunctional sexual experiences brought more frustration than any degree of satisfaction. They were attempts to fulfill needs that were not forthcoming in our sick families whose caregivers often tried their best but always hurt the ones they most loved, breeding fear and secrecy that compounded and multiplied emotional problems.

I was caught in a seesawing cycle of taboo-breaking drives followed by guilty self-recriminations. My self-esteem fluctuated from inferior to superior. I was plump, and jibes of "Fatso" hurt or angered me, I was patchy at sports and self-consciousness affected my concentration in games. I was tall and intelligent and had topped classes in some subjects when stable.

Reading developed as one of my earlier addictive escapes; at eight years of age I'd discovered that Hugh Lofting's Doctor Doolittle could spirit me out of the mundane poverty of my environment, tripping to the moon on the back of a friendly giant moth. But I recall being distraught and going into a withdrawal of sorts when I had read through the school library's collection of Doolittle's adventures. A poignant melancholy settled about me as I pondered the gap between stark reality and the safe, warm, intoxicating dreamworld of imaginings.

Thelma's drug of choice was the movies. We would go four or five times a week when Mum had the money. She used to justify this irresponsible extravagance (that meant the neglect of more urgent functional expenditures) by saying that a person would go mad looking at four walls. Such are the myriad distractions from ourselves and life's unforgiving demands.

Movies played a bigger part than I'd realized in my "pre-TV era" childhood and life with Mum. I can see now the acting-out scenarios and role modeling they provided. I would find myself "being" some screen hero I admired, especially, not having a father. Mum would indulge in "bitchy" critiques of Bette Davis or Joan Crawford after one of their performances, but nevertheless made sure she caught their next pictures.

She would often direct us in unconsciously motivated games of victim and persecutor; she would be the trapped, tortured heroine of unblemished, emotional purity whilst I'd co-star as the thankless, relentlessly unscrupulous villain, a role Norman played for real! By my later teens I'd been typecast as Charles Boyer's crazed persecutor from the film "Gaslight," opposite Ingrid Bergman. It was one of Thelma's ploys to retain a maximum of control, when I became more assertive about some of her noisome obsessions, like piling our flat with streetjunk or defleaing her cats during dinner, that she would plunge into high drama, wringing her hands and tearing at her hair, screaming hysterically that I was a beast! Asking for the reasonable is beastly to an addict.

We'd play out the drama to its bitter end, with me revealed at last, as the cruelly mocking embodiment of Satan himself, in Thelma's eyes, and what's worse, in my own, irrespective of the reality. A distorted spirituality buoyed me out of the periodic emotional thoughts. I was a naive, well-intentioned Christian-socialist and sympathetic to eastern religions. I went to Mass on Sundays and used the confessional simplicly into my early 20s. I felt God should help me, but this rarely seemed the case. When things deteriorated in my 20s, I abandoned God.

The central dilemmas in my relationship with Mum revolved, as you'll have gathered, around issues of power and control. When I subscribed to her wishes I was good, a child of God you may say; if I made my own conflicting decisions I was bad, the devil you may say, and Mum could abandon me, actually or emotionally. Mum could never volunteer that she had been wrong; it seemed that any guilt terrified her. Her mother must have been terribly hard on her.

I was unsure of myself in relationships with others and anxious to please those I valued. Some boyhood companions, and later others, exploited this willingness and I would be the kid prodded into taking the big risks in dares, like stealing. I wasn't totally bereft of integrity and could make a stand on issues I felt strongly about, but I did fear rejection.

Any bullying of the weak revolted me, especially as I had also experienced cruelty regarding my fatness—I would caretake other weaker children, and oddballs, to the puzzlement of my less sentimental companions. In a sense, those I caretook were hostages, for my comfort.

At 15, I started laboring in a tobacco factory making five pounds a week. Mum had no income by then, and we subsisted in an exasperating poverty trap. My poor education meant low paid work on junior rates. Though I worked conscientiously, I lost jobs by being unreliable. I'd stay out late nights with mates; Manly Beach became an addictive escape when we got to know some girls there. Often we could barely scrape together the ferry fares, but we'd go, in a headlong, escapist expectancy heedless of consequences. Our "drugs of choice" were Iced Paddle Pops or Pepsi. These, alloyed with the girls' companionship and the geographical escape gave to us, then, an irresistible magic more than equal to any substance, and in spite of its seeming innocence, in some ways almost as abusive.

The mornings after, I'd drag myself off to work, with Mum's alarming assistance, promising myself an early night this time(!), all the way to the factory. But come evening, Manly beckoned like a drug. My old guilty phobia with facing up late, resurfaced. This defect plagued my whole working life and cost me many jobs, often where I'd done well and received promotions. I would never let anyone know that my inner child was so fearful and full of shame behind my flippant or indifferent masks. I suffered, and my reputation did, too.

I'd hate myself and despair of ever getting anywhere in life. I felt it was a godsend in later years when I discovered night shift work and I always sought this; it became a matter of survival. Thus did my codependent defects rule much of my life. I even joined a carnival and toured the country for six months, caretaking a dozen laughing clowns. I'd send Mum half of my eight pounds pay, weekly. The couple

I worked for were so impressed, they virtually wanted to adopt me, shedding a few tears when I left. I had just turned 18. I made it back to night school at 20 and topped the school at yearend. This encouraged me to go on and attempt to matriculate for university; another two years study. It was 1961.

Being a dysfunctional teenager in the late 1950s had its moments. Surprisingly, I'd turned out quite handsome after losing my baby fat. The guys I hung around weren't into violence or vandalism, and we preferred Holly to Elvis. But we weren't above siphoning petrol if cashless, as usual, I was generally the sucker.

I couldn't afford a car, or much else for that matter. Mum was sliding into neurotic obsessiveness, and our flat looked like a garage sale—she hoarded newspapers and stacks crept to the ceilings. I couldn't bring a girl home for shame. One might take me home to meet her parents, but I wouldn't respond and couldn't explain, and it became untenable to maintain the liaison. This was all a pain of frustration, anger and depression; so my teens were full of vicissitude and serial love affairs. I gradually came to realize that it took a "new love" to assuage "the blues" of the previous.

During night studies I teamed up with a female student. We were just pals, at first, and she didn't want a romance as she was going to the United States soon. I was content to be with her as such, at first, and I got along with her better than any person I'd ever met. We spent more and more time together, and it transpired she had broken two engagements. I was hooked on her, but she kept me at elbow's length most of the time, and my fluctuating esteem caused me to vacillate the few times she cued me to make love to her. She was two years older than I and much more sophisticated; she did love me, but her agendas made her ambivalent. I hoped for a miracle.

Eventually we split after an argument over her seeming infatuation with a radio commentator, 20 years her senior, whose elocution classes she attended. I was jealous and felt used in the bargain. But I paid—I was emotionally lost without her, and just plodded along joylessly with work and study.

A couple of months before this breakup, Mum received 4,000 pounds from her mother's long delayed estate. Things had looked much brighter, but Mum's mental manageability proved catastrophic. She assured me that she was following her lawyer's advice when I had a layman's doubts on a property investment; it went ahead, and I paid in half my wages for two years. When she got into trouble, I found she had overextended "against" the legal advice. We were both broke again. Mum is the most exasperating person I've ever met apart from myself. I considered suicide then; I hadn't thrown off the loss of my student love, who was now modeling on the U.S. West Coast.

My life was devoid of flavor, and I suffered a severe flattening of affect; I used no alcohol or drugs or medical aid. I was ignorant then of what was really happening to me. I pulled through, and I just couldn't leave Thelma on the planet in her state. I've since learned I survived through adapting and going into what the eminent American psychologist termed as a "neurotic resignation" marked by "shallow living."

I dropped my studies and decided to treat life as a bit of a joke. If I hadn't had Thelma to support I would have become another "jolly swagman" and headed for "Crocodile Dundee" country. The '60s were revving up, and when I turned 25 I wished I was 15. These kids are "with-it," I thought, and joined in the youth revolution. I was no hippy and never made it to a commune or even smoked pot, but I partied with them and became obsessed with the anti-Vietnam movement. I formed a codependent friendship with a boy eight years my junior, and we used to go to demonstrations and rallies. Among the ferment of ideas and adventurous initiatives I'd have my say. My mate's sister came from leaving school in the country; she was a mature girl for 15. The first time ever I saw her face I was struck by its subtly gentle sadness. Four years later, we married.

My ex-wife is a lovely, extremely codependent person; we have a son and daughter. This marriage was not a dramatic and feverish affair. We more or less drifted into it from a lack of options. I even resisted our involvement at first because of our age difference but we discussed this and she was still willing. I still didn't have sex with her though we petted; she was 17, I was 27. Six months later, we made up for lost time. But there was a strong element of rescuing in our affair.

I became enmeshed in my wife's family in a caretaking muddle of codependent controlling and tense power struggles. The stage was set, as my wife's mother had abandoned her husband and five children one night when she decamped with one of his long lost drinking mates whom they'd put up for the weekend. He became her fourth husband, fathering her ninth and tenth children. This sounds like some Old Testament happenings, but it's closer to the insane codependent relentlessness of Greek tragedy.

The pressures of my attempts to "outmaneuver" my wife and the rest of her family left me with an alcoholic dependence at 35 and a new and anarchic chapter opened in my life. After my wife left, I patched things up. We lived apart but met spasmodically, and our daughter was born. Three years later, my wife left for the bush with her family and our two kids. They left no address, and I sorely missed the children but booze damped down this pain.

At 45, I entered an alcohol rehabilitation program after being arrested for shoplifting a bottle of rum. A famous psychologist there advocated the AA recovery program but she pushed the genetic causation as the primary factor in the disease, which I disputed with her. Nevertheless, she regarded me as sufficiently motivated to stay at the clinic's prestigious "halfway" center at Bondi Beach. I was the eldest of its recoverees.

I went through the motions of recovery appropriately, but secretly I spent more time at the city's libraries studying academic texts on alcoholism and psychology rather than honestly surrendering and opening my heart willingly to the acceptance of the Twelve Steps and loving support within the Fellowship to help me contact my own Higher Power.

I went into a borderline, psychotic mania and wrote a long rambling treatise on spirituality, psychology and alcoholism to our psychologist. She was very impressed with this effort and said that I'd do well at University if I chose to carry on with studying—then she recommended an interview with the psychiatrist.

I raced about the city in an ambience of golden certitude that "I," John A., had become privy to the secrets of the universe; "I," poor, humble John, by my faithful perseverance had been admitted to an exalted circle of knowledge granted only to "The Few;" the Popes were insiders, as were David the Psalmist, Shakespeare and Freud. I received strong messages from this trio via various quotations I'd memorized. I had a mission, I must ready myself and it would be revealed. Omens buoyed me everywhere I went, from advertisements, streetnames, etc.; I was so confident that I even had a few judicious drinks, amber beer to cool the heat of the golden ambience so to speak.

I soon realized, when the interview came up, that the psychiatrist had not yet entered "the exalted circle." She showed some promise, but had a long way yet to go, and "I" decided, was unworthy of trust. I bluffed my way through the session. Then I visited my ex-wife and children, 1,000 kilometers up country and gave them part of "The Message."

On returning, I attended a rehabilitation group drunk and the psychologist tried persuading me to re-enter the clinic, but I still felt I was on the right path and left after some mild melodramatics. I had about nine months alcohol dry-time up.

I experienced a series of dries and relapses until entering a long-term rehabilitation the day after my

49th birthday. There, with love and support, I went through a grieving process in letting go of the past and seeing the futility of my old willful attitudes. I accepted the First Step at an emotional rock-bottom from which the only release is surrender. As the Fellowship cliche goes: I had to give in to win.

A counselor there began emphasizing codependence issues in her groups and shared that she herself was a recovering codependent. This alerted me to my children's possible suffering when I realized the inescapability for any family members from some manifestation of the life-sabotaging symptoms.

I bought a copy of a book that comprehensively described and offered explanations of the causes and treatment of codependence. I intended to send it to my 20-year-old son. A quick look-through before shipping it off to him and I couldn't put it down. I experienced an excited feeling of release as I absorbed the implications of what I'd read; I'd never conceptualized boundaries. At last the jigsaw of my life came together, and I felt some real joy for the first time in years as I was now able to begin letting go of so many more of the unreasonably negative and ill-founded judgments of myself and others made in the absence of valid insights. Now I could begin to see how my and others' codependence smothered real love and healthy growth, robbing lives of sustenance and meaning. Manageability was a possibility for me with the clarifying of so many questions that had haunted me for a lifetime.

My recovery is a gradual one-day-at-a-time process now. I am learning from the experiences of others, further along than I, to "keep it simple" and moderate my old tendencies to intellectualize, which made me crazy. I attended CoDA meetings regularly as well as my alcohol Fellowship. I share honestly at meetings and on a one-to-one basis with fellow members, personally and by phone. I am learning to take on only as much as I can comfortably handle for my stage of recovery. This allows me to do some service work in my Fellowships. I do pray, asking for help and guidance and using positive self-talk and encouraging affirmations; daily readings on spiritual themes help me get in touch with my Higher Power through reflection and the counting of my blessings.

I'm 18 months into recovery in my 50th year on the planet, and faith and hope have returned to my life, and I'm learning to love myself and receive love from others. The Twelve Steps prompt me to move on in a good orderly direction. I'm getting well.

Oh, and Thelma? She is 86 now. I visit her regularly in her nursing home where she is comfortable and in good physical health. Sometimes she thinks I'm her dad, and she is largely in a world of her own now. She never got the Academy Award, but I can't help but love her. God has been kind to us.

by John A.

TWO LIVES, ONE RELATIONSHIP

Nancy's story

First, some notes on my family of origin.

My father was a retired chief petty officer for the U.S. Navy. Controlling, mentally abusive to all of his family, he was an alcoholic like my grandfather. I was a good child, but always afraid of him. I never had to be told twice to do something.

As I grew up, I was accused of wearing bandaids instead of bras because there was nothing there. At age 16, I was told to hold my fat belly in. I weighed 115 lbs; I had no butt and no belly. I didn't stand up straight because I was ashamed of my appearance so I was made to walk up and down the hall of our house with a encyclopedia on my head and was threatened I'd have to wear a back brace. I never felt pretty. I realize today how shamed and controlled I was in my childhood.

One thing that really sticks in my mind is the physical abuse. My father taught me how to use hot water by sticking my hands in a sink full of very hot dish water. He put hot sauce in my mouth if I teased someone. I felt a lot of shame, pain and resentment with my father.

My mother worked full-time, so I cleaned the house after school everyday and sometimes started dinner. My mother picked out my clothes for most of my life. I wore what was bought for me until I could pay for my own, then I was still controlled as to what I could wear.

My mother is a very self-centered, spoiled woman who wore lots of diamonds and gold. She redecorated the house every five years even though we weren't rich by any means. I resented her for having the right to pick out pretty things for herself to wear. I wore my mother's hand-me downs. My father bought me my first miniskirt. I wore the mini, the granny shoes and the Tom Jones shirt to rebel against her.

My oldest brother was the family brain but he also took a lot of crap. He was always expected to be the achiever. He committed suicide in July of '93 because he was ashamed of who he was and what his life had become. He had always searched for approval from Dad, sometimes Mom. Mom didn't get along with him. He worshipped Dad and strived to be as good as Dad wanted him to.

My brother also drank a lot. When we were in high school, he broke his arm pole vaulting, I would sit with him and write out his homework for him. I always loved him a lot.

He was there when I put my son in the hospital

for 18 months due to addictions. He would call me just to see if I was OK. He's the reason my daughter started speaking when she was three years old; he had taken her into his home and worked with her and paid her tuition to be placed in a special school. That's more unconditional love than I had felt since our grandma.

In July of 1993, my father called and told my husband that my brother had taken and laid down on the garage floor of his home and pulled the trigger of a Magnum44. I felt shock, anger and rage. I hoped it wasn't true. He had attempted this before and was stopped, but this time he made sure no one was around. I was so angry!

I will remember his bright smile in the sunlight and the sparkle of his laughing eyes in the stars. I can't change the past; I can only go forward and remember him with love. God rest his soul—he was a wonderful man who knew how to love everyone but himself. I will always miss him!!

My other older brother, the middle child, was the family clown. He was also a rebel and talented singer and guitarist. In high school, he got into fights; he didn't start them, he just finished them. He never backed down. He protected me from our older brother when we were kids. He has his own past with heavy drug and alcohol problems.

I was the youngest—the only girl—in a family considered fairly normal at the time. As the kids, we were pretty well behaved because Dad wouldn't have it any other way. As adults, we were all alcoholic and/or drug addicts. I was certainly a caretaking, controlling, people-pleaser and forgotten child who was ashamed and controlled all my life.

At the age 18, I married to get out of my father's house even though I was still in high school. I met my first husband in a bowling alley, and six months later, (April, 1970), I invited my parents to my wedding on that very day. My father refused to attend and my mother cried. Our married life started with my family disliking my husband and his family disliking me.

After being married a few months, we packed and moved to Oregon to start a life away from our families. A year later, my husband started drinking and became abusive shortly after our son was born. He used to go to strip joints and make me go so that I'd drive him home. When we returned to California in '73, we had to live with my folks for a short time while he found work. When our second child was conceived he got even more abusive.

Shortly after our daughter was born, he became very physically and sexually abusive toward me. Since I was not allowed to work and kept busy by cleaning our home, it was very intimidating to hear him tell me I was a lousy mother, lousy housekeeper and lousy in bed. I began living in fear of my life. Then I started fearing for my children's safety when he locked me out of the house.

After one physically abusive episode at breakfast, I walked into my childrens' room. My little girl was playing in her crib and my son had pulled out a suitcase and was packing his little sister's clothes. I asked what he was doing and he said, "Mommy, get me out of here before I make him bleed for hurting you. I don't like him anymore!" My little boy opened my eyes that morning. We packed what we could

carry and I tried calling my mother but she wasn't
home. I was still in awful pain and could just barely
walk but I forced myself. There I was, with my two
children—a diaper bag, a large suitcase on the
bottom of the stroller, and my little big boy on his
tricycle with built-in wagon—all of us walking three
miles to Grandma's house.

I was taken to the emergency room and after three
days of examinations, they discovered that my gall
bladder had deteriorated so badly that it had
detached itself from my body. I had major surgery
after a few months of out-patient treatment.

To my husband, I was a hypochondriac even after
the surgery! I never went back to him. In March of
'76, my divorce was final and so ended the pain I
suffered—at least that's what I thought. My ex-
husband died in the 1980s, alone in the back seat of
his car, due to self-inflicted carbon monoxide
poisoning. Pictures of his children were lined up
across the dashboard. His children have children of
their own now. I pray the chain is broken.

In 1976, I met a man in a bar. I was there with a
friend named J. We spotted a good-looking man on
the dance floor. J bought him a drink and he politely
said, "I don't know which one of you ladies bought
me the beer, but I don't drink. Would you mind if I
traded it for a Coke?" I said, "No problem."

J wanted the man so I stood back and watched.
After being raised by and married to an alcoholic, I
was impressed and interested. He and J were talking
so I went about talking to friends. I was just out of a
very bad marriage and going through a divorce so I
was out sowing my oats. I sat on a bar stool, checking

out the Marines coming through the door and everywhere else in the room. I was having a great time. I made a date for the next night to meet someone there. I showed up and in walked T. He was looking for J. They were supposed to meet there too—that's the beginning of my relationship with T. Eleven years ago we moved to Missouri where we are now.

We were married on December 23, 1978. I was controlled in this marriage too, and there was some mental abuse as well. I was ridiculed in public and at times even shamed. In the beginning of this marriage, I wanted to be loved and cared for so much that I was a subservient wife; I hung on to what I thought I had. In reality I had married another alcoholic. He never physically abused me so I thought things were OK. But there was a very painful time in our marriage.

I've included entries from my journal during this difficult time of my marriage with T.

April 28—He admitted to what I've known for years—three affairs. What about my wants, my needs?! What do I want to do?! I'm confused, lonely, unhappy, sad; I'm experiencing physical pain in my body. My life is a joke! What do I want? I want my husband!!! I want my best friend!!! I want a clean start!!!

April 29—It's more pain than I care to handle. Once, twice, three times my marriage was violated! He feels good about getting it out and getting rid of his guilt. All I feel is pain, rage, resentment, unhappiness and worthlessness. He says he loves me and wants "romance" in our marriage the way it should be. He doesn't make sense to my confused state. I don't want to be in the house with him tonight.

I am supposed to understand that his "multiple addictions" cause his problems. Give me a break. The man cheated on me and I am supposed to excuse it because it's a f___'n addiction!!! Someone cheats on their mate and because they are "in recovery" they should be forgiven—kill the bastard!!! Going to a meeting ain't going to solve this. I don't want to get into bed with him today, and maybe not tomorrow and for however long this crap takes. Does this pain end? Help me!!!!!

May 4—I have made my mind up. Love outweighs the pain. I still feel the pain but I'm hoping we can work through it all. I still need a lot of help with the violation of trust! The fact that someone else has touched him only the way I should is hard—very hard to deal with. I want to try, but I'm really scared. I still feel the anger and resentment. It has only been a week. Miracles don't happen in a week or overnight. I need to feel his love and I don't. Maybe it's my anger!! I don't feel anything and I don't feel anything coming from him. He feels guilty and shameful. Him! Him! Him! I wish he could feel this pain for five minutes! Maybe he would understand a little better. I still have a lot of feelings to come out.

May 6—Yesterday, I decided to stay with the man I love. He's a good person; it's his addictions I hate. One day at a time, I will go to therapy, and with the help of my Higher Power, things will get better, but they will never be the same.

May 29—(After a recovery conference where I attended with T.) I'm alone in the bedroom after taking a long shower. I had a very emotional weekend. I don't know how I feel anymore. I got very angry when T ignored me and was talking to a female. I know something is not right. I know there is something in there but it's jumbled up inside of me. I know I really hate life; it really sucks. I don't feel anything—nor do I want to. Where did my life go? What do I do now. Please, help me!!

May 31—I made a decision to be alone for now. I'm not angry. I don't think I'm still in pain but I need to be alone today.

It is my choice to do this. I have prayed for guidance; I have thought long and hard about it. I need this time to try to get me back on track. I am not sure who I am at this point. I feel like all I want to do is sleep. Is that a sign of depression?

I brought phone numbers so that I can make calls, but whom do I trust other than myself and my Higher Power? People say they'll listen, but whom can I trust!!?? It's 8:00 p.m., and I'm in bed still searching for feelings. I have none.

I called home earlier just to say I was OK and in a room. It's not what I wanted, but it's affordable. I drove around a lot with no destination. I was just driving and trying to figure out what I am going to do. I also thought about how I could murder the son of a bitch for cheating on me. I figured I could do it while he was sleeping—that way he couldn't stop me. But why bother? All it would do is land my ass in jail, so why not take my car and ram it into a tree or empty building without my seatbelt on? Maybe I'd get lucky and die. Then I wouldn't have to deal with all this crap. With my luck, I'd live. Why bother? I have grandchildren to think about; besides, me being dead might make him happy. I'm out of the picture anyway. Now he can play all he wants!! Just driving and thinking.

I think it's bullshit when they say that God doesn't give you anything you can't handle. What do you call all the lies? We weren't even married a year and the bastard slept with another woman and I'm supposed to forgive. Let go and let God—yeah right!!

Death is too good—an easy out—besides tying him in a sheet while he sleeps, and stabbing him 'cause he bleeds good is very messy!! It will be better to make him suffer with life, and me!!

June 1—I just want to be left alone to work out what I am going to do with the rest of my life, or what's left of it. Should I just end it and let him live with that!!??? I really need strength in my life. I need to do some real heavy soul searching. I have asked T to come and talk with me on Friday. Maybe we should, maybe we shouldn't. Maybe we should meet in a public place. I can't understand my feelings. I'm really angry—I really hate what he's done! It was the alcoholic T, but it was still T. Sexually, I feel cheap, dirty and no better than what he picked up somewhere. It's 11:05 now. I'm trying to take care of me but what is it I want? I'm not making any sense.

June 2—I'm at work eating lunch and still not sure of my feelings. Can I stay married to T—the man I have loved for 17 years!!! It's now 4:12 p.m.; I'm having trouble concentrating on work issues. I have other things on my mind. I need to get out of here as soon as possible tonight. I need to really deal with issues—the first one being my marriage!

Can I handle living with what has happened in the past? This isn't easy—can I do this??? Can I???

June 3—I don't feel any different. I love him but I don't know that I can live with the issues. Tomorrow T and I are going to talk at Denny's.

June 4—It's about midnight. I was sent home from work today at 9:00. I am alone in my motel room, listening to T's song. We talked tonight. I'm going home on Sunday. I still have a lot to work through. He tried to help me understand. It's a lot to swallow. I need to work through my pain and other issues. He cried and for a moment I felt he was on his pity pot with a poor-me attitude. At one point I wanted to smack him!!! He's crying and I'm the one who's been violated, cheated on and lied to. There are no guarantees of what tomorrow will bring. I need to get therapy and work on "me." I have to put my husband, marriage, family and life in God's hands. God will do what is needed to guide me in the right direction. I will not make any advances toward him. I want him to love me the way I deserve and need to be loved. I don't want anything dirty and unhealthy anymore.

June 16—I had my first therapy today; her name is Josephine and I think I can do this. I cried of course; my issues are tough ones. I itch because of my nerves. Life is not easy but I do have a lot to live for, at least that's the way I feel now.

My life as I understand it today:

Today, who I am and what my life is, is all due to this program I entered over two years ago. It has helped to guide me to become a woman happy with this life—the only life I am responsible for. I cannot change the past, nor do I wish to close the door on it. I have forgiven some things, some I may never forgive. I have come to believe and have shared with T that I do not need him in my life to make me happy—I choose to have him there. I believe that one day at a time I will grow and learn from the past with all its pains, sorrow and other feelings. I have Twelve Steps that keep me in a straight line. I have a Higher Power that guides me as I walk. This program of individuals, whose common problem is an inability to maintain functional relationships, is a key factor in helping me.

I decide to stay with the man I have loved all these years, and together we continue to work on our marriage. He has his program, and I, mine. I have stopped allowing others to control me and I no longer am controlled. I accept the things I cannot change and I change the things I can. I cannot bring my childrens' father back, nor can I bring back my brother. I will never really understand the reasons they died; I choose to accept that they are in a better place. I cannot change my father and mother. They did the best they could with the tools they had. I can be the person who changes; I have and will continue to better my life. I cannot change what I have done, said or felt. I can only go forward with my life.

If I can give back a little of the experience, strength and hope that was given so unselfishly to me, I will. I thank all of the people who have listened and shared with me. Most of all, I thank my sponsors who listened without passing judgment. In closing, I would like to share this verse that I choose to live by:

I expect to pass through
Life but once.
If there be a kindness
I can show.
Or any good thing I can do
Let me do it now.
For I shall not pass
This way again.

For me I live
One day at a time,
Gratefully
With the help of my Twelve Steps,
And a loving Higher Power.

Verse 1, author unknown
Verse 2, Nancy's

Terry's story

I was raised in a railroad town in New England and moved to a small farm town in my teenage years. My family was a mixture due to divorce. My grandmother was living with a man I only knew as Goldie, and my grandfather had, what my family referred to, as a live-in housekeeper. My father was raised by his aunt, who I referred to as Grandma. I never felt close to any of my family except my mother because I was her man. I was there when my father was off having one of his affairs or hunting and fishing, which always received more thought, time, and care than I did.

When my father was home and needed something done, I was included if I could carry my share of the load. If we were fixing the car, I was expected to lay out all the tools and jack the car, have the ground cover, fender covers and everything else in place before he would appear to do the work, and God forbid that anything went wrong because he would rage. I was expected to know which tool he needed before he asked for it, and the light was to be held so he could see what he was doing.

Punishment was based on the thought "spare the rod and spoil the child." It came to the point that being danced around the floor with a razor strap was no big deal, and I was tired of hearing that men don't cry, so I didn't. I felt bad when my mother begged him to stop. I wished he would have stopped so my mother would quit crying.

I knew where my father kept his pornography. When I was older and would take a girlfriend out parking I would have to check to see if my father was there with one of his girlfriends. I knew he knew I would never tell my mother; it would crush her.

My father verbally raged at my mother for things my sisters and I did or at her directly for "things any dummy would have known." My mother acted as if that was the way a loving marriage was supposed to be. She reminded us that it was no big deal because he never hit her and he always kept a roof over our heads.

My father would work overtime to provide us kids with the material things we wanted. I wish he had figured out it was his love we wanted. He would stand in the corner of the room and watch us open our packages till the tears had swollen in his eyes and he had to leave the room to get something.

I started dating young, maybe at age 12 or so, and would totally lose myself in whomever I was dating. I was afraid of losing them, which I did after a long period of time, because I hung on till they forced me away.

I learned all the right things to say and do to get a lady to love me, from opening doors to bringing their mother flowers. I worked out to keep my body in shape because my physique was important to me. The bigger and stronger I looked, the more the women would want me, I thought. I wanted to scare the guys away because I was afraid to fight. Healthy confrontation was not something modeled at home; I learned not to rock the boat.

My father did tell me that if I got a girl pregnant I was expected to marry the "slut." He also informed me that any girl I had sex with on the first date would do it for "anyone," so use a rubber.

My mother took care of everything for me because that was her job. She made my bed, washed my clothes and fixed my meals. I worked to give her money, which she used to pay my bills; she even set up my car and life insurance. I didn't have to know what was going on with my finances at all. I learned to be taken care of; I didn't know how to get my basic needs met.

I joined the Marines because it was known to be the hardest boot camp and my father said he would never be in the Marines. I thought, "Boy, would I show him that I was the best." He told everyone how proud he was of my becoming a Marine—everyone except me.

After boot camp I was on my own and knew nothing except how to work. Working was like a drug to me—it gained me recognition and put me in charge. As long as I stayed busy, I didn't feel alone and didn't have to deal with all the things I knew nothing about.

I married a high school sweetheart and just knew she would take care of me. I had learned to control her every thought. I could be charming and make her smile, or with the coldest stare, I could send chills through her bones. She knew I had run around on her while we were going together, so it must be all right.

We had lost a boy at six weeks of age, after I had agreed to a test that only gave him a five percent chance of making it; they felt there was little chance if he did not have it. He didn't make it and we were far from home. We had to get his body shipped clear across the country, so within hours of his death I made arrangements with the funeral home to have this taken care of. The only way I could handle this was to do it like a business deal—no emotions. We then had to get ourselves across the country and she was no help. I hated her for not helping. Why was I the only one who was not allowed to feel?

After two daughters and a lot of my drinking and physical abuse, she left me. I felt crushed that I would not be able to be there while our kids grew up.

I proceeded to have the greatest of times. I found all kinds of women just ready to take care of me. I lost myself in the process, as well as the hope that they would make the feeling of loneliness go away.

I met a lady who described how she thought a man should be taken care of, but I was being persuaded by her friend. The next night her friend was not there, nor was the guy she had a date with. So we talked some more and went to breakfast.

She was from a very abusive marriage and was trying to take care of two children. I knew how to be a knight in shining armor. She would give me her last $20 for food and I would bring her back $40 worth. She had three outfits so I bought her clothes. The kids were watching a small black and white TV, so I brought home a large color set.

We fought because I did not want to settle down but I still wanted her around. I did not even ask her to marry me. I just told her we would get married if she could find a baby sitter. Then it took me a long time before I told anyone because I had stated once that I'd never get married again; I was afraid of what they'd think.

Shortly after we were married, I was sent overseas for seven months, came back for a year and a half, then went back overseas. This gave me the strong feeling of being alone, which I used with my addictions to deal with the loneliness.

During my time in the service, my father died. He was a lonely, scared man. He even had my mother ask for the shot which would allow him to drift off peacefully. He had turned his back on me weeks earlier when I had gone to visit him. He had never learned to live.

I thought a college degree would make people think of me differently so I did four years of college night school in four and a half years while working days. People never noticed.

I wanted to do one more trip overseas where I could be in charge of 100 Marines to prove to everyone how good a job I could do. After all my problems with my drinking, I figured it was time to retire, so I picked up my daughter from my first marriage and moved home. Upon my arrival, I found myself in a support group for parents with children in recovery. One night I was told I was a codependent, which meant nothing to me but that I should get help so I could help my kids.

I attended my first meeting of CoDA, where women were talking about how they hated the controlling, abusive men they were married to. I introduced myself as that controlling husband they were talking about, and said I wanted to get better.

I began to understand the talk, terms and felt the feelings. Slowly the garbage was lifted and I began to feel better. Then I was able to look at everyone around me and tell you everything they needed to do to get better. A young man who was counseling the youth group looked at me one evening, while I was taking someone's inventory and told me to start working my own program. I had to learn to feel my feelings about life and not get caught up in everyone else's situations. I had to learn to recognize what I had done to cause the problem.

The idea of separating my children from their behavior was helpful for me. I learned that my love is not based on behavior or conditions but unconditional love. I started telling my children that I loved them but did not like their behavior.

I had to ask a couple of different men to sponsor me and had trouble making the first call. Someone finally asked me to sponsor them and I agreed to a deal where we would sponsor each other and it worked.

Through CoDA, I began working the Steps. I read the CoDA literature that was available on the Steps and talked in small groups about what it meant to me. A couple of men wanted to work a "workbook" on the Twelve Steps so we formed a group outside our CoDA group and spent the next 28 weeks eating, drinking and breathing the Steps so that we wouldn't break the Traditions (we were using materials other than CoDA-approved literature). I couldn't believe the progress I made. I found that each person had their own sense of how the Steps worked for them and through that I gained a sense of validation for my beliefs.

My wife was working her program and it felt so good to be able to tell her to take her problems to her sponsor because I was too close to the problem or I might even be part of the problem. We began to fight fairly with our defenses not so high. We asked each other what we heard the other one say and found we did not hear what the other was trying to communicate on the first try or even on the second try. Our misunderstandings were beginning to get worked out.

I had three affairs during our marriage. I had been struggling with forgiving myself and accepting my addiction in this area, when one night during a talk, my wife asked if I had ever had an affair. I answered, "yes" and the crushing blow was evident on her face. I had to accept whatever happened because I was the one who had made the choice. She left to get her head together. As much as it hurt both of us, my feelings about being honest were only strengthened. Months later, I told my wife that if I ever wanted to get into a relationship with someone else, she would be the first to know. It took me too long to get rid of the guilt from the past. If I started an affair with someone while still in a relationship with her, I didn't want the guilt back and no one else could ever trust me. I might do the same thing to them.

The kids expected me to go back to my drinking and told me so. I knew there was no going back.

Her brother—my best friend—committed suicide. Before I had gotten into recovery, we had shared family secrets and talked about the struggle to please our parents. If he could only learn that we have to learn to please ourselves. This happened only months after an old drinking buddy had blown his head off. He had told me they would never put him out of the service. I could have been that person whose only thing in life was to be a Marine. I questioned the saying, "God doesn't give you anything you can't handle." I now feel God showed me what I could have been.

For me commitment is the thing that takes love and made it a relationship. I have to do my part no matter what she does, or I would be running as before and feeling the guilt for not only what I did but for what I should have done. I don't have to deal with guilt if I don't do things I know I'll feel guilty for, and which I had experienced in the past.

I placed myself back on a "gratitude trip" where I am grateful for everything that happened to me. It doesn't matter if my car has a flat or my feet hurt. I force myself to think positively. Nice things happen, too, that I had not recognized in the past. Today, I have a new outlook toward my marriage. I accept the fact that my parents loved me in their own way and did the best with what they knew. I accept the fact that I had done the best I could have done for my kids with the sickness I had. I've finally let go of the past.

People have told me that men and women are different but nowhere have I found that certain feelings are for males or females. I have cried many a tear, have felt scared and alone, helpless and without hope. If we can't get past the gender stereotype and down to feelings, we will continue to struggle. To me, it doesn't matter whether a man talks to a man or woman, feelings matter the most. Honesty knows no gender; I feel compassion and long to have been nurtured by both of my parents. At first, I felt funny being hugged by a man when I came into the Fellowship because of the homophobia, but caring is not about sex. Caring is letting the other person be who they are and me being myself.

Service work gives me an opportunity to take on only what I want to do, to say no and mean it, to watch others struggle with their recovery, to allow myself to be human and make mistakes and not judge others when they make mistakes. It also allows me opportunities to accept what others have to contribute, whether it meets my expectations or not and to speak up when I disagree. I try not to control but to be myself and let others know who I really am. For me, the Traditions are not to be used to control others but to learn to conduct myself healthily within the Fellowship. For me, it is modeling the program that is more important, no matter how uncomfortable and scared I might seem as I move forward into uncharted ground. The program tells me that half Steps avail me not, so I choose to work them to their fullness. I'm human and make mistakes but that is no longer a reason to quit.

For me there is a feeling that there should be a Step 8a and 9a which should read:

Step 8a "Made a list of those persons that I had allowed to control me and became willing to confront them all."

Step 9a "Made direct confrontations with such people whenever necessary to continue my life."

These would cause me to deal with those people I had allowed to control me so that I would set boundaries and not allow that to happen anymore.

by Nancy and Terry S.

BOB'S STORY

It is difficult to know where to start because my story actually begins 65 years ago when I was less than one year old. My mother died in a fire and my father died a few months later of pneumonia. I was raised by my widowed grandmother who was overly strict and protective. I am reaching far back only to establish the source of my codependency. I grew up in a home without laughter and joy, and I harbored a deep-seated resentment and anger at my parents for having died and left me to this fate. Along with the anger, of course, came guilt for feeling that way. How can you be angry at someone for dying?

I grew up feeling inadequate and unable to have normal relationships from an early age. I was never involved with a circle of friends like other children in school. Instead, I had only one "best friend" at a time whom I proceeded to virtually smother until he did not want anything to do with me any more. This cycle repeated itself many times right into my teens. My grandmother died when I was not quite 15 and I was left practically on my own. Once again I felt guilt, this time for feeling relieved to be rid of my grandmother.

I think this explains why I went through life feeling angry, guilty, inadequate and with low self-esteem. I am married for the third time now even though I was never divorced. Both my previous wives died and I remarried in rather short order.

Up until summer 1988, I knew nothing of codependency. I had been attending Al-Anon for several years, but it did not do much for me at the time. I am not saying that it is not a good program, but probably I was not ready for it. We had some severe problems in our marriage, and my wife saw a counselor on a regular basis. She asked me to come with her for a few sessions, and one day the counselor said to us that we were so codependent that it was hard to know where one ended and the other started. It got me thinking about a problem that, up until then, I had attributed only to my wife. After all, there was nothing wrong with me; it was all her fault.

In September that year, my wife left me and I was devastated. Somehow my Higher Power led me to my first CoDA meeting. The group had just started a few months earlier, and there were only 10 or so people in attendance. I felt such warmth and unconditional acceptance that I was drawn to return for subsequent meetings and it was the turning point in my life.

Since that time, CoDA has grown in my town. Now we have 10 meetings every week, and I make it a point never to miss the meeting of my home group. I have made dozens of really good friends, and my marriage is back together better than ever before. I might add that my spouse also attends CoDA meetings, and our understanding and communication have improved 100 percent since we are both "program" people.

One of the wonderful revelations I found in CoDA is the fact that I do not have to appear all together and in control of my life. I am accepted for what I am, not for what I feel obliged to appear to be. As a boy I was taught from an early age that "men don't cry" and, if they had feelings at all, they certainly didn't show them. "Never allow anyone to see your weaknesses, because people will ridicule you and take advantage of you." "If you feel weak or hurt, you must hide that to maintain your masculine image." Since I grew up without a male role model, I tried to pattern myself after movie stars and sports figures. It created untold problems when I was trying to raise my son, because not having had a father, I did not know how to be one.

Thanks to the CoDA program, the loving support of the members and the opportunity to be of help and service to others, I am glad to say that I finally am living life and not just surviving it. Through the Twelve Steps and my increased faith in my Higher Power I am no longer angry. I have replaced anger with compassion, and as my faith grew, my fear diminished. Today I am able to face nearly anything without fear. I enjoy nature and the friendship of many people. Back in December last year I faced a cancer operation scheduled for January. I was able to enjoy the holidays with my family and face what was to be by putting it into the hands of my Higher Power. As it turned out, my Higher Power saw to it that I was cured, and I am now extremely grateful for all the good things life has to offer.

Sometimes I feel that I have overcome most of my problems, but I find that if I do not attend CoDA meetings on a regular basis, I tend to slip back into the old habits. I guess that I will never graduate, but that is no problem; I look forward to attending CoDA meetings, and I also feel good to be giving something back. Every time I do a newcomer's meeting I feel that I am gaining as much, if not more than the newcomers. It gives me a wonderful feeling to see some of the new people heal and grow over the months, knowing that I might have had a small part in it. Every time I hear people sharing and I share my feelings honestly, I feel that I am finally part of the human race.

by Bob B.

BETH'S STORY

Today, I feel like a butterfly bursting out of its cocoon. But it took almost a lifetime of insanity for me to gain the courage to peek outside of this shell. My Higher Power brought me to a path of recovery. That path of recovery is Co-Dependents Anonymous, its Twelve Step program and wonderful recovery people.

I was the fourth child of five born into an alcoholic home. I was born at an inopportune time in my family's history. I was a very quiet and a very good child. I remember hearing "what a good girl" I was all of my life.

Looking back, I believe I stepped inside a fantasy cocoon where I could be safe. Hidden inside this cocoon of "never-never land," I denied myself the opportunities to learn how to relate with people, how to appropriately express myself, and how to be assertive. Unfortunately, I never learned to switch from fantasy to reality. I stayed safely inside my cocoon of goodness.

I learned that confusion was not a safe place for me, and it was whirling all around me. My father was drinking heavily, money was tight, teenaged children were in the home and I had a toddler sister. Add to that the fact that my brother's birth occurred one year after mine.

As I put my thoughts on paper, I've become aware that I repeated this family pattern. At the height of the dysfunction in my home there were teenagers, toddlers, babies, and money was tight. I believe that part of the healing of my inner child has come as a result of watching my youngest child struggle with the same issues I did. He began his growth for freedom in second grade, but, for me, it was high school before I felt safe enough to step into "reality." My father joined Alcoholics Anonymous in the 1950s. My mother, the wonderful, loving, caring, co-dependent person that she was, taught me how to "walk on eggshells."

I learned well. I was a pretty, bright, energetic young woman. Many people said I was a Jacqueline Kennedy look-alike. (Isn't it funny how we can look so lovely on the outside and be so totally unlearned on the inside?) I encountered men who took advantage of me. The one man who both hurt and helped me most came in a lovely package. He was extremely handsome and was raised in a loving home. Church and God seemed to be number one in his life, and that was very important to me.

We met in December, became engaged in February, and married in June. We both shared the desire to raise a large family, a family in which the wife stayed home and raised the children. At one point in our marriage we were considered the "perfect" couple and family in our church. My husband was the parish council president, and I had started a ladies' Bible study group. My husband was the head of our home.

My dream had been realized! I had a lovely home, children everywhere, and church was an important part of our family life. We even had ruffled, tieback curtains hanging in every window. (Remember Dick and Jane in the first grade primer? Keep in mind, my reality had always been a fantasy.) Life seemed good; then something happened. My husband lost his job, those darling children became teenagers and money grew tighter. We functioned perfectly in perfection, but neither my husband nor I had the coping skills for imperfection.

Early in our marriage I had seen signs of rage and rigidity in my husband. Our way of dealing with this was to keep so busy that we never had time to deal with real-life issues. As confusion entered our home, my husband's rage and rigidity reared its ugly head. We began the typical cycles of an abusive home. Rather than look at ourselves and our behavior, we chose money as our issue.

My husband thought our problems would be solved if I worked outside the home. For me, it only intensified the crazy activity. My husband demanded good sex, frugal living, a spotless home, perfect kids, delicious meals, and a flawless life. Sadly, I truly believed that as long as I met those demands, I was doing all that I could to make my marriage work. It never occurred to me to look at my needs. I thought that if I performed perfectly all would be OK. No wonder the pressure and unrealistic demands became unbearable for me.

I wasn't allowed time for friends or personal interests, nor money of my own. I was caught in a vicious cycle of jumping when my husband said, "Jump," and pathetically, I just kept jumping! Because the pressure was so great and I had grown so fearful, I fled to a convent.

The nuns suggested that I seek professional counseling. I did, and the counselor began teaching me skills I could use to take care of myself, including how I could recognize some of my own needs. This was all so new to me. In the name of religion, I had grown to believe that the more giving I did, the more pleasing I was to God. I was left defeated and exhausted with no sense of self-respect.

I encouraged my husband to seek help with me and he did. Things improved, but stress recurred— particularly over money issues—and the cycle repeated itself. I believed that the more obedient I was to this man—the household head—the more obedient I was to God. Please keep in mind that this psychological abuse was a well-kept secret. I knew and the children knew. Later, my teenagers shared with me about the night their youth fellowship director was discussing families. He identified our family as the perfect model. My sad teens sat silently, knowing I was at the Salvation Army seeking refuge from their raging father.

I don't know what brought me to my senses, but on May 14, 1988, I made a decision. My husband always expected me to give him my entire paycheck.

We always lived a very frugal lifestyle, but lately I had realized that not only were our emotional needs not being met, but our physical needs were being neglected as well. I decided on that day to withhold my paycheck from him. Instead, I safely hid it in a spot I knew he couldn't find. Somehow I knew I would find the strength to deny this man his demand. I knew he was 6'2" and I was 5'7". He weighed more than 200 pounds, but that day I was determined to stand my ground.

Unfortunately, what I had feared most happened. My husband physically assaulted me. As awful as that moment was, a miracle occurred. I finally made a decision to take charge of my life. I filed for a legal separation and he counterfiled for a divorce. In that interim, from May until July, he withheld all money. Relatives, friends, and food stamps fed me and the children. Our bills went unpaid.

That fall I attended my first Twelve Step meeting— Adult Children of Alcoholics. I began to feel safe in the presence of these caring people. I remember letting the years of stored tears flow. Five weeks of meetings passed before I could stop those tears. Then a hunger to learn and to understand those Steps consumed me. I started attending a beginners' Al-Anon group as well. This group concentrated only on the first three Steps. Attending ACoA and Al-Anon were important in my growth, for it was there that I recognized my codependency.

The following May, I learned that two women—a former pastor's wife and a recovering alcoholic— had begun our community's first Co-Dependents Anonymous group. A recovery friend and I attended the meeting out of curiosity. The issues of codependency in my life rang loud and clear. I began to see that my previous 48 years had been dedicated to making others happy. Not only were they not happy, I was miserable. Walking through CoDA's Twelve Steps with a sponsor and attending meetings gave me some tools to help me deal with my life and my self-defeating behaviors. Looking back, it is my firm conviction that a loving God gave me these Twelve Steps at a time when I was desperately in need of guidance and direction.

I'm the single parent of six children. I'd been a homemaker for more than 20 years. Today I'm a full-time elementary school teacher. Every day is a challenge for me. But today, with the help of CoDA's Twelve Steps, my sponsor, the readings and attendance at meetings where there is recovery in progress, I'm unafraid to meet challenges and take risks. I've learned to own my own power and not give it away. I'm learning to stop the busyness of life and have fun. I find that living one day at a time puts my life into a manageable time frame.

I had gone into marriage and parenthood with the misconception that if I gave all of me to my husband and children, I would truly have given my family all that I could. Unfortunately, I gave away so much of me, there was nothing left. I no longer had an identity. I no longer had laughter or spontaneity. I lived in fear and terror. I was as good as a dead person.

I remember once asking my therapist, "What can I do to help my children?" She simply said, "Take care of yourself." When people take care of themselves, growth and freedom follow. Children discover innately that these persons are ideal to turn to in times of need. When I am overwhelmed by life today, I know my recovery is maintained and sustained only when I stop and take care of myself. I have no sense of serenity until my needs are in check. I know I can only give to others when I have been first true to myself. I also know when life hits rough spots, that I should first stop and think of how a particular situation is affecting me.

My Higher Power has given me a rebirth and a new sense of enthusiasm for life. And so, when I say I feel as though I'm a butterfly, I know now that my wings have given me a new and wonderful freedom.

by Beth F.

I AM A MIRACLE

Hello. My name is Peggy and I am a miracle. I was born into a dysfunctional family. I "grew up" in an environment of drugs and alcohol. I was physically, emotionally, spiritually and sexually abused as a child. I survived. I am a miracle because I no longer survive. Today I live!!!

I was the fourth of nine girls born to my parents. My first born sister died when she was three days old. My second sister was born severely physically handicapped. The next pregnancy ended in a miscarriage. I was the first "perfect" child. There were four more pregnancies, but only two others lived.

My parents separated before I was six or seven years old. I remember very little prior to that time except for violence. I remember feeling very afraid because Mommy and Daddy were fighting again because Daddy was drunk. They would always fight, hurt each other, yell and scream, and I would be afraid, and hide under my blanket or in the basement. I was afraid I'd get hit. I was afraid they would kill each other. I knew I had to do something to stop them. I just didn't know what I was supposed to do.

I tried real hard to be the "perfect" little girl I was expected to be. I got good grades in school, but never good enough. I was involved in school activities, but I could never remain involved. I always felt guilty, like I should be home cleaning the house or making dinner. I played the violin, which I hated, but my mother loved. I never practiced long enough or "good" enough. I tried real hard but I was just never good enough.

My youngest sister was born when I was five years old, and I became her mother. I had to bathe, dress and feed her before I went to kindergarten. Later on, I had to watch my two younger sisters after school because Mom always had to work since Dad didn't give her any money. There was never enough money. We ate a lot of pork and beans and scrambled eggs.

I always thought we were poor. I felt like we were poor people pretending to be middle class. I was always ashamed of where we lived, our furniture and most ashamed of what was going on inside our house. I knew this wasn't happening in anyone else's house. I was different. I never fit in anywhere although I tried really hard. I gave away prized possessions so my friends would like me. I wanted desperately to be liked and to be accepted. I wasn't.

We moved a lot. I think we moved an average of once every two years, except for 4th grade when we moved three times. It was difficult to make friends and impossible to keep them.

My mother remarried when I was about nine years old. I don't ever remember liking or trusting my stepfather. I have always believed that my mother married him for his money. They never got along. They always fought and tried to kill each other. I was always afraid of him. He was really mean to me.

I was most afraid when I had nightmares and woke up crying, and my mom would send my stepfather down to my room to "calm" me down. I was more afraid of what he was going to do to me than I was of the nightmares. When I told my mother that he was sexually abusing me, she told me that I lied. She said that he loved me, and that he would never do anything to hurt me. She didn't protect me. I wasn't important. My feelings of being afraid were not validated.

As I became a teenager I finally found a way to win my mom's approval. If I drank with Mom, she liked me. So at age 12, Mom and I started drinking together on the weekends. Alcohol had always been the center of our universe. Whenever my mom said she was going out, we knew she was going to a bar. That was where everybody went when they went "out." I didn't know there were other things to do besides go to bars. We drank when we were happy. We drank when we were sad. We drank when we were mad. We drank when we were disappointed. We drank for anything. And if the drink didn't make you feel better, there were always nerve pills to calm you down. Mom and I got along when we drank together. She liked me then. Finally, Mom liked me. And I liked the feeling I got when I drank. I was pretty, smart and funny—everything I always wanted to be and never believed I was.

Growing up if I felt sad and I cried, my mom would say, "You're tired. Go to bed!" Or if I was happy and laughing I was always "up to something". However I felt, Mom always knew there was a hidden meaning behind those feelings, and the feelings were not OK with Mom. Somehow she would "fix" me. I can remember hearing, "If you're going to continue to cry, you can stay in your bed until tomorrow morning. Nothing is that bad."

In junior high school, I discovered that I no longer needed Mom's approval. I could get boys to like me really easy. I became very promiscuous. I didn't need to get good grades, or to clean the house or to be "perfect" anymore. All I had to do was to let boys do whatever they wanted to me and they would hold me and tell me they loved me and I would be "OK." The only problem with this theory is that what really happened was that I hated myself.

I ended up hating myself so bad that suicide became the only solution to all my problems. I considered suicide as an acceptable alternative for at least the next 20 years until I entered a Twelve Step program. Several suicide attempts with drug overdoses put me in the hospital. Twice I ended up in mental wards; it was still the easier way out. No one would care if I was gone and I'd be out of everyone's way. Needless to say, my attempts at suicide were not successful. Thank God.

At 16 years old, I became a single parent of a baby boy. When I found out I was pregnant, I wasn't surprised. As a matter of fact, I was happy. I finally would have something of my own to love, that would love me back and that no one could ever take away from me. My stepfather had my son sold on the "black market" for $50,000.00 before he was even born. He asked me if I gave my son to him for $50,000.00, could he borrow the money. I hated him for even thinking that I would consider giving the baby up, and I hated him even more for centering his world around money.

I kept my son and married his father less than three months later. The next two years were sad, frustrating and painful. I had my first daughter 13 months after we were married. We lived at my mother's for three weeks at a time, then we would have a fight, and one of us would move out. The next day we'd kiss and make up and move into his parents' house. The cycle continued. It was physically, emotionally and spiritually abusive. But my fear of rejection and abandonment was so strong that I would rather tolerate this personally harmful behavior than be left alone. My fear was not financial security or the lack thereof, because I was the only one who worked. I supported my husband and two children while he played cards and rode go-carts with his friends.

I became exhausted. My world was not coming together the way I thought it would. The storybooks told me that I would get married and live happily ever after. Little babies make people happy and love each other. None of this was happening in my world. I was lonely, afraid and unhappy. I was looking for happiness, and it was hiding. My marriage had fallen apart. I just couldn't take it anymore. I had failed again.

At 17 years old, I worked in bars as a dancer. I was underage and afraid of being caught. I knew how to con and manipulate men to get what I wanted. I knew how to get affection (even if it was only temporary). I knew how to get drinks bought for me. I had learned my lessons well. My mother had taught me that all men were out to use us women, so use them first; get what you can.

I met my youngest daughter's father, and he moved in; I had captured another hostage. Again, I believed a baby would somehow bond us together. If I had his child, he would love me more than anything or anyone for the rest of his life. I lost his first child, and 10 months later, our little girl was born. Her dad loved her. There was some kind of a bond there that I didn't understand. I didn't know or understand what it was like to have a father. I was jealous.

Our relationship was abusive. It became so physically abusive that I feared for my oldest two children's lives. I knew that I deserved the beatings I got, but my kids didn't. I was afraid and alone. I had nowhere to go. My mother had moved to Florida so I couldn't easily run to her. The abuse became life threatening. I had a gun put to my head and the trigger pulled. I was tied up and beaten until I admitted doing things that I really hadn't done. I had to admit I had done them to stop the beating. I was confused. I was frustrated, and I wanted to die.

This relationship, like all the others, ended after two or three years. I was devastated again. I had failed again. I tried to commit suicide again. Again I failed. I couldn't even do that right.

I moved to Florida, a geographical change. I landed my first "successful" job in an office. I met business men and got into the "9 to 5" swing of things. At 5 p.m., everyone met at this little bar. It didn't take long for my alcoholism to kick in and save me from the frustrations of the world. I learned to drink away my pain and problems. My children became less and less important. I left them at the nursery school overnight and sometimes for several days at a time. It was more important for me to stay at the bar and drink than it was for me to pick up my kids, take them home, feed them and put them to bed. Getting drunk was more important. I would miss "something" if I left the bar. I couldn't leave.

I was in one relationship after another. They just didn't work. What was wrong with everybody? Couldn't they see how hard I tried? Didn't they understand what I needed? Why couldn't I keep a relationship together? I worked hard. I was raising three kids by myself. Didn't that mean anything?

Four years later I moved back to Pennsylvania. My children's fathers were here and they had recently been making an attempt to see them, so I decided to move back and see whom I could capture. My sister introduced me to all her friends at the bar. We went drinking several times a week, and soon I was at the bar every day drinking. I knew that if I was at the right bar at the right time, I'd find whatever it was that I was looking for.

I was a very functional alcoholic and drug addict. I had to be. I still had to be perfect. I got good jobs and was very responsible at work. I was promoted rapidly. I am a real good "adult child." I lived in a nice home. I had three kids who seemed to be dealing well with society. (They weren't drinking and drugging like their mother.) I was living with the man I was engaged to, and I was miserable. This relationship was seven years old and had died before it even started. I continually picked people who were emotionally unavailable, but I just thought they were a challenge. I knew in my mind what I wanted and how I wanted to be. I just didn't have any idea how to become that person or how to tell anyone what I needed and/or wanted from them. I had learned to be needless and wantless. It wasn't OK to need anything. I felt guilty every time I asked for something, like new shoes, because my old ones didn't fit anymore. I was always afraid to ask for anything because I was afraid I would be yelled at and humiliated for wanting or needing anything.

I hit an emotional bottom in September of 1987. I knew nothing of rehabs, detoxes or AA. I had been confronted on my drinking by my kids. My behavior had become unacceptable even to my children, whom I thought would never turn against me. I was worthless. I couldn't drink or drug the pain away anymore but I couldn't live this way either. It would kill me. The pain was too great. I stayed dry for three days before I reached AA. I walked into my first meeting and felt like I was home. For the first time in my life, I felt like I fit in. I felt accepted and I felt something even more special, something that I'm not sure has a name unless I can call it a spiritual awakening. I felt like I belonged. I felt hope. For the first time in my life I didn't feel I had to do everything myself. I knew I had friends who would help me find the answers to my numerous questions. I was finally allowed to ask questions.

I learned to follow directions and get "involved." As an adult child, I got real involved. I held four, five maybe six different positions at six different groups during my first year of sobriety. I didn't know how to do anything else except go to work and go to AA. My kids thought that I had given up being addicted to drugs and alcohol and took up being addicted to AA.

My relationship ended, but I wasn't devastated. It hurt but not like past endings had hurt. I knew that my newly found Higher Power had something special in store for me, and I was sure that he would give me the guidance I needed. Besides that, being a good, compulsive, codependent person, I had already started another relationship. I stopped drinking but my reactions to life had not changed very much. I didn't know how to do life. I always thought that I was doing things wrong, and if I could just get everybody else straightened out, I would be OK. I started to lose that feeling of acceptance and hope. I was in a relationship that was day to day, and I never felt like I knew where I stood. I certainly couldn't ask, that was against the rules.

Being the good codependent person that I was (and sometimes still am), "I put my interests and hobbies aside in order to connect with you." When the man I was dating showed me the "Patterns" and "Characteristics" of a codependent it didn't matter if I thought it applied to me or not. He had vacationed in California and brought back information on Co-Dependents Anonymous. He was starting the first meeting in Pennsylvania. He would be at this meeting, so I would too. I didn't start going to CoDA because I was in pain or wanted to change, I just wanted to be involved in everything my new hostage was involved in.

I made a regular attendance of CoDA meetings and again became very involved. But something happened in CoDA that I didn't expect. I became important to me. I started going to meetings by myself, no matter who was there. I started to learn who I was and to accept the fact that I'm a human being in recovery and that I am OK! I've learned that my feelings count, that they're a part of who I am, that I am allowed to tell other people how I feel, and they won't laugh at me or ridicule me or tell me I'm being childish. I've learned to listen to the little girl inside who is still so very scared. She's learned to trust and she comes out to learn more and more each day. She's very, very special to me because she was so deprived of living until now, that I want to give her all the opportunities she never had before.

CoDA has given me another chance to learn how to live and experience the true joy of living. I've learned to stand up for myself and to respect myself. I've learned that even if I'm afraid, I'm allowed to ask questions and I can keep asking until I get the information I need so I'm not afraid anymore. I'm learning how to do life. It's not always easy. As a matter of fact, it's really hard sometimes to accept me as I am. I have to remember that God accepts me just the way I am, just the way he made me and who am I to question Him? I keep coming back and keep working the Steps to the best of my ability and I keep growing.

I am learning how to have healthy relationships with myself and others. I no longer take hostages. I don't need to blame. I don't need to con and manipulate people. I am allowed to ask to have my needs met. I don't have secrets. I am very "shame-based" but I do not have to be ashamed of who I am. I have people in my life who love me, care about me and respect me. I don't have to allow anyone in my life who doesn't know how to treat me with respect. Everyone doesn't have to like me, but they do have to respect me. My children are no longer possessions that I cling to. They are beautiful human beings growing up in a healthy environment of love, trust and respect. I believe that we are all children of God on loan to our parents. God loaned me three beautiful children and gave me extra chances to love and nurture them into loving, caring adults.

I am growing up in CoDA. I don't have to be perfect today; I can just be me. I am allowed to make mistakes because that means I am doing something. If I'm not making any mistakes I'm probably at a standstill. I don't have to be abused today; I can stand up for myself. I have had so many opportunities to grow in CoDA that I might never had experienced. I am grateful to CoDA and to my Higher Power for doing for me what I couldn't and didn't know how to do for myself. I thank God for giving me the chance to experience the "joy of living!"

by Peggy S.

TIM'S SAFE PLACE

I was born in a large Eastern city in a middle class family—a World War II baby. Dad was supposed to go off and save the country, but he couldn't get into the service. He had a bad heart and a drinking problem. Mom and Dad hung out with a wild crowd. I don't think they wanted me to come along and spoil their fun (drinking). Mom, Dad and I soon found ourselves in Grandmom and Grandpop's house.

I felt scared and sad while growing up in this madhouse with four angry, unhappy adults. They told me I had to take care of my little brother. It was painful for me and the rest of the family, taking turns taking care of each other and no one taking care of themselves. It seemed that we all tried to do what society said was right to do. But it didn't work. Pain and sadness ruled our family. I was ashamed of my grandfather because he was the neighborhood drunk. My father left us in our early years, not long after he and my grandfather tried to kill each other with their fists as I watched and cried.

At a very young age I started to drink myself, out of curiosity. I wanted to know firsthand what was the magic of alcohol. It had taken Dad out of the house, it had made a fool out of Grandpop, and it made Mom and Grandmom upset for long periods of time. Alcohol got a lot of attention at our house. Even when I wasn't drinking, I always seemed to get into trouble. I went into the Army at the age of 17 at the strong suggestion of a judge. He said that it would teach me to be a "man." I got in just as much trouble in the Army as I did in civilian life. At 20, I left the Army with an honorable discharge, not quite a "man," yet.

After collecting unemployment for a few months, my future wife explained to me that she was pregnant. Trying to do the honorable thing, for her and everybody else, we were married. Three children later, a row home in a middle class neighborhood, wall-to-wall carpeting and a color TV set, I felt miserable. My drinking at this point was out of hand, and my life was unmanageable.

After repeated attempts at staying dry, a friend suggested I go to AA. In 1972, I attended my first AA meeting. I felt hope and at home for the first time in my life. I got heavily involved in AA. I helped to remodel two rented AA Clubhouses from 1972 to 1982. After being asked to leave the second AA rented Clubhouse, the group conscience decided to buy a meeting hall on their own as a corporation. Other members of AA and I became the proud owners of an old Church. There were soon AA meetings being held seven days a week, 365 days a year.

After 15 years of sobriety and a second failed marriage, another friend in AA asked me to go to an ACoA meeting. Being a "good" AA'er, I reluctantly said yes. At my first ACoA meeting, my eye began to twitch, pain shot up and down my leg, and I felt extreme emotion. I didn't want to go back but I knew I had to. While doing my Fourth Step in ACoA I decided to go to California to handle some unresolved issues with my father who had made a geographical move to California and died there.

While attending an AA meeting in California, I heard someone share who sounded healthy. When I approached him, I found that he was going to CoDA. I asked what that was and the next day I found myself at my first CoDA meeting feeling a new hope in a new home. The day after that, at my second CoDA meeting, I just happened to be at the right place at the right time and ran into Ken R., co-founder of Co-Dependents Anonymous. We sat and talked for a couple of hours about how CoDA had been started and how it was working in Ken's life. I gathered all the literature and information I could find and flew back to PA.

The first CoDA meeting in Pennsylvania was held at the old Church I had helped to purchase back in 1982. As the President of the Board of Directors, my request was granted to allow CoDA meetings to be held at the AA Clubhouse. The first meeting was attended by about 26 people. It has only grown from there. It is one and a half years later, and there are now over 25 meetings being held throughout the city and suburban area. We have a community group organized which supports the growth of CoDA in our area.

For the last year and a half, CoDA has opened up closed doors within me. Even though I was working the Twelve Steps of AA and ACoA, these doors wouldn't open. I still felt like something was missing until I found CoDA. I began to learn more and understand more about me. My interactions with other people became healthier. I have learned to take care of myself and to let everybody else take care of themselves. I am now learning to feel my own feelings, to share them, to be who I am and to accept myself. CoDA has helped me learn how to meet my needs instead of meeting society's needs. Today I have learned how to share my pain and sadness in a healthy and appropriate way with my friends in CoDA.

I bought a corner property with a storefront where we put the Philadelphia Area Community Group Office. This is where all the telephone calls come from those still suffering from codependency. Here we hold community group meetings and bridge the gap from CoDA International Headquarters to the individual groups.

I'm still involved in AA at the "old Baptist Church" with over 17 years of sobriety and attend meetings on a regular basis. I still attend ACoA and attend ACoA Intergroup meetings, held in my storefront, once a month. CoDA is an important part of my life. I believe that going to California, meeting Ken and getting CoDA off the ground in Pennsylvania, is God's will for me.

God has done for me what I couldn't do for myself.

by Tim.L

512

A STORY OF THE ORIGINAL SIN

I was born a daughter of the Golden West. My mother is from an aristocratic Mormon pioneer family, making me a fifth generation Mormon. My father is a cowboy, born and raised on an Indian reservation in the West. He is still a cowboy with cowboy behaviors. My mother is very Mormon and very much his wife. They have a life together.

I am the oldest of five natural children and three foster children. My youth began (as my mother would say) as an "unbaked." I was born two months premature, about six months after the unfortunate marriage of my parents. My mother considers my "illegitimacy" to be her major sin in life, and believes all of her woes are due to God's rage at her mistake, which became my life.

As a child, I asked questions about my legitimacy. I never felt wanted in the family, and quickly became an overachiever in order to "prove" my worth to the world. The whole basis for writing this story deals with my overachievement. I was a perfectionist. This did not serve me well, however, because in reality we were a very poor family. There were times we were

homeless and hungry, however, we were clean. My
mother's aristocratic genes required daily baths in
aluminum washtubs which we carried around on top
of the car. She would wash us with harsh cleanser
until our skin was raw, and she washed our clothing
with the same vigor. As a result, we were brilliantly
clean, poor kids.

My father officially joined the Mormon church
when I was eight, and we all went "through the
temple" together to be "sealed for time and all
eternity." Essentially this meant that our family and
all of those before and after us would live on the
same big block in Heaven. This was one point in my
life about which I felt forever hopeless in the literal
sense of the word. By the time I was eight years old,
I already had begun to bear the physical and
emotional scars of violent physical and sexual abuse
in the family. In addition to being the overachiever,
I had become the family scapegoat.

I realize now that a portion of the violence was
based on my parent's sense of hopelessness, but
another, more major issue was based on their jealousy
toward one another around their individual feelings
toward me. Another matter centered around the fact
that these two 18-year-old kids were raising four
children, all one year apart in age, in a car. Needless
to say, these folks did not receive the "Parents of
the Year" award, either.

In addition to our isolated family unit, we also
were a part of two very large, enmeshed extended
family systems. Incest was a part of life. Essentially,
everybody did it with everybody else. Sometimes the
sexual intimacy was forced, sometimes coerced,

sometimes mutually agreed upon. My sisters and I experienced all of these experiences. My last incestuous experience was into my later teen years when I still had no idea there was something illicit about it, other than the fact that sex among Mormons is "marital." All my sexual experiences were riddled with guilt and shame. I was raped as a small child, then as a freshman at college, then again as a student in graduate school, and finally by a "happily married" Mormon woman. There were four other attempts, and many coerced sexual situations which felt so shameful, yet seemed so normal. I knew these situations were about the "something terrible" that secretly lived inside my soul and had a life of its own. This entity still occasionally resurrects itself, however, today I embrace it, and it loses its power.

The physical abuse continued until I left for college in the fall. It is important for me to describe the physical abuse that I refer to due to the fact that my reality may be somewhat different from others. I recall being about age three when father and mother burst into the room. I think they were enraged because I was sleeping in a crib with my baby sister who was about 18 months younger than me. My mother's big skirt was flying and she was screaming. I was glad to see them initially, until I was yanked from the crib, thrown into walls and hit many times. My mind is blank after that. I can feel the terror of impending annihilation even now.

This basic scenario repeated many times until my first semester of college when I lived away from home. I remember riding in the car, and my father grabbing me and throwing me around the back seat with my younger siblings screaming. All the while he was slapping and punching me wherever the blows might land, and he was still driving.

I remember being yanked from the kitchen table and beaten, kicked and thrown around the kitchen for dropping a cucumber slice. The rest of the family sat quietly and ate their dinner. I came back to the table and ate my dinner, filled with shame and wishing I could disappear. It was very embarrassing and shameful to have it explode in front of others.

I remember having a sleepover in high school and being beaten in front of my friends with a cane from the state fair. I was a Candy Striper at the time, and when the nurse in charge asked me what happened to my legs, I said I fell. I remember my father chasing me around the house, beating and kicking me one morning before school because my skirt was rolled up to my knees. I remember him kicking me up the stairs into my room, then forcing me to take off my sweater and put on something else because I was showing off my breasts. I remember hearing his footsteps come up the gravel driveway while I was doing my homework. I'd stop studying and immediately take already clean pots, pans and plates out of the cupboards to wash so that he wouldn't attack me for being lazy.

I remember him throwing the vacuum cleaner at me, hitting me in the head because I wasn't vacuuming fast enough. I remember his accusations about my behavior with boys, coming out to get me from the car as we would drive up after a date. I was not allowed to date until I was 15 years old. My parents kept us very isolated, myself in particular.

Every day of my life at home was a threat to my existence and a reminder of my parents "original sin."

I found a way to survive. My brain was still good, and I excelled academically. I also was very popular among my peers. Our "crowd" allowed me to develop talents and some self-esteem, although I knew that if they ever found out about the "something terrible," they would certainly be disgusted and abandon me. So I became perfect at fitting in with the crowd. I also became a perfect Mormon. I set out to convert my friends and boyfriends to Mormonism and held a respectable success rate. In my senior year of high school, I admitted to my bishop I had drunk alcohol, and was publicly chastised by the school's denial of my "Individual Award." I realized imperfection was unacceptable in the Mormon church, so I began my departure (this task took 20 years to complete).

I found alcohol at age 14. It did for me what a failed suicide attempt had not done two years earlier. It deadened the pain. I began to drink regularly. My friends had parents who drank, and I would bring empty soda pop bottles and canning jars to their house in order to steal their parents' booze. We were also able to get beer and alcohol easily from their older siblings and friends. I loved it. I don't remember beatings very vividly when I was drunk.

At age 15, our family physician gave me an open prescription for daprisal (the primary ingredient being dexedrine), and suddenly I felt great. Speed and booze quickly became my drugs of choice. My perfectionism topped out my senior year in high school when I perceived I had done a less than admirable job on a school project. I attempted suicide again; however, in my naiveté, I was unaware of the word suicide. I only knew I wanted to die, and that the Day of Reckoning—when "something terrible" would be revealed—was impending. Because of that, I felt I would lose my friends, my college scholarships and my life. After taking a bottle of Midol, which I thought would do me in, I threw up. My mother walked me around all night; I went to school the next morning. I didn't die, and I believed I had pulled off the biggest lie on earth.

My college years began as bright and promising. I was 16 and "just off the farm." I had no business living on a major university campus. My life disintegrated in front of my very eyes. The month before I left for college, I attempted suicide again by hanging. All I got for my trouble was a rope burn. Three months later, I slit my wrists. Someone else in the dorm had done it and she was taken home by her parents. By contrast, my parents didn't even respond. I banged my head on the walls, starved myself and was gang-raped. I wound up somewhere in Montana with a truck driver who sexually assaulted me, and overdosed on LSD. This bright promising kid ended her first year of college with a whopping 1.5 grade point average.

Now even my brains had failed, and I was living the family shame by being less than perfect. My sophomore year was the year of two psyche hospitalizations and two unsuccessful suicide attempts. I was also in full swing of sexual promiscuity so it was a revolving door of men and "dicks." Janis Joplin was my idol. I stayed in school and during the hospitalizations, my grades improved. I lost my scholarships, but by then I was determined to finish in spite of my parents, or maybe to spite them.

My mother sent me some money in secret, but I worked, sold drugs, drove hot cars for the mob and sold my body to support myself. I believed the "something terrible" was finally out, and surprisingly it was a relief. I drank and did as many drugs as I could. Even so, by some sort of miracle, my grades returned to a 4.0 average. I had been formally rejected by the Mormon church, the "prophet" himself. The pain, sadness and shame were overwhelming without the benefit of alcohol and drugs, so I stayed loaded, worked and completed graduate school. I became a professional codependent, a.k.a., a psychotherapist. I became good friends with death, as we continued toward the top of suicide hill. I figured that it would all be over sometime, so I went headlong into my work and performed perfectly. My age surprised people; they thought I was young for all my achievements, yet I felt very old.

I also moved away from my home base, and today I believe that move was my Higher Power's way of preparing me either for death or recovery. I did not interact with my family. The other kids went into the Army, graduated high school, went on missions, got married and had kids. I just went away. My parents moved and began to live my father's dream of becoming like John Wayne and Maureen O'Hara in one of their classic movies. I lived very far away from them. I was becoming a textbook example of a workaholic. I began to experience difficulty leaving work. My profession had become an addiction which I attacked with fervor. Alcohol and drugs were my daily vitamins. I dimly perceived professional failure ahead, and bought a gun. I looked death in the face and felt sad, but it seemed inevitable. My new life away from family and religion was again in shambles, thereby proving the "something terrible" was still winning.

A woman "who knew" interfered with my plans. She drove me to a place where "executives and professionals" could "get away and rest." I agreed to go for three days. About five weeks later, I emerged clean and sober. I knew that the ignition that started my self-destruct button was drugs and alcohol. I knew if I used again I would die. I was on a pink cloud; I felt as if I had hope again.

And then the pain....

I worked harder and harder on the Steps. I wore out sponsor after sponsor. The catchword now was "needy." I had apparently built a dam in my tear ducts since I hadn't cried since I was a small child. I was a shell, an empty pit. Pain, shame, sadness and loneliness. I did what any self-respecting codependent would do. I began to get "married." Relationship after relationship. Intensity, passion, sex, total honesty, commitment, finally, all were dead. Time after time. I was still clean and sober, so I was certain the "right one" would come along and I was correct. Time after time, I dove into my work and became the best psychotherapist I could be. I got very busy, then I got sick. After a few years, I crawled along at a snail's pace and just felt the pain, loneliness, shame and sadness.

I would sit and talk with my friends, many of whom were in the chemical dependency recovery field. As we talked, we discovered there was an empty pit that we all experienced, a quiet feeling of helplessness that we would never be whole. I was relieved others felt the same way, and began to discover that as I felt those feelings, memories of a childhood survived by a teeny-weeny towhead began to surface. I remembered her, and I knew her but I could not experience her feelings except through illness. I dreamed about her and recognized her.

I worked with clients, who in their sobriety, reported many of the same experiences. Their stories began to unfold. The brutal honesty about childhood trauma began to take a new form as I watched the feelings that sometimes eeked out and sometimes exploded outwardly. I noticed they began to come alive as they reclaimed their lost childhood. I experienced some conflict in terms of how I learned to "work the program" in AA. It seemed to me that a requirement was "not to feel" and to sustain a feeling, a serenity, a gratitude. I had come to believe this pain was about me not doing it right, and that was a very familiar feeling for me. I worked diligently on the Steps and felt like a failure when I could not sustain serenity. I felt as if I might explode.

Nearly five years of total abstinence went by before I slowly began the process of working my codependence recovery. I began to uncover and discover the reality of my past and reclaim my history. This process has required a new level of rigorous honesty because I wanted it to be over and done with. My parents didn't mean to do what they did. They had hard lives. They were too young. They were uneducated. They did the best they could... yes, but...

I hold my offenders accountable for their behavior, and I have boundaries that feel healthy and growth-inducing. What is done cannot be undone. However, I daily examine my behavior and identify my feelings and actions to determine, "Is this a ghost from the past singing the same old song, or is this about me today?" Those things that are about me are now manageable, and the ghosts I simply release. I have worked through the sadness, loneliness, emptiness, and much of the shame. My pain is still blocked and safely put away somewhere, hence, the work continues. I have felt free from a life that happened to me while I was doing something else. My life is my own and there is a sense of hope and tranquillity. I don't have to be busy and productive all of the time, and at long last, I am learning to play.

The emptiness and depression occasionally might surface and I embrace it, then it loses its power. Sometimes it is a daily struggle, but it is always a relief. I still experience issues around intimacy and relationships; I still feel like I'm dancing with two left feet. However, I can and do sustain feelings over a long period of time now. My greatest gift is a sense of love and compassion for myself which has allowed me to love my son and to parent him without violence and abuse. I am also released from the sickness of my family of origin. Where there previously existed a relentless pull from them, there is now a tiny tug. I have hope. I am a precious child of God.

by Donna L.

LIFE IS POSITIVE

I'm a child of a nonfunctional family. As far as I remember, in the early ages there was a lot of caring and fear along with love in the family, which continued being present stronger and stronger (I'm 24 now). My mother was frightened by the idea of letting go, and became too close to me. So I went into my mind. My fantasy life was rich, and I felt that I was important.

I was an immature child, but not physically immature. My behavior was judged as childish, today I think, because it was freer than others. I was bad and lively during kindergarten. I wasn't part of the community. I remember I always ate my lunch separately from the others. (I think a big part of the reason was that I was sick a lot and vomited.) I would sit on the floor struggling with the food. I was ridiculed by the children because I was different. So I learned soon to feel guilty. I tended to want to be different because I liked to do what I shouldn't have, but I hid it, avoiding the pain. I thought, "If you boys do not accept me, then I don't want to be like you any more." But I didn't want to feel uncomfortable either, so I hid my feelings from them about not wanting to be like them.

I didn't have any serious friends during school. Or if I did, they were extremely shy and were let out of the leadership and groups of others, too. Me and any of the friends I did have were a support against others out there.

I chose to read. I read a lot and like many good codependents, I pleased others—mostly my parents—by being a good boy. I learned well, fit in to all of the expectations of my parents and of the outside world. And I was sad, of course; I felt alone, and was offended and angry. I wouldn't act it out. Or if I did, everybody in the family was scared, stunned and looked at me with deep disgust. I remember some humiliating slaps on the face, some hitting with a belt, and some unspoken rule in the family. I don't remember the spoken rule and I know I would have been ashamed (and I was) if I acted unaware of this rule. So I had to be cautious at home. As I write this, I'm realizing there were some hard, abusing games in my childhood, that I wasn't clear about before. I used to tell it wasn't that bad. Now I'm not sure at all how bad it was, since I remember few things from my childhood.

I got all the material support from my parents that they thought I needed—mostly food and clothing. So I wore clothes according to my mother's wish. It wasn't too far away from my taste either (as a good, innocent boy, my taste was close to my mother's). I wore a kind of hairstyle which my mother liked as well.

I became interested in girls later than the others. So I felt I was "let out of the game" as usual. I was a shy boy. When the need of sex arrived to me, I didn't dare show it, thinking that it was bad, or show or accept loving feelings from girls. I was manipulating. If I knew you wanted a relationship with me and I wanted it too with you (I wasn't clear about myself: I just felt your needs), I wouldn't let my need be shown. I would have chosen and I chose the way of giving double messages, manipulating you to show feelings first, to take that scaring first step, so I didn't have to take any responsibility over our relationship. You are the person who wanted it, you have to heal it (I expected an unhealthy relationship all the time which is to be healed and I'm not able to do that). This manipulation was unhealthy, sick behavior. And I felt sick then, too.

Since I'm a good-looking man, I've (somehow) been chosen ever in my life. I don't remember when I chose, or if I did, I was rejected (I did once, during childhood, without words, just looked at a girl, and I was rejected from the distance by a cruel grimace). So I lost all my weak courage to initiate.

I was too hungry and alone for feeling anything negative toward a relationship with a girl. And I had a habit of not knowing the difference between a sexual relationship and a friendship with a girl. By my long unfulfilled need of sexual connection, I tried to get many females into bed, being scared that my need may stay unfulfilled again.

The first girl who chose me was a "good girl." We behaved good, smiled a lot, were a polite little couple and when I felt we weren't fitting to each other, I didn't dare tell her the fact. I know this was a really uncomfortable and hurting experience because of my insincerity to her.

I feel I'm too fearful and scared of others to trust so much that I would be able to make strong bonds between us. However, this feeling hits me less and less, I still feel I wouldn't give you a chance to hurt me before I accept you totally.

I felt—as I mentioned before—sad and alone a lot. I tried to medicate this feeling with alcohol once or twice but it didn't have the expected result on me. So I didn't become dependent on it.

I didn't believe in God. In school, I learned there is no God, and it's ridiculous if I believe in any other thing than Marxism-Leninism. And I was too proud to be humble or accept a Higher Power than me. So I felt this world was empty and cold, and I felt I could run nowhere from this feeling. Another reason that I didn't believe in a God was (thanks to my perfect logical mind) because if God existed, it wouldn't allow this world to be so bad and cold.

I was proud of having difficulties in my life and seeing difficulties in the life of society, because I felt I was really somebody by the fact I had realized those problems and hardships. I was proud of myself and I looked down upon others a lot. And still, I was dependent on other people's opinion on me. They were allowed to decide whether I was proper or not, good or not, etc. And today I still feel other people, like bosses or teachers, decide whether I'm smart enough or strong enough, and everybody takes this situation for granted, so I can easily do it too.

I was called into the Army for one and a half years. It was a kind of place where I had to behave. It was already hard at that time because I had chosen and had been following some art interests to become somebody, to create a difference between me and others. You know, to be better than somebody who goes to the disco. I meant that I'm not a normal young but a "special one." They, in the Army, tried to force me back on the "good way." I was a hard game, and I came out of it as having an even better ability to hide my difference from others, and still being more proud of it. I got power and responsibility there and it was a good place to learn about my patterns; how would this shy and good boy perform if he gets big power and is sent to the high rung of the ladder.

Before the discharge from the Army, I felt worse and worse and needy, and I was seeking a group, a place where I could feel well. My girlfriend, who was really supportive of me at that time, found a humanistic movement in which we both became involved. It was self-supporting, nurturing, and great. Somehow I found the proper way of involvement there. I mean with the help of lack of free time and fear I didn't become completely dependent on groups, or experienced spiritual healers. I had friends, opportunities to act out my sexual patterns with more and more freedom and less and less manipulation. My life changed slowly. My ego became stronger, so did my trust in myself, too. I felt better. And I wasn't sure any more that there was no God.

And so I lost my safety about this. I started to behave part time to an angry and avenging God who is in the sky, over us.

Then my girlfriend found a book in a humanistic meeting, sent from America by an ACoA member, who is a dear friend of mine today. She was really interested in it and showed it to me at once. That book was written by Melody Beattie: *Codependent No More*. Somehow I started to read it, trusting my girlfriend's feeling, and I realized through my strong denial, thank God, that it was about me. I felt more and more devoted to getting free of all the patterns of my codependency, however, it was hard to read and understand that book in English. I wanted to get a method of how to heal myself (of course I didn't even think that God could help me in the work: I still wasn't sure of a Higher Power existing).

As I got some materials about Anonymous programs and read the Twelve Steps, I decided that it wasn't for me at all. However, I felt I didn't understand that method. Then I found an address of CoDA—the address of ISO, and got closer and closer to the idea of Higher Power and Twelve Steps through reading that book. I wrote a letter, asking information, expressing my willingness to be a part of the recovery, writing that I may start a group here. Within a very short time, I got a packet with 11 cassettes, a lot of printed materials, pamphlets and a welcome chip. I was on cloud nine. I started to read the materials, and I saw the reason of my not accepting the Twelve Steps was that I simply wanted a quite miraculous method without any kind of Higher Powers being involved. As I continued to work on the pamphlets and cassettes, I felt an incredible amount of wisdom and love in them. My point of view about the Twelve Steps started to change quickly. And as it got known by me that I can choose, I can give shape to my own Higher Power; however I didn't use the opportunity but I had the freedom to choose, so I felt OK.

This happened during the summer of 1990. Since then in this last half year I have learned a great amount about the core of life. Through my fear, which I have a lot, I chose Twelve Steps to be the most important thing in my life. I feel an incredible pureness, simplicity in it. And I learned a lot about my illness, codependency and about the word humility. The world became full of miracles and love to me, and my life—in spite of Hungary's quickly worsening economical situation and life-level—is becoming better and better. I can still find new things in cassettes and books replaying and rereading them as my difficulties lessen with English and with my denial.

Today I just listen to my quickly changing self which I admire and I'm grateful to CoDA for giving me the opportunity of an even deeper and more beautiful life than I ever had before.

by Gabor L.

ONCE UPON A TIME

"And they lived happily ever after…" These words followed most of the stories I had heard or read as a child. I believed and lived in them as though they were true for my own life. Princesses were adored and carried off by princes to wonderful castles where fairies lived, and the air sparkled with a silver mist.

The seduction of adventure, riches and long life were woven throughout these myths. I fantasized that my life would be like one of those fairy tales; I wanted to be saved and loved. Life was very confusing, lonely and scary for this little girl.

I was the firstborn child to a couple who knew each other less than three months when they married. Mom had a glamorous job as a stewardess, and Dad was a traveling salesman. My mother, who had been raised in a very poor Midwestern family, in a very poor Midwestern town, left as soon as she could get a ride out and was rescued by a handsome suitor. Dad was newly widowed with a young child.

My older half sister was being raised by her mother's parents and I'm sure Dad was grateful to find a mother for his daughter. So for the next few years, it was the three of them: Dad's drinking and gambling, Mom's threats and martyrdom, and Big Sis's temper tantrums. I believe that life got worse for them, and each day seemed to unravel the fabric of their spirits.

When my big sister was seven years old, I was born. I was cute and held the promise of newness. Looking back at my history, I realize that I was born the wrong sex for my parents. I have a boy's name and was raised as one until I grew secondary sexual organs. Then I was fired. The hopes of starting over with another child was a wonderful fantasy for both of my parents.

The reality is that my life started in a family that was in full-blown addiction. I didn't realize it then, but there were no choices for my family while in the throws of that death spiral. I never felt any sense of hope. It seemed like growing up took many, many years; life moved in slow motion.

Three years after my birth, my little sister was born. She was cute, chubby and funny. I took my pent-up anger out on her. I scared, teased and hurt her. I have a lot of sadness about that.

The next few years of my life, as a preteen, seem to be a muddled blur. I remember being alone a lot and trying very hard not to be noticed, when in reality, I was used as a hood ornament. I remember being the child who was sent out to represent the family. My parents needed to be recognized as "do-gooders" by their contemporaries. So I collected for the March of Dimes, swam on the local swim team

(Dad was the coach), sang in the junior choir at church (Mom was the choir director), became a cheerleader and the neighborhood babysitter.

My adolescence was a rocky road. When my older sister was almost 16, she was in a near fatal car accident. She remained in the hospital for months and was in and out of plastic surgery for years. When she was 13, my younger sister was diagnosed with an irreparable malady that required medication and constant monitoring. She needed to be kept calm at all times. There went my dumping ground, and I resented it. It seemed to me that she got sick so she could get all the attention. So there I was, the physically capable, family spokesperson/average student/doer of all odd (unwanted) family obligations that were child-appropriate. Whew!!!! This ended up being fertile ground for some nice juicy resentments. I was off and running. I didn't know where, just off and running.

By the time I finished my freshman year in high school, my father announced that we'd be moving to a new city. I was very angry, and by the time we relocated, I was beginning to act in delinquent ways, scaring even myself. Within two years, I had begun to drink and do drugs, steal the car to impress friends and go on dates with anyone who'd ask, and ended up pregnant when I was 17. I gave that child up for adoption, returned home and proceeded to get pregnant again by the same man. Three days after I graduated from high school, we got married. Seven months later I had a beautiful baby boy. It had been only one year and 11 days after I had given birth to my first beautiful baby boy.

My husband was a junior in college and a gifted athlete. Two years later, my daughter was born, and I quit work to be a full-time mom and wife. My husband had made it to the professional ranks as an athlete, so financially, we were fairly stable. We lived the life of celebrities; we were in the fast lane and traveled around with the ball club. Quaaludes and marijuana, alcohol and other drugs were there for the taking—and that we did, and more. By this time, I was probably 23 or 24 and scared to death to think of the future. My life looked very acceptable on the outside, but I felt lonely and empty on the inside.

In the spring of 1975, my husband announced to me that he had a lump in his neck and thought he would have it checked out. After an initial observation, the doctor decided that further scrutiny was necessary and my husband went in for exploratory surgery. There they found massive cancer, and within two years he was dead.

I was 26 years old with two babies, no self-esteem, a family I was scared of and worst of all, no hope for the future.

I remarried within three months, sold my business and moved my family to a Caribbean island. We bought a house in the mountains with a stream and a wonderful view of the ocean. There was no telephone, no television, and that's how I wanted it. I had my children, my art (I painted and sculpted), my husband, and my delusions. I was running as fast as I could from my past and my feelings.

Alas, the geographical cure was not to stick. We left our pretty island after six months and moved back to "the states" with kids in tow. This marriage

was doomed from the start. I was a no-show mate—
no body was "home" in my heart. We separated, I
moved my children back to my hometown where my
parents lived, and I got a good job. I tried to forget
that I had remarried. In fact, it took me several years
before I was willing to take some action and get a
divorce. I denied the marriage and called myself a
widow. My shame was so great!

I ran through a series of relationships with men
and even questioned my own sexual preferences. I
was totally and completely capable of being seduced
by anything that changed my feelings or eliminated
them. The spectrum of ways I escaped from reality
jumped from work, drugs and alcohol, to people,
money, sex, control, to—you name it—I used and
abused it.

In 1985, I met the "love of my life." My Love was
dashing, smooth, eloquent, gorgeous and alcoholic.
For me, at that time anyway, those were very
dangerous "qualities" for a man to have. The minute
he looked at me, my ability to take care of myself
flew out the window, along with my sanity. We drank
together, made wonderful love, cooked, traveled,
drank, had sex, drank—well you get the picture.

At his family reunion, nine months later, I was
literally abandoned in a blizzard in Wisconsin by My
Love, and left to find my way home. His mother told
me that I should go and find a nice man for myself.
For My Love, this was his first publicly noticeable
bottom. I was still in denial. Living on the edge is
what I did best.

I soon found myself in an Al-Anon meeting. I read
the Twelve Steps and began to look at my own

behavior. My actions were very scary and I had been going down the crapper fast. I learned the meaning of detachment and tried to apply it to My Love as much as I could. There was just one hangup. As long as I was focused on My Love, I wasn't focused on taking care of my own needs or finding out why I behaved and felt like I did. These thoughts and questions never dawned on me until I got some help and heard of Co-Dependents Anonymous. This was in January of 1986.

The lights slowly started to dawn in my brain. I was able to see how these principles could help other people, but it was so hard for me to see how they applied to my situation. I was terminally unique, and after years of shame, denial, chemical abuse and delusion, it took many meetings and hearing the same things over and over before I could really start to apply it to myself. After all, I was so different and had such unusual circumstances.

I did not like to go to these CoDA meetings. They were far too personal with those small groups and all. I wasn't even allowed to help anyone else with my suggestions or advice. This was really different and controlling, I thought. Obviously, I needed to shut up and listen.

Throughout all of this, I had been getting some outside help which helped me see patterns and traits that were not serving me any longer. These were usually things that I had mastered as a child in my dysfunctional family, and being an "adult child" was what I did best.

Much of my adult life has focused on living in fantasies. I've since learned how hard it is to live in reality, while nursing a juicy fantasy. I once saw a bumper sticker that said, "Reality is for people who can't handle drugs." Before I started recovery, I thought the word "drugs" should be replaced with "fantasies." Wow, did I have some growing up to do.

There are 24 parts to the backbone of my "recipe for living." They are called the Twelve Steps and Twelve Traditions of Co-Dependents Anonymous. After hearing the information I needed to hear through outside help, I now had a resource with which to change things. This would not have been possible for me without the program. The key for me was to take the valuable information I had received from outside help and to DO something with it.

The First Step is the only Step that I have to do as perfectly as humanly possible. Sometimes I do it less perfectly than others. Today, I'm able to admit my powerlessness. I'm willing to look at the unmanageability in my life. There is a great sense of relief for me when I tell the truth. There is a healing for me when I, once again, can be honest in the face of great fear and shame. When I am finally whipped by the lies and ready for relief, I admit my humanness, I own my humanity (humility).

There's always a gift for me. The gift is that I'm not alone and don't have to carry the lies and secrets around by myself anymore. I seem to forget to remember that I don't run the show. My disease tells me I'm alone. That is, I believe, the core of my insanity which brings me to the Second Step.

Insanity—I know it well. It seemed to rule as the dictator of my own "black-hole" existence. It kept me apart from anything that was alive and growing. I've heard that those of us who suffer from codependence are egomaniacs with inferiority complexes. How true this seemed to be for me. I was either afraid that you would find out what a fraud I was and ask me to leave the planet, or I was Queen of Everything. There was never much of an in-between. God (as I call my Higher Power), was a Power Greater Than Myself with whom I had a relationship.

As I mentioned before, my mother spent a lot of time at church, directing the choir, being secretary to the minister, and counseling engaged couples. One would assume that I had every opportunity for spiritual growth and connection. Well, I believe I tried very hard to connect and have a relationship with my mother's God. It was not to be. I could never be good enough or work hard enough or be enough. That is a tough life for a little kid.

Once I began to "work" this Second Step, I listened to other people's stories about their God, as they understood God. My sponsor told me that unless I had faith in something, anything, greater than me, I might just as well keep doing what I had been doing, expecting different results. To me, that sounded insane. She told me that if I didn't have a God, I could borrow hers until I came up with one that was fitting for me and my own purposes.

I believe the key word in this Step is the first one—"Came." This gave me the freedom to let my search for God be a process—one that worked for me and my own needs. May each of us on this road of "Happy Destiny" eat an elephant. That seems like an impossible task, but we can only accomplish it one bite at a time.

Step Three seemed like a brick wall. I was being asked to make a decision to turn my *whole* life over to the care of a God with whom I was beginning to communicate. I hadn't gotten to the trust part yet and I didn't know what to do. Fortunately, I was told that all I had to do was "make a decision." That was all I was being asked to do. This was not the place for me to step back in and try to figure out the "hows" of God's work. The actual turning over could be viewed as my willingness to continue with my Step work. The willingness to turn my will and my life over to the care of God would be necessary for me to go on to do the Fourth Step.

I believe there is a gift at the end of every Step we take. When I'm in my disease, I have no faith. I feel as though I need to know what is going to happen before I cooperate with God. That is when I'm living in the future and in my own brand of fear. Neither of those places is good for my spiritual condition. For me, the gifts related to the first three Steps are honesty, open-mindedness and willingness.

In my perfectionist way, I wanted my Fourth Step to be as clean and neat and as quick as possible (as if what I wanted had ever been what I needed). After all, someone else was going to hear all my yucky stuff. I felt that I needed to present an inventory that was socially acceptable, one that would tell most of the truth. I still believe that in my first inventory I had some of those "take it to the graves" that would never be shared with another human being. For me, those are usually about sex. After months of writing and procrastinating, writing, cleaning the toilet, and recleaning it, I was finally ready to share my resentments, talk about my fears, shame and anger, and be accountable for my part.

I shared my Fifth Step with my sponsor. It was one of the most freeing, profoundly spiritual moments of my life. The previous Steps had allowed me to gain a sense of trust and feel safe with another human being. I knew I needed to be totally honest if I was going to live happily. After all, this Step is not about telling God about my secrets. She/He already knows. It is about surrendering self-will and being willing to share that yucky stuff with another human being.

Surrendering and asking God to remove that part of me that only wants you to see what is good and honorable, that part of me that hurts others when I am in pain, that part of me that is "less than," is my charge in the Sixth and Seventh Steps. I believe that doing these two Steps is the difference between staying in disease and growing up. Allowing God to show me a better way to live is what my recovery/discovery has been about. Steps Eight and Nine are another dynamic duo. I need large daily doses of humility because I'm way behind in my quota. For all the years that I used people, blamed others for my situations and otherwise copped out, these Steps help me remember how fragile humanity is, how fragile we all are and how vital it is to my recovery that I assume responsibility for my actions and attitudes. These Steps remind me that I'm answerable to the Golden Rule: "Do Unto Others As You Would Have Them Do Unto You."

Step Ten is one heck of a way to stay on my road to recovery. When I stumble and shoot myself in the foot by resorting to old behaviors, I know what to do. By making amends and changing what I can, these actions become less and less a part of who I am as I go along my spiritual path. That is the process of taking charge, being accountable, risking, and growing up, for me.

Now that I have a few spiritual tools and the means to use them, I try to do so on a daily basis. I really want to stay teachable. I believe this to be the essence of Step Eleven. Prayer is my active contact with God. I share the good stuff and yes, the yucky stuff too. I ask for courage, open-heartedness, open-mindedness, and stillness. For me, meditation is stillness. It is my ability and willingness to receive serenity, courage and openness. Only in my stillness, am I able to listen. When I listen, I can I hear the Truth. Today I know that the God of my understanding is always there for me. I didn't always believe that. I didn't always believe.

I walk through most of my days with my head up and my heart open. I go to meetings and share my story with others. I need to hear the hope that someone else's experience has brought them. Life goes on.

But the quality of my life is grander than I ever dreamed it would be. For years now, even upon hearing the miracles in meeting rooms, the richness of life never ceases to amaze me. The truth is that I was dying and now I choose life. By working with other codependents, I've been able to stay out of self, return some of the gifts of the program, learn about myself through others, and continually make healthy choices for my life. These things were not possible for me before those brave spirits who walked before me were willing to share their gifts of life. I will be grateful all the days of my life for this chance to live.

by Hollis H.

THE ONLY CHILD

Abandonment, betrayal and the threat of violence spiritually split the hurting child and led him to a shaming, self-destructive path in a frantic search for acceptance, affirmation, and a sense of belonging.

The sense of separateness and being different are the legacies of a lifetime of confusion, loneliness and guilt. I was treated as a young adult from the very beginning and denied the happy playfulness, companionship and spontaneity of childhood. The kids in grade school called me "Grandpa."

I was raised to function alone, taught that quiet distractions, activities, reading and television would ease the pain of loneliness. I learned it was more important to please my parents than to express my feelings, and I became externally focused with no sense of personal identity. I was told I was special, smarter than the other kids, and great things were in store for me; but at the same time, I was subjected to systematic beatings, public humiliation, unmerciful criticism and constant intimidation. I grew up in confusion and terror; tension and fear became a way of life.

Both my parents had unresolved issues of acceptance from their fathers; therefore, my family life was a nightmare. My parents played me off against each other in order to get their needs met. Each, in turn, either smothered or pushed me away. My father became jealous when my mother paid too much attention to me, so my relationship with her became secret. It was warm and affectionate when he was away, cold and distant when he was at home. She instilled her fear of my father's violence in me and used it as a method of control. I felt betrayed, used and guilty. I learned not to trust my parents and began to view them as adversaries, a fear I became conditioned to and projected on everyone I met.

My father, a military policeman, was a violent, intimidating bully who parented with rigid authoritarianism and disciplined me with regular strappings. I became bonded to the physical violence and emotional abuse.

My mother was a vacillator. She was either warm, affectionate and caring or she was cold, rigid and controlling. I bonded as her surrogate spouse and this role became solidified when my dad spent a year in Europe.

Both my parents were perfectionists: unaccountable, self-righteous and pretentious. Our household looked normal, but it was a covert battlefield, where silence and rage clashed in a whispered war of wills.

Violence followed me to school. My family moved every two or three years, and I was constantly bullied for being the new kid, the cop's kid, the "Momma's boy" and the bespectacled honor student. I was rejected by my peers. I was sad and lonely—no one to turn to at home—no one to trust away from it.

By grade four, in an effort to stop the bullying, I attempted to bond with my oppressors, the delinquent faction. I became enmeshed in a gang, carried a knife and was introduced to sex, alcohol, violence, gang rape, vandalism and theft. This lasted three long years.

We moved to another city when I was 14, and in an effort to find happiness, I decided to become like the happy kids in my new school. They played sports and came from nice homes. I underwent a lot of shame and humiliation, but managed to learn enough fundamentals to make my school sports teams. I had a sense of belonging, but again I was bonding with my oppressors, this time to avoid the cruelty of the wise-cracking "jock" crowd; it was safe to be "one of the boys." I became addicted to the pornography my father kept at home, and too ashamed to have a girlfriend. In order to fill the void and gain acceptance, self-esteem and status, I became a social climber.

This pattern continued throughout university and, after four years, I was academically dismissed. By this time I was an alcoholic and addict. My only desire was to party, get drunk or stoned, play sports and be popular. My friends married, entered professions and abandoned me. I misspent an inheritance, had two untreated breakdowns and felt irreparably flawed and defective.

I turned my efforts to work, served five years apprenticeship on one of my county's most exclusive country clubs, and managed to get a turf management diploma from a technical institute. I became an assistant superintendent at the prestigious golf course and felt like I belonged to something because I wore the course insignia on my clothing. It gave me status. I also knew a lot of professional athletes and had connections in many professions. It seemed to give me importance, but inside I was lonely, scared and terribly unhappy. I had begun to drink and drug alone at home and rarely went out. I was unable to make a successful transition to superintendent of my own golf course, and smarting from that failure, I deteriorated to the point of repeated admissions to psyche wards and detox centers. I became suicidal and hit bottom.

My first year and a half of recovery was spent between psyche wards and treatment centers. I got free of alcohol, drugs, caffeine, nicotine and antidepressants. I began to work the Steps, and I became involved in service work, learning how it provided opportunities to relate with others in the Fellowship. The stored emotions of a lifetime of abuse and denial emerged. My rage, fear and resentments scared everyone around me and elicited a lot of shaming behavior. I was impatient to recover and knew I had to shift my focus.

I then spent two years looking at my family dysfunction, my adult children issues and my patterns of behavior and denial. I read the books, did the inner child work, attended workshops, started therapy for codependence issues, continued to work the Steps and evolved in service work, holding positions of group secretary, and representative and public information speaking.

My next course of action was to attempt a relationship with a co-sponsor. I was in my late 30s and had never been in a relationship. In the past, I had used and objectified women, and my contact had been limited to casual sex and one-night stands. I had never engaged in sober sex, and my sexual unions usually left me feeling shamed, trapped and wanting to run. My friend and I decided to work on the relationship and have no sex for the first year. We spent about three hours a day together, walking, talking and attempting to "therapize" and fix each other. Our well-intentioned union was an unhealthy, addictive enmeshment that became progressively toxic. After nine months, we eventually became sexual and then separated permanently in a hostile manner.

I found myself powerless over anger, rage and reactive behavior. I attacked her, shamed her and had a desire to hurt her. I was unable to be accountable for my actions and emotions, and continually dumped on her. Sometimes I had a different response. I would withdraw, isolate, become suspicious, judgmental and create an impenetrable wall of tension and mistrust. The first response resembled my relationship with my father; the second was like the one with my mother. In addition to this acting-out, I discovered it was essential for me to create conflict followed by emotional resolution, further re-enactments of the push-pull relationships of my childhood. I felt dizzy, nauseous and afraid. I turned to Co-Dependents Anonymous for help.

I admitted my powerlessness over people and saw that the unmanageability of my life stemmed from my parental enmeshment. I recognized I still did not accept myself, and that I did not feel comfortable with either men or women. I was back to Square One, sad, lonely, afraid and separate.

I viewed men as oppressors who were threatening, intimidating, shaming, sarcastic, abusive and emotionally unavailable misogynists. I didn't feel safe around them. I viewed women as treacherous, unreliable martyrs who were controlling, hypocritical and deceitful. I was angry at them. I saw myself as a defective, hopeless victim—lost, unhappy and spiritually bankrupt. I knew I was shame-based and fear-bound and saw no way out.

In spite of all this, the people in my home group accepted me, initially at a distance, but now several years later, they affirm me and have taught me to affirm myself.

I followed the path I had established in my first two Twelve Step programs, working the Steps and doing service work. I have chosen to work the Steps and Traditions as a way of life and they have begun to work their magic for me. They helped me release a lot of my shame, fear and resentment; connected me with a Higher Power and established a relationship with my inner self. I had a spiritual awakening and slowly began to connect with others in my home group. I began to reach out. I learned to be accountable for my actions and express myself in a nonconfrontational manner. I learned to respect other people; I became empathetic and learned to express my feelings. I made amends to many people and learned to admit when I was wrong. As my fears and resentments diminished, so did my anger and mistrust. I became softer and more approachable. My sense of humor returned, and I began to set goals, set boundaries and stand up for myself. My home group has been a safe place for me to listen and learn. It has also been a haven where I can speak and heal.

My service work provided the means for challenging connections with people. I performed my service at the group level, the community and state level, and I now represent my area as a delegate. Committee work has taught me the value of group conscience, helped me deal with control issues and taught me how to let go and trust the process. It is an excellent, safe environment in which to practice recovery tools. I am now better able to own my own stuff, rarely get hooked by another's issues, and when dysfunction happens, I work through it quickly in a nonthreatening manner. I still make lots of mistakes, and that's OK. My perfectionism, self-sabotage, tension and urgency to recover, like most of my issues, have diminished considerably. I trust and know that they will continue to diminish as long as I remain humble, ask for help and work my program on a daily basis. My journey is a lifelong process of ever-expanding awareness, change and acceptance. I work at self-affirmation, self-love and self-nurturance. My relationship with myself is my most important relationship. I am beginning to focus on doing things I enjoy and developing interests that I find challenging and rewarding.

I am aware that the old, negative enmeshed patterns can invade my life at any time, so I work on being in the present and focusing from that creative, non-critical and open place within myself, my true self. I no longer choose to have my life tarnished by the oppressor reality I assimilated in childhood.

In my newly developed posture of recovery, I recognize that my Higher Power is providing for me and is always available—when through prayer, I ask for His help, and then, through meditation, I listen for His guidance. I no longer feel separate. I am connected to my real self, my Higher Power, the members of my home group and my extended family in the Fellowship of CoDA. I affirm myself.

It is my hope to learn to accept myself at a level where I am able to extend this sense of warmth and respect to all people and connect by a common spiritual bond. I am exceedingly grateful for my recovery. I wish you all the best in your individual journey of discovery, recovery and self-respect. To thine own self be true.

by Ted M.

THE CELEBRATION OF A SPIRITUAL JOURNEY

No other place in the universe touches me so deeply as this place of beauty by the white shores of Lake Tahoe. My strongest connection to my Higher Power exists when I am by these shores. It is here, with the majestic Sierras, mountain streams and cool air that I first clearly heard my Higher Power speak to me.

Today I am celebrating my life, not only because of the gift of my 45 years, but perhaps, even more importantly, the past seven glorious years of recovery from codependency.

Can it be only seven years ago that I felt such tremendous pain after making one of the most difficult decisions of my life—ending my second marriage, a love-addicted relationship of almost seven years? I remember that pain. At times it felt like my soul had been ripped out of my body. I felt so empty and lost. At other times, it felt like someone had put a tourniquet around my heart and was twisting it tighter until the pressure would burst through my chest. Pain ached in my throat and throbbed in my head; I knew I desperately needed help.

I didn't know it then, but I had finally hit my codependency "bottom." At the time, I had no idea that in order to stick to that decision of cutting off my relationship with my ex-husband, I would go through a painful withdrawal and walk through many tear-filled doors of childhood memories and former relationships. This long journey began the day I found the courage to say goodbye to my abusive husband and discovered the miracle of Twelve Step programs.

Yes, finally admitting defeat, I crawled to recovery's doors. At that time, I didn't know I was being guided by my Higher Power. By the age of 21, I had locked any "God" in a room behind a cold steel door secured by double bolts. I wanted no part of religion, God, church or prayer, since my Catholic upbringing no longer served my beliefs. I'd rather think mankind was put on Earth by ancient astronauts than by any creator. Life just was—not created.

I know now that my Higher Power put that book in front of me—the one with the typical traits of a codependent—the one with which I identified so painfully. This book broke my denial and indicated that I, too, had a big role in the dysfunctional relationship I experienced with my husbands. That book steered me toward help in Twelve Step programs.

Yes, my Higher Power's guidance brought me to Co-Dependents Anonymous, but in the beginning I would never have acknowledged that fact. For too long, my second husband was my Higher Power. Today I have chosen to forget him and go on with my life. I didn't know at the time that it would feel like I had given up the alcohol in my alcoholic-like love addiction. To even think of my love as an addictive one was not in my realm of pre-recovery knowledge. All I knew was that I was tired of being a yo-yo—up and down, in and out of frequently broken promises. I thought his gambling and midlife crisis were the causes of our family breakup. Other women in his life also caused problems in our relationship, but in my mind, I could no longer compete with his true mistress—Lady Luck. No more could I live on promises and what I believed was his "potential."

For our first two years together, I thought this man could do no wrong. I later realized that I had never really known him. I had fallen in love with his glitter, so when the garbage came out, I didn't want anything to do with it. It was not part of the perfect man I had met and married; I began to do everything I could to kick the garbage out and get the glitter back. What I didn't know was that the man I met was the garbage as well as the glitter that so attracted me. Soon, very little glitter remained, and the garbage was too overwhelming to deal with anymore. By the time I had made the decision to really get out of the relationship, we had been separated twice and finally divorced, with six added sick months of in-and-out, up-and-down craziness. I had little sense of me left, a deflated (basically nonexistent) ego, and no sense of reality.

With my first gambling/alcoholic marriage, my ego had not really been touched. My husband was always sorry and going to do better; he never blamed me for the way he was. It was the steady increase of violence that was beginning to be witnessed by our son that caused me to divorce him. Two years after we divorced, I held on to hopes that he would change. I continued seeing him on my own terms until I finally slid into the relationship with my second husband.

My ego still intact, I had no idea there was something wrong with me. For so long, I thought my ego was my self-esteem, but in recovery I learned that those things I used as my criteria for self-esteem (such as doing well at work, being one of the best at whatever I tried, giving others advice or helping others) were just outside factors I used to make myself feel good. I really knew nothing about how to esteem myself from within. My new relationship was to be the one which would eventually lead me to understand the difference between ego and self-esteem; I was to definitely and painfully learn the hard way.

My second marriage was one of "it's all your fault; if it weren't for the way you are, I wouldn't gamble and stay out." I was never "enough" for him. My ego no longer existed as I tried to live up to his "loyal enoughs" or his "faithful enoughs." He could never give any clear, concrete explanation or definition of what any "enough" meant, but he expected that of me. I tried to be super wife, super mother, super housekeeper, super worker, super Miss Perfect, super whatever-you-want-and-need-me-to-be, until I "supered" out of my ego and most of any "me" I might have had left. My ego was not the only loss I suffered from this relationship; my reality was shot, too.

I can remember times my ex-husband would toss $300 across the table, and then proceed to convince me I didn't see what I saw because he hadn't even been paid that much. He'd shame and rage at me for believing a stranger's word over his. I'd always end up consciously accepting his reality and doubting what I knew in my gut to be true. I chose to believe him, for to not trust my husband was (by my upbringing) practically a sacrilege. I chose to remain a victim of whatever reality he'd paint for me to accept.

In both marriages I'd played the victim and martyr to the hilt and would dramatically tell my woes of a failed relationship to whoever would listen. Although I had no ego or reality, and very little sense of me left when I made the decision to end my second marriage for good, I knew I had to have something wrong with me that I should always get into such painful relationships. I was tired of being the victim.

I was tired of the extreme insanity it took to hold on to relationships where I didn't trust my spouses. Haunting memories of my crazy, compulsive behaviors left me feeling small and ashamed. I didn't want to find last-minute babysitters or pack the kids in the car to search one more time for the father who didn't make it home for dinner or hadn't been home for three days. I didn't want to call a long list of bars and casino haunts to cry and plead with him to come home before he blew another paycheck again. I didn't want to comb dark, smoky dives to find him, or drive slowly with locked doors down seedy alleyways, searching for his car.

I still vividly remember incredibly fearful empty fears that if I did find him, he'd be with another woman. I can also recall the stifling pain I felt when I did catch him holding hands with another woman, and when we received a postcard addressed to my husband that said, "Thank you for staying at our motel." I remember countless times of going through his wallet, listening to his telephone conversations, and cleaning his car to find proof of infidelity. Even with proof, I still would refuse to believe what my gut knew was true. I preferred to accept any story he would tell that could possibly explain such situations. I've had to forgive myself for these behaviors and for the many times I had lied for my husband to cover for his inappropriate behaviors or not making it to work.

I had been taught that the man was no more than the woman behind him. I also had been instructed that I was supposed to control not only the children, but also my husband's behaviors in order to have a good family and be a good wife and mother. Because of these instilled values, my husband's lies, inappropriate behaviors, and even his deteriorating appearance I took personally as my own failures. To keep myself and my marriage looking good, I felt I had to cover for him. The nagging, pleading, crying and constant efforts to make him see his ways helped me to avoid the thoughts of making choices which would end our painful relationship and give me back some sanity.

It was difficult to not take my pain out on my children. In fact, often I couldn't hold it back and my children would get the force of my anger, fear and temper. I realized I was in a vicious cycle of distrust and resentment. Crises ruled my life. Besides, after a crisis, there was always a very loving, humble man who treated me like a queen and bought me flowers and lots of materialistic baubles to make up for the pain he caused. I looked forward to this honeymoon time. The hard part was the tension that would soon evolve as I began to feel it was time for another crisis. Sometimes the tension lasted so long that I would do or say something just to cause a quarrel; this caused us to get to the crisis quicker. I hated that vicious cycle! It was never-ending. I also hated the verbally violent arguments which resulted from living in this hideous pattern. I always fell for the argument game and my behavior would end up as ugly as his. He would start picking on some imperfection in my character until I fought back to defend myself. Only in recovery did I learn that I had fallen for the trick of, "I'm feeling so ugly for blowing the money or cheating on you that I'm going to bring you down to my level."

Today I still know this game because (sadly) my teenage son learned it so well and tries to play it. I try to stay out of power struggles with him. I don't always succeed, but at least I now know the game and can bow out if I'm in a good place in my recovery.

When I first opened the doors to my recovery several years ago, I opened on a Twelve Step meeting that talked of codependency, and I knew I belonged. The characteristics they read fit me so well that I was sure someone had talked to my therapist or overheard my tragic story. I stayed and sobbed through my next six months of meetings. What I heard was muddled, confusing, and overwhelming at first. They would say, "Take what you need and leave the rest," and I'd often leave it all. But I was drawn back each week because I identified closely with much of what was said by the people there. Although my face was always swollen from tears and I hurt a lot when I left each time, I always felt more hopeful. I didn't understand much of the recovery language, in fact, the Twelve Steps and Twelve Traditions made little mark on my conscious mind.

I remember the meeting that I really heard the words of Step One. The blurs in my head finally dropped down to my heart and I got it! This has been mostly how I work the Twelve Steps—I live them! There are a number of things that I can intellectually understand, but in recovery this knowledge drops into my heart. Yes, I have written pages about my past using the Steps, but not until two years after I discovered them. Writing the Steps any earlier would have fed into my control issues; I was the kind of person who followed directions without question to be the perfect what-ever-was-needed-at-the-moment. I think I would have felt I had done the program and was cured if I had completed the Steps any earlier. I probably would have felt smug, secure, and a real know-it-all when humbleness was the key to my recovery. My Higher Power (as always) knew what was best for me. Every recovery issue that has reared its ugly head to confront me, has forced me to work the Steps whether I liked it or not. (I'm powerless you know.)

Yes, I now have a wonderful Higher Power in my life who guides me daily as I pray to stay out of the way and let my will go and my H.P.'s will be done. But believe me, it was no easy task to have faith in a Higher Power.

Raised Catholic, I endured much abuse in the way of instilled fear and shame. The ideas and values of this religion that were forced on me as a child helped set me up for some of my codependency issues. I was told that to get to Heaven I needed to help others and give unselfishly of myself, and nowhere in the Catechism texts did it say I needed to help myself first in order to get there. I was told that Hell was a sure thing if I did anything wrong and didn't confess. The God that was stuffed down my throat was a God who kept an accounting of my activities, and I needed three "right-goods" to offset any one "bad-wrong." He was a punishing, ferocious God if thwarted. People who were all-giving and saintly were models held up for me, to show me how I should act. I tried hard to be the perfect, good little girl so that I wouldn't go to Hell. For many years, I contemplated being a nun, for this was the ultimate symbol of goodness. I laugh at this thought now. Knowing what I know now about my rebel and sometimes naughty self, I would have been kicked out of a nunnery before I reached 20.

Religion never gave me spirituality or the tools needed to make my spiritual journey. I only found my spiritual self after I had been with Twelve Step codependency programs for a while. I realize now that it was the Higher Power of my innocence that was there for me when I almost got raped and when my husband was choking me and threatening to use a gun if I didn't do what he wanted. It was this Power that showed me to recovery's arms and to the serenity I know so often today.

When I first walked into Twelve Step meetings, I heard prayers with "God" in them and I almost left, but my gut knew I belonged there. About my third meeting, the topic was about our "Higher Power" and I freaked. I squirmed, tuned out, denied, scoffed, criticized and did all but leave. At each meeting, some things called Steps were passed around which I mostly ignored because they, too, had the word "God" in them. Finally, I experienced that meeting where I really heard Step One.

I knew my life was unmanageable; that's why I came to get help. I knew I was mostly powerless over my ex-husband, but I was still hoping recovery would give me one more hammer to help him change his life and want the family back. I wasn't sure I was powerless over all things and people. It took me longer to really understand the rest of the First Step, but one day it, too, finally "kerplunked" into my heart.

Step Two was easy in that I really felt insane, but it was harder to come to believe a power greater than me could restore me to sanity, that is if I knew what sanity was in the first place. What I had to do at first was to pick the ocean as a power greater than me. The ocean I knew I could not control. The ocean as my Higher Power worked for me quite awhile until Step Three.

I wasn't so sure I could ever totally turn my life and my will over to the ocean. What could the ocean do for me? It was basically a stationary force which couldn't help me from 400 miles away. I decided to begin to formulate an idea of a Higher Power, a special energy or universal force that loved me. My Higher Power needed to be a force that held my secret cards and knew when to deal them to me whether I thought I was ready to work with them or not.

To begin to build the faith to trust a loving, all-forgiving, all-accepting Higher Power, I had to start small. No way could I trust H.P. with all my will, let alone my life. I began to turn my will over for what I wanted the weather to be like that day. After a while I let H.P. guide me to find a lost shoe or belt. It took me about six months to get to Step Two, and about a year before I gave my Higher Power the ultimate test: my ex-husband and what he was doing with his life. I had felt so insane about this at times, like when he pierced both ears and put heart earrings in them. This was a man who had categorically sliced to nothing anyone who was the least bit effeminate. I can remember the times my hands would shake like an alcoholic having withdrawals as I would reach for the phone to say something to him that of course would make him "see the light" and change his ways. The insanity and humiliation of this behavior had to stop. For three days and three nights, I prayed off and on for release from the obsession I still had for my ex. One morning I awoke and I felt lighter and freer with a joy I cannot express in words. I knew my prayers had been answered. Although after that day I had short bouts with my obsession, I never again felt the heavy burden of that particular part of my life. I was free with Step Three. I now knew what it was like to "turn my will and my life over to a Higher

Power" and how to "go with the flow." I was now finally free to really focus on me! I was ready for Step Four.

But oh for Step Four! My belief is that Step Four actually brought me to recovery. I knew something was wrong with me, but I just didn't know what. I began looking at myself and what I needed to do to quit living in the extremes and to find balance in my life. A counselor once told me early in recovery that each day I needed to take up every ideal, principle, and value I had within me and decide which ones were my own and which ones were stuffed in there by society, parents, religion, school and such. Daily affirmations and meetings helped me in this area.

I was totally afraid to do Step Four formally, as my low self-esteem could not have taken any type of criticism. Looking at one little thing at a time was painful enough without writing pages about all of them. Perhaps if I had known then that the Fourth Step was as much about acknowledging the positive side of me as well as the character flaws, I wouldn't have taken two years to be ready to tackle this job on paper. Further, I doubt I would have been able early on to accept any positives about myself since my self-worth was nil, and I didn't really believe I had much goodness left.

What I believe now is that my Higher Power guides me to and through each Step. My H.P. helps me work on what issues I need when it's time to do them. My H.P. continuously amazes me by putting the right meeting, the right page, the right person in front of me when I need to learn more about myself. I feel certain I have done, and will continue to do my Steps as my Higher Power presents them to me.

Step Five has been easier for me in recovery than it was in my childhood religion. I used to fabricate lies just to have something to confess, but for recovery, I've been blessed with wonderful friends who don't judge and make me feel "less than" if I share my darker side with them. Much of my Fifth Step is done in my meetings when I expose myself and become vulnerable. I'm much more committed to working on my character limitations once I share them with other human beings. I feel much lighter and more joyful when I can free myself from the burden of my secrets and darker self. I have to learn to accept and love the whole me to grow in recovery. Step Five helps me do this.

Step Six is my nemesis. Someone once compared the Twelve Steps to the Twelve Apostles. Well, Step Six is my Judas Step. I can easily give up many of my character limitations to my Higher Power. I hardly have to stop at Step Six with these, but on the other hand, there are certain survival behaviors that have served me well throughout the years. It is much harder to give up a survival behavior that still allows me to control my world. The key for me to remember is that it's still my control, my will that I'm fighting in Step Six, and not the will of my Higher Power.

Many times I get quite stuck on Step Six and just pray "to be willing to be willing to be willing" to turn my character limitations over to my H.P. My food addiction is a good example of how I get stuck on this Step. Chocolate chip cookies always have been my friends. It is my belief at this point in my recovery that I can avoid men in the world who care more about physical appearances and not personalities if I have enough weight on my body. I want someone in my life who loves me for me no matter what weight I'm at. When I get into a mutual chemistry relationship when my weight is up, I can lose 15 pounds in a month. He is my safety valve because I don't have to fear as much that he might go away or that he doesn't care about me for me. I'm praying to let go of this character limitation and my control, but the fear is so great. My food addiction is one of the most complicated and longest used of all my addictions. It's physically not healthy for me to indulge in this addiction, but sometimes it works so well for me. I try to pray daily to turn this one over to my H.P., and I do for short periods of time, but just a compliment from a man can send me right back into it. I have faith that one day when the time is right and my H.P. says, "Here's the card," I'll be able to stop letting my fear cause me to give up my personal power to some unknown men out there who have no clue they even have it. One day I'll be able to cross over to Step Seven on this issue, and my H.P. will take care of those chocolate chip cookies instead of me. My goal is to one day have harmony in all parts of me: intellectual, spiritual, emotional and physical. I'm praying for that day.

Step Eight was difficult for me because I had already made amends to basically everyone in the world. I had been sorry for everything, and when I wasn't blaming others and the world for my woes, I was busy blaming myself and making constant apologies for my behavior. What I realized was that the person at the top of the amends list was me. I had to forgive myself for so many things, especially for my dysfunctional parenting and the choices I made that left my children basically fatherless. I have to believe my children will find their own Higher Power and serenity even though my actions and choices have possibly impeded their journey. They are my hope to break this chain of pain that has been passed on for so many generations. I have always been my own worst critic, and I am learning to accept myself with all my human frailties. I have to understand and remember I don't have to be perfect, and I need to forgive those times my compulsive behaviors have in some way hurt others.

Step Nine was also fairly easy once I let go of what I expected to be the outcome of any amends I needed to make. I had to realize that this Step was designed to free me from my own guilts and shames which block my progress toward my really living life. This Step wasn't necessarily designed to make people forgive me or to force them to make amends back. Sometimes I make amends and the person hasn't had a clue what I did. A good example of this is when I discover I've manipulated and tried to control someone. They may not know or even understand my motives for the amends, but it doesn't matter because I have to free myself from my guilt before it builds into shame. I not only make amends by direct apology, but also by writing a letter that is never sent when the apology could somehow hurt the person involved. My best kind of amends to others is to not say anything and just change my behavior toward them or others that may enter my life in the same way. Step Nine is a Step where I can really free me!

Step Ten allows me to get out of those heavy places where shame can easily trap me. My meetings, affirmations, and daily dealings with life help me to stay current with what character limitations need to be worked on and what amends need to be made. It has been difficult to be in a place of recovery where the "a-ha's" are fewer and farther between, and I have to work more often with the subtleties of my disease. The joy-bursts I feel when I achieve recognition and partial mastery over some character fault also are not as frequent. I lived for those joy-bursts of hope, but now I'm learning to be satisfied with victories that aren't always so easily seen or understood. I'm also learning to listen to the faint rumblings in my gut more frequently. When something feels uncomfortable for me, I don't dismiss it with a shrug as often. Step Ten helps me to acknowledge those gut-rumblings and figure out what aspect of my life needs work.

Step Eleven sounds so easy but the reality is that although my life goes so much better when I'm in constant contact with my Higher Power, there are many days I wake up forgetting to pray for guidance and the time to find the silence to hear my H.P.'s will. I can always tell when I forget to begin my day with affirmations and prayers because my life becomes difficult and my behaviors are more dysfunctional; it's definitely much more difficult to go with the flow.

It would be fantastic to say that I do this Step faithfully every day, but the truth is I too often forget it and end up doing my old behaviors. My CoDA meetings help me to remember to do this Step. I can really tell the difference when I'm going with the flow with the Steps instead of fighting upstream against life's current. I've learned that when I resist life, life resists me. The most important aspect of this Step is that it leads me to focus on gratitude. It is here I am thankful daily for my life, recovery and spirituality.

Step Twelve is often my surprise Step. I never know when my Higher Power will put me in a situation where I can share my program. I feel like this Step is my dropping-seeds Step. I can never be sure if the seeds will take root, but it's not for me to stay and make sure every seed is productive. When asked, I share the gifts of the program of Co-Dependents Anonymous, and it's H.P.'s after that. Another aspect of my Twelfth Step is the service I can give to my program. With the type of control issues I had when I first entered the program, I knew service wasn't the place for me.

About two years into Twelve Step programs, I finally decided to take the chance and began to take on more responsible roles in my meetings. I definitely had to face my control issues and continue to do so today. Many times I find myself beginning to make decisions on my own which could affect other members of the Fellowship. It is difficult for me, in my impulsiveness, to wait for a group conscience. I've been caught in the middle of situations and blamed for things that went wrong. I've had frequent bouts with my ego, too. It's hard to let go of my ideas, beliefs and projects when they're not accepted. On the other hand, I've learned so much about myself and my control issues from being in service. I've met so many more wonderful people working their program than I would have by isolating in my meetings.

For the last four years, I've been working on the community, state and national levels of CoDA. The various positions of service to which I have been elected have given me the chance to get to know more about myself and our program. I have done things alone that I would never have attempted when I started recovery. To travel to my first national conference by myself, not knowing a soul or what to expect was terrifying, but my Higher Power saw to it that I was given the opportunity to face these fears. The best gift of my service has been to watch the trustees, committee chairs and other people working their program, too. There is such a joy in seeing someone be human, become aware, let go, and make amends to a whole delegation. The decisions and issues faced at the service conferences are true evidence that this program of Co-Dependents Anonymous is truly being guided by a power much greater than any known force.

My Step Twelve is one of the most precious of my Steps. It helps me out of my tendency to stay isolated and forces me to face many control issues with which I might otherwise not have to deal. It helps me to give back some of the miracles I've experienced in my recovery.

The Twelve Steps of this spiritual program help me to live my life in a more balanced way. They have much more meaning for me than the Ten Commandments that I was taught as a child. I never thought I could take someone else's life, steal, or commit adultery. Where many of the Ten Commandments have no bearing on who I feel I am, the Twelve Steps all apply to my life and how I need to live in order to stay in a spiritual place. I am grateful to these Twelve Steps and my Higher Power for showing the way to a fuller life through working them.

My recovery, the Twelve Steps and my meetings have been the best gifts of my life. The events of my life—bad and good—have also been my gifts. When I started recovery, it was not at all feasible for me to believe I would ever have been able to forgive my ex-husband, let alone see him as a gift to me. Today, I do forgive him, and he was my gift. Because of these gifts in my life which have led to the recovery I feel today, I now have a spiritual path and a Higher Power. I've found serenity, and I'm learning to live life. No longer do I have to play the role of victim, and I know I don't have to rely on survival techniques to always get me by.

I've learned how to esteem myself from within by first of all learning what my wants and needs are and then by setting boundaries. I've learned to say no when I need to say no, and to maintain who I am without always trying to please others. I've learned how to reparent and nurture myself as well as all the little children inside who need healing. I am slowly even becoming a better parent to my own children. Further, I have stopped giving up much of my personal power by people-pleasing and putting others on pedestals. I've reclaimed much of my personal power. I'm more grounded in my reality. My recovery has not been a quick fix or painless. I've shed many tears, often wanted to stop working, and backslid countless number of times. The fact is, I know I can never go back. I'm aware now and can't undo what I know in my heart. My life and serenity are at stake.

That is where I am today in my recovery. I cannot conceive what my life would be like if I hadn't found Co-Dependents Anonymous. I can remember the time my mom asked me when I would stop going to meetings. My family's belief is that recovery is just a phase, a fad I'm going through. My answer to her came easily. "Mother," I calmly replied, "when will you be able to stop going to church?" The church of my choice includes CoDA meetings, Lake Tahoe, and all the universe.

Recovery has been very good to me, but, on the other hand, I know I've worked hard to get to this birthday celebration. I still have faith that I will one day overcome my toughest codependency issues like my control over my weight and my fear that I might choose an unhealthy partner. These tougher issues will require much footwork, focus, and daily dedication. I believe, however, that with my Higher Power's guidance, the Twelve Steps, the Twelve Traditions and my support friends, I will one day be free of these issues and be able to bring my whole being into harmony with the universe—this beautiful universe so evident to me on this beautiful spring day of celebration. I humbly and gratefully sit by the healing waters of Lake Tahoe, eagerly ready to walk where my Higher Power will guide me along this miraculous journey called recovery— one day at a time.

by Vicki F.

APPENDICES

CoDA's First Six Years

Ken and Mary R., founders of Co-Dependents Anonymous (CoDA), believe they were spiritually guided in translating the principles of Alcoholics Anonymous (AA) into a life-sustaining program of recovery for codependence.

Ken and Mary believe that seeds of inspiration were planted within them as they experienced a movie depicting the life of Mohandas Gandhi. Both were moved by Gandhi's courageous efforts to help the people of India gain their freedom and independence. Witnessing how one person's work could have such far-reaching effects, they began to think about their own lives and how they might make a difference.

Both Ken and Mary had been in recovery from alcoholism and drug abuse for many years and were well aware of the Twelve Step way of life. They prayed together, in earnest, for God to show them the way.

Mary:

"Passing on the gifts of recovery was so important to us. We were willing to make ourselves available to our Higher Power, to use us in whatever way He chose, so that we might somehow make a difference in this lifetime."

After praying, as they had learned through their Twelve Step recovery experience, they "let go and let God."

During the next three or four years, Ken and Mary experienced both hardships and triumphs. Although they didn't realize it at the time, a Higher Power was at work in their lives, preparing them for what was to come. Ken was working as the Director of Treatment in a residential facility that treated codependence and other addictive behaviors. Both Ken and Mary had begun therapy to deal with their own codependence issues. Over time, they had felt an ever increasing need for fellowship with other codependents.

Ken:

"I found that many of the patients in treatment for codependence were facing the same dilemma that Mary and I were facing. Once they returned home, these patients found little or no fellowship or support to help them in working the Twelve Steps for codependence issues.

It was becoming clear that it was time for me to explore the idea of starting a support group for codependents."

Ken and Mary saw the value in maintaining the spiritual principles found in the Twelve Steps and Twelve Traditions of Alcoholics Anonymous.

Mary:

"We wanted a group specifically focused on the issues of codependence and recovery from codependence, but it had to be based on the Twelve Steps, Twelve Traditions, and principles found in Alcoholics Anonymous. We wanted a group where we could work on our codependence issues both individually and as a couple." During the summer of 1986, Ken and Mary discussed their ideas for a group at length. Then, seeking support, they presented their ideas to friends in recovery. Ken was pleasantly surprised that people were open to the idea.

"It was an exciting time. Everyone was enthusiastic. We held an organizational meeting at our home, inviting anyone who had expressed an interest. Mary M., Renee P., and Craig B. attended. Together we determined the information, materials and steps we'd have to take to hold the first meeting. We adopted the name Co-Dependents Anonymous."

Since AA had over 50 years of success with alcoholism recovery using the Twelve Steps and Twelve Traditions, the group agreed to adopt AA's Steps and Traditions as the heart of the CoDA program. Ken contacted Alcoholics Anonymous for written permission to adapt the Twelve Steps and Twelve Traditions. Permission was granted as long as CoDA was willing to print AA's original Steps and Traditions along with those of CoDA. Mary M. agreed to compile a list of codependent characteristics. The list would help people attending the meeting to identify their issues of codependence. Ken agreed to write the Preamble, the Welcome, the meeting format, and to adapt the Steps and Traditions for CoDA's needs.

The next step was to find a meeting place. Mary recalls how difficult a task that was.

"Weeks went by. We called churches and schools, but could not find any that would be willing to house CoDA's first meeting. The problems we faced were 'not enough space,' 'high liability insurance rates,' 'no time available on the schedule' and extremely high rents. Finally, I spoke with a priest at a church in Phoenix. He graciously agreed to rent CoDA a meeting space. Later, we discovered that one of the initial members of the Board of Trustees belonged to that church." During this time, Craig B., Renee P., and Mary R. had been accumulating supplies and spreading the word about the meeting. Wendy Lee B. designed the trademark and flyer, and Jenise A. created the CoDA Teddy Bear which became the first CoDA logo. And so it began. The first meeting of Co-Dependents Anonymous was held on October 22, 1986, and drew approximately 30 people. Some people came out of curiosity. Some were friends and came to support Ken and Mary. Others came because they had tried different programs and had not found the type of support they needed.

Ken R. chaired the meeting and shared his story. Afterward the meeting broke into small groups for sharing.

Ken:

"It was the first time that any of us were able to openly and freely hear the experience, strength and hope of recovery from codependence. Through the depth and vulnerability of the sharing that took place, it was apparent to many of us that Co-Dependents Anonymous was a program truly inspired by a loving

Higher Power. God had indeed answered the prayers we had uttered four years before."

The following Wednesday, Mary R. shared her story. Attendance at the second CoDA meeting had doubled in size. Within four weeks, the meeting had grown to over 100 people. During the first month, CoDA had to change meeting rooms three times to accommodate the growing number of members.

As the weeks went on, excitement and enthusiasm for the support that CoDA offered continued to build. More CoDA meetings began forming in the Phoenix area. Within the first six months of CoDA's existence, two informational magazine articles were written about the program. These articles, along with meeting starter packets, were distributed by a local treatment center to patients returning to their homes all over the country. Through these and similar efforts, meeting representatives began registering their groups throughout the United States, as well as Sweden. Many people had already pioneered independent codependence support groups throughout the country. They adapted their groups to CoDA's structure and registered them as CoDA groups. Ken and Mary soon realized that CoDA needed a development plan and a structure to aid its rapid development. Again, they turned to their Higher Power for help.

Ken:

"Our prayers were answered through Jim S. He had a solid background in Twelve Step program structure, both on the local and national level, and a working knowledge of the law. Jim was a valuable addition to our group. He graciously offered us his time, direction, experience and services."

They decided to adopt an organizational structure similar to that of Alcoholics Anonymous. AA had survived and grown for more than 50 years with the understanding that each member would have a voice in the decisions and direction of the program.

Mary:

"We recognized that as CoDA's individual members continued to grow and evolve, so would its organization and structure. We decided to adapt AA's Conference Plan and Service Structure to CoDA's needs as a starting point. We wanted the membership of CoDA as a whole to continue to explore and expand. We felt this could be accomplished through the wisdom and guidance of a loving Higher Power, the Twelve Traditions, and a group conscience vote at the annual CoDA Service Conference."

Jim guided Ken and Mary through the process of adapting the AA structure for CoDA's purpose. He also helped them to incorporate a National Board of Trustees and, later, a National Service Office. Jim, with the help of Lane S., wrote the Articles of Incorporation and Bylaws for which CoDA was established. CoDA was incorporated on February 10, 1987.

Jim suggested they appoint seven members with diverse skills and occupations to form the initial CoDA Board of Trustees. The first meeting of the Board was held on February 25, 1987. In attendance were Bill T., Donna P., John M., Donna L., Bill S., Jim S., John J., and Ken and Mary. Ken was elected as Chairperson; John M. became Vice-Chairperson. Mary was elected as Treasurer, and Donna P. became Secretary.

Committees were established to effectively balance the work load of addressing CoDA's growing needs. Each Trustee was charged with the responsibility of recruiting CoDA volunteers to support the committees which included a Finance Committee, the Bear Facts Committee (the original national CoDA newsletter which is now called Co-NNections), a Hospital and Institution Committee, a Literature Committee, an Executive Committee and the National Service Office (N.S.O.).

The Board accepted the challenge to implement a National Service Structure and Conference Plan so that each member of CoDA would have an opportunity to take part in its business and growth. Through the dedication, long hours spent, and love of the first Board of Trustees, CoDA was able to reach and support many individuals in need of recovery from codependence. The National Service Office operated out of Ken and Mary's home for the first seven months.

Mary:

"Our home phone number became CoDA's first national number, and a Glendale, Arizona, post office box became CoDA's first national mailing address. We received hundreds of phone calls and letters from people wanting information about the disease of codependence and about the Co-Dependents Anonymous program. We spent many nights reading letters, corresponding with the CoDA Fellowship, and returning phone calls. We often shared tears of joy reading the many letters people wrote describing the help they received at their local CoDA meetings."

Ken:

"Times were often overwhelming; we answered phone calls for help at 3 a.m.; attempted to operate on not enough sleep; and tried to balance family, recovery, careers and marriage. In addition to answering N.S.O. correspondence, we mailed meeting starter packets, processed registrations and finances and still tried to find time for ourselves! What carried us through was the love and strength of our Higher Power, and the loving support of recovery friends such as Barbara and Curly M., Bill S., John M., Donna L., and many other people too numerous to mention." As the number of calls and letters grew, it became clear that a formal National Service Office needed to be established. Again, Ken and Mary's prayers for help were answered—this time through a CoDA recovering family. Jack M., Betty Lou M., John M. and Nancy M. graciously donated office space, equipment and furniture for the National Service Office. The computer equipment is still in use today.

Nancy M. volunteered to manage the N.S.O. and later accepted the volunteer title of Administrator. She devoted much of her time and skills developing a volunteer force that could meet the fast-growing needs of CoDA. The many hours she spent organizing and managing the National Service Office paid off. Within six months, CoDA had received enough donations to begin paying its own rent! The Board saw this as the achievement of a primary goal, whereby CoDA could maintain autonomy and adhere to the Traditions.

When CoDA was approximately seven months old,

the Board of Trustees began the work of planning CoDA's first National Conference. Elected CoDA representatives from cities nationwide, and Sweden, were invited to participate. On October 2, 1987, just three weeks short of CoDA's first birthday, the first CoDA National Service Conference was held in Phoenix, Arizona.

Mary:

"We were very pleased with the attendance. There were 29 representatives from seven states, the Board of Trustees and the N.S.O. employees. Many people described the experience as a cooperative, intensely spiritual business meeting. There was a profound sense of love, caring and unity. Some people referred to it as the spiritual birthing of CoDA on a national level." At the Conference, Ken and Mary and the Board of Trustees relinquished the future direction of CoDA to the membership and to the guidance of a loving Higher Power as expressed through the group conscience vote. The previous year's work by Ken and Mary, the Board of Trustees and their committees was reviewed by the Conference. Plans for the following year were outlined and set in motion by Conference members.

With the continued growth of CoDA, there was a tremendous need for development of CoDA literature, including a national newsletter and material for use in hospitals and institutions. Also needed was financial support to develop a CoDA Teen Program and to support the National Service Office.

Ken explains the overall mood of the Conference:

"There was an enormous feeling of excitement generated during those three days as CoDA's foundation was solidified in the form of a working Service Structure. Conference members returned home, charged with the responsibilities of implementing the CoDA Service Structure. By developing Group Representatives, Community Committees, State Committees and Assemblies to open the voice of CoDA to each member, we were able to establish a more effective way of communicating."

Many Conference members volunteered to serve on and support the Standing Committees of the Service Conference. It is largely through their efforts, struggles and consistency and those of succeeding Conference members, that CoDA exists today as a worldwide program. CoDA grew to approximately 4,000 meetings with a membership of approximately 100,000 within the first six years.

At the 1990 National Service Conference, Ken R. resigned as Chairperson of the Board of Trustees and as Chairperson of the Service Conference. Mary R. resigned as Trustee of the Board of Trustees. They both continued to serve as nonvoting Trustees and Advisors until fully resigning at the 1993 National Service Conference. Today they continue to be of service to CoDA as members, Founders, and as guided by a loving Higher Power.

The CoDA Service Conference has grown and expanded since its organization. The CoDA Board of Trustees has varied between seven to fifteen members. Chosen for their diverse talents, skills and abilities, Trustees demonstrate an overwhelming level of commitment to carry on the unending work of service to CoDA.

Today, the CoDA, Inc. Board is responsible for managing the day-to-day business of CoDA, responding to the service needs of the Fellowship and coordinating functions of the Conference Committees.

The CoDA Conference Committees have continued to meet the needs of the CoDA Fellowship. The current committees (as of this printing) are Hospitals & Institutions, Convention, Service Conference, Service Structure, Outreach, Literature, Finance, Co-NNections, Issues Mediation, and Translation Management. The members of each committee work diligently and lovingly, providing a tremendous amount of support, information and guidance.

The Fellowship of Co-Dependents Anonymous is and will continue to grow and expand worldwide. As it does, the needs of the Fellowship will continue to grow and expand as well. With the help of God, the volunteer service organization of CoDA and you, the individual members of CoDA, CoDA will continue to be a strong and viable worldwide resource for the support of recovery from codependency and will continue to fulfill its primary spiritual aim—to carry our message of recovery to those who still suffer from codependency, until the need to do so no longer exists.

How To Get In Touch With CoDA

Co-Dependents Anonymous, Inc.

P.O. Box 33577

Phoenix, AZ 85067-3577

Phone: 602-277-7991

Website: www.coda.org

How To Order CoDA Literature

CoDA Resource Publishing (CoRe)

P.O. Box 670861

Dallas, TX 75367-0861

Voice Mail: 214-340-1777

Fax: 214-340-6066

E-Mail: coreorders@coda.org

Order online at: www.coda.org/estore

Order Form Available for
Download
at www.coda.org

CoDA Materials Available from CoRe

Service Items
Fellowship Service Manual (FSM): CoDA's Organization & Procedures

CoDA Meeting Starter Packet

Pamphlets
What is CoDA?

Welcome to CoDA

Am I Codependent?

Attending Meetings

Communications & Recovery

Boundaries

Booklets & Handbooks
Tools for Recovery Booklet

Common Threads of Codependency Booklet

Crosstalk Handbook

Making Choices Booklet

Carrying the Message–Living the 12th Step Booklet

Peeling the Onion Booklet

Newcomers Handbook

Twelve Steps Handbook

Building CoDA Community, Healthy Meetings Matter

Sponsorship: What's in it for me?

Workbook
The Twelve Steps & Twelve Traditions Workbook

Special Items
Affirmations Booklet
Serenity Bookmarks (set of four)

Spanish Literature
Paquete Para Principiantes
Manual de Instrucciones Para Nuevos
Participantes
Estableciendo Limites en la Recuperacion
¿Soy codependiente?

Books
Co-Dependents Anonymous Book
In This Moment Daily Meditation Book

CDs
The Twelve Steps
Newcomers/Sponsorship
Codependency & Shame
Ken R: I Feel Like I've Come Home
Anita F: How Empty of Me To Be So Full of You
Newcomers/Sponsorship
Pat: The Promises, Carmen N: A Pocket Full of Anger
Jim: I Didn't Need Any One, Any More, Mary: I
    Don't Surrender Easy
Wes: Turning Points
Hollis: Walking My Road of Happy Destiny
Karmann: Hope for a New Day, Ann D: I Thought
    I Would Be OK As an Adult
Larry V: Recovery is the Greatest Gift, Wally:
    Recovery, The Wildest Thing, Judith: CoDA is
    God's Program

Culle V: I Have a Family Today, Mike D: Look
Inside For All Your Gifts, Sherrill S: Women's
Issues

Jim: Who's Got My Soul?, Phyllis: I Met My
Inner Child, Charles C: Relationships and
Intimacy

Posters

Serenity Prayer

The Twelve Steps

The Twelve Traditions

CoDA Opening & Closing Prayers

Meeting Announcement Poster

Medallions

CoDA Antique Bronze Birthday/Anniversary
Medallions—beginning with One Year

Chips

CoDA Colored Aluminum Acknowledgement
Chips—One, Two, Three, Six, and Nine Months
and Welcome Home

NOTES

NOTES

NOTES

NOTES

NOTES

NOTES

NOTES

NOTES

NOTES

NOTES

NOTES

NOTES